The European Union and its Constitution
From Rome to Lisbon

Dr Laurent Pech

CLARUS
PRESS

Published by
Clarus Press Ltd,
Griffith Campus,
South Circular Road,
Dublin 8.

Typeset by
Compuscript Ltd,
Shannon Industrial Estate,
Shannon,
Co. Clare.

Printed by
MPG Books Ltd
Victoria Square, Bodmin, Cornwall.

ISBN
10 Digit No.
1-905536-13-5

13 Digit No.
978-1-905536-13-9

This publication was grant-aided by the Publication Fund of *National University of Ireland*, Galway.

FOREWORD

No democratic state in the world is without its critics. No government of any democratic state satisfies the wishes of all the legitimate interest groups within its jurisdiction. In most democratic systems, critics call for changes in government policy, or for changes of government. Rarely do they call for the abolition of the state and its replacement by some other order.

International organisations come in for their share of criticism. The United Nations Organisation is widely respected, yet widely criticised for what are perceived to be its weaknesses and failures. For all that, even its most ardent critics do not call for its disbandment. Nor do they call for Member States to withdraw from it as a statement of their dissatisfaction.

In terms of popular political comment, the EU lives in a kind of twilight zone between statehood and the status of an international organisation. It is somehow more than each and less than either. This book sets out to cast the light of rigorous analysis on that twilight zone. This kind of rigorous analysis is sadly lacking in much of the current debate about the EU. As the author remarks:

> "For marginal political forces keen to attract attention, EU-bashing represents an effective strategy as the media favour oversimplification and controversy."

Several chapters are prefaced by pairs of utterly contradictory assertions about the nature or activities of the EU, taken from participants in debate about political and constitutional issues. This entity, this polity, with the mission of removing barriers to communication and commerce between its members and between those members and the rest of the world, has ferocious critics on both the left and the right, for diametrically-opposed reasons. The Left, heirs of the rhetoric of international brotherhood, sees its integrationist impulses as the servants of capitalism. The Right, avowed advocates of economic liberalism, sees its attachment to common rules, as unwarranted interference with mercantilist freedoms. Each claims that the EU polity robs states of their right and liberty to order things according to their wishes. Each analyses the EU in the same terms and using the same yardsticks as are applied to arguments about the activities of the governments of states. Laurent Pech identifies the fallacy of each of these approaches.

> "Contrary to what critics explain, the EU is no super-state in the making but an original and unprecedented system of government by, of, and for the Member States, with

conferred and *limited* powers, which is perfectly democratic in light of its 'consociational' nature."

Debate about the EU and its policies and actions has been bedevilled by the false premises exposed in this book. That much was evident in the French and Dutch referendum debates on the proposed Constitutional Treaty and in a succession of referendums on EU issues in Ireland. Indeed, the confusion engendered by the failure of most participants in the debate to appreciate the specificity of the EU enterprise has led directly to a peculiarly Irish form of nonsense in the matter. Where else in the world is a government obliged by the decision of a Constitutional Court to finance the publication, in the name of public information, of flatly contradictory and largely misleading claims about the intent, nature and consequences of freely entered-into international activities which it carries out at the direct behest of the electorate, consulted by democratic referendum? Yet this is precisely what has happened in Ireland as a result of the activities of the constitutional Commission set up in response to the Supreme Court judgment in the *McKenna* case.

The acuity and the clarity of the analysis in this book are such that I felt like standing up and cheering as I came to the end of each chapter. It should be required reading for every participant in the debate on the forthcoming referendum on the EU Lisbon Treaty.

Alan Dukes,
Director General,
Institute of International and European Affairs

ACKNOWLEDGMENTS

I am grateful to Donncha O'Connell, Dean of the Faculty of Law at the National University of Ireland in Galway, for suggesting that I revisit and—dare I say—defend the European Union's "constitutional" system during which time the 50th anniversary of the signing of the European Community Treaty was celebrated. This book would not have come into being without his support, and has benefited greatly from his helpful comments.

Special acknowledgment is also due to Tracy Bruen, Ursula Connolly and Anna-Louise Hinds who have read and commented on various sections of this book. Thanks should be offered to those of my colleagues who did not refrain from expressing their rather sceptical views on the idea and current developments of European integration. I also wish to thank Michael Coyne for reminding me that a coffee break is supposed to be a moment of relaxation. I am indebted to David McCartney, Director of Clarus Press, for his efficiency and help in the production of this book.

Finally, I would like to express my deep gratitude to my wife, Julia. Not only has she been extremely tolerant of my frequent absences, she also made sure to comfort me with delicious meals after each long day spent at writing. This book is dedicated to her.

TABLE OF CONTENTS
AT A GLANCE

DETAILED TABLE OF CONTENTS

INTRODUCTION

United Ever More Closely?

Human wills change, but what is there here below that does not change? The nations are not something eternal. They had their beginnings and they will end. A European confederation will very probably replace them. But such is not the law of the century in which we are living. At the present time, the existence of nations is a good thing, a necessity even. Their existence is the guarantee of liberty, which would be lost if the world had only one law and only one master.
Ernest Renan (1882)[1]

One impression predominates in my mind over all others. It is this: unity in Europe does not create a new kind of great power; it is a method for introducing change in Europe and consequently in the world.
Jean Monnet (1962)[2]

Explaining the European Union (hereinafter "EU") is an exercise fraught with perils. Its precise political and legal nature remains mysterious. To some extent, the EU embodies a baroque and unprecedented supranational entity and its decision-making processes may reveal, at times, some Byzantine characteristics. An American scholar observed that "while [the EU] maintains many of the fixed physical trappings of a state ... its genius is its indeterminacy".[3] To paraphrase Jacques Delors, president of the European Commission from 1985 to 1994, this genial "indeterminacy" has produced an unidentified political object with the distressing consequence that it remains an entity difficult to explain and to relate to the layperson. Furthermore, although political elites realise that their countries need the EU to effectively confront today's challenges, most politicians are reluctant to communicate on European affairs. Indeed, it is always more rewarding to project an image of absolute control over national affairs while shifting the blame to "Europe" whenever it is politically convenient. Unsurprisingly, therefore, the EU offers modern sophists a fertile ground to spread disingenuous opinions without much opposition. The constitutional

---

[1] E. Renan, "Qu'est-ce qu'une nation", reproduced in G. Eley and R. Grigor Suny (eds), *Becoming National: A Reader* (Oxford University Press, New York, 1996), p 53.
[2] J. Monnet, "A Ferment of Change", (1962) 1 *Journal of Common Market Studies* 203, reproduced in B. Nelsen and A. Stubb, *The European Union. Readings on the Theory and Practice of European Integration* (2ⁿᵈ ed, Lynne Rienner Publishers, London, 1998), p 26.
[3] J. Rifkin, *The European Dream* (Polity, London, 2004), p 229.

debate has revealed, in particular, the continuous strength of the following claims: that the EU is akin to a "superstate" exercising a new dominance from Brussels to the detriment of the Member States' sovereignty, that the EU suffers from a "democratic deficit", and finally, that it embodies either a neo-liberal bias or, alternatively, favours socialist (over)regulation.

Regardless of the merits of these respective claims there is, however, a straightforward explanation for this apparent European desire for originality and complexity. As Jean-Claude Piris points out, "for nearly half a century, the path taken by European integration has not followed any pre-established Cartesian model. It is for political reasons ... that the complex system of governance of the EU and its many complicated decision-making rules have been established and refined by its Member States in successive treaties".[4] Among these successive treaties, the two most fundamental ones are the Treaty Establishing the European Community (hereinafter "EC Treaty") and the Treaty on European Union (hereinafter "EU Treaty"). To put it concisely, the EC Treaty is heir to Robert Schuman's Declaration of 9 May 1950, a declaration inspired by Jean Monnet, in which the Foreign Minister of France calls for a "European federation indispensable to the preservation of peace". Officially signed in Rome in 1957, the EC Treaty (also known and referred to as the Treaty of Rome[5]), set up the rules governing what was then the European Economic Community (hereinafter "EEC") and the European Atomic Energy Community. In 1993, the Member States decided to rename the EEC the European Community (hereinafter "EC"). Dropping the word "economic" was seen as a symbolic step to mark the expanding role of the Community beyond the economic field.

As is well known, Ireland had to wait until 1973 to secure membership of the EEC. The Irish application had been blocked for several years along with the British one, due to the French President's opposition. Charles de Gaulle feared that the United Kingdom would try to undermine European integration from within and would simply act as a trojan horse for American interests. As it happens, the European project lost momentum following the British and Irish accessions up until the mid-1980s, but this was surely a coincidence. At this stage, under the leadership of Jacques Delors, the European Commission launched a campaign to complete a genuine European internal market by the end of 1992 which gave a new impetus to the EC. More fundamentally, the signature of the EU Treaty in Maastricht, also in 1992, marked a new ambitious step towards closer integration. This Treaty not only paved the way for the creation of the Euro but also

---

[4] J.-C. Piris, "Does the European Union have a Constitution? Does it need one?", *Harvard Jean Monnet Working Paper* 5/00, p 60 (available at: http://www.jeanmonnetprogram.org/papers).
[5] Technically speaking, two Treaties were actually signed in Rome in 1957: The Treaty establishing the European Economic Community (EEC) and the Treaty establishing the European Atomic Energy Community (EURATOM).

established a new "creature", the European Union, whose main purpose was to improve intergovernmental co-operation in foreign affairs, defence, justice and home affairs.

One should note that, technically speaking, the EC and the EU are not the same thing. As the current EU Treaty puts it, in a somewhat opaque manner: "The Union shall be founded on the European Communities, supplemented by the policies and forms of cooperation established by this Treaty".[6] This division between the EC and the EU is, however, artificial in practice. It has become common practice merely to refer to the EU even though, strictly speaking, the EC Treaty and the EU Treaty offer two distinct sets of legal rules with different legal effects. Realising, *inter alia*, that these two Treaties offer "a confusing and incoherent mess",[7] the Member States acknowledged in 2001 that the Treaty of Nice fell short of simplifying the current legal framework.[8] The drafters of the "EU Constitution" sought to achieve this result by repealing the EC Treaty and EU Treaty and replacing them with a new text. The decision to abandon the constitutional text in June 2007 unfortunately means that the present Treaties will continue to remain in force. Indeed, the Member States agreed that a new Treaty, initially branded as the "Reform Treaty" but subsequently referred to as the "Lisbon Treaty", will not merge into one new text but "merely" amend them.[9] In conformity with the aborted text, however, the Lisbon Treaty grants exclusive legal personality to the "Union" which shall replace and succeed the European Community. The expression "European Community" will therefore be replaced by "European Union" throughout the Treaties. This also explains the decision to rename the EC Treaty the Treaty on the Functioning of the European Union. Before assessing further the scope of the Lisbon Treaty, it is imperative to understand why the idea of a European constitution proved to be so controversial and whether the strident criticism it gave rise to was completely justified.

The formal title of the defunct "EU Constitution" is the Treaty Establishing a Constitution for Europe. In Ireland and in the United Kingdom, the prevailing term— Constitutional Treaty—is a slightly different one. This is actually in line with what the former French President Valéry Giscard d'Estaing argued for in his first speech as President of the Convention on the Future of Europe (known as the European Convention), the ad hoc body in charge of drafting a constitutional text from 2002 to 2003. Emphasising the ambitious goal of the European Convention—to open the way towards a Constitution

---

[6] Article 1 TEU. It is important to note that references to EU Treaty articles and to EC Treaty articles are respectively made in the form "Article ... TEU" and "Article ... TEC".

[7] D. Chalmers *et al.*, *European Union Law* (Cambridge University Press, Cambridge, 2006), p 41.

[8] See Treaty of Nice: Declaration on the future of the Union, [2001] OJ C80/85.

[9] References to new EU Treaty articles and to EC Treaty articles as amended or inserted by the Lisbon Treaty are respectively made in the form "new Article ... TEU" and "new Article ... TEC". Although the EC Treaty will be eventually renamed the Treaty on the Functioning of the European Union (TFEU), the abbreviation TEC will nevertheless be used for the sake of clarity.

for Europe—he recommended that, "in order to avoid any disagreement over semantics", the new text should be called a Constitutional Treaty for Europe.[10]

One may ask: does it really matter whether the text is called a constitution or a constitutional treaty? Undeniably, the quarrel over semantics is fought, above all, for symbolic political purposes. This does not mean that the quarrel is unimportant.[11] To some extent, eurosceptics are not entirely wrong when they fear that the use of the word "constitution" may lead to acceptance of the idea that the EU should be treated as some sort of federal state. Were the term "constitution" to be widely accepted, the legitimacy and authority of the European legal order would be considerably strengthened. This is why Michael Howard, former Leader of the UK Conservative Party, vehemently argued that only countries had constitutions. It is important, however, to understand that "for decades it has been commonly understood that, despite its formal treaty format, the structural architecture of the Communities and subsequent Union were better explained with a constitutional vocabulary than with that of international law".[12] In a famous opinion, the European Court of Justice bluntly stated that the EC Treaty "albeit concluded in the form of an international agreement, none the less constitutes the constitutional charter of a Community".[13] This use of constitutional terminology has proved controversial ever since. However, it is entirely reasonable to contend that the EC/EU has, since its origin, been operating on the basis of what may be described as a constitutional text.

Numerous works have discussed the differences between a constitution and a treaty.[14] A constitution is typically understood as the fundamental law with supreme legal force which lays down the rules governing the organisation and exercise of state power as well as the fundamental rights of citizens. Furthermore, according to orthodox constitutional theory, the concept of constitution relates, in principle, only to states and the making of a constitution is usually understood as an act of sovereign self-determination. Accordingly, until the time comes when a European treaty is put to the peoples of the Member States for direct approval in a European-wide referendum, a proper European "constitution" cannot emerge. This was certainly the case with the Constitutional Treaty. To enter into

---

[10] See Secretariat of the European Convention, Speeches delivered at the inaugural meeting of the Convention on 28 February 2002, Brussels, 5 March 2002, CONV 4/02, Annex 4, p 20.

[11] See e.g. the insightful analysis of M.P. Maduro, "The Importance of being called a constitution: Constitutional authority and the authority of constitutionalism", (2005) *International Journal of Constitutional Law* 357.

[12] J. Weiler, "On the power of the Word: Europe's constitutional iconography" (2005) 3 *International Journal of Constitutional Law* 173, at 176.

[13] Opinion 1/91, [1991] ECR I-6079, para 21. See also Case 294/83, *Les Verts* [1986] ECR 1339, para 23.

[14] For two concise yet informative studies, see P. Eleftheriadis, "Constitution or Treaty?", *The Federal Trust Online Paper* 12/04, July 2004 (available at: http://www.fedtrust.co.uk/eu_constitution); L. Diez-Picazo, "Treaty or Constitution? The Status of the Constitution for Europe", in J. Weiler and C. Eisgruber (eds), *Altneuland: The EU Constitution in a Contextual Perspective*, Jean Monnet Working Paper 5/04 (available at: http://www.jeanmonnetprogram.org/papers).

force, national ratification in all the Member States was required, in the same way as any other European treaty. In my view, however, the term "constitution" does not necessarily refer to a unique and hierarchically superior legal instrument if we consider, for example, the distinctive experience of the United Kingdom. As is well known, the absence in the United Kingdom "of a constitution in the form of a written single document with special overriding status"[15] has not led British lawyers to conclude that they lack a constitution. Accordingly, the EU can be said to already possess a constitution as both the EC Treaty and EU Treaty offer a set of justiciable written rules that define the main organs of government and powers, are viewed as superior law and can only be amended by special procedures.[16] Similarly, although the Constitutional Treaty did not obviously pursue the objective of giving birth to a new and sovereign state entity, it included some characteristic and decisive components of any constitution. For instance, it clearly organised the government of the entity to which it applies and it also guaranteed human rights. As far as substance is concerned, therefore, the comparison with the constitution of a state appeared relevant. This understanding of the concept of constitution may not fully satisfy orthodox constitutional theory but it explains why this book is entitled "the European Union and its Constitution", regardless of the tragic fate of the 2004 "EU Constitution", the story of which will now be briefly addressed.

The idea of a formal constitution for the EU was first seriously discussed in policy and academic circles during the 1980s.[17] The political debate on the subject is more recent, beginning essentially in 2000 with a speech made by the German Foreign Minister Joschka Fischer, where he called for a European constitution modelled on the German Constitution.[18] This led to the Laeken Declaration of December 2001,[19] in which EU leaders agreed to call for a Convention on the Future of Europe to draft a text with the laudable aims of making the EU more democratic, more transparent and more efficient. Three basic challenges were also identified: how to bring citizens closer to the European ideal and the European institutions, how to organise politics in an enlarged Union and how to develop the Union into a stabilising factor and a global model. The European

---

[15] P. Birkinshaw, "Constitutions, Constitutionalism and the State", (2005) *European Public Law* 31 at 33.
[16] P. Craig, "Constitutions, Constitutionalism, and the European Union", (2001) 7 *European Law Journal* 125 at 127.
[17] See in particular the "Spinelli initiative" which led to the adoption of a *Draft Treaty on European Union* by the European Parliament in 1984 (OJ C77/33). Altiero Spinelli is the founder of the European Federalist Movement and a former Commissioner.
[18] See J. Fischer, "From Confederacy to Federation: Thoughts on the Finality of European Integration", in C. Joerges, Y. Mény and J. Weiler, *What Kind of Constitution for What Kind of Polity? – Responses to Joschka Fischer* (European University Institute, 2000), p 19.
[19] See European Council of Laeken, Presidency Conclusions, 14–15 December 2001, Annex I: Laeken Declaration on the future of the European Union, in *Bulletin of the European Union* 2001, No 12, pp 19–23.

Convention, composed of members representing all the relevant parties,[20] adopted a draft Constitution in July 2003 and presented it to the European Council, i.e. the EU institution which brings together the Heads of State or Government of the Member States and the President of the Commission.

Despite what some critics have suggested,[21] this "Convention method" was certainly not undemocratic. In fact, it achieved new levels of openness and inclusiveness in comparison with previous procedures used to prepare other European treaties. Furthermore, all significant viewpoints were represented. Noel Treacy, the then Irish Minister for European Affairs, rightly pointed out that the Convention was, in reality, an unprecedented "open exercise, bringing together for the first time public representatives from across the full spectrum of European opinion. This is quite apparent from a glimpse at the Irish membership: John Bruton, Dick Roche, Pat Carey, John Gormley and Proinsias De Rossa—a broad church by any reckoning".[22]

Criticism appears particularly absurd when one compares the drafting of the EU Constitutional Treaty with the manner in which national constitutions were created. It would certainly be difficult to argue, for instance, that the Irish Constitution, Bunreacht na hÉireann, was widely debated and open to amendments from all political forces and civil society in the period 1935–1937, despite the fact that it was narrowly approved in a plebiscite. Similarly, in France, the drafting of constitutional texts—and the French have had more than sixteen in two centuries—has always been an exercise conducted in relative secrecy with citizens only involved at the ratification stage. Finally, regarding the EU Constitutional Treaty, one should note that the text submitted by the European Convention was not legally binding on the Member States. Democratically elected Heads of State or Government of the Member States had the final say on the content of Constitutional Treaty. And indeed, in order to secure a consensual agreement between the Member States, the draft Constitution submitted by the European Convention had to be amended extensively. Once these amendments were formalised, the Treaty Establishing a Constitution for Europe was officially signed by the Member States in Rome on 29 October 2004.

Some have regretted that the Constitutional Treaty was unlikely to be popular bedtime reading among Europe's citizens. One may retort that it would seem quite challenging to

---

[20] The European Convention brought together representatives of the governments of the 15 Member States and the 13 candidate countries, representatives of their national parliaments, representatives of the European Parliament and of the European Commission, 13 observers from the Committee of the Regions and the European Economic and Social Committee, plus representatives of the European social partners and the European Ombudsman.

[21] See e.g. Mary Lou McDonald, MEP, Sinn Féin National Chairperson, Letters Section, *The Irish Times*, 7 April 2005.

[22] Letters Section, *The Irish Times*, 8 April 2005.

find anyone who would read one's own national constitution for relaxation. Yet such constitutions can be legitimate and effective. More seriously, it was often claimed that the Constitutional Treaty is both too long and too obscure.[23] By contrast, the US Constitution is presented as the model which Europeans should emulate. To quote a characteristic utterance, Jack Straw has suggested that "size is important" and that "the smaller the better when it comes to constitutions".[24] It may be worth discussing the aesthetic attributes of the Constitutional Treaty in more detail to offer a good example of double-standards and constitutional ignorance, unfortunately two typical features of any popular discussion on the EU.

Although it is a familiar practice among common-law authors, comparing the EU Constitutional Treaty with the US Constitution is defective. The American document was written more than two centuries ago. Its founding fathers were obviously not faced with the same challenges as Jean Monnet or Paul-Henri Spaak when creating an institutional structure based on shared sovereignties and market integration. Furthermore, one may argue that the "pocket-size" of the US Constitution has left the US Supreme Court with no choice but to be judicially creative in order to cope with the evolution of American society. Undeniably, with 448 Articles, the EU Constitutional Treaty was not a short one. This simply reflects the Member States' insistence on maintaining the strictest control over the evolution of law-making at EU level. In other words, the Member States wanted the Constitutional Treaty to be extremely detailed because they wanted to control exactly how much competence they gave to the EU and how much power they gave to its institutions to exercise these competences.[25] Yet, when compared with modern constitutions of federal states such as Germany (146 articles) or India (395 articles), the Constitutional Treaty did not appear excessively long. Furthermore, commentators tend to forget that constitutional texts are often accompanied by certain laws of constitutional value, which detail, precisely, the manner in which specific provisions of the constitution should be applied. For instance, the French Constitution is rather short (89 articles) but its content is further specified by several comprehensive "organic laws".

Certainly, the EU would benefit from offering its citizens a more concise basic law, setting aside all provisions dealing with process (e.g. the provisions governing the adoption of the EU's annual budget) in protocols and/or organic laws. The Constitutional Treaty was

---

[23] The Constitutional Treaty is split into four parts. Part I details the new institutional framework of the Union in about 60 articles. Part II incorporates the European Charter of Fundamental Rights "proclaimed" in Nice in December 2000. Part III contains the detailed provisions on policy and procedure for many of the articles in Part I. Part IV contains the usual technical provisions that deal with details regarding the entry into force of the agreement and the repeal of previous agreement(s). In total, the Constitutional Treaty offered a long but nonetheless legible single text of 448 articles, to compare with the current EC and EU Treaties, which respectively consist of 53 articles and 314 articles.

[24] J. Straw, "A constitution for Europe", *The Economist*, 10 October 2002.

[25] J.-C. Piris, *The Constitution for Europe* (Cambridge University Press, Cambridge, 2006), p 59.

still quite an improvement compared to the current European Treaties. Although, as Peter Norman put it, it is doubtful whether this text "would appeal, as Giscard hoped, to the average intelligent secondary school pupil",[26] he conceded that "the constitutional treaty has a beginning, a middle and an end that an ordinary mortal can follow".[27] To that effect, the Constitutional Tready's Preamble and the first eight articles defining and setting out the objectives of the EU can be read and understood without difficulty, and compare well with national constitutions. Regardless of its alleged complexity, one must understand that it is precisely because the EU is not a federal state that it needs a relatively more complicated set of rules. Jack Straw eventually realised this much in 2004:

> "Here lies a paradox about the EU, and also the root of our collective ambiguity towards it. Were it a superstate, writing its constitution would be easy, and the result short. ... It is precisely because the EU is not a superstate that it needs a more complicated rule-book spelling out, policy by policy, the areas of its competence."[28]

Notwithstanding its aesthetic merits, the Constitutional Treaty has been denounced, quite intriguingly, by eurofederalists and eurosceptics alike. Irrespective of one's theoretical point of view on the desirability of a formalised constitution for the EU,[29] the Constitutional Treaty, while offering innovative improvements to the current institutional framework and promising to make the EU more manageable and more accountable, did not offer radical changes. It did, however, clarify the EU's values and the role that the EU should play in the world.[30] In the end, it seems legitimate to argue, as one well-informed commentator observed, that "while the plot and the set may look impressive, the play itself is not revolutionary".[31] This is why, in most instances, British eurosceptics appeared to be so widely off the mark when they denounced the imminent arrival of a European Leviathan. In reality, European federalists should have been the ones disappointed with the Constitutional Treaty. But as Lord Kerr, former secretary general of the European Convention, contended:

> "Those who would have wished for something more far-reaching, perhaps a real 1787 founding Constitution rather than another Treaty among sovereign states, need to

---

[26] P. Norman, *The Accidental Constitution. The Making of Europe's Constitutional Treaty* (2nd ed, EuroComment, Brussels, 2005), pp 315–316.

[27] *ibid.*

[28] J. Straw, Charlemagne, *The Economist*, 8 July 2004.

[29] See in particular the original views developed by J. Weiler, "In defence of the status quo: Europe's Constitutional *Sonderweg*", in J. Weiler and M. Wind (eds), *European Constitutionalism beyond the State* (Cambridge University Press, Cambridge, 2003), p 7.

[30] See G. de Búrca, "The Drafting of a Constitution for the European Union: Europe's Madisonian Moment or a Moment of Madness?", (2004) 61 *Washington and Lee Law Review* 555.

[31] K. Nicolaïdis, "Our European Demoi-cracy. Is this Constitution a Third Way for Europe?", in K. Nicolaïdis and S. Weatherill (eds), *Whose Europe? National Models and the Constitution of the European Union* (Oxford University Press, Oxford, 2003), p 137.

beware of letting the best become the enemy of the good. ... And Treaty form means that the slowest ship sets the convoy's pace. That's life."[32]

The great irony, therefore, is that the Constitutional Treaty was "in fact a Eurosceptic constitution, entrenching the status quo, though the Eurosceptics seem too short-sighted to have noticed it".[33]

As is well-known, the French "Non" and the Dutch "Nee" in 2005 proved ultimately fatal to the Constitutional Treaty. At the Brussels meeting of the European Council in June 2007, the Member States finally agreed "that, after two years of uncertainty over the Union's treaty reform process, the time has come to resolve the issue and for the Union to move on".[34] It was agreed to abandon the "constitutional concept" and to convene an intergovernmental conference, i.e. a group consisting of a representative of each of the Member States' governments,[35] to draw a new treaty which will amend the two existing Treaties. This was a difficult decision to make considering the fact that 18 countries—representing a *majority* of the Member States and of the EU population—had already ratified the Constitutional Treaty.[36] From a legal perspective, however, the rules governing the entry into force of the Constitutional Treaty were clear-cut: unanimous ratification was required for this text to enter into force. Such unanimity, no matter how practically absurd in a union of 27 Member States, is actually the clearest indication that the Member States continue to retain the entirety of the *pouvoir constituant*, the supreme power to decide their own constitutional arrangements.

The "period of reflection"[37] that the Member States agreed to in June 2005 thus led to the demise of the constitutional project. As advocated by Nicolas Sarkozy in 2006, before he became the President of France, the new Lisbon Treaty—also known as the "Reform Treaty"—will merely amend the existing Treaties and not replace them. However, contrary to his suggestion of adopting a "mini-treaty" of 10–15 articles,[38] the Lisbon Treaty will dramatically amend the EU Treaty and EC Treaty. Indeed, to the palpable satisfaction of those countries reluctant to completely discard the Constitutional Treaty, the Lisbon

---

[32] J. Kerr, "Best on offer", EU Constitution Project Newsletter, The Federal Trust, July 2004, p 10.

[33] V. Bogdanor, "A Constitution for a House without Windows", EU Constitution Project Newsletter, The Federal Trust, July 2004, p 6.

[34] European Council of Brussels, Presidency Conclusions, 21–22 June 2007, Doc No 11177/07, 23 June 2007, p 2 (available at: http://www.consilium.europa.eu/ueDocs/cms_Data/docs/pressData/en/ec/94932.pdf).

[35] One representative of the European Commission and three representatives of the European Parliament were also be involved in the work of the intergovernmental conference.

[36] Austria, Belgium, Bulgaria, Cyprus, Estonia, Finland, Germany, Greece, Hungary, Italy, Latvia, Lithuania, Luxembourg, Malta, Romania, Slovakia, Slovenia, Spain.

[37] See e.g. A. Duff and J. Voggenhuber, MEPs, *Report on the period of reflection: the structure, subjects and context for an assessment of the debate on the European Union*, European Parliament, A6-0414/2005, 16 December 2005.

[38] N. Sarkozy, "EU reform: What we need to do", *Europe's World*, Autumn 2006, p 56.

Treaty retains most of its innovative provisions. In the much-quoted words of Irish Prime Minister Bertie Ahern, "90 per cent of it is still there".[39] This explains why eurosceptics continue to oppose the new text on the ground that the Lisbon Treaty is the EU Constitutional Treaty in all but name.

The most significant departure from the Constitutional Treaty is indeed the abandonment of the word "constitution". As Andrew Moravcsik judiciously observed in June 2005 :

> " ... the central error of the European constitutional framers was one of style and symbolism rather than substance. The constitution contained a set of modest reforms, very much in line with European popular preferences. Yet European leaders upset the emerging pragmatic settlement by dressing up the reforms as a grand scheme for constitutional revision and popular democratisation of the EU."[40]

With the benefit of hindsight, it is clear that the use of the word "constitution" was not the most sensitive choice, not only because the term constitution is (though erroneously) synonymous in the mind of most voters with intangibility, therefore dramatising the debate, but also because it spectacularly raised expectations. And these expectations could only be dashed by the reading of a document of 448 articles which did not revolutionise the nature of European integration and did not fundamentally alter the complexity of its current decision-making process. This diagnosis has now been accepted by the Member States.

The agreement found in the Lisbon Treaty, however, came at a price. Instead of the promised "simplified" Treaty, the new Treaty, as liberal British MEP Graham Watson noted in June 2007, "reads like the instructions for building a Japanese pagoda translated into English by a Chinese middle-man".[41] To use another popular diagnosis, the Lisbon Treaty has been compared to a "treaty of footnotes". The description is not entirely warranted as it is based on a reading of a draft text agreed by the European Council at its Brussels meeting on 21–22 June 2007. This draft text guided the work of the intergovernmental conference which was in charge of drawing up a fully-fledged treaty before the end of 2007. Yet it was already clear from this draft text that the new treaty was not going to ease citizens' understanding of the EU. On the contrary, the Lisbon Treaty multiplies pointless or incomprehensible declarations and protocols as well as the number of areas where some Member States, i.e. the United Kingdom and Ireland, can "opt-out" from the adoption and application of EU law. It is more than a little ironic that previous critics of the

---

[39] Editorial, "Constitution no more", *The Irish Times*, 25 June 2007.
[40] A. Moravcsik, "Europe without illusions", *Prospect*, July 2005, p 22.
[41] European Parliament, Debate on the EU summit and Germany presidency, Press release IPR08363, 27 June 2007.

Constitutional Treaty now find it an "easily understandable"[42] text by comparison to the new Treaty.

Without a doubt, the Lisbon Treaty is unlikely to make the EU more transparent and bring it closer to its citizens. It only partially fulfils the four objectives announced in the 2001 Declaration on the future of the Union and which were: (1) to establish and monitor a more precise delimitation of powers between the EU and the Member States, reflecting the principle of subsidiarity; (2) to clarify the status of the EU Charter of Fundamental Rights of the European Union; (3) to simplify the Treaties with a view to making them clearer and better understood without changing their meaning; (4) to improve the role of national parliaments in the European architecture. Arguably, the Lisbon Treaty only satisfies the second and fourth objectives. The depressing truth is that the Constitutional Treaty, by contrast, offered an answer to all of them.

Although the Constitutional Treaty is now officially abandoned and the Lisbon Treaty not yet ratified, this book will extensively examine their provisions and compare them to the rules currently in force with a view to addressing all the major and prevalent "constitutional" controversies previously identified: the superstate argument, the democratic deficit accusation and the EU's alleged ideological bias. It is argued that the EU is not and should not become a state (Part I) and that the treatment of the EU as a democratically deficient entity is misguided (Part II). It is also contended that the EU legal framework is neither neo-liberal nor socialist, but offers a balanced framework which does not pre-empt the political direction of EU legislative intervention (Part III). Generally speaking, one should note that the objective of this book is not to propose reforms, but rather to clarify what ought to be the terms of the debate while highlighting the inconsistencies of eurocritics. Indeed, before suggesting reforms, a correct diagnosis should be articulated.

---

[42] Jean-Claude Juncker, Prime Minister of Luxembourg, quoted in Editorial, "Constitution no more", *The Irish Times*, 25 June 2007.

PART ONE

A Misguided Analogy:
The European Union as a "Superstate"

We have not successfully rolled back the frontiers of the state in Britain, only to see them reimposed at a European level, with a European superstate exercising a new dominance from Brussels.
Margaret Thatcher, Speech at the College of Europe, Bruges, 20 September 1988

We are creating a model, admittedly by reference to inherited principles, but in circumstances so extraordinary that the end result will be unique, without historical precedent.
Jacques Delors, Speech at the College of Europe, Bruges, 17 October 1989

Whereas the preamble of the 1787 Constitution of the United States affirms: "We the People of the United States, in Order to form a more perfect Union … do ordain and establish this CONSTITUTION for the United States of America", Article 1 of the present EU Treaty states that "By this Treaty, the HIGH CONTRACTING PARTIES establish among themselves a EUROPEAN UNION, hereinafter called 'the Union'." The contrast is patent: in the United States, the American People acted as a constituent power to adopt the new nation's fundamental law, while in Europe, *only* the Member States are said to have decided "to establish a European Union" by unanimously ratifying a treaty.[1]

A brief glance at the aborted EU Constitutional Treaty might suggest a more ambitious move towards the "United States of Europe". Indeed, according to its Art I-1(1), the Union is said to reflect "the will of the citizens and States of Europe to build a common future". As a result, the Constitutional Treaty, albeit not established by the "People" of Europe, appeared to be more ambitious than the EU Treaty, which currently speaks of the "peoples" of Europe and not of an indeterminate group of citizens. As for the formal emphasis on the Union's dual legitimacy,[2] the original reference to the will of the citizens of Europe was immediately followed by an important qualification: Art I-1(1) confirmed that the EU

---

[1] See preamble of the EU Treaty.
[2] As Jacques Delors put it, "the nature of the European integration process, since it began, has been to reconcile two sources of legitimacy: that of the Member States, reflected in intergovernmental procedures, and that of common institutions based on a direct relationship with European citizens", foreword to the study of J.-L. Quermonne, "The Question of a European Government", Notre Europe, Research and European Issues No 20, November 2002, p 5 (study available at: http://www.notre-europe.asso.fr).

is dependent on the powers conferred on it by the Member States to attain objectives they have in common. Remarkably, the decision in June 2007 to replace the Constitutional Treaty with a "Reform Treaty"—now referred to as the "Lisbon Treaty"—did not lead to the complete discarding of this provision. As amended by the new Treaty, Art 1(1) of the EU Treaty reads:

> "By this Treaty, the HIGH CONTRACTING PARTIES establish among themselves a EUROPEAN UNION, hereinafter called 'the Union' on which the Member States confer competences to attain objectives they have in common."

In line with the Constitutional Treaty, the Lisbon Treaty does not, therefore, alter the ultimate truth of European integration: the EU is and will remain the creation of each Member State. To push the US analogy further, the European Treaties could be said to be more reminiscent of the Articles of Confederation of 1777 which provided that "Each state retains its sovereignty, freedom, and independence, and every power, jurisdiction and right, which is not by this confederation expressly delegated to the United States, in Congress assembled". Indeed, the EU may only act if it has the power to do so, power conferred on it by an *exclusive* and *unanimous* decision of the Member States. Analogies with constitutional texts of federal states should, nonetheless, be brought into play with care as they may lead to the implied assumption that the EU is itself a state or a federal polity. As we shall see, the EU does not and will not have any independent sovereignty. The Lisbon Treaty itself will not change the nature of the present relationship between the Union and the Member States: the EU continues to be a creature of the Member States who retain the ultimate political authority.

As a result, the EU is certainly no "superstate"—an imprecise but prevalent assertion—and the possibility of a superstate ever emerging reveals some phantasmagorical thinking. The superstate fear was reignited by the inclusion in the Constitutional Treaty of a new provision on the "symbols of the Union".[3] The EU was to have its own flag, its own anthem (the "Ode to Joy" from the Ninth Symphony by Ludwig van Beethoven), its motto ("United in diversity"). The Constitutional Treaty also provided for a "Europe day" to be celebrated on 9 May. This date corresponds to the Schuman Declaration. On 9 May 1950, Robert Schuman, the then Foreign Minister of France, made a decisive speech on the future of Europe and proposed the creation of the European Coal and Steel Community. The "constitutional" consecration of all these symbols has been fiercely contested as they are traditionally associated with nationhood and statehood, hence the description of the EU as a proto-state in the making. This criticism led the Member States to agree to drop any reference to the symbols of the EU in the Lisbon Treaty. The lack of any Treaty provision referring to the symbols of the EU is nevertheless rather pointless since these symbols are and will continue to be used. For instance, the circle of 12 yellow stars on a

---

[3] Article I-8 of the EU Constitutional Treaty (hereinafter "EU CT").

blue background was adopted as the European flag by the Council of Europe in 1955 and by the EU Heads of State and Government at the Milan Summit in June 1985.[4]

The fact that the EU possesses its own flag or its own motto does not substantiate, however, the hasty conclusion that the EU will become the "United States of Europe". It would certainly be more appropriate to describe it as a community, or better, a voluntary association of European States which consensually administer or co-ordinate a certain number of policies at European level. The major difficulty with the EU is that it cannot escape comparison with traditional constitutional phenomena, but such comparisons are misplaced. It is certainly true that the "founding fathers" themselves thought of Europe in terms of a federal state in the making. Robert Schuman, in his aforementioned declaration, set out the ultimate goal of European integration:

> "By pooling basic production and by instituting a new High Authority [*currently known as the European Commission*], whose decisions will bind France, Germany and other member countries, this proposal will lead to the realization of the first concrete foundation of a European federation indispensable to the preservation of peace."

However, as European integration has always evolved by a successive set of compromises between "federalists" and "sovereignists", the EU is, and will remain, an ongoing "experiment in transnational politics".[5] Therefore, even though the qualification may certainly appear frustrating, the original political and legal nature of the EU makes it a *sui generis* entity: an entity not bestowed with statehood but whose legal system is reminiscent of a federal state.

---

[4] Technically speaking, the European Council unanimously approved the proposals contained in the report produced by the ad hoc Committee on "A People's Europe". See Bulletin of the EC, Supplement 7/85.
[5] See H. Wallace, "Designing Institutions for an Enlarging European Union", in B. de Witte (ed), *Ten Reflections on the Constitutional Treaty for Europe* (Robert Schuman Centre, Florence, 2003), p 86.

CHAPTER ONE

The Non-State Nature of the European Union

The difficulties in overcoming long-established concepts and paradigms are clear in the European constitutional debate. This is especially true with regard to the debate about the "state nature"[1] of the EU. It is not surprising. The state continues to be the paradigmatic model of organisation for the exercise of public power. Yet, the state is an historical product. In fact, before the state emerged as a distinctive and successful model in the sixteenth century, other models had been put into practice, such as the Greek *Polis*, the Roman *Civitas* or the Empire.

A brief and pragmatic assessment of the EU could easily lead to the conclusion that it does not have the means and resources that one expects of a state apparatus. The director of human resources of the Dublin City Council manages a staff of approximately 6,200 for a population of almost 500,000.[2] To supervise a Union of nearly 450 million inhabitants, European institutions are staffed with approximately 40,000 agents, about 24,000 of them employed by the Commission. One may thus wonder about the discernment of commentators such as Myers who speaks of "the growth of that vast and insidious Eurocracy emanating out of Brussels. This is the gravest enemy of a prosperous Europe, with its army of civil servants imposing mountains of regulations which no democratically elected politician has ever approved."[3] As with the United States where the average American citizen believes that 20 percent of the US federal budget is devoted to foreign aid when in fact the actual number is well under 1 percent (or one-thirtieth of the military budget), some deep-seated ignorance also reigns in Europe regarding the size of the EU budget.[4] The 2006 budget corresponds to €120 billion compared to €270 billion for the French budget or $420 billion for the US defence budget. In other words, the European budget continues to represent a very small share of public expenditure across the EU, about 2 percent of the total.

---

[1] J. Shaw and A. Wiener, "Paradox of the European Polity", in M. Green Cowles and M. Smith (eds), *The State of the European Union: Risks, Reform, Resistance, and Revival* (Oxford University Press, New York, 2000), p 81.

[2] See Dublin City Council's website: http://www.dublincity.ie/your_council/our_organisation.

[3] K. Myers, An Irishman's Diary, *The Irish Times*, 20 May 2005.

[4] In 2001, the Commission adopted gross national income (GNI) instead of gross domestic product (GDP) to determine the ceiling of EU revenue. And as a percentage of EU GNI, the EU budget fell from 1.05 percent to 0.98 percent over the period from 1992 to 2003. For an excellent synthesis, see the report of the House of Lords, EU Committee, *Future Financing of the European Union*, 6th report of Session 2004–05 (HL Paper 62).

Futhermore, the six biggest net contributor countries—Germany, France, Austria, Sweden, the Netherlands and the United Kingdom—have remained reluctant to accept a ceiling for EU spending exceeding 1 percent of the gross national income of the Member States. In short, the Member States do not appear willing to grant the EU anything more than meagre financial resources, and are always extremely careful not to extend the nature and level of the EU's resources. In addition to this unhelpful evidence to support the superstate hypothesis, the EU does not have the power to levy taxes nor to run a deficit. As for the "own resources" of the EU—strictly speaking of the EC—it is an unfortunate term. As a matter of fact, the EU is mostly funded by direct transfers from the Member States. The traditional own resources, i.e. customs duties, agricultural levies and VAT contributions, provide for approximately one-third of total EU budget revenues.

Regardless of these human and fiscal constraints, the administrative constraints are numerous. The implementation and control of EU law is primarily left to national administration and national courts. These administrative constraints are evident in the Irish debacle over illegal dumping.[5] A European obligation requires that all municipal landfills hold permits for waste disposal. This originates from a directive first approved in 1975 imposing on the Member States a number of obligations regarding waste management. Not only did Ireland transpose the 1975 "waste directive" extremely late, Irish authorities also failed to put in place an effective permit procedure and have tolerated unauthorised activities in numerous places around Ireland. Although Ireland's failure to comply with the "waste directive" has long been documented, it took 30 years for EU institutions and, more precisely, the European Court of Justice, after the Commission started examining formal complaints in 1997, to condemn Ireland for "general and persistent" flouting of EU rules on waste disposal.[6] This example plainly reveals that the administration and implementation of European rules, given the size of the European civil service, is essentially left to the ultimate goodwill of national authorities.

Such a brief overview may be valuable if only for the sake of putting the EU into the appropriate context.[7] Yet it does not formally answer the statehood question.

(I) The Concept of State

The state is a tangible reality of national and international life. Full understanding of the state remains difficult, however, due to its numerous definitions. Such plurality could be

---

[5] See Editorial, "Time to clean up on waste", *The Irish Times*, 27 April 2005. On Irish environmental policy, see generally B. Flynn, *The Blame Game: Rethinking Ireland's Sustainable Development And Environmental Performance* (Irish Academic Press, Dublin, 2006).

[6] Case C-494/01 *Commission v Ireland* [2005] ECR I-3331.

[7] On the plurality of constraints imposed on EU institutions and, therefore, the near elimination of any threat of a European superstate, see the incisive analysis of A. Moravcsik, "In Defence of the Democratic Deficit: Reassessing Legitimacy in the European Union", (2002) 40 *Journal of Common Market Studies* 603, pp 607–610.

explained by the diversity of points of view adopted by their authors. For instance, the sociologist may assimilate it with the product of the differentiation between governors and the governed, while the historian could understand it as the institutionalisation of the nation. The political scientist may identify it as the abstract and permanent holder of power whereas the jurist could comprehend it as a system of norms governing a sovereign polity.

An inquiry about the constitutive elements of the state could shed some interesting light on the notion of statehood. To answer the question "what is a state *in abstracto*?", one may look first at what a state *in concreto* is. The definition offered in the classic work of the French Law Professor Carré de Malberg,[8] affirms that a state is a human community situated on a defined territory with an organisation endowed with the ultimate power to command and coerce its members. Such a "continental" definition does not in reality differ much from the one offered in Black's Law Dictionary: "A people permanently occupying a fixed territory bound together by common-law habits and custom into one body politic exercising, through the medium of an organised government, independent sovereignty and control over all persons and things within its boundaries, capable of making war and peace and of entering into international relations with other communities of the globe."

By focusing on the conventional conditions pertaining to the creation and existence of a state, it can thus be asserted that the EU may only be characterised as a state if the following elements are cumulatively present: a People or Nation; a territory; and a sovereign capacity of action both internally and externally. Each of these elements will now be considered in turn.

(a) A European People?

Theoretically, a state cannot come into existence without a "People". The People here discussed should not be reduced to the more precise notion of population. According to the eminent Austrian legal academic Hans Kelsen, the term denotes an abstract unity, insofar as its members belong to the same state system. Quite significantly, the concrete diversity of the People is of no relevance for the legal recognition of a single sovereign People. Alternatively, the concept of nation could be used to identify the sovereign entity presiding over the creation of a state. Historically, reference to the nation was used in the aftermath of the French revolution. In truth, the problem in France at the time of the French Revolution of 1789 was in determining which new abstract entity could substitute the People to replace the King. This new abstract entity was to be known as the Nation. Therefore, Art III of the Declaration of the Rights of Man and of the Citizen of 1789 asserted that "The principle of all sovereignty resides essentially in the Nation.

---

[8] R. Carré de Malberg, *Contribution à la théorie générale de l'État* (Sirey, Paris, 1920–1922).

No body and no individual may exercise authority which does not derive expressly therefrom." The word "Nation" was used to demonstrate that the sovereignty which belonged exclusively to the King had now passed to the citizens of France, i.e. the Nation.

Legally speaking, the birth of a state could coincide with the emergence of a People or a Nation as the new sovereign entity. Indeed, the simple ratification of a constitutional text by referendum, for instance, implies the pre-existence of a People, although it may not formally exist until after the text is ratified. In other words, a new constitutional order can emerge as soon as a human community decides to adopt a new fundamental "contract" where the capacity to act as a single People is recognised. A brief reading of the preamble of the Constitutional Treaty may therefore offer a preliminary answer to the question of a European People:

> "CONVINCED that, while remaining proud of their own national identities and history, *the peoples of Europe* [emphasis added] are determined to transcend their former divisions and, united ever more closely, to forge a common destiny ..."

The reference to the peoples, not to a people, implies that the first element in the definition of a state is missing. The Constitutional Treaty therefore did not depart from the current wording of the EC Treaty, which again emphasises the plurality of the peoples composing our "Community":

> "DESIRING to deepen the solidarity between their peoples while respecting their history, their culture and their traditions ... RESOLVED to continue the process of creating an ever closer union among the peoples of Europe, in which decisions are taken as closely as possible to the citizen in accordance with the principle of subsidiarity ... "

Quite in contrast, the often quoted Preamble of the US Constitution states "We the People of the United States" and offers, as a result, an interesting point of comparison. To reinforce the argument, one may also quote, for example, the Preambles of the Irish Constitution and of the more modern German Constitution. They read, respectively: "We, the People of Éire, ... do hereby adopt, enact, and give to ourselves this Constitution"; "Conscious of their responsibility before God and men, moved by the purpose to serve world peace as an equal part in a unified Europe, the German People have adopted, by virtue of their constituent power, this Constitution."[9]

---

[9] This is the text as amended by the 36th Amendment, i.e. the unification amendment. The original text of 1949 avoided the term Constitution and stressed the temporary character of the so-called Basic Law (*Grundgesetz*).

It must be emphasised that the diversity of the European peoples from a historical or cultural point of view—if one assumes there is more diversity than unity—is not an obstacle to its legal recognition as such. However, for a European *demos* to emerge as the new "*pouvoir constituant*", it would have been necessary for the Constitutional Treaty to be enacted in its name and adopted through an act of sovereign self-determination. This would require the organisation of a European-wide referendum with the adoption of the text by a simple majority of Member States and of the European population as a whole. No "*saut constitutionnel*" of this sort is foreseen and, therefore, the constituent power will remain with the European peoples.

(b) A European Territory?

One of the key elements for a state to emerge is to have a territorial space defined by borders where it could exercise its *imperium*. The trouble with the EU is that its ultimate borders are far from being well defined. Furthermore, special provisions govern the relationship between the EC and a great number of infra-national entities. For instance, if common policies apply to the French overseas departments, the Azores, Madeira and the Canary Islands, they must take account of the structural, social and economic situations of those "regions". In addition, a distinct set of rules deal with the situation of "*non-European* [emphasis added] countries and territories which have special relations with Denmark, France, the Netherlands and the United Kingdom".[10] Greenland, New Caledonia or Bermuda are among the "countries" mentioned. To render the situation even more confusing, a special provision exempts a certain number of countries and territories from the scope of Treaty rules. Hence, the EC Treaty does not apply, for instance, to the Faeroe Islands nor to the sovereign base areas of the United Kingdom in Cyprus. As a result, the territory of the Union cannot be said to perfectly equate the territories under the control of the Member States. Moreover, its external borders are constantly expanding with no apparent end in sight.

The question of a predetermined European territory has been a widely discussed topic in the context of Turkey's prospective EU accession. For instance, according to former French President Valéry Giscard d'Estaing, Turkish membership should be opposed since Turkey is not a European country.[11] The crucial question is, therefore, whether the current Treaties require candidate countries to be "European" in some geographical sense. Faced with fresh applications for admission after the fall of the Berlin Wall, the EU decided to opt for the easy way: to define "objective" criteria instead of defining the outer limits of Europe. In Copenhagen in 1993, the European Council—the reunion of the Heads of State or Government of all the Member States—*unanimously* approved the principle of the Union's

---

[10] Article 182 TEC.

[11] V. Giscard d'Estaing, "Pour ou contre l'adhésion de la Turquie à l'Union Européenne", *Le Monde*, 9 November 2002.

enlargement. However, candidate countries were asked to fulfil the following criteria: the stability of institutions guaranteeing democracy, the rule of law, human rights and respect for and protection of minorities (political criterion); the existence of a functioning market economy as well as the capacity to cope with competitive pressure and market forces within the EU (economic criterion); and the ability to take on membership obligations including adherence to the aims of political, economic and monetary union (criterion concerning adoption of the Community *acquis*). A few years later, the Treaty of Amsterdam put a particular emphasis on the political criteria. According to Art 49(1) TEU, which governs the conditions of eligibility and procedure for accession to the Union, any European State which respects the principles of liberty, democracy, respect for human rights and the rule of law, may apply to become a member of the Union:

> "Any European State which respects the principles set out in Article 6(1)[12] may apply to become a member of the Union. It shall address its application to the Council, which shall act unanimously after consulting the Commission and after receiving the assent of the European Parliament, which shall act by an absolute majority of its component members."

The Constitutional Treaty illustrated a similar logic although it slightly expanded the demand imposed on any prospective candidate by requiring it to respect the Union's values, and also to be "committed to promoting them together".[13] Furthermore, the list of these values (formerly called "principles") was also fairly inflated:

> "The Union is founded on the values of respect for human dignity, freedom, democracy, equality, the rule of law and respect for human rights, including the rights of persons belonging to minorities. These values are common to the Member States in a society in which pluralism, non-discrimination, tolerance, justice, solidarity and equality between women and men prevail."

This type of clause obviously does not answer the question of the Union's ultimate boundaries. If the EU shall be open to all European States that respect its values, it remains unknown as to what exactly amounts to a "European" State. On their own, the "universal" criteria for membership set out at the Copenhagen Council do not exclude the admission of Turkey[14] or, say, Israel. In any event, the admission of any new Member State is

---

[12] "The Union is founded on the principles of liberty, democracy, respect for human rights and fundamental freedoms, and the rule of law, principles which are common to the Member States."

[13] Article I-1(2) EU CT.

[14] In its Communication of October 2004 the European Commission found that Turkey sufficiently fulfils the Copenhagen political criteria and recommends opening accession negotiations with Turkey. See *Recommendation of the European Commission on Turkey's progress towards accession*, COM (2004) 656 final. In December 2004, the European Council decided that the Union would open accession negotiations with Turkey on 3 October 2005.

dependent on the agreement of each of the current Member States as well as the consent of the European Parliament. The Constitutional Treaty simply did not alter the current situation on accession. This was plainly demonstrated on 3 October 2005, when the EU British Presidency kept alive the promise to launch membership talks with Turkey after some last-minute bargaining with Austria—until then one of the staunchest opponents to Turkish membership.

To answer the concerns of those worried by the prospective accession of Turkey, the Member States agreed that the Lisbon Treaty should reproduce the Constitutional Treaty's provision dealing with EU membership and reinforce the conditions of eligibility for accession to the EU. Accordingly, the present reference to the principles of liberty, democracy, respect for human rights and the rule of law is replaced by a general reference to the Union's values and the addition of a commitment to promoting such values. In other words, once the Lisbon Treaty enters into force, prospective members will have to respect additional European "values" such as equality and the rights of persons belonging to minorities.[15] They will also have to demonstrate their commitment to promoting them although the provision remains silent as to how to do so. The bar for membership is also raised by the insertion of a new sentence agreed in June 2007: "The conditions of eligibility agreed upon by the European Council shall be taken into account." The so-called Copenhagen criteria will therefore become legally binding although one may well argue that they are already indirectly guaranteed by a series of provisions in the EC and the EU Treaties. However, no mention is made of the indefinite yet recently popular notion of "absorption capacity", i.e. the EU's capacity to integrate new members.[16] France and the Netherlands were keen to link any future enlargement with the demonstration that the EU could continue to adequately function. Had they succeeded in convincing their European partners, the situation would not have been dramatically different. Since the EU Treaty does not define the Union's final boundaries and that the Copenhagen criteria are too vague to be operational, the decision to accept a new Member State is, ultimately, a political one.

Some subjectivity will inevitably colour any discussion of what the term "European" means. To follow William Wallace, one may argue that "what Europe you see depends on where you live. 'Europe' is a movable set of myths and images, both positive and negative, embedded in national histories and vernacular literature."[17] And yet the eminent author

---

[15] See new Art 2 TEU.

[16] For the European Commission, absorption capacity or integration capacity is "about whether the EU can take in new members at a given moment or in a given period, without jeopardizing the political and policy objectives established" by the European Treaties. See European Commission Communication, Enlargement Strategy and Main Challenges 2006–2007, Annex 1 – Special Report on the EU's capacity to integrate new members, COM(2006) 649 final, p 17. Available at: http://ec.europa.eu/enlargement/key_documents/reports_nov_2006_en.htm.

[17] W. Wallace, "Where does Europe End? Dilemmas of Inclusion and Exclusion", in J. Zielonka (ed), *Europe Unbound* (Routledge, London, 2002), p 79.

immediately appreciates that the EU is unworkable without clear boundaries. Ultimately, it may not be possible to end the discussion on the Union's boundaries. Indeed, it could be argued that the simple fact that boundaries are undefined embodies the uncertainty about the ultimate nature of the EU. If it were a state, it would have fixed borders. If there is no European People, it cannot be firmly stated where the borders of the EU should end. Answering the question about borders requires us first to clarify the nature of the EU. The fact that its borders remain somewhat fuzzy might justify the qualification of a "post-modern" state[18] or, the even more creative comparison with a neo-medieval empire.[19] In any case, such analysis clearly indicates that the EU cannot be said to fulfil the second element which presides over the emergence of a state: the existence of a fixed and hard external border.

The last element to indicate the existence of a state is the presence of an organised government, a state apparatus governing all persons and things within the boundaries of its territory. While an essential condition prior to the international recognition of a new State by its peers, its study would not offer any fruitful conclusions with regard to the EU. More fundamental is the debate over the *attributes* organised governments are supposedly bestowed with: a sovereign capacity to act and command. Undeniably, more than just a constitutive element, sovereignty is indeed the essence of statehood and its key legal attribute. It is therefore not surprising that the question about the EU's alleged sovereign capacity is a fertile field of interrogation and heated debate. Before exposing a personal thesis, according to which European integration has not led to the emergence of a European entity with sovereign capacity, one must demonstrate that the concept of sovereignty does not preclude the transfer of (sovereign) powers at the European level.

(c) The Absolute and Inalienable Characters of Sovereignty

Sovereignty is the key legal element which differentiates a state from other legal entities. An abstract principle, the meaning of which is complex, sovereignty is often used to characterise the entity—the state being the personification of the Sovereign[20]—possessing the legitimate political authority to issue norms which could be imposed upon individuals.

---

[18] See J. Caporaso, "The European Union and Forms of State: Westphalian, Regulatory or Post-Modern", (1996) 34 *Journal of Common Market Studies* 29, pp 44–48.

[19] J. Zielonka, "How New Enlarged Borders Will Reshape the European Union", (2001) 39 *Journal of Common Market Studies* 507, pp 509–511. For Jan Zielonka, the neo-medieval empire is characterised by overlapping authorities, divided sovereignty, diversified institutional arrangements, multiple identities and last but not least, by soft-border zones that undergo regular adjustments.

[20] It should not be assumed that popular sovereignty, as the main source of public authority, is a tradition shared across Europe. For instance, in the United Kingdom, the "constitution" does not refer to the people as the constituent power. On the contrary, the orthodox view of sovereignty is that Parliament exercises power by virtue of its own right and is therefore omnicompetent. For a clear overview of British constitutionalism and alternative visions of the constitution, see K. Armstrong, "United Kingdom – Divided on Sovereignty", in N. Walker (ed), *Sovereignty in Transition* (Hart, Oxford, 2003), p 327.

While the existence of a People, a well-defined territory and a political authority commanding such territory may be essential for a state to emerge, to subsist and to be recognised by its peers, sovereignty is the fundamental legal attribute of statehood.

Sovereignty is nonetheless a historical product.[21] A French scholar, Jean Bodin, produced the first substantial work on the notion in 1576: *Les six livres de la république.* For the renowned author, sovereignty is the inherent quality of a state, "the distinguishing mark of a commonwealth". And the principal feature of "sovereign majesty and absolute power is the right to impose laws generally on all subjects regardless of their consent." Whereas Bodin accepted the possibility that sovereignty can reside in different persons or bodies, the theory of the divine right of kings locates sovereign power in the hereditary monarch. Royal power flows directly from God. The royal prerogative is thus absolute and is not subject to limitations except for the obligation to respect the laws of God and nature, the "fundamental laws" of the kingdom, and treaties. As implied by the famous dictum, *Regia maiestas non moritur* (the King never dies), sovereignty was also meant to be of a permanent quality. Indeed, while the King's "body natural" may perish, his "body politic" always remained. With the clear triumph of the monarchy over internal forces that threatened the existence of the French nation as such, and as doctrines of *jus divinum* and natural law began to lose their binding character, the problem of how to limit royal absolutism arose. Looking to the English system as a model, Montesquieu, in *De l'Esprit des Lois* (1748), developed a political analysis that focused on the idea of constitution as "the indispensable term to describe the fundamental order of a state, the models of political existence of a nation or people, the essential disposition of the elements or powers composing a form of government".[22]

While these historical developments contextualise the emergence of the concept of sovereignty—and it can already be seen that a constitution could serve as a limitation on the concrete exercise of sovereignty by the State—its nature and substance need to be further explained. In a few words, the essential nature of sovereignty is classically said to be supreme (*summa potestas*). Within its territory (internal sovereignty), the state is said to enjoy sovereignty when it has a monopoly on rule-making and on the legitimate use of force. More abstractly, a state is sovereign insofar as its authority is said to be initial (the state is at the source of the new legal order), unlimited (entire freedom to determine how to exercise its sovereign authority without reference to any external or anterior norm) and unchallengeable (no superior authority exists within its territory).

Sovereignty has also an external face. In this context, it essentially encompasses a negative element and another type of capacity: the state does not know a superior authority

---

[21] This analysis is based on L. Pech, "Rule of Law in France", in R. Peerenboom (ed), *Asian Discourses of Rule of Law* (Routledge, London, 2004), p 79.
[22] K. Baker, "Constitution", in F. Furet and M. Ozouf (eds), *A Critical Dictionary of the French Revolution* (Harvard University Press, Cambridge, 1989), p 481.

and the state has the capacity to negotiate rules of coexistence and co-operation with rival states; its equals. In this regard, it may be useful to recall what the Permanent Court of International Justice affirmed in the celebrated case of the S.S. Wimbledon:

> "The Court declines to see in the conclusion of any treaty by which a State undertakes to perform or refrain from performing a particular act an abandonment of its sovereignty. No doubt any Convention creating an obligation of this kind places a restriction upon the exercise of the sovereign rights of the State, in the sense that it requires them to be exercised in a certain way. But the right to enter into international engagements is an attribute of State sovereignty."[23]

The presentation seen above is undeniably too systematic. Further details are required in order to eliminate a series of common misunderstandings associated with the concept of sovereignty.

Firstly, as sovereignty is said to be unlimited, one could assume that state organs acting on behalf of the Sovereign could undertake any action they see fit. Sovereignty should not, however, be confused with absoluteness or arbitrariness. By the term unlimited, it should be understood that the Sovereign is the *source* of ultimate political authority, not that the Sovereign has total power. And undeniably, in a democracy, it is usual for the holder of sovereignty to (voluntarily) submit the exercise—through a state—of its power to some limitations by adopting a constitution. Article 1 of the Italian Constitution is interesting in this regard: "Sovereignty belongs to the people, who exercise it in the manner, and within the limits, laid down by the Constitution". However, a written constitution may not even be an imperative. Indeed, the magnificent idea of the rule of law leads to an identical result. Albert Van Dicey defined it, in his *Introduction to the Study of the Law of the Constitution*, as "the absolute supremacy or predominance of regular law as opposed to the influence of arbitrary power, and excludes the existence of arbitrariness of prerogative, or even of wide discretionary authority on the part of the government".[24] In the end, it is unproblematic to conclude that there could be no "lawful State" when there are no limitations on state powers. Many illustrious authors could be referred to. For instance, in his theory of the state, Kant defined it as the union of a multitude of men under laws of justice. Any lawful state has to be a state governed by the law of reason, i.e. based on the principles of freedom of every citizen, equality and individual autonomy. Therefore, sovereignty could certainly not be interpreted as giving *carte blanche* to public authorities.

Nor in its external dimension, should sovereignty be understood as an absolute. In a world of equals, any state can freely decide an agreement with its peers, i.e. in a sovereign

---

[23] PCIJ Series A No. 1 (1923), p 25.

[24] A. Van Dicey, *Introduction to the Study of the Law of the Constitution* (Reprint 8th ed, 1915, Liberty Fund, Indianapolis, 1982), p 120.

manner, to limit their sovereignty for common purposes. For instance, Art 1 of the Irish Constitution affirms the sovereign right of the Irish nation to determine its relations with other nations while Art 29 not only affirms Ireland's adherence to peace and friendly co-operation amongst nations, but also affirms the acceptance of generally recognised principles of international law as its rules of conduct in its relations with other States.[25] Within this framework, which clearly demonstrates the will of the Sovereign to *voluntarily* adhere to ideals of international justice and peaceful co-existence, the constitutional text also mentions the possibility of Ireland becoming "associated for the purpose of international co-operation in matters of common concern".[26] Is such international co-operation a threat to the preservation of national sovereignty?

As sovereignty is often mistaken for inalienability, the concept is also occasionally understood to exclude any limitation or transfer of "sovereign" powers to external entities. In a few words, the Sovereign has the sovereign authority to limit its sovereignty. There is no legal obstacle for such action and, in fact, some constitutional texts specifically refer to the feasibility of some limitations of sovereignty. However unexpressed, the idea is inherent in Art 29 of the Irish Constitution. A more affirmative example is to be found in the preamble to the French Constitution of 27 October 1946, a legally binding text. Paragraphs 14 and 15 assert respectively that the French Republic "faithful to its traditions, shall respect the rules of public international law" and that "subject to reciprocity, France shall consent to the *limitations upon its sovereignty* [emphasis added] necessary to the organisation and preservation of peace". When first faced with the delicate task of clarifying the relationship between EC law and French constitutional law, the *Conseil constitutionnel* drew an uneasy distinction between limitations of sovereignty, constitutionally valid, and transfers of sovereignty, which require a prior revision of the constitutional text.[27] This distinction between limitation and transfer is, however, far from clear. And in the so-called Maastricht decision,[28] the *Conseil* finally held that respect for national sovereignty does not preclude France from participating in the establishment of a permanent international organisation enjoying legal personality and decision-making powers on the basis of transfers of powers decided on by the Member States. Interestingly, such is the nature of the EU according to the *Conseil constitutionnel.* There is, nonetheless, an ultimate boundary. Should an international agreement involve a clause which directly conflicts with the French Constitution or jeopardises the "essential conditions" for the exercise of national sovereignty, authorisation to ratify the agreement would require prior revision of the

---

[25] See generally G. Biehler, *International Law in Practice: An Irish Perspective* (Thomson Round Hall, Dublin, 2005).

[26] Article 29.4.2° of the Irish Constitution.

[27] See Decision no. 71-76 DC of 30 December 1976 on the EC Council Act of 20 September 1976 concerning the election of the members of the European Parliament by direct universal suffrage.

[28] Decision no. 92-308 DC of 9 April 1992. See also the Amsterdam Decision no. 97-394 DC of 31 December 1997 and the Decision no. 2004-505 DC of 19 November 2004 on the Treaty establishing a Constitution for Europe.

Constitution. Such was the case with the Maastricht Treaty, the Amsterdam Treaty and finally, the Treaty establishing a Constitution for Europe. On each occasion, the French Constitution was amended to allow the Republic to "participate in the European Communities and in the European Union constituted by States that have freely chosen, by virtue of the treaties that established them, to exercise some of their powers in common".[29] It is worth noting that the French Constitution already indicates that the EU is *constituted by States*, meaning the EU is *not* considered, from a French point of view, as a sovereign entity.

The constitutional logic governing European integration is no different in Ireland. As *Crotty v An Taoiseach*[30] made it abundantly clear, any new Treaty substantially altering the scope or objectives of the EU will require the intervention of the sovereign People.[31] This holds true whenever there is an alteration to the constitutional functions granted to national authorities. An amendment to the Irish Constitution will then be necessary. As they were deemed to contain reforms altering the essential scope and objective of the founding European Communities, each major European treaty since 1986 was followed by an amendment to the Irish Constitution. As a concrete result, Art 29.4 of the Irish Constitution lists, in a somewhat non-aesthetic manner, all the European Treaties that the State was authorised to ratify and all the organisations it was authorised to become a member of: The European Coal and Steel Community of 1951, the European Economic Community of 1957, the European Atomic Energy Community of 1957, the Single European Act of 1986, the Treaty on European Union of 1992, the Treaty of Amsterdam of 1997 and finally, the Treaty of Nice of 2001.

To conclude on the inalienable character of sovereignty, if the constitutional text forbids any transfer or limitation of sovereignty, the *pouvoir constituant*, i.e. the People (or its representatives acting in the name of the Sovereign), could always either amend the Constitution or refuse to amend it. And when it does so, it simply exercises its independent power to revise its own creation. Technically, there could be no constitutional provision out of reach of the amending power of the Sovereign. And if the Sovereign decides to transfer "sovereign" powers to the European level—understood as powers classically associated with the State such as monetary power—it has the "sovereign" right, the ultimate political authority to consent to such a result.

---

[29] Article 88-1: "The Republic shall participate in the European Communities and in the European Union constituted by States that have freely chosen, by virtue of the treaties that established them, to exercise some of their powers in common."

[30] [1987] IR 713.

[31] For an introduction to the relationship between Irish constitutional law and EC law, see generally G. Hogan and G. Whyte, *J.M. Kelly: The Irish Constitution* (4th ed, LexisNexis Butterworths, Dublin: 2003). For a concise and clear overview, see also C. Costello, "Ireland's Nice Referenda", (2005) 1 *European Constitutional Law Review* 357.

With the hope that some of the usual confusions about the unlimited and inalienable characters of sovereignty have now been dissipated, the case remains to be made about the alleged sovereign capacity of the EU.

(II) SQUARING THE EUROPEAN CIRCLE: THE TRANSFER OF "SOVEREIGN" POWERS WITHOUT TRANSFERRING SOVEREIGNTY

In a few words, the EU is not a sovereign entity although it exercises important "sovereign" powers (or competences[32]). A customary source of misunderstanding lies in the understanding of sovereignty both as a quality and as a sum of powers. The view defended here is that a state could transfer all its "sovereign" powers, e.g. the monetary power and even the power to conduct external relations and national defence, without losing its sovereignty as long as any additional conferral of competence is the subject of unanimous agreement between Member States. The Constitutional Treaty simply did not change the nature of the relationship between the EU and the Member States and neither will the Lisbon Treaty: the EU will continue to lack independent sovereignty and the Member States will remain the masters of the EU's amendment procedure. Even with an understanding of sovereignty as a sum of powers, the argument about a European superstate does not sustain a simple reading of the current and foreseen provisions describing the exclusive and shared powers of the EU. History has yet to see a *Leviathan* emerging from a situation where a non-state organisation has no police power, no power to declare war or no exclusive control over international relations. True, if the EU has the ultimate authority to decide where power lies, there will be no obstacle for the eurosceptics' nightmare to become a reality. Yet, one should not indulge in dreadful thinking!

(a) Attribution of Powers to the EU

Before analysing further the limits of the EU's powers *in abstracto*, it is important to list the areas in which the EU may intervene to refute the common charge according to which the EU is omnipotent. A didactic way to proceed—although not uncomplicated—is to distinguish between different types of legislative power: exclusive, concurrent and complementary.[33]

Exclusive power covers areas in which the EU alone may adopt rules. In principle, any national intervention is excluded with the sole exception of legal gaps needing to be filled. As a result, this is the sole category where the EU has a monopoly of action. Yet, it should be emphasised that these areas are under the exclusive control of the EU only because the Member States agreed *unanimously* to it. The five areas falling within the exclusive power

---

[32] The term competence has been denounced as "Euro-speak" by *The Economist*, "Snoring while a superstate emerges?", 8 May 2003.

[33] For a bright introduction, see F. Mayer, "Powers-Reloaded? The Vertical Division of Powers in the EU and the New European Constitution", (2005) *International Journal of Constitutional Law* 493.

of the EU are as follows:[34] customs union; competition rules necessary for the functioning of the internal market; monetary policy;[35] the conservation of marine biological resources; and common commercial policy. While one should not deduce from a comparison with the constitution of a federal state that the EU is itself a state or an entity of federal nature, it may be interesting to offer a view of Art 73 of the German Constitution, if only to put into perspective the extent of the Union's exclusive powers:

> "The [German] Federation has exclusive power to legislate in the following matters:
> 1. foreign affairs and defence, including the protection of the civilian population;
> 2. citizenship in the Federation;
> 3. freedom of movement, passport matters, immigration, emigration and extradition;
> 4. currency, money and coinage … ;
> 5. the unity of the customs and trading area, treaties on commerce and on navigation, the freedom of movement of goods … ;
> 6. air transport;
> 6a. the traffic of railroads owned completely or mainly by the Federation … ;
> 7. postal affairs and telecommunication;
> 8. the legal status of persons employed by the Federation … ;
> 9. industrial property rights, copyrights and publishing law;
> 10. cooperation between the Federation and the States [Länder] concerning a) criminal police, b) protection of the free democratic basic order … and c) protection against activities in the federal territory which, through the use of force or actions in preparation for the use of force, endanger the foreign interests of the Federal Republic of Germany, as well as the establishment of a Federal Criminal Police Office and the international control of crime;
> 11. statistics for federal purposes."

Reading the German Constitution certainly helps dilute the criticism on the alleged stylistic insufficiencies of European Treaties in general and of the Constitutional Treaty in particular. Anyone familiar with constitutional law knows how concision could not easily be reconciled with the demands of legal certainty. Particularly striking was the lack of consistency on the part of authors complaining about the length of the Constitutional Treaty while, at the same time, arguing against the lack of transparency of its provisions. A shorter text—absent an extensive organic law—offers more room for judicial interpretation. As a result, if one fears judicial activism, it is inconsistent to criticise European Treaties for not being pocket-sized documents.

---

[34] See new Art 2 B TEC. This provision lists areas which presently fall within the exclusive competence of the EU.

[35] For the members of the Eurozone.

The notion of shared powers is another source of controversy. As of today, most EU powers fall into this category: internal market; social policy (but *solely* for the aspects strictly defined in the Treaties); economic, social and territorial cohesion; agriculture and fisheries; environment; consumer protection; transport; trans-European networks; energy (but *solely* for the aspects strictly defined in the Treaties); areas of freedom, security and justice; and common safety concerns in public health matters (again *only* for the aspects defined in the Treaties).[36] True, these shared powers are not actually "shared" inasmuch as Member States may no longer legislate in the field covered by EU legislation except to the extent necessary to implement EU law. European intervention is said to pre-empt national intervention. Therefore, the shared powers can actually become progressively "exclusive" whenever the EU acts. Nevertheless, it would be wrong to assume that European intervention is always synonymous with complete harmonisation. Of critical importance is the fact that EU action in these areas is subject to compliance with the principles of subsidiarity and proportionality, principles whose meaning and scope will be examined when dealing with the alleged federal character of the EU. It is also important to note that national legislative intervention is required in most cases. Besides, contrary to the exclusive powers listed above, it is always possible for the EU not to act, or for the Member States, acting through the Council of Ministers,[37] to repeal EU legislation. In such circumstances, the Member States retain maximum legislative scope at the national level. Undoubtedly, despite the wishes of those who argue for a return of powers from Brussels, the Constitutional Treaty did not "repatriate" powers to the Member States. However, this was not a decision from "Brussels" but the unanimous choice of national governments. In any event, to answer continuous concern about the scope of Union's powers, the Lisbon Treaty includes a Declaration which expressly states, for the first time, that the Member States may always "decide to amend the Treaties on which the Union is founded, including either to increase or *to reduce* [emphasis added] the competences conferred on the Union in the said Treaties".[38] In other words, "repatriation" of power at the national level is entirely feasible as long as the Member States unanimously agree to do so. The Lisbon Treaty also refers to a new Protocol to be annexed to the Treaties and which clarifies that when the EU has taken action in an area of shared competence, "the

---

[36] A quotation of Art 74 of the German Constitution dealing with "concurrent legislative powers" would, again, require a great length of space. Indeed, no less than twenty-six matters are stated. The main areas of shared powers include civil law, criminal law and execution of sentences (1); the law relating to residence and settlement of aliens (4); public welfare (7); the law relating to economic matters (11); labour law (12); the regulation of educational and training grants and the promotion of scientific research (12); land law (18); measures against human and animal diseases (19); protection regarding the marketing of food (20); artificial insemination of humans, research on manipulations of genes, and regulations for transplantation of organs and living (26).

[37] What we call the Council of Ministers is formally known, since 1993, as the Council of the European Union. It consists of a representative of each Member State at ministerial level who is authorized to commit the government of that State. The change of vocabulary has led to much confusion with the European Council, i.e. the reunion of the leaders of the Member States at least twice a year. The Constitutional Treaty rightly suggested to return to the denomination "Council of Ministers".

[38] Declaration in relation to the delimitation of competences, [2007] OJ C306/256.

scope of this exercise of competence only covers those elements governed by the Union act in question and therefore does not cover the whole area".[39] These unprecedented explanations should reassure those who are—wrongly—convinced that the EU can legislate in any area it sees fit.

The last category of power could be labelled "complementary powers". This category covers areas in which the EU is limited to co-ordinating or supporting the action of the Member States: one may mention, for instance, economic and employment policies, the protection of human health, industry, culture, tourism, education, civil protection and administrative co-operation. Although these are areas where the EU already intervenes, the Lisbon Treaty creates new individualised legal bases to increase transparency. The most important point, however, is that the acts adopted by the EU in these areas do not entail harmonisation of Member States' laws or regulations. In addition, if the EU has power to support the actions of the Member States, EU measures cannot supersede national competence. In other words, EU intervention in these areas can only "complement" Member States' intervention.

As a final point, one should regret that the Constitutional Treaty was abandoned. With the exception of very few and unremarkable new areas, the Constitutional Treaty did not extend the Union's powers but essentially consolidated the existing powers in a clearer framework more than it created new ones. There was certainly room for criticism regarding the indefinite or unclear aspects of some provisions, yet one has only to read the constitutional texts of some federal States to understand that the Convention's performance fares well in comparison.[40] Unfortunately, the Lisbon Treaty does not attempt to further consolidate and rationalise the current rules on allocation of powers between the EU and the Member States. In line with the Constitutional Treaty, it only requires the reading of a single set of five articles to get a broad picture of "who does what" in Europe.[41] Unfortunately, it also increases the complexity of the current legal framework by adding articles, protocols and declarations emphasising that the EU shall only act within the limits of competences conferred upon it by the Member States and that competences not conferred upon the EU in the Treaties remain with the Member States. This is rather pointless since the present Treaties already state this. These clarifications may nonetheless be useful to the extent that they clearly indicate that the EU cannot act in new areas without the Member States having previously consented to these grants of power.[42]

---

[39] Protocol on the exercise of shared competence, [2007] OJ C306/158.

[40] For a view on the Constitutional Treaty arguing that it actually generated more confusion than clarity, see S. Weatherill, "Competence", in B. de Witte (ed), *Ten Reflections on the Constitutional Treaty for Europe* (Robert Schuman Centre, Florence, 2003), p 45.

[41] New Art 2A to 2E TEC (formerly Art I-13 to I-17 EU CT).

[42] For a similar view, see P. Craig, "Competence: clarity, conferrral, containment and consideration", (2004) 29 *European Law Review* 323.

(b) The Kompetenz-Kompetenz Issue

German lawyers like to refer to the expression *Kompetenz-Kompetenz* to express the idea that a state has always the ultimate authority to decide on the limits of its own power or to decide with whom power lies. The key question is therefore whether the EC/EU has the power to determine the scope of its own powers. An apparently straightforward answer could be deduced from Art 5 of the Treaty of Rome: the EC does not have independent sovereignty as "the Community shall act within the limits of the powers conferred upon it by this Treaty and of the objectives assigned to it therein". This provision lays down the principle at the heart of the Treaty's legal system, which jurists call the principle of "conferred competence" whereby the EC—and more generally the EU—may act only if it has the competence to do so. Two major rules could be derived from such a principle: first, it is *not* for the European institutions to add or extend their powers; and secondly, to adopt a legal act, European institutions must always find a legal basis in the Treaties allowing the act envisaged to be adopted.[43] The Lisbon Treaty does not alter the present legal regime. On the contrary, it multiplies references to the principle of conferral and confirms that the powers not conferred upon the EU in the Treaties remain with the Member States.

It has been argued that these legal niceties will be insufficient to restrain the EU from intervening outside the scope of the Treaties. The American experience, for example, may lead to some justified scepticism with regard to the legal constraints imposed by the principle of conferral. As a matter of fact, the Constitution of the United States created a (federal) government of enumerated powers. Amendment X (1791) could not have been more restrictively drafted: "The powers not delegated to the United States by the Constitution, nor prohibited by it to the States, are reserved to the States respectively, or to the people." It was therefore assumed, as James Madison wrote, that "the powers delegated by the proposed Constitution to the federal government are few and defined. Those which are to remain in the State governments are numerous and indefinite."[44] Nevertheless, the subsequent interpretation, for instance, of the Commerce Clause,[45] certainly led to a drastic enhancement of the federal government's power with as a result, no apparent limitation on federal power. The question therefore is how could we exclude such "expansive" interpretation in the case of the EU? The litigious aspect of the question is apparently fuelled even more once Art 308 TEC is taken into consideration:

> "If action by the Community should prove necessary to attain, in the course of the operation of the common market, one of the objectives of the Community, and this

---

[43] As the principle of subsidiarity governs not the attribution of powers but only the exercise of powers previously conferred on the Union, it will be studied below.

[44] The Federalist No 45.

[45] Article I, s 8, cl. 3: "Congress shall have power to regulate commerce among the several states." In the landmark ruling *Gibbons v Ogden* (1824), Chief Justice Marshall defined the US Congress's power to regulate foreign and interstate commerce to embrace every species of commercial intercourse as long as the commercial transaction does not entirely occur within the boundaries of a single state.

Treaty has not provided the necessary powers, the Council shall, acting unanimously on a proposal from the Commission and after consulting the European Parliament, take the appropriate measures."[46]

Despite the apparent constraints of Art 5 TEC previously mentioned, it must be said that Art 308 TEC, the so-called "flexibility clause", has been used in a somewhat critical manner which seemed to validate the argument of EU's critics.[47] Indeed, its broad interpretation appeared to nullify the restraints one could draw from the principle of conferral. The rationale behind this provision, however, is clear and legitimate: the necessity to guarantee some flexibility to deal with unexpected challenges. Yet several conditions are attached to the use of this clause.

First, a measure has to attain a Community objective. True, the objectives set out in the European Treaties are numerous and somewhat imprecise. Among the objectives already mentioned in the treaties are the Union's aims to promote economic and social progress and a high level of employment; to maintain and develop the Union as an area of freedom, security and justice; and to promote a harmonious, balanced and sustainable development of economic activities and a high level of protection and improvement of the quality of the environment. The Lisbon Treaty offers some new objectives: the aim of maintaining a highly competitive social market economy; the commitment to combat social exclusion and discrimination; the promotion of scientific and technological knowledge; the promotion of territorial cohesion. Clearly, the wording is broad and the objectives' scope appears to be quite indefinite.

The ratification of the Lisbon Treaty will not be an obstacle, however, for a continuing strict interpretation of the condition according to which Art 308 TEC could be relied upon only insofar as the EC Treaty has not provided the necessary powers.[48] Therefore the Council of Ministers must not rely on Art 308 TEC whenever a more specific legal basis could be found in the Treaty.[49] True, a more "elastic" interpretation characterises the

---

[46] The US Constitution also offers such an apparently open-ended provision. According to Art I, s 8, cl 18, the Congress shall have power "to make all Laws which shall be necessary and proper for carrying into Execution the foregoing Powers, and all other Powers vested by this Constitution in the Government of the United States, or in any Department or Officer thereof".

[47] Although they are also subject to criticism, Arts 94 and 95 TEC will not be examined as the European Court of Justice has now placed strict limits on their use. Generally speaking, these two articles allow the adoption of harmonisation measures for "the establishment and functioning of the internal market". In the Case C-376/98 *Germany v EP and Council* [2000] ECR I-8419, the Court of Justice annulled Directive 98/43/EC designated to harmonise the law relating to the advertising and sponsorship of tobacco. In doing so, the court strictly restricted the scope of the "harmonisation" articles, recalling that they do not vest in the Community a general power to regulate the internal market and ruled that it will always verify whether the measure whose validity is at issue in fact pursues the objectives stated by the Community legislature. Due to the lack of a proper legal basis, the directive was finally annulled.

[48] Opinion 2/94 on Accession by the Community to the ECHR [1996] ECR I-1759.

[49] Case 45/86 *Commission v Council* [1987] ECR 1493.

final condition, that the legislation must be *necessary* to attain a Community objective. Nonetheless, the rule is clear: the "flexibility clause" must not be used to extend European competence beyond the framework established by the Treaties. As stated in a Declaration agreed in June 2007:

> "[The Member States underline] that, in accordance with the settled case-law of the Court of Justice of the European Union, Article 308 ... being an integral part of an institutional system based on the principle of conferred powers, cannot serve as a basis for widening the scope of Union powers beyond the general framework created by the provisions of the Treaties as a whole and, in particular, by those that define the tasks and the activities of the Union. In any event, Article 308 cannot be used as a basis for the adoption of provisions whose effect would, in substance, be to amend the Treaties without following the procedure which they provide for that purpose."[50]

Furthermore, one must note that a unanimous decision of the Council of Ministers is at all times required. The latter condition should help us realise one enduring truth of European integration: the EU cannot be granted more powers without the agreement of the Member States. In other words, the EU has no sovereignty in its own right. It does not derive its authority from a European *demos* but remains the creature of the Member States. If the blame game needs to be played regarding the powers conferred upon the EU, criticism should be addressed to the Member States and, in particular, to national executives.

Some have contemplated the idea of deleting Art 308 entirely. The drafters of the Constitutional Treaty rightly decided to retain it, calling it the "flexibility clause", although it was more precisely reformulated and its potential use tightened.[51] The Lisbon Treaty preserves these improvements. For instance, the use of the flexibility clause to adopt harmonisation measures in policy areas where the EU rules out harmonisation is prohibited.[52] Furthermore, to increase the transparency of the process, proposals to use the flexibility clause must be sent to national parliaments. Finally, the rule of unanimity within the Council of Ministers is preserved, with the new additional and not superfluous requirement to obtain the consent of the European Parliament rather than to simply inform it. Accordingly, it is for national parliaments and the public opinion to make sure that national governments do not agree to a possible extension of the Union's areas of competence without prior discussion and parliamentary approval.

---

[50] Declaration on Art 308 of the Treaty on the Functioning of the European Union, [2007] OJ C306/263.
[51] See Article I-18 EU CT.
[52] This is not to say that Art 308 TEC authorises such harmonisation. The novelty lies in the codification of the principle whereas under the Treaties, such harmonisation is forbidden on a case-by-case basis. For example, where the Community has competence to support Member States' action in the field of employment under Art 129 TEC, the same article states that "those measures shall not include harmonisation of the laws and regulations of the Member States".

Yet, despite all the textual constraints, judicial activism may still allow their circumvention. In other words, the European Court of Justice may well act as the ultimate arbiter of the allocation of competence between the EU and the Member States and may authorise an undue extension of EU powers. And, for some commentators, judicial activism is indeed inherent in its case law. In a few words, the European Court of Justice was set up in 1952 and is located in Luxembourg, hence the name "Luxembourg Court" to describe it on occasion.[53] The Court is composed of one judge per Member State and its mission is to "ensure that in the interpretation and application of this Treaty the law is observed".[54] The Court can hear various types of action. In particular, it has competence to rule on applications for annulment of EC acts, to hear actions against Member States for failure to fulfil obligations and to give references for a preliminary ruling, this last type of action being specific to EC law.[55] In fulfilling its mission, the Court has been accused of transforming itself as a law-maker. An American commentator can, however, be relied on to briefly qualify such diagnosis, especially where criticism originates from the United Kingdom:

> "Like their common-law counterparts, European judges must often fill in legislative gaps and arrive at conclusions based upon broadly worded legal language. Anyone who has ever read a 'Code' knows that it invites, indeed often requires, law-making by judges. Nevertheless, the mystique that judges can only apply the law, not create it, weighs heavily in the minds of many Europeans."[56]

However, in some cases, it remains legitimate to wonder about the scope of the interpretative power of the European Court of Justice. The doctrine of implied powers as elaborated by the Court could indeed be used as a possible example of alleged undue "federal" extension. Such is the archetypal diagnosis as formulated again by *The Economist*: "Just as decisions of the Supreme Court drove the expansion of federal power in the United States, so the ECJ has helped to establish a federal legal order in Europe."[57]

To synopsise the jurisprudence, in a series of cases in the 1970s, the Luxembourg Court developed the doctrine of implied external competence to justify that in some instances competence flows *implicitly* from specific Treaty provisions or their general

---

[53] A common mix-up is made by journalists between the European Court of Justice and the European Court of Human Rights. The latter is located in Strasbourg and was set up under the Convention for the Protection of Human Rights and Fundamental Freedoms of 4 November 1950. The Convention itself is a product of the Council of Europe, a political institution independent from the EU and which was founded on 5 May 1949.

[54] Article 220 TEC. A Court of First Instance was set up in 1989 to help the Court of Justice cope with an ever-growing backlog of cases.

[55] To ensure the effective and uniform application of EC law, national courts may, and sometimes must, turn to the Court of Justice to obtain from it the clarification of litigious issues concerning the interpretation of EC law. A reference for a preliminary ruling may also seek review of the legality of an act of EC law (see Art 234 of the TEC).

[56] R. Folsom, *European Union Law in a Nutshell* (3rd ed, West Group, St. Paul, 1999), p 66.

[57] "Government by judges?", *The Economist*, 17 January 2004.

structure. In particular, the Court argued that external powers may be derived from the existence of internal powers in specific areas whenever it is necessary to fulfil the objectives set out by the Treaties.[58] If the doctrine of implied powers is certainly an example of judicial creativity, it remains a well-known and ancient doctrine in constitutional law.[59] Furthermore, there could be no implied power where there is no initial power. Indeed, it is the existence of an initial power which justifies the existence of any other power when *reasonably* necessary for the exercise of the former. And in most cases, the recognition of an implied power for the Community was the logical consequence of a reasonable interpretation of Treaty provisions.

True, such positive assessment may be challenged. True also, the need for a degree of flexibility in the allocation of powers between the EU and the Member States, is a potential threat to a strict compliance with the principle of conferred powers. In this regard, a key question is who should act as the ultimate arbiter in a case of conflict or to use the classic adage, *quis custodiet custodes ipsos?* As a matter of EC law, the judicial monitoring of compliance is the exclusive task of the European Court of Justice. If European institutions act *ultra vires*, the Court of Justice will nullify the act without any power for the national courts to intervene. However, the Court's monopoly on the judicial monitoring limits to some extent the scope of our argument according to which the EU has no independent sovereignty. Indeed, there is no absolute guarantee that European institutions will act within the limits of their powers. Persuasive arguments could be raised to justify the ultimate position, the power of the final say granted to the Luxembourg Court. Without it, the effectiveness and uniform application of EC law across the Union could be undermined. But what if the Court does not "impartially" fulfil its mission?

There is always the potential for national constitutional courts to scrutinise EU norms with regard to their constitutions in order to determine whether European norms are within the terms of that Member State's accession to the EU. For instance, the German Federal Constitutional Court made it clear, in its *Maastricht* decision, that Germany's acceptance of the European legal order is conditional:

> "If, for example, European institutions or governmental entities were to implement or to develop the Maastricht Treaty in a manner no longer covered by the Treaty in the form of it upon which the German Act of Accession is based, any legal instrument arising from such activity would not be binding within German territory. German State institutions

---

[58] Case 22/70 *Commission v Council (so-called ERTA case from European Road Transport Agreement)* [1971] ECR 263.

[59] See the renowned case of *Mac Cullogh v Maryland*, 17 US 316 (1819). Chief Justice Marshall declared for the Court that the relevant clause of the US Constitution gives Congress the means to carry out its expressly granted powers: "Let the end be legitimate, let it be within the scope of the constitution, and all means which are appropriate, which are plainly adapted to that end, which are not prohibited, but consist with the letter and spirit of the constitution, are constitutional."

would be prevented by reasons of constitutional law from applying such legal instruments in Germany. Accordingly, the German Federal Constitutional Court must examine the question of whether or not legal instruments of European institutions and governmental entities may be considered to remain within the bounds of the sovereign rights accorded to them, or whether they may be considered to exceed those bounds."[60]

In other words, the German Constitutional Court has reserved, *in principle*, its right to review EC law (and *a fortiori* EU law) as applied in Germany, to ultimately guarantee that European institutions do not go beyond the bounds set forth by the Treaties. For the European Court of Justice, however, national courts do not have the power to declare acts of the European institutions invalid.[61]

Strictly speaking, due to the absence of a federal hierarchy between national courts and the European Court of Justice, an open conflict on the validity of EC law would be impossible to solve through legal means only. Politics would, inevitably, engage. However, in light of the existing working relationship between the Court of Justice and national courts, it is unlikely that a national court would ever challenge the Court of Justice's jurisdiction. On the other hand, a lack of clear hierarchy is not in itself regretful. It allows national courts to act as latent checks on any future temptation by the European Court of Justice, through the use of the teleological or purposive method of interpretation, to validate any undue expansion of EC's powers. In any case, the political control carried out by Member States during the legislative procedure limits to a great extent the likelihood of such expansion. The issue of potential conflict between the European Court of Justice and national courts will be dealt with in more detail when the issue of EC law supremacy will be addressed. The main point here is that some national courts have ruled that they retain the (theoretical) power to set aside EC law if adopted *ultra vires*.

Notwithstanding the question of who is the ultimate judicial arbiter in Europe regarding the lawful exercise of EU powers, an unambiguous conclusion can be formulated: legally speaking, the EU can only act where Member States have agreed to grant it the power to act. Powers not conferred on the EU remain with the Member States. In other words, the EU does not and will not possess the *Kompetenz-Kompetenz*.

(c) Internal Dimension of Sovereignty: State Monopoly on Legitimate Coercion

As Max Weber famously postulated, a state is a human community that claims the monopoly of the legitimate use of physical force within a given territory. Unmistakably,

---

[60] BVerfGE 89, 155. The German decision is translated and reprinted in (1994) 33 *International Legal Materials* 388, pp 422–423 for the excerpt quoted above. On this decision, see D. Grimm, "The European Court of Justice and National Courts: The German Constitutional Perspective after the Maastricht Decision", (1997) 3 *Columbia Journal of European Law* 229.
[61] Case 314/85 *Foto-Frost* [1987] ECR 4199.

the EU does not have such a monopoly, lacking any power of coercion. To ensure the proper application of its law, the EU must rely on national authorities. Therefore, to claim European statehood in those circumstances is hardly convincing.

Competition policy may be the only field where the EU comes close to undertaking action linked to the exercise of police power.[62] To enforce European competition law, the Commission is granted the power to enter any premises of the relevant companies, without prior request, in order to investigate a possible infringement.[63] By extension, the Commission has the power to search the private homes of directors, managers, and other staff members insofar as it is suspected that business records are being kept there. Tough powers of this type are, however, strictly circumscribed. The assistance of the Member States through the disposal of national officials is decisive. Moreover, European inspections are subject to prior authorisation of the national judicial authority and control. Accordingly, it is unproblematic to conclude that it would be inaccurate to compare the Commission, even in its mission to enforce European competition rules, to some equivalent of the American FBI.

The reading of the Lisbon Treaty makes it effortless to draw the following conclusion: the EU will not gain any police power. This text swiftly restates the current situation: the Union "shall respect their essential State functions, including ensuring the territorial integrity of the State, maintaining law and order and safeguarding national security. In particular, national security remains the sole responsibility of each Member State".[64] Such restraint on European potential intervention is already clear under the current treaties which forbid European law to "affect the exercise of the responsibilities incumbent upon Member States with regard to the maintenance of law and order and the safeguarding of internal security".[65] One may note, in passing, that the scope of the applicable current provisions may be nonetheless more limited as they are strictly linked to specific titles in the Treaties: Title VI of the EU Treaty on police and judicial co-operation in criminal matters and Title V of the EC Treaty on visas, asylum, immigration and other policies related to free movement of persons. In other words, the Lisbon Treaty appears to expand the scope of the constraint on potential EU action since the preservation of national power in the field of law and order is supposed to guide the formulation of all EU policies.

Irrespective of the express respect of essential state functions, the EU will continue to pursue the goal of offering its citizens an area of freedom, security and justice. What does such an immodest expression mean? The development of the EU as an area of freedom,

---

[62] See e.g. A. Dashwood, "States in the European Union", (1998) 23 *European Law Review* 201, p 213.
[63] See Art 20 on the Commission's power of inspection in Council Regulation No 1/2003 of 16 December 2002 on the implementation of the rules on competition laid down in Arts 81 and 82 of the Treaty [2003] OJ L1/1.
[64] New Art 3a(2) TEU. With the exception of the last sentence, introduced in June 2007, the provision reproduces Art I-5 EU CT.
[65] See Arts 33 TEU and 64 TEC.

security and justice refers to a key objective set out by the Amsterdam Treaty and further developed by the Nice Treaty. The basic goal is for the EU to ensure the free movement of persons whilst guaranteeing their security by tackling cross-border crime, as well as promoting judicial co-operation. Given the ineffectiveness of purely national policies, the EU may complement Member States' action in the areas of terrorism, human trafficking, sexual exploitation of children, drug trafficking, arms trafficking, corruption and fraud. As far as the area of justice is concerned, the primary aims are to promote co-operation between the judicial authorities and to simplify the legal environment of European citizens. The cornerstone of judicial co-operation is the principle of mutual recognition of decisions and enforcement of judgments, thus allowing judicial decisions of one Member State to be recognised and enforced by the authorities of another Member State.

A lot of confusion characterises the debate about the Union's competence to intervene in the above-mentioned areas. What the EU offers is merely a framework of co-operation and co-ordination in order to ease citizen's daily life (freedom aspect) and to fight cross-border crime (security aspect). Above all, *Eurojust* and *Europol* should not be confused with any European police power. Established by a Council Decision on 28 February 2002, Eurojust is an agency of judicial co-operation for the investigation and prosecution of serious cross-border crime. Its scope of intervention is limited and each Member State is represented either by a senior prosecutor, judge or police officer. Its mission remains limited to serious crime affecting two or more Member States and Eurojust has yet to gain the power to require national authorities to prosecute. In other words, the Lisbon Treaty does not suppress the freedom of national authorities to refuse the undertaking of a criminal prosecution on the basis of specific evidence. Also, formal acts of judicial procedure will still be carried out by the competent national officials. In any case, it is arguably difficult to deny the added-value of a body whose prime mission is to facilitate co-operation between investigating and prosecuting authorities in serious criminal cases.

Similarly, Europol clearly corresponds to a genuine need. Europol is the agency responsible for supporting (and not overriding) Member States in combating serious organised crime when two or more Member States are affected. By comparison with current legal provisions, the Lisbon Treaty, which merely reproduces here the Constitutional Treaty, should be understood as a simple rewording exercise in order to provide greater legislative flexibility for developing Europol's structures and tasks. The apparent extension of Europol's mandate to terrorism and forms of crime which affect a common interest covered by an EU policy ought to be considered, in reality, as an exercise of increased transparency. Indeed, the 1995 Europol Convention already gives Europol the task of supporting Member States' law enforcement activities with regard to serious forms of international crime, including terrorism and drug trafficking among many others.[66] In

---

[66] Council Act of 26 July 1995 drawing up the Convention based on Art K.3 of the Treaty on European Union, on the establishment of a European Police Office (Europol Convention).

any event, with a staff of approximately 490 people, Europol clearly cannot be compared to an EU police force irrespective of the alleged broadening of its mandate. As long as Europol is not given the right to carry out "operational action" without the involvement of the Member States' competent authorities,[67] Europol will remain an instrument of co-operation between the Member States, not the police force of a new sovereign entity.

Even though the EU cannot claim any *monopoly of the legitimate use of physical force*, two issues have proved particularly controversial in the context of the development of the EU as an area of freedom, security and justice. The first issue is about the potentiality of a European-wide harmonisation of criminal law. The second deals with the establishment of a European Public Prosecutor.

More than a clear-cut policy of harmonisation of criminal law, co-operation in the field of criminal matters will continue to be governed by an emphasis on the setting up of minimum European rules. In practice, the Lisbon Treaty provides for minimum rules to facilitate judicial co-operation in criminal matters with *a cross-border dimension* on the mutual admissibility of evidence between Member States, the definition of individual rights in criminal procedure and rights of victims.[68] It is important to point out that the Lisbon Treaty only codifies an initiative launched in October 1999 by the Member States themselves. In order to guarantee the principle of mutual recognition of judicial decisions, the Member States agreed to envision a certain degree of harmonisation in the field of procedural rights. However, few important measures have been implemented so far, the only major exception being the European Arrest Warrant.[69] Apart from an inappropriate sense of national superiority, it is difficult to see why the aim of setting minimum standards in the field of criminal procedure ought to be rejected as long as the differences between the legal traditions and systems of the Member States are taken into account. For those criminally prosecuted in a Member State of which they are not a national, such minimum standards will in reality be the guarantee of their procedural rights and will certainly improve tangible compliance with rights already protected by the European Convention on Human Rights. Furthermore, such procedural approximation both facilitates the collaboration between law-enforcement agencies of the Member States (and the EU bodies

---

[67] Article III-276(2)b EU CT.

[68] European institutions are already working on these issues. See the Proposal for a Council Framework Decision on certain procedural rights in criminal proceedings throughout the European Union, 28 April 2004, COM(2004) 3289 final. The Commission's proposal foresees minimum standards in areas such as access to legal advice, access to interpretation and consular assistance. These "common minimum standards" are built on the requirements of the ECHR and do not deprive Member States of the freedom to maintain or adopt higher standards. More problematic is the scope of the decision as it would apply to all proceedings taking place within the EU. It may be argued, however, that such a result is indeed "necessary" (within the meaning of Art 31 TEU) to effectively facilitate judicial co-operation between Member States.

[69] Council Framework Decision of 13 June 2002 on the European arrest warrant and the surrender procedures between Member States (2002/584/JHA) [2002] OJ L190/1.

acting in the field), and the application of the principle of mutual recognition, as it strengthens mutual trust between national authorities.

In any case, the Lisbon Treaty largely reproduces provisions previously contained in the Constitutional Treaty and which are strongly protective of national interest. If a *single* Member State considers a European legislative proposal to affect fundamental aspects of its criminal justice system, the procedure is suspended. In the case where no consensual solution can be found by the European Council within a period of four months, the authorisation to proceed with "enhanced co-operation"[70] is deemed to be granted if at least one third of the Member States still wish to implement the proposal between themselves. In other words, the Member States willing to go further will be enabled to proceed while reluctant Member States will not be obliged to participate.[71] The so-called "emergency brake clause" has been described as "so vague that it is unclear how it will work".[72] Such criticism is largely unjustified as "constitutional" provisions are always open-ended and it is hard to see how the relevant clauses could be better drafted if only for the sake of concision. Furthermore, Member States are certainly the ones to blame with their insistence on details to preserve themselves from any future expansive interpretation.

A more legitimate uneasiness relates to the harmonisation of *substantive* criminal law. It is often assumed that further European legislative harmonisation may lead to limitations on the right to trial by jury and on *habeas corpus*, with the underlying assumption that these traditional notions only exist in common law legal systems. As respectable and important as these legal practices are, one must also accept that a "certain degree of approximation of substantive criminal law (i.e. the definition of constituent elements of a given crime, and penalties foreseen for it) is necessary given that certain crimes have a transnational dimension and cannot be notably addressed effectively by the Member States acting alone".[73] The Lisbon Treaty merely offers a limited list which does not, in reality, modify the current areas where the EU can already intervene: terrorism, trafficking in human beings and sexual exploitation of women and children, illicit drug trafficking, illicit arms trafficking, money laundering, corruption, counterfeiting of means of payment, computer crime and organised crime.[74] Furthermore, the Union's scope of action is limited. It can

---

[70] Enhanced or closer co-operation is the procedure allowing groups of Member States to co-operate on specific issues when all Member States do not wish to. Provisions on enhanced co-operation were first introduced by the Amsterdam Treaty and have yet to be used.

[71] The Lisbon Treaty extends this mechanism to legislative proposals concerning the European Public Prosecutor and police co-operation.

[72] "The right verdict on the constitution", *The Economist*, 24 June 2004.

[73] European Convention, Final report of Working Group X "Freedom, Security and Justice", CONV 426/02, Brussels, 2 December 2002, p 9.

[74] True, the list could be amended and consequently extended. This is a welcome development as the EU must have the option to respond to changing patterns of crime. In any case, any amendment has to be decided by unanimity, with the consent of the European Parliament.

define criminal offences and sanctions only in the areas of particularly serious crime with a cross-border dimension or where the approximation of national criminal laws "proves essential to ensure the effective implementation of a Union policy in an area which has been subject to harmonisation measures".[75] And as explained before in the field of criminal procedure, an additional "emergency brake" clause is again included. Finally, two general safeguard clauses limit European legislative intervention: The EU will have the obligation to respect the different legal traditions and systems of the Member States and the adoption of EU directives shall not prevent Member States from maintaining or introducing a higher level of protection for individuals. It is thus difficult to imagine what additional safeguards could have been included without completely annihilating the likelihood of any effective EU intervention. Yet, to appease everlasting British concerns about the future of its common law tradition, the Lisbon Treaty extends the scope of the 1997 Protocol on the position of the United Kingdom and Ireland to include the Treaty sections on judicial co-operation in criminal matters and on police co-operation. The 1997 Protocol currently allows the United Kingdom and Ireland to selectively participate in the adoption of measures taken under the present EC Title IV on visas, immigration and asylum. The Lisbon Treaty, therefore, gives the United Kingdom the right to "opt-out", that is, the right not to comply with measures adopted in the field of justice and police co-operation unless it chooses to take part. This is a "major change from the text of the Constitutional Treaty"[76]. The Irish Government reserved at first its position, but in October 2007 the Taoiseach formally announced that the Irish Government will follow the United Kingdom and ask to benefit from the new right to opt-out from decisions adopted in the police co-operation and criminal law areas. The irony, of course, is that the United Kingdom and Irish Governments have been constantly pushing for more EU co-operation in fighting crime and terrorism. It would seem that the Irish Government partially realised the incongruity of the situation which explains why the Taoiseach made it clear that Ireland intends to participate in future developments in police and judicial co-operation to the maximum extent possible and, more importantly, to review the situation in three years' time.[77]

The Irish decision to join the UK in October 2007 was not without controversies. First of all, there was no consensus within the Cabinet itself. Dick Roche, Minister for European Affairs, urged the Government not to "slavishly follow" the British.[78] The lawyers

---

[75] An example would be fraud. See e.g. Council Act of 26 July 1995 drawing up the Convention on the protection of the European Communities' financial interests [1995] OJ C 316/48.

[76] Statewatch Analysis by S. Peers, "British and Irish opt-outs from EU Justice and Home Affairs (JHA) law", EU Reform Treaty Analysis no. 4, 26 October 2007, p 7. On a highly complex subject, this analysis offers an excellent synthesis and is available at: http://www.statewatch.org/news/2007/oct/eu-reform-treaty-uk-ireland-opt-outs.pdf.

[77] Dáil Statement by the Taoiseach on the Informal European Council, (18/19 October) on Wednesday, 24 October 2007.

[78] S. Collins, "Cabinet likely to reject key parts of EU crime plan", *The Irish Times*, 8 October 2007.

working at the Department of Justice and the Attorney-General's office proved more resilient. They appeared to have convinced a majority of Ministers and the Taoiseach that no other option could be contemplated on the grounds that Ireland and Britain share the same common law identity as well as a Common Travel Area which has been in existence since the foundation of the Irish State in 1922. Minister for Justice Brian Lenihan felt required to add that "if Ireland had opted in while Britain opted out, EU police could have come into this country to arrest people".[79] As an editorial in the *Irish Times* sensibly argued, the legal case against the Lisbon Treaty's justice and home affairs provisions "is weak, although it draws on conventional thinking in the Department of Justice, the Attorney General's office and the legal profession".[80] The main opposition party, Fine Gael, also condemned the decision. Its Justice spokesman Charlie Flanagan judiciously remarked that the Government "has not explained why, if our different legal system is such an obstacle, it chose not to opt out of the European constitution that contained much the same provisions as the reform treaty".[81] The Government replied that it had received strong advice from Attorney-General Paul Gallagher to follow the British decision to opt-out, but without publication of this advice, it is rather difficult to be convinced. If the decision to opt-out makes political sense from a domestic point of view, it seems obvious that the arguments raised by the Taoiseach and the Minister for Justice lack substance. This was actually plain to see when, in a rather embarrassing development soon afterwards, Irish citizens learnt that senior officials were working on a plan to end the Common Travel Area between Ireland and Britain following the development of an electronic border control system by Britain by 2009.[82] There is an obvious solution to this ridiculous situation: Ireland should join the Schengen system.[83] Regarding the preservation of the common law features of the Irish legal system, it may be sufficient here to quote the Director of Public Prosecutions (hereinafter "DPP") who recently rejected "the idea that there was that judicial co-operation within the European Union is made impossible by the divide between civil and common law systems".[84] The DPP was also entirely right to point out that the Government must identify which features of Ireland's common law legal system should be regarded as non-negotiable and what are the current or potential threats to such features.[85]

If some strident screams have accompanied the discussion on the European harmonisation of criminal law in the United Kingdom and Ireland, what may be the

---

[79] S. Collins, "FG and Sutherland attack Government's EU opt-out", *The Irish Times*, 10 October 2007.

[80] Editorial, "EU opt-out not way forward", *The Irish Times*, 8 October 2007.

[81] S. Collins, "FG and Sutherland attack Government's EU opt-out", *The Irish Times*, 10 October 2007.

[82] "Irish will need passports to visit Britain from 2009", *The Irish Times*, 24 October 2007.

[83] This is also the position now advocated by *The Irish Times*. See Editorial, "Border controls', *The Irish Times*, 13 November 2007.

[84] J. Hamilton, "The interplay between EU and domestic counter-terrorism laws', speech at the ERA-ICEL Seminar on terrorism and EU Law, Dublin, 1 November 2007, p 22 (speech on file with author). See also Paul Cullen, "DPP backs judicial co-operation in EU", *The Irish Times*, 3 November 2007.

[85] J. Hamilton, "The interplay between EU and domestic counter-terrorism laws", *op. cit.*, p 24.

boldest move in the Constitutional Treaty was the idea of setting up a European Public Prosecutor (hereinafter "EPP"). Remarkably, the Lisbon Treaty retains this innovative reform. Often described as one of the Britain's "red lines", the proposal to create an EPP was fiercely opposed by the British Government, essentially on pragmatic grounds as there is no alleged need for such an authority. In Ireland, the former Minister for Justice Michael McDowell went as far as to say that the EPP proposal is part of the agenda of a "small but well positioned group of integrationists" which would undermine the common law system in Ireland and the United Kingdom.[86] More seriously, the creation of a separate prosecution authority, with no accountability to national parliaments, was also seen as highly problematic. Such attachment to the rule of law at EU level is ironic given the practices of national governments that often pay scant regard to such lofty standards. In any case, due to some dissension between Member States, an unfortunate compromise has been devised in which the setting up of the EPP's office is left to the Council to decide under the fulfilment of two conditions: it must adopt *unanimously* a law for this purpose, but this has to be after obtaining the European Parliament's consent. As a result, it is a euphemism to say that the EPP has little chance ever to occur.[87]

This is quite an unfortunate outcome as the Member States have shown hardly any will to tackle fraud against the Union's finances, a major rationale behind the idea of an EPP.[88] Once more, inconsistency is a key feature of eurosceptics' talk. They are certainly never shy about emphasising the need for Brussels to get its own house in order, but fraud is unlikely to be effectively tackled without an EPP. On practical grounds, however, it may convincingly be argued that Eurojust could certainly fulfil the mission foreseen for the EPP if it was granted additional powers, therefore avoiding any future overlap. In addition, some significant legal issues do need to be dealt with, for example the notion of prosecuting a case in a national court according to specific rules of procedure, as well as judicial review applicable only to the EPP, or how to adequately safeguard individual freedoms and basic rights. However, it must be emphasised that the EPP would certainly have recourse to existing national authorities to conduct its investigations, and there is no question of creating a Community court to hear cases on the merits. Again, if the EU was a state, it would be a dramatically weak one. There is, however, no need to speculate further, as criminal prosecution will remain an exclusive national responsibility.

To conclude, internal law and order are, and will remain, the responsibility of the Member States. To answer critics obsessed with the emergence of a European *polizeistaat*,

---

[86] Quoted in M. Brennock and D. Staunton, "Proposal to curtail referendum rule on EU issues", *The Irish Times*, 6 May 2005.

[87] In a new development, the Lisbon Treaty offers an additional option. In the absence of unanimily in the Council, a group of (at least nine) Member States may decide to set up an EPP.

[88] See the arguments put forward by the European Commission in its Green Paper on Criminal Law, Protection of the Financial Interests of the Community and the Establishment of a European Prosecutor, COM(2001) 715 final.

it must be repeated again and again that harmonisation of laws governing national police forces remain excluded. The Lisbon Treaty, for instance, reiterates that the provisions on police and judicial co-operation in criminal matters "shall not affect the exercise of the responsibilities incumbent upon Member States with regard to the maintenance of law and order and the safeguarding of internal security".[89] Furthermore, the implementation of coercive measures is and will be the exclusive responsibility of competent national authorities. The Lisbon Treaty may still be praised for enhancing the European Parliament's role. It also gives national parliaments the right to evaluate the legal norms being produced in the area of freedom, security and justice. In the end, no matter how hard it is to reconcile with the rule of law which the EU is allegedly founded upon, the Member States have decided to exclude any European judicial control over the exercise of their police power.[90] This may be the ultimate evidence that the Member States have retained the freedom to set aside the rule of law in the name of preserving their sovereignty.

(d) The External Dimension of Sovereignty: EU's Power in Security and Defence Matters

To echo Art I, s 8, cl 11 of the US Constitution, does the EU have the power to declare war or to use a more modern formulation, i.e. does it have any (independent) competence in security and defence matters? A brief overview of the current European Treaties should lead again to the conclusion that the EU remains the creature of its founding entities. Since the Maastricht Treaty, however, there is a clear will to assert Europe's regional and global role and to increase its military credibility.[91] To the dismay of some, and especially the United Kingdom, France is especially keen on emphasising the need for a "*Europe puissance*". The defence component of European integration is thus growing but under the strict and ultimate control of the Member States. In practice, this means that the pace of reform is gradual, if not extremely slow, as it has to accommodate sovereignty concerns and divergent views about what should be the nature and role of the EU in the world.

Article 17 TEU states that the Common Foreign and Security Policy (hereinafter "CFSP") shall include all questions relating to the security of the EU and refers to the possibility of setting up a common defence through the development of the Common Security and Defence Policy hereinafter "CSDP"). Paragraph 2 of the same article specifies that security questions include the so-called Petersberg Tasks,[92] in particular "humanitarian

---

[89] See Art 33 TEU and Art 64 TEC.

[90] Article 35(5) TEU prevents the European Court of Justice from reviewing the validity or proportionality of national policy operations or national measures concerned with "the maintenance of law and order and the safeguarding of internal security".

[91] See the conclusions of the Cologne European Council meeting in June 1999.

[92] These tasks were established in June 1992 at the Ministerial Council of the Western European Union (hereinafter "WEU") held at the Petersberg Hotel, not far from Bonn, and were subsequently introduced in the TEU with the Amsterdam Treaty. Set up in 1948 by the Treaty of Brussels, the WEU is a European organisation for the purposes of co-operation on defence and security. The WEU is now more or less an empty shell as almost of its structures and operational capabilities were transferred to the EU.

and rescue tasks, peacekeeping tasks and tasks of combat forces in crisis management, including peacemaking". In line with the Constitutional Treaty, the relevant provisions of the Lisbon Treaty are largely built upon Art 17 of the current TEU.[93] Unanimity is still required for a European common defence policy to occur. As a result, one can hardly argue that the new Treaty will lead to a common defence against, for example, Ireland's will. It will still be up to the Irish people to decide whether or not to eventually amend Art 29.4.9° of the Irish Constitution which states that Ireland "shall not adopt a decision taken by the European Council to establish a common defence". However, the Lisbon Treaty does expand slightly the scope of the Petersberg Tasks since the EU shall be provided with "an operational capacity" for use in peacekeeping missions, conflict prevention or, when necessary, to strengthen international security.

On the other hand, two important caveats are strikingly evident. First, the Lisbon Treaty requires the EU to act in accordance with the principles of the United Nations Charter and with respect for the specific character of the security and defence policy of certain Member States. As a result, the US-inspired and flawed doctrine of pre-emptive war is, constitutionally speaking, unthinkable.[94] Secondly, the Member States will provide the civilian and military capabilities required for performing these tasks. An independent European army is thus excluded: a further example that the EU essentially remains a framework of co-operation. True, the scope of the CSDP is defined in very broad terms and no geographical limit is placed on the Union's action. However, not only does such breadth characterise the current state of affairs, it does not imply European sovereignty on security and defence matters. In other words, the broad definition of the CSDP only exists to serve the pragmatic understanding of the Member States. They need to be able to modify their policies according to the changing patterns of security threats.

To fear the militarisation of the EU via the Lisbon Treaty is without foundation as it does not change the current truth: the Member States have already the potential to define any defence policy they see fit as long as there is *unanimity* to do so. And when unanimity is present, Member States could agree, for instance, on the objective of a 60,000 strong

---

[93] For an analysis emphasising the high degree of continuity between the current Treaties and the Constitutional Treaty, despite some extensive reformulation, see W. Wessels, "A 'Saut constitutionnel' out of an intergovernmental trap? The provisions of the Constitutional Treaty for the Common Foreign, Security and Defence Policy", in J. Weiler and C. Eisgruber (eds), *Altneuland: The EU Constitution in a Contextual Perspective*, Jean Monnet Working Paper 5/04 (available at http://www.jeanmonnetprogram.org/papers/04/040501-17.htm).

[94] For a defence of an international order based on effective multilateralism, see the EU security strategy drafted by J. Solana: *A Secure Europe in a Better World*, Brussels, 12 December 2003. Mr Solana is High Representative of the CFSP, a post created by the Amsterdam Treaty. The post is held by the Secretary-General of the Council of Ministers and is therefore the voice of the Member States as far as they have mandated him. The Lisbon Treaty provides for the High Representative to be replaced by a "High Representative of the Union for Foreign Affairs and Security Policy".

military "rapid reaction force". Known as the "Helsinki Headline Goal", the Member States' initial goal was, by *voluntary* co-operation, to be able to deploy military forces capable of the full range of Petersberg Tasks within 60 days and for at least one year. Faced with limited resources, the Member States have since decided to set up smaller "battle groups" of 1,500 people which are intended to respond rapidly to any humanitarian crisis or to an urgent request by the UN. Remarkably, Ireland has already agreed to contribute to one of the foreseen 13 battle groups.[95] One should also note that some Member States, on behalf of the EU, have already conducted some crisis-management operations. For example, the EU decided to put in place, as from 1 January 2003, a policing mission in Bosnia and Herzegovina to take over the United Nations policing operation, with contributions from volunteer Member States. Police co-operation, with the possibility of providing a force of up to 5,000 policemen, was indeed an idea developed at the Feira European Council (1999) and Gothenburg European Council (2001). The aim is to offer a civilian force to fulfil the Petersberg Tasks. In addition to a police force, the European Council agreed to provide up to 200 judicial experts, a team of experts in public administration and, finally, to provide "assessment teams" as well as "intervention teams" to assist humanitarian actors through emergency operations.

Is such flexibility in terms of security goals detrimental to national sovereignty? To understand the principles governing the CFSP and in particular the CSDP, it may be worth briefly mentioning its historical antecedent.[96] In 1970, the Member States decided it was time to increase their political co-operation in foreign policy matters to answer to the famous question asked by Henry Kissinger: "If I want to talk to Europe, who do I phone?"[97] Real progress, however, has been elusive. Indeed, due to the importance of diplomacy, the sensitivity of defence policy in some Member States and its close association with sovereignty, the area has remained governed by a large inter-governmental element. In other words, the Commission,[98] the European Parliament[99] and the European Court of Justice are largely excluded from foreign and military matters

---

[95] See Defence (Amendment) Act 2006.

[96] See e.g. B. White, *Understanding European Foreign Policy* (Palgrave Macmillan, Basingstoke, 2001). For a more theoretical approach, see T. Christiansen and B. Tonra (eds), *Rethinking European Union Foreign Policy* (Manchester University Press, Manchester, 2004).

[97] Progress in the establishment of a common foreign policy or even a common defence policy was seriously delayed since the French National Assembly failed to ratify in 1954 the Treaty establishing the European Defence Community. Quite an ironic result considering the fact that such failure to ratify led to a NATO monopoly, reinforcing in turn the unwillingness of European States to break from what appeared to be the most solid military alliance. What France alone refused in 1954 became soon after (see the Fouchet Plan in 1960) an obsession of French foreign policy in subsequent decades.

[98] The Commission still retains a right to submit legislative proposals and controls budget execution.

[99] At present, the European Parliament is informed of developments in CFSP by the President of the Council, and by the High Representative. It is thereby informed of progress and decisions taken in CFSP matters. The Parliament may also submit resolutions to the Council.

which remain under the exclusive control of the Member States. The Lisbon Treaty does not alter the eminence of Member States in security matters. Certainly, in what may be the only real innovation brought about by the Constitutional Treaty and maintained by the Lisbon Treaty, a new post of Union Minister for Foreign Affairs will be created. One should note, however, that the official terminology has been amended in 2007 with the EU minister for foreign affairs now to be called the High Representative of the Union for Foreign Affairs and Security Policy. Regardless of this pointless semantic change, the (illusory) aim remains identical: to bring more coherence and to make the Union's voice in the international arena more audible. Indeed, at present, no less than four persons could represent the EU internationally, i.e. the head of Government of the Member State holding the Presidency of the Council (which rotates every six months); the High Representative based at the Council; the Commission President; and the Commissioner for External Relations. The Lisbon Treaty reduces the number to two: the European Council President and the Minister for Foreign Affairs, the latter reuniting into one the functions of the present High Representative and the Commissioner for External Relations.

Overall, the entry into force of the Lisbon Treaty is unlikely to alter the current equilibrium. The Lisbon Treaty reflects the provisions of the EU Treaty which rule out the possibility of applying qualified majority voting with regard to decisions having military or defence implications. Furthermore, it maintains the principle according to which expenditure arising from operations having military or defence implications shall not be charged to the budget of the Union. It is left to the Member States taking part in an operation to finance it, unless the other Member States accept otherwise.

The major issue, however, is not finance but relates to the alleged threats raised by the Lisbon Treaty to the neutrality of some Member States. In this regard, two novelties are worth mentioning: the mutual defence clause and the solidarity clause. First contained in the Constitutional Treaty,[100] both clauses deal with modern security challenges which could emerge from outside the EU or from inside it, meaning in the latter case, threats from non-State entities. The question is, evidently, to what extent should these provisions be interpreted as a threat to Irish neutrality? Ireland, and five other Member States (Austria, Finland, Sweden, Cyprus and Malta), are said to be neutral or non-aligned countries. Yet these neutral/non-aligned countries co-operate with NATO under the Partnership for Peace Programme (hereinafter "PPP") and take part in the Euro–Atlantic Partnership Council (hereinafter "EAPC"). Furthermore, the vast majority of Member States (21 out of 27) are members of NATO and are therefore bound by the collective defence clause under Art 5 of the North Atlantic Treaty signed

---

[100] See respectively Art I-41(7) EU CT and Art I-43 EU CT.

in Washington in 1949.[101] It is therefore surprising that that the inclusion of a similar provision in the Constitutional Treaty proved to be a source of deep contention. It appears that some Member States are unwilling to assume their duty of assistance to a fellow EU State victim of armed aggression outside the US-dominated NATO framework. Since the initial provision establishing a similar obligation on participating Member States was deemed overreaching, it was agreed in 2004 to adopt a "light" version of NATO's Art 5. The European mutual defence clause now reads:

> "If a Member State is the victim of armed aggression on its territory, the other Member States shall have towards it an obligation of aid and assistance by all the means in their power, in accordance with Article 51 of the United Nations Charter."[102]

Clearly, the reference to an "obligation" of "aid and assistance by all the means in their power" is not as explicit and constraining as the commitments contained in the NATO Treaty. And in its initial version, the reference to an obligation of aid and assistance referred to military means or other. Furthermore, to answer Irish concerns, it was clearly stated that the Constitutional Treaty "shall not prejudice the specific character of the security and defence policy of certain Member States". The Lisbon Treaty merely reiterates the same point.[103]

Surprisingly, Ireland, whose economic development was initially dependent on Europe's (economic) solidarity, felt no embarrassment when it opposed the inclusion of a mutual defence clause. The British opposition is also puzzling. If a Member State is ready to assume its duty within the context of NATO, why should it refuse mutual assistance within the EU framework? The answer is obviously dictated by geopolitical concerns. To put it bluntly, the United Kingdom never bought the idea of a common defence in the EU, hence the insistence on unanimous voting to keep ultimate control over the process. Unwilling to undermine NATO (a mantra so often repeated that no one even wonders about its ultimate justification), the British Government has argued about the ineffectiveness of duplicating military obligations, to the palpable satisfaction of the US Government.[104] Unable to prevent the

---

[101] North Atlantic Treaty, Art 5, first para reads: "The Parties agree that an armed attack against one or more of them in Europe or North America shall be considered an attack against them all and consequently they agree that, if such an armed attack occurs, each of them, in exercise of the right of individual or collective self-defence recognised by Article 51 of the Charter of the United Nations, will assist the Party or Parties so attacked by taking forthwith, individually and in concert with the other Parties, such action as it deems necessary, including the use of armed force, to restore and maintain the security of the North Atlantic area." Germany, Belgium, Denmark, Spain, France, Greece, Italy, Luxembourg, the Netherlands, Portugal and the United Kingdom, with the notable exception of Denmark, are also members of the WEU and have therefore entered into a similar, if not wider, commitment under Art V of the Brussels Treaty (23 October 1954).

[102] New Art 28A(7) TEU (formerly Art I-41(7) EU CT).

[103] *ibid.*

[104] See e.g. Foreign and Commonwealth Office, *A Constitutional Treaty for the EU: The British Approach to the EU Intergovernmental Conference*, White Paper, September 2003, para 95 (available at: http://www.fco.gov.uk).

inclusion of the mutual assistance clause, though in a diluted form, the United Kingdom successfully lobbied for the inclusion of a reference to NATO which remains, for those EU States which are members of it, "the foundation of their collective defence".[105] Despite this direct and unambiguous reference to NATO, some analysts, in particular in the US, clearly saw the EU Constitution as a threat to the Atlantic Alliance.[106] It appears, nevertheless unrealistic to expect the EU to ever offer a common and independent defence policy. The Lisbon Treaty, in line with the Constitutional Treaty, does include a provision allowing for "permanent structured cooperation" among a limited group of Member States[107] but the emergence of a "defence Euro-zone" is likely to be limited to France and Germany and is unlikely to present a credible alternative to the Atlantic Alliance.

Apart from the mutual defence clause, the drafting of a solidarity clause has also proven to be a challenging task. Public opposition to it was, however, softened by the events of 9/11, and this was later reinforced by the Madrid bombings. While it can generally be argued that law based on exceptional circumstances makes bad law, a solidarity clause, as such, is definitely legitimate and should have been included long ago. Yet, it took a lengthy discussion for some Member States to accept a legal obligation "to act in a spirit of solidarity".[108] If the emphasis on terrorism-related threats seems somewhat overblown, the reference to a duty of solidarity in the event of a natural or man-made disaster should already have been enshrined in the Treaties.[109] Overall, the circumstances in which the solidarity clause may be implemented do not suffer criticism even though the precise content of such duty remains to be specified by legislation adopted by the Council of Ministers. The only condition laid out is for the solidarity clause to be implemented at the request of political authorities of the relevant Member State. However, there should be no misplaced apprehension about sovereignty as, once again, if the EU is under an obligation

---

[105] New Article 28A(7) TEU. The draft Constitutional Treaty in its July 2003 version was less deferential to NATO: "In the execution of closer cooperation on mutual defence, the participating Member States shall work in close cooperation with the North Atlantic Treaty Organisation." Furthermore, in its 2004 official version, there is an additional reference to NATO in the para 2 of Article I-41 EU CT. With reference to the progressive framing of a common EU defence policy, it is stated that the policy of the EU "shall respect the obligations of certain Member States, which see their common defence realised in the North Atlantic Treaty Organisation, under the North Atlantic Treaty" with a supplementary guarantee of permanent allegiance: "… and be compatible with the common security and defence policy established within that framework."

[106] See e.g. J. Cimbalo, "Saving NATO from Europe. A Threat from Within", *Foreign Affairs*, 83, November–December 2004, p 111.

[107] To compare with current Art 27b TEU: "Enhanced cooperation pursuant to this title [*CFSP*] shall relate to implementation of a joint action or a common position. It shall not relate to matters having military or defence implications."

[108] New Art 188R TEC (formerly Art I-43 EU CT).

[109] One may wonder why Denmark should still be part of the EU when it has excluded itself from the implementation of the solidarity clause (see declaration No 39 annexed to the Constitutional Treaty). In the unfortunate event of a terrorist attack or a disaster located in Denmark, should we feel compelled to act in a spirit of solidarity with a country which refuses to commit itself to help in similar circumstances?

to mobilise all the instruments at its disposal, including military resources, these resources shall be made available by the Member States.

To argue about the "militarisation" of the EU, following the inclusion of the mutual defence and solidarity clauses, is ludicrous. The solidarity clause merely confirms the multi-dimensional aspect of European integration: Economic objectives have always been accompanied by reference to political objectives. Therefore, the EC cannot be mistaken for an organisation whose primary concern is economics. Member States have long agreed to "lay the foundations of an ever closer union among the peoples of Europe" (preamble to the TEC), and "to deepen the solidarity between their peoples" (preamble to the TEU). The codification of a duty to act in a spirit of solidarity should be positively viewed as it demonstrates that European solidarity is not an empty slogan. As for the mutual defence clause, the Lisbon Treaty only offers a diluted version of the NATO clause which today binds 21 Member States out of 27. Finally, the EU is, and will remain under the Lisbon Treaty, a "soft" power with very limited military capacities in comparison with the US.[110] The civilian aspect of its goals and means of action is overwhelming. In addition, the emphasis on the United Nations Charter and respect for international law is a feature one would like to see enshrined in the US Constitution.[111] In the end, the EU will remain a non-state power as none of the changes transgress "a crucial threshold: the defence of national sovereignty".[112] For instance, the Union minister for foreign affairs could only act when "mandated" by the Council and will remain accountable to Member States, an additional illustration of the consolidation of the EU as a union of States. The insistence on preserving a pre-eminently intergovernmental decision-making process and unanimous voting has a price, however: it will prevent the EU from becoming genuinely effective, with the probable perspective of seeing European citizens disappointed, once again, with their collective impotence when faced with the next Srebrenica.

(e) The External Dimension of Sovereignty: The EU's International Capacity

The attribute of legal personality associated with a monopoly on treaty-making power is the final key feature of statehood. The fact that the Lisbon Treaty confers legal personality on the EU[113] as well as treaty-making powers could prompt us to question our prior

---

[110] See R. Kagan, *Of Paradise and Power: American and Europe in the New World Order* (Knopf, New York, 2003).

[111] See e.g. new Art 3(4) TEU: "In its relations with the wider world, the Union shall uphold and promote its values and interests and contribute to the protection of its citizens. It shall contribute to peace, security, … as well as to the strict observance and the development of international law, including respect for the principles of the United Nations Charter."

[112] Wessels, "A 'Saut constitutionnel' out of an intergovernmental trap?", p 31. See also D. Thym, "Reforming Europe's Common Foreign and Security Policy", (2004) 10 *European Law Journal* 5. For this author, the reform of Europe's CFSP does not pave the way for the federalisation of European foreign policy.

[113] In line with the Constitutional Treaty, the Lisbon Treaty provides for the "Union" to have legal personality (new Art 46A TEU).

assessment that the EU lacks the essential characteristics of a state. Critics actually often claim that the Constitutional Treaty's substitute text, by giving "the new European Union its own legal personality" will "enable the newly constituted EU to sign treaties with other states" and will "establish the constitutional form of a supranational state for the first time".[114] It can, however, be argued that the EU already benefits from an implicit legal personality.[115] Furthermore, the attribution of treaty-making power, i.e. the power to negotiate and conclude international agreements, should not be confused with that of a state. In fact, where any state possesses the totality of international rights and duties recognised by international law, the rights and duties of the EU are and will remain dependent "on its purposes and functions as specified or implied in its constituent documents and developed in practice".[116] To put it forward differently, if the EU becomes a subject of international law on its own, such development will not lead to a situation where Member States will individually lose their own status as subjects of international law.

The issue of legal personality figured prominently in the work of the European Convention.[117] In essence, the concept of legal personality means the capacity to bear legal rights and duties under the law.[118] To understand the added-value of the explicit conferral of legal personality on the EU—a rather intricate topic—one must realise that under the current rules, only the EC (and not the EU) has legal personality.[119] As interpreted by the European Court of Justice, the legal personality of the EC also implies acknowledgment of its external capacity, i.e. the right to conclude treaties, the right to become a member of an international organisation, etc. in all policy areas falling within its competence.[120] In other words, it was always clear for the European Court of Justice that the EC has treaty-

---

[114] A. Coughlan, "Revised EU agreement has radical implications", *The Irish Times*, 28 June 2007.

[115] See e.g. A. Tizzano, "La personnalité internationale de l'Union européenne", (1998) 4 *Revue du marché unique européen* 11.

[116] Advisory Opinion of the International Court of Justice (ICJ) on *Reparation for Injuries suffered in the Service of the United Nations*, ICJ Reports, 1949, p 174. The ICJ ruled on the rights and duties of the UN as an international organisation. In its judgment, the court derived the UN's legal personality from its Charter and the functions it was empowered to fulfil.

[117] A Working Group on Legal Personality was set up with the mandate to examine the consequences of explicit recognition of the Union's legal personality and the consequences of a merger of the Union's legal personality with that of the Community.

[118] See Art 282 TEC: "In each of the Member States, the Community shall enjoy the most extensive legal capacity accorded to legal persons under their laws; it may, in particular, acquire or dispose of movable and immovable property and may be a party to legal proceedings. To this end, the Community shall be represented by the Commission."

[119] Art 281 TEC: "The Community shall have legal personality." To be entirely accurate, each of the European Communities: the EC, Euratom and the ECSC (the ECSC Treaty has ceased to exist in 2002) is expressly declared, by its respective founding Treaty, to have legal personality.

[120] Case 22/70 *Commission v Council (ERTA case)* [1971] ECR 263, para 14.

making power whenever such power flows implicitly from other provisions of the EC Treaty creating internal powers for the Community.[121]

As previously mentioned, the EU has not yet been granted explicit legal personality. The reason lies in the specific circumstances surrounding its creation. The EU was originally established by the Maastricht Treaty as an encompassing framework aimed at including the pre-existing Communities and two newly born intergovernmental pillars: the Common Foreign and Security Policy (hereinafter "CFSP") and Justice and Home Affairs (hereinafter "JHA"). The justification behind this structure was to make clear that the CFSP and JHA would be operating according to methods different to the "Community method". Under the Community method, the Commission proposes a legal act to be adopted by the Council of Ministers in association with the European Parliament under the scrutiny of the European Court of Justice. In other words, where the EC is governed by a supranational philosophy, by contrast, the CFSP and JHA are governed by intergovernmental co-operation. The division between the EC, the CFSP and JHA led to a common description of the EU as a "three pillar" structure.

It may be useful to add that the first pillar is the set of rules one could find in the TEC, thus presiding over the functioning of the EC. The second pillar refers to the CFSP, and the third pillar deals with JHA, renamed in 1997 "Police and Judicial Co-operation in Criminal Matters".[122] While a single institutional framework presides over the functioning of the EU,[123] the respective powers of each European institution varies considerably according to the pillar concerned. In other words, the same institutions serve the three pillars but their powers and the decision-making processes vary, thus creating a political creature likely to be misunderstood.[124] To take two striking examples: the

---

[121] In Opinion 1/76 [1977] ECR 741, the European Court of Justice held that: "Whenever Community law has created for the institutions of the Community powers within its internal system for the purpose of attaining a specific objective, the Community has authority to enter into the international commitments necessary for the attainment of that objective even in the absence of an express provision in that connexion" (para 1).

[122] The current designation of the third pillar is the result of a further set of amendments to the TEU and TEC, introduced by the Treaty of Amsterdam. The "1992 version" third pillar was reduced in size and changed in scope as certain matters were transferred into the first pillar. As a result, the third pillar has been renamed Police and Judicial Co-operation in Criminal Matters. The term *Justice and Home Affairs* is often used to cover both the third pillar and the transferred areas.

[123] Article 3 TEU: "The Union shall be served by a single institutional framework which shall ensure the consistency and the continuity of the activities carried out in order to attain its objectives while respecting and building upon the *acquis communautaire*."

[124] Even for the connoisseurs, the evolution towards a more flexible arrangement with, for instance, opt-out clauses or enhanced co-operation schemes, drastically complicates the feasibility of presenting a clear view. See e.g. B. de Witte, "The Pillar Structure and the Nature of the European Union: Greek Temple or French Gothik Cathedral ?", in T. Heukels, N. Blokker and M. Brus (eds), *The European Union after Amsterdam – A Legal Analysis* (Kluwer Law International, The Hague, 1998), p 51.

European Parliament has almost no genuine role in the second[125] and third[126] pillars, whereas it can decisively influence law-making within the first pillar. As for the European Court of Justice, its jurisdiction differs radically in each pillar.[127] The latest treaties to date, the Treaty of Amsterdam and the Treaty of Nice, did not attempt to end the pillar structure of the EU, nor did they explicitly confer legal personality on it.

While there was no breakthrough on these issues, the Treaty of Amsterdam introduced a new provision giving the EU treaty-making power in the fields covered by Title V (Provisions on a common foreign and security policy) and Title VI (Provisions on police and judicial co-operation on criminal matters).[128] After Amsterdam, Art 24 of the TEU purposefully states that "Agreements concluded under the conditions set out by this Article shall be binding on the institutions of the Union". In more practical terms, it necessarily implies that the EU has the capacity *as such* to enter into international agreements, insofar they relate to Title V and Title VI of the EU Treaty. Without much doubt, it could therefore be concluded that the EU has already—although implicitly—legal personality.[129]

As a result, not only does the EC have legal personality and treaty-making power but so does the EU. Should it, therefore, be assumed that the EC/EU possesses at least one element required for the identification of a state? Not so, as the EC/EU can only conclude international agreements in respect of the matters which fall within its powers. Certainly, the explicit conferral of legal personality on the EU would heighten "its profile on the world stage"[130] and clarify its legal status since the EU would become a subject of international law. This means that the EU would then be able to avail itself of all means of international action (right to conclude treaties, right of legation, right to submit claims or to act before an international court or judge, right to become a member of an international organisation or become party to international conventions, right to enjoy immunities) as well as to bind the EU internationally.[131]

---

[125] See Art 21 TEU.

[126] See Art 39 TEU.

[127] While the court is fully competent within the framework of the EC (with the exception of Art 68 TEC), it has no jurisdiction with regard to legal acts adopted in the framework of the CFSP and has a restricted jurisdiction in the third pillar (see Art 35 TEU).

[128] Article 24 as amended by the Treaty of Nice now reads: "1. When it is necessary to conclude an agreement with one or more States or international organisations in implementation of this title, the Council may authorise the Presidency, assisted by the Commission as appropriate, to open negotiations to that effect. Such agreements shall be concluded by the Council on a recommendation from the Presidency. (...) 5. No agreement shall be binding on a Member State whose representative in the Council states that it has to comply with the requirements of its own constitutional procedure; the other members of the Council may agree that the agreement shall nevertheless apply provisionally. 6. Agreements concluded under the conditions set out by this Article shall be binding on the institutions of the Union."

[129] An additional indication is provided by Art 254 TEC (as amended by the Treaty of Nice) which refers to the "Official Journal of the European Union" and not the Official Journal of the European Communities.

[130] European Convention, Final report of Working Group III on Legal Personality, CONV 305/02, Brussels, 1 October 2002, para 19.

[131] *ibid.*

To respond to the superstate fixation, two important remarks ought to be made. First, one must repeat that the EU as a new subject of international law will *coexist* alongside the Member States as subjects of international law. As a rule, the EU and the Member States shall act within their respective sphere of powers. This means, for instance, that only the EU may negotiate and conclude international agreements in an area of *exclusive* EU competence such as the common commercial policy. In practice, the Commission is responsible for conducting negotiations, in consultation with a committee appointed by the Council of Ministers. By contrast, in areas of *shared* competences, each individual Member State has the power to conclude international agreements.[132]

Second important remark: no extension of the Union's competence will result from the conferral of legal personality and treaty-making power.[133] To allude again to the 1949 advisory opinion of the International Court of Justice on the legal personality of the United Nations, the rights and duties of the EU are similar to that of an international organisation, as they depend on its purposes and functions as specified in the texts governing the institution. The EU may thus be thought to be legally distinct from its Member States. It does not, however, have the authority to act outside the tasks given to it by the constitutive treaties. In short, the EU is not sovereign and as a result, cannot be said to be in a similar position to a state.

To avoid common misunderstandings, it is important to stress that while the EU has treaty-making powers, it does not mean that Member States have no say in the conduct and negotiation of international agreements falling within the exclusive competence of the EU. The Council of Ministers, i.e. of the representatives of national executives, remains a critical actor. It is, therefore, incorrect to argue that the Lisbon Treaty, by giving the EU its own legal personality, will allow the EU "to enter into treaties without the agreement of national governments".[134] As a matter of fact, the Council is left with the decisive power "to authorise the opening of negotiations, adopt negotiating directives, authorise the

---

[132] See e.g. Art 174(4) TEC: "Within their respective spheres of competence, the Union and the Member States shall cooperate with third countries and with the competent international organisations. The arrangements for the Union's cooperation may be the subject of agreements between the Union and the third parties concerned. The first subparagraph shall be without prejudice to Member States' competence to negotiate in international bodies and to conclude international agreements."

[133] When the Amsterdam Treaty brought into existence a new Art 24 in the TEU, a Declaration was annexed to the Treaty of Amsterdam, which reads as follows: "[t]he provisions of Articles 24 and 38 of the Treaty on European Union and any agreements resulting from them shall not imply any transfer of competence from the Member States to the European Union." Regarding legal personality, a new Declaration annexed to the Lisbon Treaty states that "[t]he Conference confirms that the fact that the European Union has a legal personality will not in any way authorise the Union to legislate or to act beyond the competences conferred upon it by the Member States in the Treaties."

[134] Editorial, "Put it to the people", *The Sunday Times*, 17 June 2007.

signing of agreements and conclude them".[135] Where international agreement covers matters over which powers are shared between the EU and the Member States,[136] the Member States remain free to exercise these powers themselves, by concluding the agreement on their own behalf as long as they ensure close co-operation with European institutions.[137] And in the case of an international agreement covered partly by the exclusive competence of the EU and partly by the competence of the Member States, the Member States must approve the part of the agreement that comes within their national competence in accordance with their respective constitutional requirements. As for the EU, it can only approve aspects that come within its competence.[138] The fact that the Lisbon Treaty finally gives an explicit legal personality to the EU will not put an end to the obligation to conclude mixed agreements, together with the Member States, in situations where "Europe" does not have an entirely exclusive competence. And the European Court of Justice has demonstrated it would not accept a claim of European exclusive competence without a precise legal basis.[139]

The distinction made above between situations where the EU has exclusive competence and situations where competence is shared further explains why, in some instances, the EU has a representation of its own to the exclusion of the Member States or in addition to them. For instance, as the EU has exclusive competence in fisheries matters, it has full member status acting alone in the North West Atlantic Fisheries Organisation.

---

[135] New Art 188N(2) TEC. Current Art 300(1) of the TEC states that "Where this Treaty provides for the conclusion of agreements between the Community and one or more States or international organisations, the Commission shall make recommendations to the Council, which shall authorise the Commission to open the necessary negotiations. The Commission shall conduct these negotiations in consultation with special committees appointed by the Council to assist it in this task and within the framework of such directives as the Council may issue to it. In exercising the powers conferred upon it by this paragraph, the Council shall act by a qualified majority, except in the cases where ... the Council shall act unanimously."

[136] The so-called "traditional mixed agreements". The situation is slightly more complex when an agreement falls within the EC domain and at the same time falls within the EU domain. The agreement is said to be a cross-pillar agreement and its legal regime could be quite difficult to come to terms with.

[137] In 1991, the Court of Justice, referring to an agreement that fell partly within the competence of the EC and partly within that of the Member States, emphasised the need "to ensure close cooperation between the Member States and the Community institutions, both in the process of negotiation and conclusion and in the fulfilment of the commitments entered into. That obligation to cooperate flows from the requirement of unity in the international representation of the Community", Opinion 2/91 [1993] ECR I-1061, para 36. Moreover, Art 11(2) TEU stipulates that Member States "shall refrain from any action which is contrary to the interests of the Union or likely to impair its effectiveness as a cohesive force in international relations".

[138] See e.g. Council Decision 94/800/EC of 22 December 1994 concerning the conclusion on behalf of the European Community, *with regard to matters within its competence* [emphasis added], of the agreements reached in the Uruguay Round multilateral negotiations [1994] OJ L336/1.

[139] In its Opinion 1/94, the court rejected the Commission's contention that the Community had exclusive external competence in all matters covered by the GATT Agreement, including services, transport and intellectual property. It concluded that the exclusive competence of the Community, in which ratification by the Member States is not required, was limited to the area of trade in goods.

As "trade" is, in most cases, a shared competence, the EU is represented in its own right in conjunction with the Member States in the World Trade Organization. In other words, the Member States and the EU (as such) have, therefore, 28 votes. The reservations raised that the Constitutional Treaty generally threatened Member States' membership of international organisations were unfounded.[140] Similarly, the Lisbon Treaty neither extends the list of the EU's exclusive powers nor gives the EU the right to become a member of international organisations to the detriment of the Member States. It is, therefore, ludicrous to argue that the EU is about to take on Member States' own membership, for instance, the United Kingdom's seat in the UN Security Council.[141] A Declaration agreed in June 2007 further confirms, if need be, that the new provisions dealing with the Common Foreign and Security Policy "will not affect the existing legal basis, responsibilities, and powers of each Member State in relation to the formulation and conduct of its foreign policy, its national diplomatic service, relations with third countries and participation in international organisations, including a Member State's membership of the Security Council of the United Nations".[142] The emergence of the EU as a "global power" in lieu and place of its Member States is, therefore, not to be feared or expected.

CHAPTER ONE – CONCLUSION

With regard to traditional legal and political concepts, the EU is undoubtedly a difficult object to classify as it does not easily fit into customary classifications. More troubling for legal purists, it is often described as the "pooling" of national sovereignties, apparently undermining the indivisible and inalienable characteristics of sovereignty. It has therefore been suggested "not to try to build an alternative, more Europe-friendly doctrine of sovereignty", but rather to abandon the concept of sovereignty in the legal discourse on integration.[143] This may be desirable, but the cultural attachment to the concept, and the political use made of it to attack European integration, renders elusive such a prospect in the short run. Furthermore, it may not be necessary to abandon the concept as critics

---

[140] With the exception of the reference to the OSCE, new Art 188P TEC (formerly Art III-327(1) EU CT) is a plain restatement in a single article of the current Arts 302, 303 and 304 of the current TEC. It reads as follows: "The Union shall establish all appropriate forms of cooperation with the organs of the United Nations and its specialised agencies, the Council of Europe, the Organisation for Security and Cooperation in Europe and the Organisation for Economic Cooperation and Development. The Union shall also maintain such relations as are appropriate with other international organisations."

[141] The Lisbon Treaty only requires that when the EU has defined a position on a subject which is on the UN Security Council agenda, the United Kingdom and France (or other Member States sitting provisionally) shall request that the Union Minister for Foreign Affairs be asked to present the Union's position (new Art 19(2) TEU, formerly Art III-305(2) EU CT). Such an obligation could hardly be interpreted as a surrender of the UN Security Council's seat.

[142] Declaration no 14 concerning the common foreign and security policy, [2007] OJ C306/255.

[143] B. de Witte, "Sovereignty and European Integration: The Weight of Legal Tradition", in A.-M. Slaughter *et al.* (eds), *The European Court and National Courts–Doctrine and Jurisprudence* (Hart Publishing, Oxford, 1998), p 303.

often confuse sovereignty with absolute power or a sum of powers, whereas sovereignty should more appropriately be seen as a quality: the quality of the entity bestowed with ultimate political authority. Our essential argument is that the EU does not, and is unlikely to ever, have the competence to decide with whom competence lies. To simplify, the EU is not and will not become a state. It is and will remain the creature of the Member States who retain the ultimate political authority. Ironically, one may even argue that the Lisbon Treaty reinforces the "conservatory elements" of the Union's constitutional order.[144] As a result, statehood is indubitably an inappropriate characteristic to attribute to the EU. It is essential to realise that the understanding and relevance of traditional concepts is being challenged by European integration, not to mention the globalisation of economic forces and the subsequent call for new forms of governance.[145] Therefore, one relevant question is whether traditional concepts are still able to make sense of the complex nature of the EU. Before offering a possible answer, an inquiry into the federal character of the EU is required in order to interrogate further myths about the European "superstate".

---

[144] Professor Alan Dashwood distinguishes the "conservatory elements", those elements designed to preserve the position of the Member States, from the "constitutionalising elements" such as the doctrine of supremacy and the doctrine of direct effect. See A. Dashwood, "States in the European Union", (1998) 23 *European Law Review* 201, p 201.

[145] For a challenging introduction to these issues, see the work of A.-M. Slaughter, *A New World Order* (Princeton University Press, Princeton, 2004).

CHAPTER TWO

Fitting the European Union into Procruste's Bed: The Federal Question

In a seminal speech at Humboldt University on 12 May 2000, Joschka Fischer, the German Minister of Foreign Affairs, had "a very simple answer" to Europe's problems: "the transition from a union of states to full parliamentarisation as a European Federation", meaning "nothing less than a European Parliament and a European government which really do exercise legislative and executive power within the Federation".[1] In his call for a European Federation, however, Joschka Fischer used the word *Föderation* and not *Bundesstaat*. In fact, the German Minister was cautious enough to argue that "the existing concept of a federal European state [*Bundesstaat*] replacing the old nation-states and their democracies as the new sovereign power shows itself to be an artificial construct which ignores the established realities in Europe".

(I) THE EUROPEAN UNION'S PUZZLING CONSTITUTIONAL ESSENCE

The answer to Fischer's call for a somewhat mysterious "Federation" is to be found in the most fundamental article of the aborted Constitutional Treaty, Art I-1(1):

> "Reflecting the will of the citizens and States of Europe to build a common future, this Constitution establishes the European Union, on which the Member States confer powers to attain objectives they have in common. The Union shall coordinate the policies by which the Member States aim to achieve these objectives, and shall exercise on a Community basis the powers they confer on it."

The former German Minister may have felt disenchanted as this definition of the Union was very conservative and to some extent only offered an unpretentious and rather inelegant restatement of the current Art 1 TEU:

> By this Treaty, the HIGH CONTRACTING PARTIES establish among themselves a EUROPEAN UNION, hereinafter called "the Union".

---

[1] J. Fischer, "From Confederacy to Federation: Thoughts on the Finality of European Integration", in C. Joerges, Y. Mény & J. Weiler (eds), *What kind of Constitution for what kind of Polity?* (The Robert Schuman Centre for Advanced Studies, Florence. 2000), p 24.

"This Treaty marks a new stage in the process of creating an ever closer union among the peoples of Europe, in which decisions are taken as openly as possible and as closely as possible to the citizen. ... "

The Lisbon Treaty largely preserves the present clause. It will only insert the following sentence, earlier contained at Art I-1 of the Constitutional Treaty, at the end of the first paragraph: "... on which the Member States confer competences to attain objectives they have in common". In order to more precisely understand the original constitutional essence of the EU, it may be useful to scrutinise several elements of the provisions mentioned above as well as to explain the absence of familiar concepts such as the concept of federalism.

In fact, the word "federal" was initially mentioned in the Constitutional Treaty. In October 2002, Article I-1 read as follows: This Constitution establishes "a Union of European States which, while retaining their national identities, closely coordinate their policies at the European level, and administer certain common powers on a federal basis".[2] For eurosceptics, a mere mention of the "f" word was like a red rag to a bull. Although the word only referred to the exercise of certain powers and not to the nature of the EU, i.e. it did not imply that the EU was a federal state, it proved to be a step too far. As the governing principle of the European Convention was to reach consensual decisions, the word "federal" was removed—a move welcomed by the British and Irish Governments—and Valéry Giscard d'Estaing could only confirm that the subsequent version of Art I-1 had to be viewed as a provision conciliating federalist and intergovernmentalist beliefs. He said:

"In the course of the debate, extreme solutions were gradually set aside. The idea of creating a single European federal state which would ultimately swallow the identity of the Member States, which some people supported at the beginning of our work, was gradually abandoned as inappropriate to the structure of the new Europe. Similarly the watering down of Europe in a Confederation comprising only unshared, individual interests, by depriving it of the means of action it needs, was rejected almost unanimously."[3]

The fact that the word "federal" has not reappeared in the Lisbon Treaty further confirms that, as previously argued, the Member States have decided to reinforce the "conservatory elements", i.e. those elements designed to preserve their institutional pre-eminence, of the Union's constitutional order.

---

[2] European Convention, Preliminary draft Constitutional Treaty, CONV. 369/02, Brussels, 28 October 2002, p 8.

[3] European Convention, Oral report presented to the European Council in Thessaloniki, 20 June 2003, p 10 (available at http://european-convention.eu.int/docs/speeches/9604.pdf).

"Reflecting the will of the citizens and States of Europe ...": This phrase has not survived the abandonment of the Constitutional Treaty. Euro-enthusiasts should not, however, be overly concerned. Since the provision did not refer to the will of a European people, not even the sole will of European citizens, its added value was rather unclear. It appeared to solely imply that the EU would have derived, as it already does today, its legitimacy from the citizens in specific circumstances, for instance, when they elect their representatives to the European Parliament. However, even in this situation, elections to the European Parliament are held in each Member State. This illustrates the continuing pre-eminence of the Member States and national boundaries. In any event, what is certain is that the Constitutional Treaty was not going to be the fruit of an act of self-determination of a European *demos*, of a new European sovereign.[4]

"By this Treaty, the HIGH CONTRACTING PARTIES establish among themselves a EUROPEAN UNION": This provision offers the clearest indication that the EU remains the creature of the Member States. The fact that the term "European Union" has not been replaced with the term "United States of Europe" is another illustration of the conservatory nature of the Lisbon Treaty. This is due, in particular, to the insistence of successive British Governments which, despite the British origin of that phrase,[5] have continuously opposed any reference to the United States of Europe. As a result, the term "European Union" remains with the diminutive "Union" used as shorthand.

"... [O]n which the Member States confer powers to attain objectives they have in common": The Lisbon Treaty has retained this implied reference to the principle at the heart of the Treaty's legal system, the principle of conferred competence whereby the EU may act only if it has the competence to do so, to make it a defining element of the EU. Unlike the Constitutional Treaty, however, the Lisbon Treaty does not get rid of the reference to the emblematic expression "an ever closer union". Some members of the Convention on the Future of Europe found this expression to be inappropriate as it could give "the impression that further transfer of competence to the Union is in itself an aim and objective of the Union".[6] The dispute over the expression appeared nonetheless futile as the Preamble of the EU Charter of Fundamental Rights actually states that "the peoples of Europe, in creating an ever closer union among them, are resolved to share a peaceful future based on common values".[7] What is more decisive, in reality, is the formal link

---

[4] To compare with the preamble of the Constitution of the Swiss Federation: "In the name of God Almighty! *We, the Swiss People and the Cantons,* being mindful of our responsibility towards creation, ... determined, with mutual respect and recognition, to live our diversity in unity, ..., *hereby adopt the following Constitution* ..."

[5] See Churchill's speech at Zurich University on 19 September 1946.

[6] European Convention, Final report of Working Group V on Complementary Competencies, CONV 375/1/02, Brussels, 4 November 2002, p 2.

[7] Furthermore, the Preamble of the Constitutional Treaty contained a similar expression as it mentioned the peoples of Europe being "united ever more closely".

established between the conferral of competence and the notion of common objectives. This makes it clear that the EU does not rest on a shared identity but on shared objectives, therefore limiting the potential development of the EU as a traditional political community. As suggested by a well-inspired observer, the EU could accordingly be described as a community of project more than a community of identity.[8]

Finally, one should note that the Lisbon Treaty does not reproduce the sentence: The Union "shall exercise on a Community basis" the powers conferred on it. As previously revealed, this phrase replaced in 2003 the expression "on a federal basis" initially mentioned by Art I-1 of the Constitutional Treaty. Unfortunately, the new formulation was as unclear as its predecessor. The drafters had certainly in mind what is now known as the Community method. In basic terms, the expression is used to describe the process according to which norms are adopted under the EC pillar: the Commission proposes a legal act to be adopted by the Council of Ministers in association with the European Parliament under the scrutiny of the European Court of Justice. It was, all the same, a little awkward to refer to the Community method as the Constitutional Treaty proposed to merge the EC with the EU, with the latter gaining legal personality. Furthermore, it has always been clear that a strong intergovernmental logic should continue to govern the EU's external policy and to a lesser extent, police and judicial co-operation. In the end, one should not regret that the Lisbon Treaty makes no reference to the expression "Community basis".

While the scrutiny of the "constitutional" definition of the EU offers some partial elements which help dissolve the superstate dispute, it remains essential to answer the question whether or not the EU is a federal entity, despite the complete absence of the word in the current Treaties or in the Lisbon Treaty.[9]

(a) A Debate Governed by Traditional Concepts of Constitutional Law

Any debate on the federal character of the EU is a delicate exercise. The dispute is frequently governed by implicit reference to constitutional law and the shared assumption that federalism means the existence of a federal state.[10] Furthermore, as constitutional theory knows of only two types of grouping of states—the confederation of states and the federal state—the assumption is that the EU is either a confederation or a federation. The following passage offers a perfect example of both a dependence on traditional constitutional law's categories and a deep misunderstanding of the current and prospective nature of the EU:

---

[8] K. Nicolaïdis, "Our European Demoi-cracy. Is this Constitution a Third Way for Europe?", in K. Nicolaïdis and S. Weatherill (eds), *Whose Europe? National Models and the Constitution of the European Union* (Oxford University Press, Oxford, 2003), p 144.

[9] If one obviously excludes the few references made to the *Federal* Republic of Germany.

[10] For a general overview, see M. Burgess, *Federalism and the EU: Building of Europe, 1950–2000* (Routledge, London, 2000).

"[The Constitutional Treaty] establishes what is legally, constitutionally and politically quite a new EU: in effect a European Federation, based like any state upon its own constitution, in which the existing member-states are reduced to the constitutional status of regions or provinces of the superior entity. The constitution does this by giving the European Union its own legal personality and corporate existence [*sic*] separate from and superior to any of its individual member-states for the first time, just as with any federal state."[11]

Remarkably, the same author has adopted a similar understanding of the Lisbon Treaty:

"Politically and constitutionally, however, the most important thing the new treaty would do would be to give to the new European Union that it would establish the constitutional form of a supranational state for the first time, making this new union separate from and superior to its 27 member states. This would make the EU just like the United States of America in that the US is separate from, and constitutionally superior to, California and New York. Similarly, Germany is separate from and superior to Bavaria and Saxony."[12]

This interpretation does not do justice to the *sui generis* nature of the EU and erroneously identifies the conferral of legal personality with the acquisition of sovereign capacity. As previously exposed, the EU cannot be compared to a state and no European Treaty is likely to ever transform it into one. This inaccurate description of the Constitutional Treaty and of the Lisbon Treaty's effects on the nature of the EU is still interesting as it shows the prevalence of traditional legal dichotomies, i.e. state versus international organisation, confederation versus federal state, etc. Unfortunately, the EU has a mixed nature which makes it difficult to comprehend in light of conventional concepts. Before discussing the potentiality of a new way of conceptualising the EU, a detour via classic constitutional theory may be profitable since it may dispel some conventional misinterpretations.[13]

Although inspired by German authors, the distinction between confederation of states and federal State was first clearly exposed by Louis Le Fur in 1896.[14] His typology has since inspired multiple and dispassionate debates about the possible formulae for groupings of states. Broadly speaking, the terms "confederation" and "federation" designate two idiosyncratic modes of distribution of authority/power between political institutions within

---

[11] A. Coughlan, "New EU Constitution would establish a federation", Letters Section, *The Irish Times*, 11 November 2004.

[12] A. Coughlan, "Revised EU agreement has radical implications", *The Irish Times*, 28 June 2007.

[13] For such a detour, see the instructive contribution of C. Leben, "A Federation of Nation States or Federal State", in Joerges, Mény & Weiler (eds), *What kind of Constitution for what kind of Polity?*, p 99.

[14] L. Le Fur, *État fédéral et confédération d'États* (Panthéon-Assas, Paris, 2000), with a foreword by Charles Leben.

a composite state as opposed to a unitary state. More precisely, in a confederation, sovereign states are associated in order to collectively exercise certain powers. An essential aspect is that the confederation does not itself possess sovereignty. The governing principle is that of aggregation between sovereign entities within a framework, habitually formalised through the adoption of a treaty where decisions are taken on a unanimity basis. A right to withdraw is generally recognised for each participating member. If such a model has the advantage of preserving the sovereignty of the contracting parties, the unanimity requirement reduces the efficiency of the decision-making process as the search for permanent consensus is far from being always the most optimal choice. Historically, Switzerland is the most ancient example of confederation (from 1291 to 1848) while the United States briefly experienced it (from 1781 to 1787). Germany was also a confederation before transforming itself into a federation, as Switzerland and the United States previously did.

To promptly define the notion of federation, it suffices to say that a federation is a *State* composed of *states*. Where the confederation of states does not constitute a new state, the federation necessitates the creation of a new entity, the federal State. Whereas in a confederation, the association itself does not possess sovereignty, the federal State—being a state—possesses such a quality. The states within a federal State do not, however, disappear. To preserve its founding entities, the federal State is organised according to three principles (the "laws" of federalism): the principles of superposition, of participation and of autonomy. Briefly said, the principle of superposition indicates the duality of constitutional and legal orders in a federal State. Both the federal State and federated states possess legal personality but *only* the former is a subject of international law. An additional element specific to the federal State is worth mentioning: federal law has primacy and is directly applicable. Secondly, the principle of participation implies the association of federated states to the decision-making process at federal level. Such participation usually entails involvement in the amendment procedure of the federal constitution and in law-making through an upper house of parliament. More precisely, any amendment to the federal constitution typically does not require unanimous agreement from the federated states. As for the second legislative chamber, each federated state generally elects the same number of representatives regardless of their respective populations. Finally, the principle of autonomy essentially means that federated states retain a power of constitutional self-organisation and a sphere of exclusive competence to the exclusion of any intervention from the federal State. However, the allocation of competence finds its source in the constitution of the federal State under the ultimate judicial control of a federal Supreme Court.

(b) The EU's Mixed Character

The temptation to make the EU fit into traditional dichotomies is always present. It is important to point out, however, that Europe's "founding fathers" chose pragmatic ways to build a peaceful and stronger union among the peoples of Europe rather than arguing interminably on the best possible model. To quote the Schuman Declaration, the aim was to build Europe "through concrete achievements which first create a *de facto* solidarity". In other words, the EU was built in an incremental manner by the successive addition of functions at the European level. As a result, such a political system is undoubtedly unique and difficult to classify. However, if Hans Kelsen is to be believed, as the foundation of the EU lies in treaties whilst the Member States retain their status as subjects of international law, the EU can only be a confederation. This analysis is at the crux of the French Constitutional Council's interpretation of the EU's nature: under the current Treaties as well as under the Constitutional Treaty, the EU remains "a permanent European organisation" with legal personality and with powers conferred on it by its Member States.[15] On the other hand, if the EU was to really espouse the legal nature of a confederation or of a specialised international organisation, it would be a considerable regression. The reality is unfortunately more complex than the concepts offered so far by mainstream legal theory.

To expose the multifaceted nature of the EU, it may be constructive to briefly list the elements which typify a confederation as opposed to a federal State, although as previously analysed, the EU cannot be said to be a State. As for the elements which typify a confederation, the following elements could be listed:

- ○ The fundamental status of the EU is to be found in treaties, the ratification of the Constitutional Treaty would not have changed this state of affairs as it formally had the legal nature of an international agreement;
- ○ The Member States remain the "masters" of the treaties as any amendment to the current Treaties ought to be adopted by unanimity;
- ○ The foundation of the political and legal authority (i.e. the sovereignty) of the Member States is to be found in their own constitutions and they retain their status as direct subjects of international law;
- ○ The most powerful institution in the decision-making process remains the Council of Ministers, and within the Council, unanimity voting or veto procedures govern essential policy areas transferred to the European level;
- ○ The prospective right to voluntarily withdraw from the EU;
- ○ Finally, the EU does not have any taxation power of its own.

On the other hand, a set of facts also indicate a surpassing of the confederate stage:

- ○ The EC possesses legal personality and treaty-making powers as does the EU under the Lisbon Treaty;
- ○ A European citizenship complements national citizenship;
- ○ The existence of a catalogue of powers and in particular a list of shared powers, whereas in a confederation, there is a simple mention of a few exclusive powers conferred on the confederation;
- ○ The existence of a legislative body directly representing the peoples of the Member States and of an independent executive organ (the Commission) representing the "European interest" and collectively accountable to the European Parliament;

---

[15] Decision no. 2004–505 DC, 19 November 2004, para 6.

- ° The increasing number of areas where qualified majority voting has replaced unanimity in the Council of Ministers;
- ° A legislative procedure where the European Parliament has acquired powers of "codecision" in most areas of EU policy, meaning that the Parliament's role acts as a co-legislator on almost equal footing with the Council of Ministers;
- ° The existence of a European Court of Justice responsible for enforcing European law and with jurisdiction over disputes, among others, between the Member States and the EU;
- ° Finally, the law of the EC is directly applicable, may be directly effective and has primacy over the law of the Member States.

In the end, the EU could be said to have a singular nature. As Jacques Delors famously described it, European integration has produced an unidentified political object and, one might add, one with an uncertain destination. Joschka Fischer may be right to speak of a "federative union of sovereign states" (*Staatenverbund*). Interestingly, and this is not a coincidence, such was the original concept set out by the German Federal Constitutional Court in its famous *Maastricht* ruling. The notion of *Staatenverbund* was distinguished from the more traditional notions of confederation (*Staatenbund*) and of federation (*Bundestaat*). Before considering, however, any "third way" to categorise the EU, two issues of vast political and legal importance must be scrutinised: the supremacy of European law and the principle of subsidiarity.

(II) Assessing the Evidence of a Federal State in the Making

Taken as critical evidence of a federal State in the making, the principle of supremacy of EC law is subject to some phantasmagorical thinking and, as a result, the public can easily be misled.

(a) European Union Law as the Supreme Law of the Land

The supremacy (or primacy) of EU law over national law is frequently the object of gloomy "analysis". Forgetting that acceptance of such supremacy was one of the conditions of Irish entry to the EU (then known as the EEC), critics liked to portray the EU Constitutional Treaty as a threat to national constitutions:

> "I believe that our political leaders have failed to uphold allegiance to Ireland's Constitution in their covert ceding of powers to Brussels. ... This constitution turns the EU into a super-state with its own legal personality and an existence separate from, and superior to, member-states. ... We need a Europe of equal nations, not a Europe with a constitution which will take precedence over Ireland's Constitution and our courts."[16]

---

[16] D. Scallon, "Vote on EU constitution should not be rushed", *The Irish Times*, 1 November 2004.

Coming from Dana Rosemary Scallon, a former MEP, this lack of basic knowledge leaves one surprised. The supremacy of EU law is not only a long established principle, it is also entirely justified and more limited in scope than the former MEP assumed. Indeed, as adequately and concisely presented by the Taoiseach Bertie Ahern:

> "Where the European Union does have a power, obviously Union law has primacy over those of the member-states. The alternative would be anarchy, if people did not have to implement the rules they have agreed. But the European Constitution does not replace national Constitutions, which remain supreme in the national sphere."[17]

Critics are still right to point out that the principle of supremacy of EC law is reminiscent of a federal legal system. It is also exact to stress that the present EC Treaty does not explicitly guarantee the EC law must prevail over national laws.[18] At last, the Constitutional Treaty offered the first express reference—later abandoned in 2007—to this principle by providing that "The Constitution and law adopted by the Union's Institutions in exercising powers conferred on it shall have primacy over the law of the Member States."[19] This provision compares well (if stylistic considerations are excluded) with the provision of the German Basic Law which states that "Federal law takes precedence over State [Land] law".[20] A similar clause, although more detailed and rigid, could also be found in the US Constitution:

> "This Constitution, and the Laws of the United States which shall be made in Pursuance thereof; and all Treaties made, or which shall be made, under the Authority of the United States, shall be the supreme Law of the Land; and the Judges in every State shall be bound thereby, any Thing in the Constitution or Laws of any State to the Contrary notwithstanding."[21]

In the seminal decision *Mac Cullogh v Maryland*, Chief Justice Marshall interpreted this to mean that "the government of the United States, then, though limited in its powers, is supreme; and its laws, when made in pursuance of the constitution, form the supreme law of the land".[22]

---

[17] B. Ahern, "Neither neo-liberal nor socialist, but a balanced Constitution for Europe", *The Irish Times*, 29 November 2004.

[18] It has been argued, however, that the principle of supremacy had already been "constitutionalised" through the ratification of the Treaty of Amsterdam. Indeed, the Protocol on the Application of the Principles of Subsidiarity and Proportionality, which is annexed to the Treaty, maintains that subsidiarity "shall not affect the principles developed by the Court of Justice regarding the relationship between national and Community law". These principles obviously include the principle of supremacy.

[19] Article I-6 EU CT.

[20] Article 31: "*Bundesrecht bricht Landesrecht*".

[21] Article VI, cl 2 of the US Constitution.

[22] 17 US 316 (1819).

Notwithstanding its federalist nature, the doctrine of EC/EU[23] law supremacy is utterly warranted and plainly implied by the Treaty of Rome signed in 1957. In any case, its scope is more limited than most critics assume: EU law is only supreme over national law in areas of EU competence. Furthermore, the doctrine does not allow the European Court of Justice to nullify domestic law nor does it allow for interference with the constitutional arrangements of the Member States. It "merely" requires that every national court must, in a case where EU law is applicable, apply it and set aside any provision of national law which may conflict with it.

As the Court of Justice itself has stated:

"The EEC Treaty, albeit concluded in the form of an international agreement, none the less constitutes the constitutional charter of a Community based on law. As the Court of Justice has consistently held, the Community treaties established a new legal order for the benefit of which the States have limited their sovereign rights, in ever wider fields, and the subjects of which comprise not only Member States but also their nationals. … The essential characteristics of the Community legal order which has thus been established are in particular its primacy over the law of the Member States and the direct effect of a whole series of provisions which are applicable to their nationals and to the Member States themselves."[24]

The above excerpt is a concise summation of European case law and more precisely, of the two seminal decisions issued by the "Luxembourg Court" at the beginning of the 1960s: the decision *Van Gend en Loos v Nederlandse Administratie der Belastingen* and the decision *Costa v ENEL*.[25] The first decision, *Van Gend en Loos*, although more concerned with the doctrine of direct effect than of supremacy, is still worth exploring. The ruling offers for the first time, the bold vision—some would say the "political" vision—of the European Court of Justice. Faced with what could appear as an innocuous question: whether the application of a duty on imports represented an unlawful increase with regard to the relevant Treaty provision, the Court had to initially rule on the more delicate issue of its "direct effect". To put it differently, could the applicant directly invoke a provision of the EC Treaty before national courts?

---

[23] Ms Scallon has accused her contradictors of confusing EC and EU law, that there is no such thing as "Union law", that only EC law has primacy, etc. See "Debate on the EU Constitution", Letters section, *The Irish Times*, 23 November 2004. True, the doctrine of supremacy is a doctrine of Community law and does not formally apply to the norms produced under the second (CFSP) or third (PJCCM) pillars. Nonetheless, norms produced by EU institutions (no matter the pillar) generally benefit from the treatment given to international norms. Furthermore, the "constitutionalisation" of Union membership in each Member State has generally led to an "immunity" regime for EC/EU norms alike, meaning they are protected from legal challenges based on any point of national law. And for didactic purposes (see the numerous textbooks entitled "EU Law"), one may generically speak of EU or Union law to encompass the entirety of norms being produced under the EC pillar and the two intergovernmental pillars.

[24] Opinion 1/91 (Draft Treaty on a European Economic Area) [1991] ECR I-1061.

[25] See respectively Case 26/62 [1963] ECR 1 and Case 6/64 [1964] ECR 585.

To rule on the issue, the European Court of Justice relied heavily on the so-called teleological method of interpretation: "To ascertain whether the provisions of an international treaty extend so far in their effects it is necessary to consider the spirit, the general scheme and the wording of those provisions." In other words, the Court read the Treaty of Rome with the intention of underlying the aims of the Community enterprise as a whole. And from the objectives of this Treaty (to establish a common market, "the functioning of which is of direct concern to interested parties in the Community") and its preamble which refers not only to governments but to peoples, the Court deduced that "the States have acknowledged that Community law has an authority which can be invoked by their nationals before their courts and tribunals." As a result, the Treaty provision prohibiting customs duties was held to produce direct effect and to create individual rights that national courts must protect. From then on, individuals have been able to invoke a Community provision (when considered "justiciable"[26]) before national courts. With the benefit of hindsight, it would be difficult to argue against the doctrine of direct effect: it has enabled individuals to act against their own Member States and oblige national authorities to be consistent about their European obligations. In Ireland, for instance, the protection of the environment or social rights would have remained a "dead letter" without active citizens relying directly on EC law to institute legal proceedings before national courts. The most decisive aspect of the ruling, however, resides in the characterisation of the EC as a "new legal order of international law for the benefit of which states have limited their sovereign rights, albeit within limited fields, and the subjects of which comprise not only Member States but also their nationals." In other words, the European Court of Justice stressed the autonomy and original nature of the Community legal system, distinguishing EC law from the law of "other" international organisations. Contrary to international law, as a matter of principle, EC law could be relied upon by individuals even in circumstances where the Member States did not expressly authorise such "direct effect".

If the "federal" aspect of such self-assured affirmation is transparent, a subsequent ruling, *Costa v ENEL*, was going to complete the loop.[27] Faced with a technically imperfect request from an Italian court asking the Court to decide upon the validity of a provision of national law—the European Court of Justice can *only* decide upon the validity of EC law or interpret EC law—the Luxembourg Court took the opportunity to affirm its supremacy. In fact, the Court had to answer an argument raised by the Italian Government according to which the national court was obliged to apply national law, and could not send a request to the European Court of Justice. This interpretation was found to be clearly in breach of the EC Treaty. A national court can always send a request for a preliminary ruling to the European Court of Justice whenever it raises a question relating to the

---

[26] To have direct effect, the legal provision must be sufficiently precise and unconditional, i.e. it must not leave discretionary power to the Member States.

[27] Case 6/64 [1964] ECR 585.

interpretation of the Treaty. This outcome, while not surprising, was accompanied by the following "unexpected" statement:

> "[T]he law stemming from the Treaty, an independent source of law, could not, *because of its special and original nature* [emphasis added], be overridden by domestic legal provisions, however framed, without being deprived of its character as Community law and without the legal basis of the Community itself being called into question."

Despite the absence of any explicit legal basis, the Court of Justice again deduced the principle of EC law supremacy from the spirit and general scheme of the EC Treaty. Accordingly, as far as the Court of Justice is concerned, when in conflict, all binding instruments of EC law shall prevail over *any* provision of national law, but only in the areas of Community competence.

Again, the federal character of the principle of supremacy cannot be denied. Unsurprisingly, the lack of a formal legal basis has prompted much criticism. The judicial finding is, however, a logical consequence of the general economy of the 1957 Treaty. Without EC law having primacy (in a situation of conflict!) over national law, any Member State could escape from their European obligations by subsequently passing a contradictory law. As the European Court of Justice perfectly emphasised, the executive force of EC law cannot simply vary from one State to another. Ultimately, the legal unity of the Community and the effectiveness of EC law require the principle of supremacy.

The supremacy doctrine can nevertheless be viewed with some apprehension. Indeed, it necessarily implies that EC law[28] ought to have primacy over any conflicting provision of national law, including constitutional provisions.[29] In short, EC law takes precedence over Member States' constitutional provisions.[30] For a number of people, this is quite a shocking statement. Yet, what would be the situation otherwise? Obligations under EC law could be subsequently violated by a Member State through constructive interpretation of the national Constitution or a subsequent constitutional amendment. And if national courts could examine the validity of EC law under national law, it would lead to legal

---

[28] Including not only the Treaties but also secondary legislation, individual decisions issued by the Council and Commission, general principles of law as well as the rulings of the Court of Justice.

[29] C-11/70 *International Handelsgesellschaft* [1970], para 3: "Therefore the validity of a Community measure or its effect within a Member State cannot be affected by allegations that it runs counter to either fundamental rights as formulated by the constitution of that state or the principles of a national constitutional structure."

[30] It may be interesting to note that the European Court of Human Rights has also affirmed the authority of the European Convention on Human Rights over provisions of constitutional value: "The political and institutional organisation of the member States must accordingly respect the rights and principles enshrined in the Convention. It matters little in this context whether the provisions in issue are constitutional or merely legislative", case of *United Communist Party of Turkey v Turkey*, 30 January 1998, Reports 1998-I, para 30.

chaos.[31] In other words, no functioning European legal order would be possible without the supremacy doctrine. On the other hand, the self-appointed guardians of national constitutions often fail to mention that supremacy of EC law is both latent and limited. Latent, as the principle does not need to be relied upon if there is no conflicting national provision. Limited, as conflicting national law is not void *per se*, meaning national law remains effective and is only inapplicable within the sphere where Community law produces legal effects.[32] Where there is no EC law, there is no potential supremacy debate. And one should bear in mind that the EU may act only if the Treaties have given it the power to do so.

(b) The role of National Constitutional Courts

A number of national constitutional courts have shown extreme reluctance to accept the principle of EC/EU law supremacy over national constitutions. Such opposition has inspired Miguel Maduro to suggest that "if an alien were to land on earth and (let us assume the impossible …) were to be interested in the relationship between European law and national law, his perception of reality would vary considerably depending on whether he would land on the European Court of Justice or some national constitutional courts."[33] Undeniably, national constitutional courts have maintained the view by which they retain the ultimate power to overrule European law, should it infringe upon their basic values in the national constitution.[34]

The first "warning shot" was delivered in 1974 by the German *Bundesverfassungsgericht*, the Federal Constitutional Court, in its *Solange I* decision, challenged the European Court of Justice by ruling that it reserves the power to set EC law aside in the case of a European norm violating German fundamental rights.[35] However, with the development of effective European protection in the area of fundamental rights, the German Constitutional Court finally agreed in the so-called *Solange II* decision that it will no longer exercise its (potential) jurisdiction.[36] Yet, as the *Maastricht* decision made clear, the German Court has not given

---

[31] And if a national court believes that an EC measure violates, for example, fundamental rights, it may only refer the question of the measure's validity to the Court of Justice for a preliminary ruling, and then must follow that ruling.

[32] See e.g. Case C-10/97 *IN.CO.GE. '90* [1998] ECR I-6307, para 21.

[33] M. Maduro, "Contrapuntal Law: Europe's Constitutional Pluralism in Action", in Neil Walker (ed), *Sovereignty in Transition* (Hart, Oxford, 2003), p 502.

[34] It is important to note first that there is no (more) disagreement about EC secondary legislation (i.e. regulations and directives) overriding national legislation in cases of conflict. Secondly, the likelihood of a conflict is not between EC primary law (i.e. the founding Treaties and amending Treaties) and national legislation, but between EC secondary legislation and national constitutions. Indeed, any new EU treaty presupposes ratification before entering into force, meaning preventive constitutional review evacuates all potential conflict with the national constitution. And if there is such conflict, the "Sovereign" could accept to overcome it by amending its constitution.

[35] BVerfGE 37, 271, reported in English at [1974] 14 CMLR 540.

[36] BVerfGE 73, 339, reported in English at [1987] 3 CMLR 225.

up the right to set aside EC law in the (highly) hypothetical situation of a direct and inescapable conflict with the German Basic Law.[37] The French *Conseil Constitutionnel* has recently followed a similar path. Whilst the European Court of Justice denies national courts the capacity to declare EC secondary legislation invalid, the *Conseil Constitutionnel* ruled in 2004 that it might, under exceptional circumstances, do just that.[38] Yet the French *Conseil* rightly and forcefully emphasised it would only recognise jurisdiction for itself in a precisely limited situation: when explicit and specific constitutional provisions enter directly into conflict with European provisions. As far as EC primary law is concerned, it is entirely immune from constitutional review by virtue of constitutional amendment following each major European Treaty.

The issue of the supremacy of EC primary law was similarly addressed in Ireland. Following the decision in *Crotty v Taoiseach*,[39] each major amendment to the Treaty of Rome has been followed by a popular referendum. By virtue of the positive answer received from the sovereign People—in all cases but one[40]—constitutional amendment has authorised the Irish State to pursue European integration. With regard to the primacy of EC secondary legislation, however, the British model was followed. A general constitutional provision guarantees constitutional "immunity" for the entirety of acts adopted by the EC/EU, as well as for the legal norms adopted by the Irish State when these are "necessitated"[41] by its European membership:

> "No provision of this Constitution invalidates laws enacted, acts done or measures adopted by the State which are necessitated by the obligations of membership of the European Union or of the Communities, or prevents laws enacted, acts done or measures adopted by the European Union or by the Communities or by institutions

---

[37] BVerfGE 89, 155, reported in English at [1994] 1 CMLR 57. See also the *Bananas* case, BVerfGE 102, 147 and the *European Arrest Warrant* case, BVerfG, 2 BvR 2236/04, 18 July 2005. In the controversial *Grogan* case, Walsh J. appears to echo the German motivation by stating that "any answer to the reference from the Court of Justice will have to be considered in the light of our own constitutional provisions. In the last analysis only this Court can decide finally what are the effects of the interaction" of the relevant articles of the Irish Constitution, *SPUC v Grogan* [1989] IR 753, pp 768–769.

[38] French Constitutional Council, 10 June 2004, Decision no. 2004-496 DC.

[39] [1987] IR 713.

[40] The Nice Treaty agreed in 2000 was rejected by Irish citizens in a referendum held in 2001. After obtaining from its partners a guarantee that nothing in the Nice Treaty would or could oblige Ireland to depart from its policy of military neutrality, the Irish Government organised a second referendum in 2002. The Nice Treaty was finally approved by 62.89 percent of the vote. See generally B. Laffan and A. Langan, "Securing a "Yes": From Nice I to Nice II", *Notre Europe*, Policy Paper No 13, April 2005; C. Costello, "Ireland's Nice Referenda", (2005) *European Constitutional Law Review* 357.

[41] The Irish Supreme Court clarified the meaning of the term "necessitated" in two landmark cases: *Meagher v Minister for Agriculture* [1994] 1 IR 329; *Maher v Minister for Agriculture and Food* [2001] 2 IR 139. For a discussion of these two cases, see G. Hogan and G. Whyte, *J.M. Kelly: The Irish Constitution* (4th ed., LexisNexis Butterworths, Dublin, 2003), paras 5.3.63–5.3.76.

thereof, or by bodies competent under the Treaties establishing the Communities, from having the force of law in the State."[42]

In the United Kingdom, s 2(1) of the European Communities Act 1972 provides for EC law to be directly applicable and s 3(1) requires any question as to the meaning or effect of any of the Treaties to be determined in accordance with the principles laid down by the European Court of Justice.[43] As interpreted by Lord Bridge in the long-running *Factortame* case, the 1972 Act illustrates a voluntary limitation, by the British Parliament, of its sovereignty to accommodate the well-established principle of EC law supremacy:

> "Thus, whatever limitation of its sovereignty Parliament accepted when it enacted the European Communities Act 1972 was entirely voluntary. Under the terms of the 1972 Act it has always been clear that it was the duty of a United Kingdom court, when delivering final judgment, to override any rule of national law found to be in conflict with any directly enforceable rule of Community law."[44]

However, in both countries, the acceptance of supremacy is voluntary and conditional: The Irish People could always amend the Constitution to provide otherwise, while the British Parliament could expressly enact that a national provision should take effect notwithstanding the European Communities Act 1972. There is also the German option to attach reservations to the constitutional acceptance of the European legal order and the supremacy of its law:

> "To realise a unified Europe, Germany participates in the development of the European Union which is bound to democratic, rule of law, social, and federal principles as well as the principle of subsidiarity and provides a protection of fundamental rights essentially equivalent to that of this Constitution. The federation can, for this purpose and with the consent of the Senate [*Bundesrat*], delegate sovereign powers."[45]

As a result, the transfer of powers to the EU is made conditional on the respect of several principles, such as subsidiarity, and on the more precise requirement that the EU must offer "equivalent" protection regarding fundamental rights. In the end, the Federal Constitutional Court retains, *in principle*, the power to scrutinise the respect of the conditions foreseen by the German Constitution.

---

[42] Article 29.4.10° of the Irish Constitution. See also the (Irish) European Communities Act 1972.

[43] On the UK's position with regard to the supremacy of EC law, see the emblematic opinion of Lord Justice Laws in *Thoburn v Sunderland City Council* [2002] 1 CMLR 1461 and more generally, the helpful report of the House of Lords, EU Committee, *The Future Role of the European Court of Justice*, 6th Report of Session 2003-04 (HL Paper 47), para 82.

[44] *R. v Secretary of State for Transport, ex p. Factortame Ltd (No 2)* [1991] 1 AC 603, pp 658–659.

[45] Article 23(1) of the German Constitution.

However hard it is to cope with, especially for legal minds accustomed to hierarchical thinking, such plurality of supreme and final interpretations over the scope and primacy of European law should be accepted. Theoretically speaking, the enforcement of European "federal" law may thus be ultimately dependent on both the European Court of Justice and the 27 constitutional/supreme courts. One should not fear anarchy as national courts will be extremely careful before ever setting aside EU norms. Although highly unlikely in light of the history of the past 40 years, their potential intervention also acts as a "virtual" check on the European Court of Justice. Ultimately, the originality of such a co-operative framework—the relationship between the national courts and the European Court of Justice is often described as being a dialogue among equals—is an additional indication that the EU should not be compared to a federal state.

(c) Restricting the Supremacy of European Union Law: The Potential Impact of the Lisbon Treaty

The decision to abandon the Constitutional Treaty has resulted in the unfortunate removal of the supremacy clause. Instead, the Lisbon Treaty will annex a new Declaration to the European Treaties which "recalls that, in accordance with well settled case-law of the EU Court of Justice, the Treaties and the law adopted by the Union on the basis of the Treaties have primacy over the law of Member States, under the conditions laid down by the said case-law".[46] In addition, for no apparent reason other than to restate the obvious, the Member States agreed to annex the opinion of the Legal Service of the Council to the Final Act of the Intergovernmental Conference in charge of drafting the Lisbon Treaty, which states:

> "It results from the case-law of the Court of Justice that primacy of EC law is a cornerstone principle of Community law. According to the Court, this principle is inherent to the specific nature of the European Community. At the time of the first judgement of this established case-law (Costa/ENEL, 15 July 1964, Case 6/64) there was no mention of primacy in the treaty. It is still the case today. The fact that the principle of primacy will not be included in the future treaty shall not in any way change the existence of the principle and the existing case-law of the Court of Justice."[47]

It should now be easier to understand how hypocritical and ill-advised is the decision not to reproduce the supremacy clause into the Lisbon Treaty. First, the criticised clause merely codified the current case law of the European Court of Justice[48] and formalised a long-

---

[46] Declaration no 17 concerning primacy, [2007] OJ C306/256.

[47] European Council, Opinion of the Legal Service, Doc no 11197/02 JUR 260, 22 June 2007.

[48] See Declaration No 1 annexed to the Constitutional Treaty which states that Article I-6 reflects existing case law of the Court of Justice of the European Communities. This is precisely the reason why the French *Conseil Constitutionnel* concluded in November 2004 that Article I-6 of the Constitutional Treaty did not necessitate any amendment to the French Constitution. For a brief but incisive criticism of the French decision in English, see A. Arnull, "A Preemptive Strike from the Palais Royal", (2005) 30 *European Law Review* 1.

established principle of international law: the state may not plead its national law, including constitutional provisions, to escape its obligations under international law, including its treaty obligations. Secondly, the principle of supremacy remains but instead of having a single and concise provision recalling its existence and scope, citizens will have to look at the Treaties with a magnifying glass to locate it. Finally, despite affirmations to the contrary, the insertion of a supremacy clause into the Treaties would not have given the European Court of Justice new and superior powers over national courts and would not have extended the scope of the doctrine of supremacy.[49]

Instead of deploring the fact that EU law will continue to have primacy over the law of Member States, eurosceptics would be well-advised to welcome the Lisbon Treaty as it appears, like the Constitutional Treaty before it, to take into account the rulings issued by several constitutional courts according to which the primacy of EU law is not of an absolute nature.[50] This aspect has completely escaped the attention of EU scaremongers. As a result, it would be particularly incongruous to oppose the text on the grounds that it advances the cause of European integration without paying due regard to national specificities embodied in national constitutions. The Lisbon Treaty, like the Constitutional Treaty before it, actually has the opposite effect. Several provisions could be relied upon to make our case.

A new Art 3a TEU on the relations between the Union and the Member States further develops the current provision in the EC Treaty ("The Union shall respect the national identities of its Member States"[51]) and requires, for the first time, that the EU shall respect the constitutional structures of the Member States as far as they reflect national identities:

> "The Union shall respect the equality of Member States before the Treaties as well as their national identities, inherent in their fundamental structures, political and constitutional, inclusive of regional and local self-government. It shall respect their essential State functions, including ensuring the territorial integrity of the State, maintaining law and order and safeguarding national security. In particular, national security remains the sole responsibility of each Member State."[52]

Such a provision could give national courts the option to argue the respect of the fundamental constitutional structures to impair the uniform application of EU law. It

---

[49] It could be deduced, however, from the abolition of the pillar structure that the doctrine of supremacy would have applied to the areas of Common Foreign and Security Policy and of Police and Judicial Cooperation in Criminal Matters. The doctrine's material scope therefore appeared to expand.

[50] For recent studies arguing along the same lines, see the challenging article of M. Kumm, "The Jurisprudence of Constitutional Conflict: Constitutional Supremacy in Europe before and after the Constitutional Treaty", (2005) 11 *European Law Journal* 262; P. Cassia, "L'article I-6 du traité établissant une Constitution pour l'Europe et la hiérarchie des normes", (2004) *Europe*, étude 12.

[51] Article 6(3) TEC.

[52] New Art 3a(2) TEU (formerly Art I-5(1) EU CT).

seems, therefore, that Member States agreed to codify the German *Solange II* ruling, according to which the transfer of powers to the EU cannot allow for the modification of the specific character of the German constitutional order.[53]

The German reservation in *Solange I* also appears to be reproduced in a provision of the EU Charter of Fundamental Rights which states that "Nothing in [the Charter] shall be interpreted as restricting or adversely affecting human rights and fundamental freedoms as recognised, in their respective fields of application, by Union law and international law … and by the Member States' constitutions."[54] The reference to national constitutions could be interpreted as an exception to the principle of supremacy. Therefore, if our reading is correct, on the basis of the EU Charter itself, a constitutional court will be empowered to set aside any piece of EU secondary legislation on the ground of a violation of a national standard of protection regarding a particular fundamental right.

Last but not least, eurosceptics may come to regret the disappearance of the supremacy clause contained in the Constitutional Treaty. Indeed, the clause itself contained an implied reference to the German warning issued with regard to the Maastricht Treaty, and to some extent, legitimised it.[55] By stating (unnecessarily, as it is legally obvious) that the supremacy of EU law could only be relied upon where the EU exercises powers conferred on it, the Constitutional Treaty appeared not to exclude national control of EU secondary legislation in exceptional circumstances. Clearly, national courts would demonstrate ultra-sensitivity before ruling that the EU acted *ultra vires* and, therefore, the problem may remain forever a virtual one. Nevertheless, the important point is that national courts could have found in the Constitutional Treaty itself the legal basis for doing so, with the consequence of a permanent and invisible check on the Luxembourg Court.

In the end, regardless of what the European Treaties state, from a national perspective, EU law is and will continue to have primacy insofar as the national constitution says so: Article 88-1 of the French Constitution and Art 29(4)10° of the Irish Constitution, etc. Although lacking a formal constitution, the situation is similar in the United Kingdom under the "constitutional" EC Act 1972.[56] No European Treaty or Constitution is likely

---

[53] Professor Papier, the President of the *Bundesverfassungsgericht*, recently argued that, in Germany, the transfer of sovereign rights to the European Union "is restricted by a guarantee of identity (Art 23.1 sentence 3 and Art 79.3 of the Basic Law (*Grundgesetz*)). A violation of this core of constitutional provisions, which also include, for instance, democracy and respect for human dignity, could therefore be identified by the Federal Constitutional Court as an exercise of supranational sovereign power that is not covered by the Community Treaties and be declared inapplicable in Germany", quoted in House of Lords, *The Future Role of the European Court of Justice*, para 43.

[54] Article 53 Charter (formerly Art II-113 EU CT).

[55] A similar approach was subsequently taken by the Danish Supreme Court in *Carlsen v Prime Minister*, judgment of 6 April 1998, reported in English at [1999] 3 CMLR 854.

[56] The EC Communities Act is often described as a "constitutional statute" in the sense that the British Parliament, to derogate from it, must explicitly and unequivocally state its intention.

to ever modify the current interpretation of most national constitutional courts according to which the supremacy of EU law remains ultimately conditional: EU norms have primacy over national law but not over national constitutions. Such departure from the position of the European Court of Justice is not surprising as the EU does not organise a formal hierarchy between national courts and the Luxembourg Court. Yet, the doctrine of supremacy has been applied for more than 40 years without any case of open or strident conflict between EU/EC law and national constitutions, with the sole exception of the *Kreil* case.[57]

In its ruling in *Kreil,* the European Court of Justice confirmed that a Directive on equal treatment between men and women can be applied to military forces. This interpretation conflicted with the German constitutional provision barring women from army jobs involving the use of arms. Since it was found by the Court to be too broad and discriminatory, the provision was judged incompatible with EC law. As a result, the German Parliament decided to amend the relevant provision of the German Constitution without much resistance, as there had been prior domestic discussion about the merits of the ban. It follows from the *Kreil* case that the supremacy of EC law over national constitutional provisions is not a purely theoretical question. Yet, as previously stated, the supremacy of EC law is both latent and limited in scope. Relatively complex, the case law of the Luxembourg Court could easily lead critics to confuse the public with bold affirmations on the invasive nature of European law, as the discussion surrounding abortion in Ireland has demonstrated.

Despite contrary popular belief, the European Court of Justice never found the Irish constitutional ban on abortion to be in violation of EC law in the case of *Grogan.*[58] In reality, the Court declined to intervene and the main question referred to the European Court of Justice was whether Irish law on the provision of *information* about abortion services abroad was compatible with the EC Treaty provisions on the freedom to supply services. Even if the Court—as we would argue it should have ruled—had declared that EC law applied to the provision of information about abortion services abroad, even when not distributed on behalf of an economic operator, the Luxembourg Court could still have concluded that the Irish legislation was justified on the ground of public policy.[59] In any case, it was left to the "Strasbourg Court", i.e. the European Court of Human Rights, to

---

[57] Case C-285/98 [2000] ECR I-69. For further references, see M. Trybus, "Sister in Arms: European Community Law and Sex Equality in the Armed Forces", (2003) 9 *European Law Journal* 631.

[58] *SPUC v Grogan,* Case C-159/90 [1991] ECR I-4685. An injunction was sought by the Society for the Protection of Unborn Children (SPUC) against the activities of various students' unions who provided information on abortion clinics in the UK. For the Court, as the information was not distributed on behalf of an economic operator established in another Member State and furthermore, as it was distributed for free, the requirement of Art 50(1) of the TEC according to which services are "provided for remuneration" was consequently not fulfilled. For further references, see D. R. Phelan, "Right to Life of the Unborn v. Promotion of Trade in Services: The European Court of Justice and the Normative Shaping of the European Union", (1992) 55 *The Modern Law Review* 670.

[59] See Article 46 TEC.

rule that the Irish "absolute" provisions violated the right of freedom to information contained in Art 10 of the European Convention. Although pursuing the legitimate aim of the protection of morality, Irish rules were judged manifestly disproportionate.[60]

Grogan is illustrative of the fact that the European Court of Justice is always careful not to enter into conflict with national constitutional courts. Undeniably, the doctrine of supremacy has far-ranging consequences. To be accepted in the non-hierarchical European judicial system, the Luxembourg Court must demonstrate self-restraint when the issue of an alleged violation of EC law by a constitutional provision is not crystal-clear. This is a wise attitude. The European judicial branch, whenever it is feasible, should let European and national political actors forge a consensual resolution. As a matter of fact, as the original Irish constitutional provision "on the right to life of the unborn", and the legislation related to it, infringed so dramatically the right to access information and the right to free movement, the Irish Constitution was eventually amended.[61]

Hence another key point: a Member State should be careful not to overreach. The inflexible defence of a public policy enshrined in a constitution can, in the long run, isolate a State unless it is a convincingly pressing public interest. If so, the Member State may invoke the means to exclude European norms. This is the case with abortion. Indeed, the Constitutional Treaty did not repeal the Protocol no. 17, which was annexed to the EU Treaty in 1992, and according to which Art 40.3.3 of the Irish Constitution is protected from challenge under EU law.[62] Such a protocol, however, creates an appalling precedent with regard to an effective protection of fundamental rights against an oppressive majority. And effectively, such precedent was referred to by Poland to issue a *unilateral* declaration where the primacy of its laws on morals over the EU Charter of Fundamental Rights is affirmed, irrespective of the lack of direct competence of the Union in such matters.[63] In any event, the abortion debate is an additional indication if such were needed that the EU does not organise a rigid hierarchy

---

[60] *Open Door Counseling and Dublin Well Woman v Ireland*, 29 October 1992, A-246 (1993). Before the ruling of the European Court of Human Rights, the Irish Supreme Court denied the existence of any constitutional right to information about the availability of a service of abortion outside the State as such recognition could potentially have the consequence of destroying the guaranteed constitutional right to life of the unborn. See *Attorney-General (Society for the Protection of Unborn Children (Ireland) Ltd) v Open Door* [1988] IR 593.

[61] The Thirteenth Amendment of the Constitution Act 1992 provided that Art 40.3.3° (the right to life of the unborn) shall not limit freedom to travel between Ireland and another state. Furthermore, the Fourteenth Amendment of the Constitution Act 1992 provided that the same Article 40.3.3° shall not limit freedom to obtain or make available information relating to services lawfully available in another state.

[62] Protocol No 31 annexed to the EU CT reads as follow: "Nothing in the Treaty establishing a Constitution for Europe or in the Treaties or Acts modifying or supplementing it shall affect the application in Ireland of Article 40.3.3 of the Constitution of Ireland."

[63] First issued in 2004, the Lisbon Treaty reproduces the unilateral declaration adopted by Poland and which provides that "The Charter does not affect in any way the right of Member States to legislate in the sphere of public morality, family law as well as the protection of human dignity and respect for human physical and moral integrity."

between its law and national constitutions. When a conflict potentially occurs, practise has shown that either a pacifying judicial interpretation or a formal neutralisation at the European or national level, will pave the way for a quiet resolution between the relevant parties.

To conclude on the principle of EU law supremacy, the coexistence of the European Court of Justice and national constitutional courts should be considered in a positive light. If the Luxembourg Court can hardly show any flexibility for fear of opening a Pandora's box, the position of the national courts is entirely consistent with the fact they must abide by the text voted upon by the Sovereign. The construction of Europe may have led to a new legal order, but its legal foundation and legitimacy resides within the consent of each national sovereign. It is, therefore, legitimate for national constitutional courts to affirm that the authority of EU law lies ultimately in each constitutional provision recognising its existence and its (relative) primacy. The (potential) plurality of legal interpretations of EU law is the clearest sign that the European legal order cannot be compared simplistically to a federal one. As with the nature of the EU itself, the European judicial system can be said to be *sui generis*. Indeed, the co-operative framework organised by the Treaty of Rome has created an intermediary system. It is not quite comparable to a federal system where, in a situation of conflict, a federal Supreme Court can directly and ultimately nullify any ruling from any state court. However, the European judicial system is much more developed than an international system where the supranational court remains "foreign" to national courts. The entrenchment of the supremacy doctrine would not have altered such constitutional pluralism. The Constitutional Treaty merely codified what the Luxembourg Court held as long ago as 1964. Member States had no choice but to accept this doctrine since they know they must preserve themselves from unilateral behaviour which could be detrimental to their national interests.

(III) FURTHER EVIDENCE OF THE *SUI GENERIS* NATURE OF THE EUROPEAN UNION

The new procedure for monitoring respect for subsidiarity and the formalisation of a new right to withdraw from the EU reinforce the idea of the *sui generis* character of the EU and certainly undermine any serious grounds for arguing about the emergence of a European superstate. On the contrary, the originality of the European institutional framework and governing principles leads us to construe the EU as the ultimate political experiment in pluralist statehood.

(a) The Subsidiarity Principle

To answer concerns about increasing centralisation and the enactment of unwarranted legislation at EU level, the principle of subsidiarity was introduced by the Maastricht Treaty (1992). At present, Art 5(2) of the EC Treaty provides that:

> "In areas which do not fall within its exclusive competence, the Community shall take action, in accordance with the principle of subsidiarity, only if and in so far as the objectives of the proposed action cannot be sufficiently achieved by the Member States

and can therefore, by reason of the scale or effects of the proposed action, be better achieved by the Community."[64]

While it remains true that the meaning of subsidiarity is far from clear,[65] it certainly cannot be interpreted as a basis to claim novel powers. The principle of subsidiarity merely regulates the exercise of current European *non-exclusive* powers or competences, i.e. environment, consumer protection, transport, etc. To act in those areas, the EU must demonstrate the added value of its intervention.[66] Subsidiarity does not make possible the "invention" of a new power, it regulates the exercise of shared or complementary powers already conferred on the EU by the Member States acting unanimously.

Enshrined in the EC Treaty, subsidiarity is a legal principle and, therefore, the European Court of Justice can eventually check that it has been complied with. Yet, to judge if the objectives of the proposed action can be "better" achieved by the EU is certainly not an easy task for the Luxembourg Court. In reality, rather than calling for a full judicial reasoning the subjective character of subsidiarity calls, in essence, for a political assessment.[67] It is thus unsurprising to discover that the Court has yet to annul an act on the grounds of substantive infringement of the principle of subsidiarity. To do so would pave the way for considerable judicial activism as it would require the Court to define "better" by evaluating, for instance, economic data in order to determine whether European action is more efficient than national intervention. If all the Member States or a qualified majority of them have decided that European action brings about some "added value", how could the Court, other than on procedural grounds, strike down a legislative proposal in the name of subsidiarity? As a result, it could be argued that there could never be a substantive constitutional test in this domain for the simple reason that it is not the task of a court to adjudicate on the added value or the scale and effects of any European action.

Less subjective is the principle of proportionality, referred to in the third paragraph of Art 5 TEC, under which any action by the EU must not go beyond what is necessary to achieve the objectives of the Treaty of Rome. Of general application and already firmly established in the case law of the European Court of Justice, proportionality essentially guarantees that the means used by the EU should be appropriate and the least intrusive in order to achieve the objectives pursued. Better suited to judicial control, the principle of

---

[64] Subsidiarity is also mentioned in Art 2 TEU: "The objectives of the Union shall be achieved as provided in this Treaty and in accordance with the conditions and the timetable set out therein while respecting the principle of subsidiarity…"

[65] Its historical roots are nevertheless distinguished. It could be traced back to medieval times as a governing principle of the Catholic Church and could also be discovered in the work of Althusius.

[66] The German influence is clear. Article 72(2) of the German Constitution states that in the field of concurrent legislative powers, "the Federation has legislation if and insofar as the establishment of equal living conditions in the federal territory or the preservation of legal and economic unity necessitates, in the interest of the state at large, a federal regulation."

[67] A. Toth, "Is Subsidiarity Justiciable", (1994) 19 *European Law Review* 268.

proportionality has not captivated the attention of the public. Critics have rather focused on the principle of subsidiarity. And, in fairness, several examples could easily come to mind where it appears that EU action did not comply with the latter principle.[68] On the other hand, one could confidently report "that the alleged European regulations governing the shape of toilet bowls, requiring that fishermen wear hair nets, and banning square gin bottles—all cited in breathless exposés in the British press—have never existed."[69]

If one is convinced of the legitimacy and usefulness of the principle of subsidiarity, it could be argued that political monitoring of the principle is required. While it reaffirmed that the use of EU powers is governed by the principles of subsidiarity and proportionality,[70] the Constitutional Treaty considerably reinforced such monitoring. It did so, however, without introducing a new Competence Court as suggested prior to the Convention.[71] In addition to reproducing the provisions of the Constitutional Treaty, the Lisbon Treaty further enhances the role of national parliaments. To discover the main innovations, one must read the legally binding Protocol on the Application of the Principles of Subsidiarity and Proportionality, which will be annexed to the existing Treaties once the Lisbon Treaty enters into force.[72] The information of national parliaments is increased with the new obligation for the Commission to directly send its proposals to the national parliaments as well as to the European Parliament. This will remedy the nonchalant attitude shown by some national governments when it comes to their duty to inform their respective parliaments on EU legislative developments.

The most innovative and most debated aspect of the Constitutional Treaty was the so-called "yellow card" or "early warning mechanism".[73] The Lisbon Treaty contains a

---

[68] See e.g. the Directive of 29 March 1999 relating to the keeping of wild animals in zoos, [1999] OJ L94/24.

[69] T. Reid, *The United States of Europe* (The Penguin Press, New York, 2004), p 57.

[70] According to new Art 3b(3) TEU: "Under the principle of subsidiarity, in areas which do not fall within its exclusive competence, the Union shall act only if and insofar as the objectives of the proposed action cannot be sufficiently achieved by the Member States, either at central level or at regional and local level, but can rather, by reason of the scale or effects of the proposed action, be better achieved at Union level". The fourth paragraph of new Art 3b(4) TEU deals with proportionality and states that "the content and form of Union action shall not exceed what is necessary to achieve the objectives of the Treaties."

[71] See the proposal of a Constitutional Council made by J. Weiler, "The European Union Belongs to its Citizens: Three Immodest Proposals", (1997) 22 *European Law Review* 150, at 155. Interestingly, it appears that a similar debate has agitated the United States where it was suggested to set up a Court of the Union composed out of the Chief Justices of the State Supreme Courts. For further references, see Mayer, "Powers-Reloaded? The Vertical Division of Powers in the EU and the New European Constitution".

[72] [2007] OJ C306/150.

[73] The EU Committee of the House of Lords has offered an instructive report on the question: *Strengthening national parliamentary scrutiny of the EU–the Constitution's subsidiarity early warning mechanism*, 14th Report of Session 2004-05 (HL Paper 101). The Committee concludes that the principle of subsidiarity needs to be applied more rigorously if it is to be effective. This is quite a departure from a previous viewpoint which favoured the inclusion of "the principle of subsidiarity only in the preamble to the new Treaty, so as to avoid litigation as to the validity of Council and Commission legislation" as stated in House of Lords, Select Committee the European Communities, *Political Union. Law-Making Powers and Procedures*, 17th Report of Session 1990-91 (HL Paper 80), para 122.

similar provision which will confer on national parliaments a formal role in monitoring the compliance of EU legislation with the principle of subsidiarity. Concretely, any national parliament will be able, within eight weeks (from six weeks as agreed in 2004) of transmission of the Commission's proposal, to issue a reasoned opinion as to why it considers that a legislative proposal does not comply with the principle of subsidiarity. This reasoned opinion or "yellow card" must be taken into account by the Council and the Commission. The most remarkable aspect of this innovative procedure is that national parliaments, if they can gather at least one-third of all the votes allocated to them,[74] will have the power to ask the responsible institution—in most cases the Commission[75]—to re-examine the relevant draft piece of legislation. If the responsible institution decides to maintain rather than to amend or withdraw the contested legislative proposal, it must respond to the yellow card by giving its reasons, thus increasing accountability. An additional innovation is that the European Court of Justice will have jurisdiction to hear actions on grounds of infringement of the subsidiarity principle brought by a Member State on behalf of its national parliament. Decisively, the Committee of the Regions may also bring such actions, therefore bypassing national governments which could be reluctant to institute legal proceedings.[76]

The "yellow card" procedure has often been dismissed as being too weak or non-existent since "national parliaments are invited to speak up if they think subsidiarity has been flouted, but the European Commission is merely obliged to take note".[77] Indeed, the Commission retains the option of maintaining the draft piece of legislation. Furthermore, the Member States appear not to be under any obligation to bring an action before the European Court of Justice on behalf of their national parliaments. With this criticism in mind, Jack Straw summed up the situation perfectly well: "We're told yellow cards don't matter. Well I've seen enough Blackburn Rovers players get yellow cards to know that they do matter."[78] In political terms, although the Commission is under no obligation to amend or withdraw its legislative proposal, it would seem unrealistic for the Commission to ignore political pressure coming from several Member States. The relevant Member States could in any case withdraw their support, making it practically impossible for the legislative proposal to satisfy the demanding threshold required under the qualified majority voting system for the Council of Ministers to adopt an act. And if national executives do not comply with the yellow card addressed to the Commission by their own

---

[74] Each national Parliament shall have two votes. And in the case of a bicameral system, each of the two chambers shall have one vote. The threshold is one-quarter in cases of proposals in the field of justice and home affairs.

[75] The legislative proposal could also originate from the European Parliament, a group of Member States, the Court of Justice, the European Central Bank or the European Investment Bank. All should take account of the reasoned opinion issued.

[76] However, the Committee of the Regions may *only* bring actions against European legislative acts for the adoption of which the Treaties provides that it be consulted.

[77] *The Economist*, 26 June–2 July 2004, p 13.

[78] Jack Straw's Press conference with the President of the European Parliament, 28 April 2004.

parliament, national parliamentarians should remember their power to hold them to account.

Some Member States were, nevertheless, keen to strengthen the procedure laid down in the Constitutional Treaty. As agreed in June 2007 at the Brussels European Council, the Lisbon Treaty will provide for an additional procedure (often known as the "orange card"). If a simple majority (rather than one-third of them as in the yellow card procedure) of national parliaments, where the codecision procedure is applicable, raise concerns, the Council of Ministers or the European Parliament[79] will have the power to override the Commission's decision to maintain its proposal. To a great extent, this new option only formalises what would have been *de facto* possible under the previous mechanism. In any event, more than legal constraints, what appears decisive is the potential creation of a new political dynamic with an improved accountability of European institutions. The clear recognition of the role of national parliaments in monitoring the application of the principle of subsidiarity, while enhancing further the democratic pedigree of the EU, is also likely to increase a sense of "ownership" with regard to European norms. It may further develop a supranational discussion and allow national parliaments to regain some breathing space with respect to their executives. More than the Commission, indeed, it is the Member States (i.e. the national executives) who will be constrained by the yellow card device. Furthermore, the legal importance of this new mechanism should not be underestimated. With the obligation for the Commission to offer a detailed statement in every EU legislative proposal, as well as to give its reasons in responding to a yellow card, the European Court of Justice might find itself with more opportunities to receive pleadings invoking a breach of subsidiarity.[80] The inclusion of national parliaments by the granting of an "objection power" cannot be dismissed for not going far enough. If effectively and seriously used, with substantive arguments raised, the orange card procedure also offers a genuinely innovative and novel reform. It has the potential to act both as a check on national executives reunited at the EU level, and to guard against unnecessary EU legislation. It is hard to conceive of a similar mechanism at the national level to balance the rubber-stamping by partisan parliaments of executive initiatives. In any case, a red card device, along the lines proposed by some Member States, triggering the automatic withdrawal of a European legislative proposal, may have actually weakened the pressure brought on the Commission by the use of a yellow (or orange) card. It could also have led to more demagogy as well as the exportation of internal conflicts between national legislatures and executives at the European level.

If there is room for criticism, it is with regard to the eight-week deadline. An eight-month period would certainly have been a more realistic period for national parliaments to

---

[79] Respectively by a majority of 55 percent of its members or a majority of the votes cast.
[80] It will not be possible for the European Court of Justice to rule that the simple mention of subsidiarity in the recitals of legislation is sufficient, irrespective of the lack of evidence offered by the Commission. For such an attitude, see e.g. Case C-377/98 *Netherlands v European Parliament* [2001] ECR I-7079.

co-ordinate answers to a European legislative proposal and send a reasoned opinion. However, it was necessary to balance efficiency concerns against legitimacy concerns. The European decision-making process being cumbersome enough, the timescale set by the Protocol may be a positive factor as it demands promptness from national parliaments. And in reality, it does not take much effort to foresee potential legislative proposals through "green papers", or "white papers", or the simple reading of the Commission's five-year work plan.

The yellow (or orange) card device is yet another illustration of the non-existence of an EU superstate. It is therefore difficult to follow those who affirm that the Constitutional Treaty or the Lisbon Treaty represent "a further shift in the balance of power away from national parliaments towards a centralised European state."[81] Such misrepresentation ignores two facts: first, the Lisbon Treaty, in line with the Constitutional Treaty, considerably increases the role of national parliaments,[82] offering them, as previously stated, a real chance to regain political leeway with respect to their executives; secondly, the domination of the executive branch over the legislative branch in the decision-making process is a trend which has characterised all parliamentary regimes since the end of World War II. Undeniably, there is no supranational structure of governance more dominated by its Member States than the EU while, simultaneously, better organised so as to take account of national, regional and local interests and to respect the diversity of these interests. The new reference to the regional and local level authorities in the Protocol on subsidiarity could, incidentally, serve as a perfect illustration of that argument. If additional evidence of the *sui generis* character of the EU is required, the right to withdraw from the Union also offers a pointed demonstration of the erroneous character of the superstate fixation.

(b) The Right to Withdraw

The future insertion in the EU Treaty of an "exit clause" or, more precisely, of a new right to withdraw from the Union could be interpreted as the ultimate evidence that the EU is a voluntary association between sovereign states.[83] A Member State wishing to withdraw would be obliged to notify the European Council, which will consider the matter and define negotiating guidelines. The EU will conduct negotiations with the Member State on this basis, and the Council of Ministers will conclude an agreement specifying the arrangements for withdrawal taking into account the framework for its future relationship with the Union. The procedure is far from making the withdrawal unachievable. The Council of Ministers can conclude the agreement, acting not by unanimity but by a

---

[81] See e.g. M. Ferris, "Transfer of power to Brussels is bad for democracy", *The Irish Times*, 28 August 2004; A. Coughlan, "Revise EU Agreement has radical implications", *The Irish Times*, 28 June 2007.

[82] See the Protocol on the role of national parliaments in the European Union, [2007] OJ C306/148, and Protocol on the application of the principles of subsidiarity and proportionality, [2007] OJ C306/150.

[83] This innovation was first agreed during the drafting of the Constitutional Treaty. See Art I-60(1) EU CT: "Any Member State may decide to withdraw from the Union in accordance with its own constitutional requirements." The Reform Treaty provides for the insertion of this provision into the EU Treaty (see new Art 49A TEU).

qualified majority of 72 percent of its members. The Council must also obtain the consent of the European Parliament. If, two years after the notification of its wish to withdraw, no agreement can be concluded, the European Treaties will cease to apply to the relevant State.

The new provision on voluntary withdrawal from the EU is a formal recognition of Member State's sovereignty. No similar provision exists in the current Treaties. Indeed, they are said to have been concluded for an unlimited period,[84] and do not provide any right to withdraw. Yet no one doubts, irrespective of the present Treaty provisions, that a Member State with the clear will to withdraw could unilaterally do so (with definite damaging consequences if it fails to consult its partners), as the ultimate foundation of European integration is to be found in the Constitution of each Member State. Moreover, the 1969 Vienna Convention on the Law of International Treaties generally authorises a state to withdraw from a multilateral treaty lacking a withdrawal clause as long as one essential condition is fulfilled: the State has obtained the consent of all the States parties.

Writing before the inclusion of a withdrawal clause in the EU Treaty, a US law professor observed that "by denying that member states have a right to secede, the law of the European Union is committed to something like Madison's theory, that the sovereign states which created the Union thereby irrevocably surrendered part of their own sovereignty."[85] The inclusion of a voluntary right to withdraw is therefore politically symbolic and legally noteworthy. If sovereignty is understood to be the unchallengeable authority to self-determination, the new withdrawal clause is the clearest sign that the EU does not bring about a superstate, nor does it set in motion an irrevocable federal organisation. It was therefore ludicrous to argue that the Constitutional Treaty "destroys the legal basis for Irish national independence in the same way the Act of Union with the British Empire did at the end of the 18th century."[86]

To reiterate the facts, the provision on voluntary withdrawal from the Union, which the Lisbon Treaty reproduces, states that the withdrawal will take effect *in any event* two years after notification. This clearly distinguishes the EU from a federal state. It may be an over-simplification but the presence of a similar clause might have prevented the US civil war. The Canadian Supreme Court with regard to a potential secession of Québec, has more recently ruled that the *belle Province* cannot invoke a right of self-determination to dictate the terms of a proposed "secession" to the other parties of the federation. This

---

[84] Both Art 51 TEU and Art 312 TEC read: "This Treaty is concluded for an unlimited period."
[85] J. Goldsworthy, "The Debate About Sovereignty in the United States: A Historical and Comparative Perspective", in N. Walker (ed), *Sovereignty in Transition* (Hart, Oxford, 2003), p 444.
[86] Mr. Roger Cole of the Peace and Neutrality Alliance quoted in D. de Bréadún, "Euro-sceptic wants deferral of Irish vote on EU constitution", *The Irish Times*, 30 August 2004.

is so even in the situation of a clear majority vote in Québec.[87] Such a ruling would be unthinkable under the proposed withdrawal clause.

The formal recognition of a right to withdraw from the EU ought to be welcomed. It will finally allow the political debate to refocus on the benefits of European integration and the reasons for further pursuing the experience. It also offers the potential of increased consistency from some Member States who conveniently blame the EU for any national misfortune. With a well-defined procedure for exiting the Union, there is hope for a more responsible debate by reminding citizens that the EU is the creature of the Member States whose sovereignty allows them to quit. The blame game may then shift from the EU to national governments, once citizens assimilate the fact they now have a clear way out of the Union. This potential effect may well explain the opposition of the British Government to having such a right enshrined in the EU Treaty. The existence of a withdrawal clause may also put an end to the old refrain according to which the key decisions affecting the lives of British or Irish people ought to be made domestically and not in Brussels. Such an assertion is particularly laudable in the case of a small economy such as Ireland's. What would be its influence on the definition of the norms governing its trade were Ireland not a Member of the EU? In a globalised world, it is somewhat amazing that those keen on emphasising the cardinal value of national sovereignty do not realise that it can mostly be exercised by pooling it with the hope of gaining real collective power at European level.

(c) *Tertium non datur*

Where the allocation of powers between the EU and the Member States appears to indicate a "federalisation" of the Union, the enshrining of principles such as subsidiarity and proportionality, added to the fact that the Member States dominate the decision-making process, create an original system of government. Examples could easily be multiplied. The supranational aspects of policy-making are always mixed with intergovernmental mechanisms. Furthermore, European institutions cannot implement European norms but must rely instead on national or infranational institutions. Political science has coined an appealing concept to describe the functioning of the European polity. It has been presented as a model of "multi-level governance".[88] The term itself is now widely used although its precise meaning is likely to vary with each author. Broadly speaking, the notion is used to typify the pluralist and interlocking character of the European decision-making process. As opposed to the concept of state, the EU is seen not as a centralised and pyramidal system but rather as a framework of government open to various public and private actors

---

[87] *Reference by the Governor in Council concerning the secession of Quebec from Canada* [1998] 2 SCR 217, para 151.
[88] See e.g. G. Marks, F. Scharpf, P. Schmitter and W. Streek (eds), *Governance in the European Union* (Sage, London, 1996); I. Bache, M. Flinders (eds), *Multi-Level Governance* (Oxford University Press, Oxford, 2004).

with an overall "layered" functioning, meaning different levels (supranational, national, infranational) of authorities participating in the definition of public policies.

As a result of this complex functioning, any discussion on the nature of the EU is likely to lead to an impasse due to its *sui generis* character or, as some would say, its Byzantine character. To put it succinctly, the EU is more than a confederation but it has yet to reach the federal stage. A key issue is whether a third category can be discovered, i.e. one that would allow the coexistence of an independent European legal order with the preservation of the statehood of its founding Member States.[89] Clearly, this resembles the problem of squaring the circle. The simplest solution, the transformation of the EU into a federal state, cannot be relied upon, as it is still considered *casus belli* in many Member States. Typically, Fischer, in his speech at the Humboldt University of Berlin, refused such a solution and provided food for thought by evoking a third category: a "Federation" (*Föderation* and not *Bundesstaat*). Unfortunately, *Föderation* and *Bundesstaat* are translated, in English and French, by a similar word: federation, thus implying nothing less than a federal state. In a similar vein, Jacques Delors previously elaborated on a "Federation of Nation States", reminiscent of a past attempt made by the eminent Aristide Briand, a French Prime minister, who spoke in 1929 of an association of European States which would establish a federal relationship between them without infringing upon their sovereignty.[90]

The crucial problem is thus to offer a convincing conceptual framework where the historical relationship between the state and the notion of federation could be set aside. And the above proposals, when analysed in detail, regrettably appear to lead to a simple duplication of the federal State at the European level. The only way forward may be to work on the concept of sovereignty and to think of a "federation" (a word not derived from federal would certainly help), whatever the nature and intensity of the powers being transferred to it, which would not lead to the disappearance of the international legal personality of the Member States. Inspired by the work of the German jurist Carl Schmitt, a recent theoretical attempt has been made to develop a convincing third category: a federation based on a "federative pact".[91] The authors of the pact, the sole holders of the *pouvoir constituant*, would continue to exist as political units in a Federation with no statehood. In other words, the new "Federation" is an alternative model to the (Federal) State, such as the previous competing models of the Greek *polis* or of the Empire. In this "Federation", Member States do not renounce their status as sovereign states but agree to

---

[89] On this quest for the academic holy grail, see recently V. Constantinesco, "Europe fédérale ou Fédération d'Etats-nations", in R. Dehousse (ed), *Une Constitution pour l'Europe* (Presses de Sciences Po, Paris, 2002), p 115.
[90] See T. Chopin, *L'héritage du fédéralisme? Etats-Unis/Europe*, Notes de la Fondation Robert Schuman, 2002, p 8.
[91] See the stimulating analysis by O. Beaud, "Fédéralisme et souveraineté : notes pour une théorie constitutionnelle de la Fédération", (1998) *Revue du droit public* 115.

set up a legal entity with international and internal legal personality. Its legal foundation lies not on a treaty as with a confederation, nor on a constitution as with a federal state but on a "federative pact" (*Bundesvertrag*) or to use recent terminology, a "constitutional treaty". Indeed, the federative pact cannot be assimilated into a treaty as it results from the decision of a plurality of sovereign bodies. Furthermore, unlike a constitution, it is an inter-state pact, although from a material point of view, the pact may resemble a constitution. Fundamentally, the "Federation" is not organised on a hierarchical basis: it does not possess the *kompetenz-kompetenz* and its law is supreme only in those areas where it has been given the power to act.[92]

Naturally, "this sort of Hegelian transcendence of opposites" may leave one sceptical.[93] But if one accepts to redefine the external aspect of sovereignty, a third category, a *tertium genus*, may finally come to emerge as a convincing (and legitimate) alternative. After all, state and sovereignty are historical products.[94] Subsequently, there is no obstacle, if only intellectual, to the acceptance of a new constitutional model which would allow Member States and the "Federation" to retain their status of international law subjects while the foundation of the Federation would continue to remain in the national constitutional texts. The EU has already innovated by its association of European and national citizenships. The Constitutional Treaty was another example of a new hybrid: materially a constitution, formally a treaty. Where constitutional theory now sees duality and hierarchy, we have to think in terms of plurality and interdependence, hence to admit the idea of a "Federation" without a (federal) state. As a mode of organisation, a European "Federation" would not imply a state or a single *demos*. And if the word "Federation" cannot be detached from the state paradigm, we might as well continue to describe the EU as a voluntary association of States.

CHAPTER TWO – CONCLUSION

The superstate allegation, although indefinite, has marked European debate. In fairness, the original nature of the EU makes any understanding of it a demanding exercise. The drafting of the Constitutional Treaty only reinforced the temptation to rely on traditional categories of constitutional law to interpret, or dare I say, to misrepresent the evolution of the EU. And indeed, it has been endlessly repeated by critics that the Constitutional Treaty and its successor, the Lisbon Treaty, will have the legal effect of turning the EU into a

---

[92] For a study arguing that the current EU framework allows the European and national constitutional orders to coexist on an equal and non-hierarchical footing, see I. Pernice, "Multilevel constitutionalism in the European Union", (2002) 27 *European Law Review* 511.

[93] C. Leben, "A Federation of Nation States or Federal State", p 110.

[94] In the US, the potentiality of a third category has already been discussed. See L. Backer, "The Extra-National State: American Confederate Federalism and the European Union", (2001) 7 *Columbia Journal of European Law* 173. This article examines the ways in which John C. Calhoun's theories of multi-state association, suppressed in the US after the Civil War, now shape the European debate over the nature of the Union's political organisation.

European federal state in which existing Member States are reduced to the constitutional status of provinces.

It is difficult to know where to begin with this kind of statement.

On pragmatic grounds, it could easily be demonstrated that the Union is no Leviathan. A brief look at the EU and US budgets clearly demonstrate the miniscule size of the Union's budget. Whereas the US budget amounts to 20 percent of US gross domestic product, the EU budget turns around 1 percent of EU gross domestic product.[95] Furthermore, the size of the EU budget is formally capped at 1.27 percent of EU gross domestic product, while recent discussions have indicated the willingness of major Member States to further reduce the cap to 1 percent. The question needs to be echoed: has the world ever seen an alleged *super*state in the making where the size of the budget is formally capped, not to mention the obligation to adopt balanced budgets and the non-existence of a European income tax? The structure of public expenditure similarly reveals the mythical aspect of the superstate line of "reasoning". The three main posts of expenditure in the United States are social security, health and national defence whereas in the EU, to the clear dismay of Tony Blair, agricultural policy and regional policy cannibalise more than three-quarters of the resources.

In light of its relative economic insignificance, it appears somewhat unreal that Europeans should spend so much energy on institutional and legal quarrels. In any event, in legal terms, the EU cannot be a superstate as it is not even a state: there is no European People, no precisely defined European territory and the EU does not possess a sovereign capacity of action, neither internally nor externally. In these circumstances, to speak of a superstate makes simply no legal sense. To put it differently, as the discussion on the question of *kompetenz-kompetenz* has demonstrated, the EU ultimately remains the creature of the Member States. Indeed, as suggested by Peter Ludlow, the Union is a government by, of, and for, the Member States.[96] In no way does the Lisbon Treaty alter this description. In the end, there is no evidence of a federal European state in the making. It can, thus, be compellingly argued that "the Union is not some Frankenstein creation over which there may be little or no control".[97] Some sense of ridicule should therefore accompany every description of the EU, to quote Nietzsche, as the new coldest of all cold monsters.

What, then, is the nature of EU? The EU is often portrayed as a *sui generis* entity, an original one that could hardly be described in terms of a coherent "constitutional

---

[95] See H. Enderlein *et al.*, "The EU Budget. How Much Scope for Institutional Reform", European Central Bank, Occasional Paper No 27, April 2005, p 12.

[96] Quoted in B. Groom, "Forging a united future", *Financial Times*, 27/28 March 2004.

[97] See House of Lords, *The Future Role of the European Court of Justice*, para 89.

system".[98]Such an outcome is hardly surprising considering that the EU has historically been the fruit of successive compromises, essentially between the proponents of a federal Europe and the advocates of a Europe of nations. These compromises have finally produced a unique entity, a supranational non-state polity. It is, therefore, unfortunate that even advocates of the "European dream" still continue to rely so heavily on the concept of state to make sense of the EU: "Lest there be any doubt on this score, the EU's draft constitution ... makes clear that a new transnational political institution is being born that, in its every particular, is designed to function like a state."[99] In reality, the EU is the fruit of successive compromises, which have led to the emergence of a fruitful experiment. It is, therefore, imperative that we refrain from our natural tendency to think of the EU in statal terms.[100] Ultimately, the fact that the organisation of the EU is said to be *sui generis* "suggests nothing more than a deviance from a historical understanding of appropriate forms of organisation as historically understood."[101] The only way forward may be to escape state-centric and hierarchical thinking and this is why, to some extent, legal science proves to be sterile with its *summa divisio* between confederation and federal state. Political science has shown the way forward with its recourse to the notion of multi-level governance, a fruitful notion as it gives an immediate sense of the fluid and hybrid nature of the EU. And if it appears indispensable to offer a simple alternative to the phantasmagorical allegation of a European superstate in the making, the EU may be more appropriately described, not as a state, but as a decentralised network owned by its Member States.[102] In this regard, we should never tire from repeating that decisions are made not *by* Brussels but *in* Brussels.

---

[98] J.-C. Piris, "L'Union européenne a-t-elle une constitution? Lui en faut-il une?", (1999) *Revue trimestrielle de droit européen*, pp 631–632.

[99] J. Rifkin, *The European Dream* (Polity, London, 2004) p 208. In all fairness, the author later qualifies his own diagnosis. Evoking the work of the renowned sociologist Ulrich Beck, he concludes (p 229): "The EU, then, is less a place than a process. While it maintains many of the fixed physical trappings of a state ... its genius is its indeterminacy."

[100] See e.g. Jo Shaw who suggests that "the challenge for the EU is that of capturing the essence of postnationalism, and combining it with understanding the process of building a new kind of polity which is based on the existing diversity of the member states", "Postnational Constitutionalism in the European Union", (1999) 6 *Journal of European Public Policy* 579, at 586.

[101] Backer, "The Extra-National State", p 217.

[102] For a straightforward and refreshing analysis, based on the work of Manuel Castells, of the EU as a "decentralised network", see M. Leonard, *Why Europe will run the 21ˢᵗ century* (Fourth Estate, London, 2005), especially chaps 1 and 2.

PART TWO

Let It Be: The European Union's
Democratic Deficit

Hence, it clearly appears, that the same advantage which a republic has over a democracy, in controlling the effects of faction, is enjoyed by a large over a small republic,—is enjoyed by the Union over the States composing it.
The Federalist No 10 (1787)

I think we have a peculiar idea of our government being perfect without knowing really and truly how it works.
General Lucius D. Clay[1]

The Union's "democratic deficit" has become such a cliché that anyone can get away with the charge without explanation. Quotations could easily be multiplied. For instance, in a strongly worded editorial on "Europe and democracy", the leading French newspaper, *Le Monde*, asserted in 2004 that "the first shortcoming of Europe is its democratic deficit".[2] There is, however, no trace in the column of the newspaper's understanding of what a democracy is and of what the notion of deficit relates to. Contrary to popular belief, there is no such thing as a democratic deficit. The term itself is "almost meaningless",[3] although one could concede it has served a useful purpose. It has, at least, obliged political actors to take democracy seriously at the European level.

There have been several attempts to remedy the so-called deficit, e.g. the Laeken Declaration, adopted by the Member States in December 2001.[4] This declaration denoted a clear consensus: there was a "crisis of legitimacy",[5] and offered a solution: European

---

[1] Former Governor of the US-occupied zone in post-war Germany, quoted by N. Ferguson, *Colossus. The Rise and Fall of the American Empire* (Penguin Books, New York, 2004), p 76.

[2] "Le défaut premier de l'Europe est son déficit démocratique", *Le Monde*, 29 October 2004.

[3] "The alliteration "democratic deficit" is so widely used and abused when discussing the European Union that it is now almost meaningless", S. Hix, "Elections, Parties and Institutional Design: A Comparative Perspective on European Union Democracy", (1998) 21(3) *West European Politics* 19, at 19.

[4] European Council, Laeken declaration on the future of the Union, SN 273/01, 15 December 2001.

[5] Impossible to be exactly measured, legitimacy is equally hard to define. To follow Philippe Schmitter, legitimacy "is a shared expectation among actors in an arrangement of asymmetric power such that the actions of those who rule are accepted voluntarily by those who are ruled because the latter are convinced that the actions of the former conform to pre-established norms. Put simply, legitimacy converts power into authority – *Macht* into *Herrschaft* – and, thereby, establishes simultaneously an obligation to obey and a right to rule." See P. Schmitter, "What is there to legitimise in the European Union ... And how might this be accomplished?", in C. Joerges, Y. Mény, J. Weiler (eds), *Mountain or Molehill? A Critical Appraisal of the Commission White Paper on Governance*, Jean Monnet Working Paper no. 6/01, p 1 (available at: http://www.jeanmonnetprogram.org).

institutions should be brought "closer" to its citizens. In the face of such apparent common sense, it could be argued that the elements of such a crisis needed to be substantiated other than by a simple reference to poor voter turnout or some unsuccessful referenda. Secondly, the "closeness" of public authorities does not bear an evident relationship with the notion of democracy. It may even be argued that the notion of closeness is so indeterminate that it also makes it completely inane. This is not to say that there is no need, for instance, to increase accountability or to enhance the transparency of the European decision-making structures and processes. In fairness, the Union's institutional architecture and effective functioning are certainly difficult to apprehend. And, considering the fact that the EU is generally a decisive source of legal norms directly applicable within national legal orders, it would be foolish not to recognise the importance of reforming its norm-making procedures. As a matter of principle, transparency, accountability and equal representation, among other elements in any democracy, are definitely essential.[6] However, they should be permanent goals for any system of government.

As the Lisbon Treaty does not fundamentally alter the institutional framework which has been patiently and painfully articulated over the last 50 years, does it imply a perpetuation of the Union's infamous democratic deficit? What if there is no such thing as a democratic deficit? The accusation is easily professed on both ends of the political spectrum. Yet, in most, if not all cases, no further explanation is provided to our fellow citizens. One may think, for instance, of Gerry Adams's charge that the 2004 Irish EU presidency "could have acted to address a wide range of concerns about the growing lack of democracy within the EU".[7] Apparently, not only is there a lack of democracy, according to the leader of *Sinn Féin*—a party widely known for its attachment to the rule of law and pure democratic canons—but, more worryingly, it is increasing. In most cases, the self-proclaimed defenders of European democracy obscure more than they clarify the debate. Indeed, as long as the nature of the Union's democratic deficit is not precisely defined, the discussion is likely to last in a way that could resemble a fruitless pub discussion on the respective merits of beer as opposed to whiskey.

In other words, the critical point is that critics of the EU rarely share their understanding of "democracy" with their audience. This is a decisive aspect of the debate. Undeniably, to condemn the EU for its deficient democratic credentials, one must have a clear idea of what they are. Unfortunately, "very rarely, if at all, is there more than cursory acknowledgment of the uneasy co-existence of competing visions and models of democracy which, in turn, should inform both diagnosis, prognosis and possible remedy of democratic

---

[6] See e.g. C. Lord, *Democracy in the European Union* (Sheffield Academic Press, Sheffield, 1998). The author argues that a democracy, to deserve such label, has to satisfy the following criteria: authorisation (of leader and power relations); accountability (rulers have to be accountable to the people); representation (decisions should be representative of public needs and values) and finally, a shared sense of political identity.
[7] Quoted in M. Hennessy, "Adams says citizenship poll 'is about the rights of children'", *The Irish Times*, 25 May 2004.

shortcomings."[8] A key problem in the debate is that democratic theory has developed in the context of the nation-state. In addition, our instinctive understanding of what the concept of democracy means is certainly marked by some sense of ethnocentrism and personal axiological preference. As a result, diverse medication can be prescribed to a "patient", the EU, which is neither a state nor a nation. If a plurality of competing diagnoses is noticeable, there is a dominant and popular view linking the Union's democratic deficit with the alleged weakness of the European Parliament. The inability of national parliaments to influence the behaviour of their executive at the European level is also often criticised.

Underlying this dominant thesis is the belief (positively or negatively appraised) that that the EU is progressively establishing itself as a state. Therefore, the EU is often analysed with particular regard to the principles of the separation of powers and the responsibility of the executive before the legislative power. The Union's institutional architecture leaves, however, little margin for the application of these two principles. Europe thus suffers the accusation of a democratic deficit. Such diagnosis is, however, inadequate. To begin with, not only is the conventional, parliamentary-based understanding of the democratic deficit defective as the EU is neither a state nor a nation, it also rests on an idealised model of representative democracy. Moreover, it is clearly incoherent to criticise the EU for a supposed lack of democracy and simultaneous fear a loss of national sovereignty. The more democratic the EU, the more state-like it will become. That is the dilemma. In any event, the model of parliamentary democracy, with its majoritarian features, if directly transposed at the European level may, in reality, lead to a genuine crisis of legitimacy for a polity characterised by and celebrated for its heterogeneity. In other words, the alleged Union's democratic deficit could actually be democratically justified as long as European citizens want the EU to remain the product of its constituent parts, the Member States and an entity which acts in an extremely consensual manner in the name of the peoples of Europe.

Naturally, the fact that the EU is a democratically legitimate entity does not preclude it from having some democratic shortcomings. Yet, before identifying and remedying these shortcomings, the notion of democracy should first be appreciated as neither static, nor monolithic. History appears to indicate that the democratisation of national political structures has been progressively undertaken and has been differently understood.[9] This is why one may proclaim that "today the term democracy is like an ancient kitchen midden packed with assorted leftovers from twenty-five hundred years of nearly continued usage".[10] In this regard, it is important to point out both the current challenges faced by the classical model of parliamentary democracy and the ensuing transformation and complexity of the

---

[8] J. Weiler, U. Haltern and F. Mayer, "European Democracy and Its Critique", (1998) 18(3) *West European Politics* 4, at 5.

[9] The tremendous work of Pierre Rosanvallon on the notion of democracy in France is, unfortunately, not available in English. See in particular, *Le peuple introuvable: Histoire de la représentation démocratique en France* (Gallimard, Paris, 1998).

[10] R. Dahl, *Dilemmas of Pluralist Democracy* (New Haven (Conn.), 1982), p 5, quoted in A. Peters, "European Democracy After the 2003 Convention", (2004) 41 *Common Market Law Review* 37, at 37–38.

mechanisms guaranteeing the democratic legitimacy of public decisions. For instance, the emphasis on the rule of law, on the protection of fundamental rights, and on the importance of the "civil society", make it clear that a democracy cannot be any longer reduced to the direct election of representatives. Any democratic assessment of the EU must, therefore, be undertaken in light of its specific nature and with due regard to the model of parliamentary democracy as effectively applied at national level. If there is an imperative for the EU to further its "democratisation",[11] such concern should be a permanent one for national democracies as well. In the end, our conclusion can be enunciated as follows: if the EU is judged for what it currently is—an organisation reflecting the will of the peoples (the plural is important) and States of Europe, on which the Member States confer limited competences to attain common objectives[12]—it cannot be said to suffer from a democratic deficit. The establishment of a European federal state with parliamentary features may have the merit of sounding familiar but, in reality, such a solution may undermine the democratic legitimacy of the EU. It would run counter to the Union's telos as articulated in the first line of the Preamble of the EC Treaty which states: "Determined to lay the foundations of an ever closer union among the peoples of Europe ...."[13] As Joseph Weiler observes: "thus, even in the eventual promised land of European integration the distinct peoplehood of its components was to remain intact—in contrast with the theory of most, and the 'praxis' of all federal states which predicate the existence of one people".[14]

Ultimately, the democratic pedigree of the EU may not suffice as an explanation of the lively discussion around the alleged Union's democratic deficit. Andrew Moravcsik has already compellingly demonstrated that if judged with regard to the actual functioning of national democracies, there is no substantial evidence that the EU is less transparent, less responsive or less accountable than the Member States.[15] The success of the democratic deficit charge may, therefore, be better explained as the expression of cultural unease with a non-state and non-nation polity.[16] Furthermore, created in a rather top-down approach,[17] the EU's consensual (and therefore complex) functioning annihilates, to some extent, ideological debate over the course of action. The insufficient politicisation of European public affairs may certainly be regrettable. It does not justify, however, the treatment of the EU as a democratically deficient entity.

---

[11] By "democratisation", we understand the steps taken to improve authorisation, accountability, and representation. See Lord, *Democracy in the European Union*, p 15.

[12] See Article I-1 EU CT.

[13] J. Weiler, "Fischer: The Dark Side", in C. Joerges, Y. Mény & J. Weiler (eds), *What kind of Constitution for what kind of Polity?* (The Robert Schuman Centre for Advanced Studies, Florence, 2000), p 240.

[14] *Ibid.*

[15] A. Moravcsik, "In Defence of the 'Democratic Deficit': Reassessing Legitimacy in the European Union", (2002) 40 *Journal of Common Market Studies* 603, at 605.

[16] P. Schmitter, *How to Democratize the European Union... And Why Bother?* (Rowman & Littlefield, Lanham, 2000), p 15.

[17] A similar approach has characterised, for instance, the formation of England or France where a central authority preceded any national feeling of belonging. By contrast, an *ethnos-demos-politeia* sequence characterised the historical process of nation-building in Germany. See Schmitter, *ibid.*, p 118.

CHAPTER THREE

Viewing Democracy through Rose-Tinted Glasses

Joschka Fischer offered a dark picture when he mentioned, in his famous speech, delivered on 12 May 2000, at the Humboldt University in Berlin, the existence of a perilous tension between the "communitarisation" of economy and currency and the lack of political and democratic structures. According to the former German Foreign Minister, the salvation lay in taking "productive steps to make good the shortfall in political integration and democracy, thus completing the process of integration".[1] If the current "shortfall" in democracy is not specified, the end of the process of integration, to follow Fischer's line of argument, is to be attained when a "European Federation" is set up. In other words, Europe will organise itself somewhat in the form of a federal state, as experienced in Germany. Underlying this diagnosis is obviously the idea that Europe should obey, to a large extent, the principles and practices of national democracies. The analogy, however, is likely to create some confusion. Indeed, in most instances, the EU is compared to an idealised model of parliamentary democracy while critics do not pay due regard to the fact that the EU is neither a state, nor a nation. Furthermore, viewed in light of the actual functioning of national democracies, the evidence of the Union's alleged democratic deficit is far from compelling.

(I) Understanding the Litany

The discussion on the democratic legitimacy of the EU is dominated by a "parliamentary tropism",[2] i.e. a constant analogy with the model of parliamentary democracy. In brief, it is alleged that the EU suffers from a democratic deficit because the European Parliament lacks the powers of a genuine parliament while national parliaments cannot hold their respective governments accountable.

(a) The Parliamentary Tropism

With European institutions having gained additional competences over the last 50 years, the temptation to evaluate the EU in light of national political systems proves difficult to

---

[1] J. Fischer, "From Confederacy to Federation: Thoughts on the Finality of European Integration", in C. Joerges, Y. Mény & J. Weiler (eds), *What kind of Constitution for what kind of Polity?* (The Robert Schuman Centre for Advanced Studies, Florence, 2000), p 22.

[2] The expression is borrowed from P. Magnette, *Le régime politique de l'Union européenne* (Presses de Sciences Po, Paris, 2003), p 240.

resist. As a result, the legitimacy of the Union's institutional architecture can be questioned. Indeed, contrary to teaching of Montesquieu, not only is there a confusion of powers but the EU apparently functions without a proper parliament. According to the prevailing view, the reinforcement of the powers of the European Parliament must, therefore, be considered as the main ingredient to put an end to the democratic concerns one might have. Understandably, the European Parliament itself was keen to rely on such a diagnosis. With members elected by direct universal suffrage since 1979, the European Parliament, in order to gain political strength, naturally stressed that its own legislative powers remained weaker than those of national legislatures whereas the competences transferred to the EU were mostly of a legislative nature. As a result, the European Parliament criticised the insufficiently democratic nature of European decision-making.[3] The issue of accountability also appeared to be fertile ground for criticism. With a Council of Ministers accumulating legislative and executive functions, yet remaining unaccountable at the European level, the European Parliament could easily deduce that the institutional architecture was not in conformity with the model of parliamentary democracy[4] as applied in all the Member States.

Surprisingly, the European Parliament's verdict was rather easily accepted by the European Commission as well as the Council of Ministers, and is now offered as a universal truth. For instance, the glossary containing terms relating to European integration available on the EU's official website offers the following definition:

"The democratic deficit is a concept invoked principally in the argument that the European Union suffers from a lack of democracy and seems inaccessible to the ordinary citizen because its method of operating is so complex. The view is that the Community institutional set-up is dominated by an institution combining legislative and government powers (the Council) and an institution that lacks democratic legitimacy (the Commission—even though its Members are appointed by the Member States and are collectively accountable to Parliament). ... The Maastricht, Amsterdam and Nice Treaties have triggered the inclusion of the principle of democratic legitimacy within the institutional system by reinforcing the powers of Parliament with regard to the appointment and control of the Commission and successively extending the scope of the codecision procedure. ... "[5]

---

[3] See e.g. European Parliament, Resolution on the democratic deficit, [1988] OJ C187/229.
[4] The notions of parliamentary democracy and of representative democracy are often used interchangeably. To define them succinctly, a representative democracy is government by the people, exercised through elected representatives. The notion of parliamentary democracy is slightly more precise as it implies that these representatives sit in a parliament, in other words, a legislative assembly upon which the executive branch is politically dependent.
[5] http://europa.eu.int/scadplus/glossary/democratic_deficit_en.htm, glossary consulted on 1 July 2005.

This definition is instructive insofar as it implies a widespread acceptance of the view linking democratic legitimacy with parliamentary representation and effective legislative power for the legislative branch. The cultural force of the parliamentary model of democracy, as classically described and applied at the national level, could also be deduced from the definition once found under the heading "institutional balance", i.e. the principle according to which each Community institution has to act in accordance with the powers conferred on it by the Treaties. In order to combat the democratic deficit "affecting" the Union, it was suggested that the European Parliament's powers ought to be increased to correct the "asymmetry" between the Council and the Parliament. Remarkably, the glossary no longer refers to the notion of democratic deficit but states that the influence of the Parliament "has increased considerably", even though "there is still an imbalance between the legislative powers of the Council and those of Parliament, since legislative power is only really shared by the two institutions" in the areas covered by the codecision procedure.[6]

The European Court of Justice did not dissent from the parliamentarian vision. Again, the representative principle is deemed to be a key element in any (national) democracy. Consequently, the Court of Justice has always rigorously protected the European Parliament's prerogatives on the grounds that the Parliament allows the "people" to participate in law-making. Thus, in the so-called *Isoglucose* ruling, a case involving the abolition of subsidies on the production of a sugar substitute, the Court solemnly emphasised the importance of the consultation procedure[7] provided for in the EC Treaty:

> "The consultation ... is the means which allows the Parliament to play an actual part in the legislative process of the Community. Such power represents an essential factor in the institutional balance intended by the Treaty. Although limited, it reflects at Community level *the fundamental democratic principle that the people should take part in the exercise of power through the intermediary of a representative assembly* [emphasis added]. Due consultation of the Parliament in the cases provided for by the Treaty therefore constitutes an essential formality disregard of which means that the measures concerned is void."[8]

---

[6] http://europa.eu.int/scadplus/glossary/institutional_balance_en.htm, consulted on 1 July 2005. The co-decision procedure, introduced by the Maastricht Treaty in 1992, is now the procedure that governs the majority of cases. An act cannot be enacted without Parliamentary approval (see Article 251 TEC). In other words, the procedure amounts to a legislative veto over selected matters if conciliation through direct negotiations with the Council cannot be achieved.

[7] The consultation procedure enables the European Parliament to give its opinion on a proposal from the Commission. The Council of Ministers must therefore consult the European Parliament before voting on the Commission proposal. Contrary to the codecision procedure, the influence of the Parliament is rather limited under this procedure as the Council is not bound by the Parliament's position.

[8] Case 138/79 *Roquette Freres v Council* [1980] ECR 3333, para 33.

Unsurprisingly, this orthodox view was also adopted by the European Court of First Instance when it held that the democratic legitimacy of measures adopted by the Council derives from the European Parliament's participation in the decision-making process. Such a statement is again justified in the name of a fundamental democratic principle that the people must share in the exercise of power through a representative assembly.[9]

In a similar fashion, national courts have quickly associated democratic legitimacy with control exercised by the parliamentary branch. In its famous ruling on the Maastricht Treaty, the German Constitutional Court saw the institutional weakness of the European Parliament as the main shortcoming in the democratic credentials of the EU:

> "According to its own definition as a union among the peoples of Europe, the European Union is an alliance of democratic States which seeks to develop dynamically; if it performs sovereign tasks and exercises sovereign powers, it is in the first instance the peoples of the individual States which must, through their national parliaments, provide democratic legitimation for such action. As the functions and powers of the Community are extended, the need will increase for representation of the peoples of the individual States by a European Parliament that exceeds the democratic legitimation and influence secured via the national parliaments, and which will form the basis for democratic support for the policies of the European Union."[10]

The dominant understanding of the democratic deficit at the European level can effortlessly be inferred from the above excerpt: there is a lack of parliamentary control over the Council of Ministers, whereas control via national parliaments is assumed to be the essence of democracy and the source of political legitimacy. The orthodox view, expressed by the German Constitutional Court is certainly shared by other national constitutional courts all across Europe. It is not surprising, then, that an additional component of the democratic deficit, widely discussed from the mid-1990s onwards, is related to the parallel diminishing role of the national parliaments.

(b) The Double Democratic Deficit

In a 1998 resolution, the European Parliament claimed that the democratic deficit was one of the reasons for discontent with the EU. Indubitably aware that its own position would be reinforced if it associated national parliaments to its quest for more authority, it also found it "unacceptable" that there were EU policy areas in which powers of democratic

---

[9] Case T-135/96 *UEAPME v. Council* [1998] ECR II-2235, para 88. Interestingly, from the broad consideration that the EU is founded on the principle of democracy, the first-instance judges also deduced that, in the absence of the participation of the European Parliament in the definition of the specific norms at issue, the participation of the people must be otherwise assured. In the present case, the participation of the people was said to be assured through the participation of social partners.

[10] (1994) 33 *International Legal Materials* 388, p 420. The German Court's references to specific articles of the Maastricht Treaty are omitted.

control had been taken away from national parliaments without being "replaced by scrutiny by the European Parliament,[11] hence the concept of double democratic deficit.[12]

The 2004 Constitutional Treaty clearly attempted to offer an answer to the double democratic deficit as conventionally understood. First of all, national parliaments were given, for the first time, a role to play in monitoring the application of the principle of subsidiarity. Secondly, the Constitutional Treaty strengthened, albeit modestly, the current provisions dealing with the scrutiny by national parliaments of their national governments when they act at EU level through the Council of Ministers. Remarkably, the Lisbon Treaty, while further strengthening the power of national parliaments to examine EU legislative proposals and to give a reasoned opinion on subsidiarity, mostly reproduces the provisions agreed in 2004. The constant emphasis on the role of national parliaments shows that it is now commonly accepted that enhancement of national parliaments' involvement would bring the citizens closer to Europe and strengthen the democratic legitimacy of the EU.[13] These concerns are not new and have already been addressed. Following the signature and ratification of the Maastricht Treaty, a number of parliaments succeeded in securing a better involvement in the work of the EU through new information and consultation mechanisms.[14] Greater parliamentary involvement was further guaranteed by the Amsterdam Treaty, with a specific protocol annexed to the Treaty on the role of national parliaments. The protocol essentially calls for national governments to ensure that their own national parliament receives Commission proposals for legislation within a reasonable time period. More importantly, a six-week period is foreseen between a legislative proposal and the date when it is placed on a Council agenda for decision. During this time period, which the Lisbon Treaty extends to eight weeks, it is up to national parliaments to make sure that their views are taken into consideration by their governments.

It would be unfair to blame the "EU" for the relative efficiency of current mechanisms. The level of accountability at the national level is dependent, in reality, on the willingness of the executive power in each Member State to submit to its legislative branch. The "Danish model" is now a generic term which describes the most effective model with regard to national parliamentary scrutiny. Indeed, the Danish Parliament—the *Folketing*—appears to exercise the tightest control over the government since the Danish Government should seek a "mandate" from the parliamentary committee in charge of European affairs

---

[11] Resolution on improvements in the functioning of the Institutions without modification of the Treaties—making EU policies more open and democratic, [1998] OJ C167/211.

[12] See e.g. G. Laprat, "Réforme des Traités: Le risque du double déficit démocratique", (1991) 351 *Revue du Marché Commun* 710.

[13] See e.g. European Convention, Final report of working group IV on the role of national parliaments, CONV 353/02, Brussels, 22 October 2002, p 2.

[14] To put the involvement of national parliaments into perspective, see e.g. K. Hussein, "The Europeanization of Member States Institutions", in S. Bulmer and C. Lequesne (eds), *The Member States of the European Union* (Oxford University Press, Oxford, 2005), pp 297–302.

before the Council's meetings in Brussels.[15] Member States are entirely free to adopt the Danish model, even though this model is obviously the product of political and cultural factors that do not exist in all countries. Yet, in a majority of Member States, despite legislative reforms and even constitutional amendments,[16] parliamentary participation in European affairs and scrutiny of governmental action remain far from being satisfactory in practice or at least could certainly be improved.

In a comprehensive study, Ireland was categorised, along with some other Member States, as a "slow adapting" parliament, unwilling or unable to affect their government's stance on European affairs.[17] In fairness, such categorisation had been made before the adoption of the European Union Scrutiny Act 2002 which improves, to a great extent, the Oireachtas' scrutiny of proposals to be adopted by the Council of Ministers of the EU. As a matter of fact, every proposal for a legal instrument to be made or drawn at EU level must now be laid, as soon as possible once the proposal is made, before each House of the Oireachtas by the Minister of the Government having official responsibility, and be referred by that Minister to the appropriate committee. Regrettably, the Act is less ambitious than the Bill introduced in 2001. Indeed, under the Bill, it was foreseen that no Minister would be able to commit his/her State to any proposed legal instrument unless the proposal had been laid before each House. More importantly, the Bill gave each House the power to adopt a resolution within 21 days, rejecting the proposal. In the Act, however, the Minister shall now simply "have regard to any recommendations made to him or her from time to time" by the Houses of the Oireachtas. Furthermore, the Act does not sanction the adoption of a proposal prior to its scrutiny by the Sub-Committee on European Scrutiny.[18]

---

[15] See the diagnosis of A. Maurer, "National Parliaments in the European Architecture: Elements for Establishing a Best Practice Mechanism", European Convention, Working Group IV, Working document 8, Brussels, 9 July 2002.

[16] See e.g. Art 23 of the German Constitution. According to its para 2, the House of Representatives (*Bundestag*) and the States (*Länder*), through their representation in the Senate (*Bundesrat*), "participate in matters of the European Union. The Government has to thoroughly inform the House of Representatives and Senate at the earliest possible time". Paragraph 3 of the same Article further requires the Government to allow "for statements of the House of Representatives before it takes part in drafting European Union laws" and "during deliberations". Article 88-4 of the French Constitution offers a similar framework: "The Government shall lay before the National Assembly and the Senate any drafts of or proposals for instruments of the European Communities or the European Union containing provisions which are matters for statute as soon as they have been transmitted to the Council of the European Union. It may also lay before them other drafts of or proposals for instruments or any document issuing from a European Union institution. In the manner laid down by the rules of procedure of each assembly, resolutions may be passed, even if Parliament is not in session, on the drafts, proposals or documents referred to in the preceding paragraph."

[17] Maurer, "National Parliaments in the European Architecture", p 25.

[18] In his First report, the Chairman of the Sub-Committee on European Scrutiny had to express (in a very diplomatic manner) his concerns about the number of proposals which were adopted prior to scrutiny by the Sub-Committee. See the First Annual Report on the Operation of the European Union Scrutiny Act 2002, House of the Oireachtas, October 2004.

However unsatisfactory the current situation may be, it is important to stress that the EU has no direct responsibility for the information or scrutiny gap that members of the public may resent and characterise as a "democratic deficit". The Amsterdam Protocol laid out all the appropriate principles to increase access to European information and, more precisely, European legislation. With regard to the Council's alleged undue secrecy, one may fairly contend that the situation before the Amsterdam Treaty was unsatisfactory. As the transparency of voting within the Council of Ministers was not guaranteed, it was almost impossible for national parliaments to hold their governments accountable. Secret voting was a convenient tool for governments to blame "Brussels" or uncompromising partners for decisions adopted in Brussels. As amended by the Amsterdam and Nice Treaties, the EC Treaty now states that "when the Council acts in its legislative capacity, the results of votes and explanations of vote as well as statements in the minutes shall be made public".[19] Since the 2002 European Council of Seville, further progress has been made: it was affirmed that the Council should from now on legislate with "open doors". Accordingly, the Council's rules of procedures were first amended in 2004.[20] As a result, the presentation by the Commission of its most important legislative proposals and the ensuing debate in the Council shall be open to the public. Furthermore, the vote on legislative acts, the final Council deliberations leading to that vote and the explanations of voting must also be available. In practice, it means that "Council deliberations shall be open to the public through transmission of the Council meeting by audiovisual means, notably in an overflow room. The outcome of voting shall be indicated by visual means."[21] Further reform has been implemented in 2006. In particular, the Member States have agreed, despite some resistance from the UK government, that all Council deliberations on legislative acts under the co-decision procedure shall now be open to the public.[22] Increasing transparency of voting within the Council of Ministers certainly complements the goal of increasing the effectiveness of parliamentary control. The current balance seems perfectly reasonable. Transparency should not come at the price of annihilating effective decision-making within the Council. At the European level, to accommodate divergent national interests, governments may need to follow bargaining strategies. To further increase the transparency of the Council's work runs the risk of transferring real decision-making to other locations. It may also tempt governments into excessive "nationalism" at the expense of the common good.

In the end, it is important to realise that the real obstacle to effective national parliamentary control is not the alleged lack of transparency within the Council of

---

[19] Article 207(3) TEC.

[20] Council Decision of 22 March 2004 adopting the Council's rules of procedures [2004] OJ L106/22.

[21] Article 8(1): Council deliberations open to the public and public debates. See also Art 9: Making public votes, explanations of votes and minutes and Article 10: Public access to Council documents.

[22] See Presidency Conclusions of the Brussels European Council, 16 June 2006, 10633/06, Annex I "An Overall Policy on Transparency" and Council Decision of 15 September 2006 adopting the Council's rules of procedures [2006] OJ L285/47.

Ministers, but the lack of enthusiasm from national governments and—somewhat unsurprisingly—from the parliaments themselves. As exemplified in Ireland by the European Union Scrutiny Act 2002, it is the executive power that has shown a certain reluctance to effectively increase the parliament's powers in order for it to counterbalance the government's policy choices. Ireland need not be singled out.[23] In most Member States, regardless of their formal powers, parliamentarians tend to act as a rubber stamp for the executive. In others words, national parliaments do not generally make use of their powers to scrutinise the action of their governments at EU Council meetings. The explanation surely lies in a mix of political reasons: the parliamentary majority does not want to embarrass a government composed from its ranks and it remains difficult for a parliamentarian to publicise its opposition to a European legal draft and, therefore, to gain political or electoral benefit from such opposition. In any event, information about legislation and access to it is not, today, the most problematic issue; the quantity of legislation is. Such a diagnosis is not, however, specific to European law-making. If the democratic deficit is understood as a lack of tools offered to national parliaments to scrutinise EU policies, one can easily argue today that there is no more "deficit".

Viewed in this light, the fact that the Lisbon Treaty does not revolutionise the situation with regard to the role of national parliaments cannot be negatively appraised. Indeed, the Amsterdam Protocol had already, and correctly, enumerated the key principles that ought to be guaranteed and developed. In line with the provisions of the defunct Constitutional Treaty, the Lisbon Treaty merely reaffirms the importance of national parliaments' ability to express their views on the work of the EU, and to enhance scrutiny by individual national parliaments of their own governments in relation to EU activities.[24] No alteration is made to the following fundamental rule: the enhancement of the role of national parliaments is a matter for the particular constitutional organisation and practice of each Member State.

Incidentally, one may note the striking inconsistency of the eurosceptics in this area: they easily complain about the lack of involvement of national parliaments in EU affairs without mentioning the complete autonomy of the Member States in this domain. Indeed, as recalled by the Protocol on the role of national parliaments in the EU (protocol annexed to the EC Treaty), "scrutiny by individual national parliaments of their own government

---

[23] This is obviously no excuse for preserving the status quo. The Irish legislation needs further improvements to guarantee an effective scrutiny. In approximately 14 months, the Irish Sub-Committee on European Scrutiny considered in the region of 450 documents and referred—worst-case scenario—25 percent of all proposals examined to sectoral joint committees of the Oireachtas for "further scrutiny". Without the power to reject the proposal for a legal instrument and the possibility to make this rejection binding on the government, the option to refer EU draft proposals for further scrutiny serves no real purpose.

[24] The incorporation of the "Convention method" will lead, however, to an unprecedented involvement of national parliaments. According to new Art 48 TEU, where the European Council decides to amend the Treaties, it may convene a Convention which will notably be composed of representatives of the national Parliaments (formerly Article IV-443 EU CT).

in relation to the activities of the Union is a matter for the particular constitutional organisation and practice of each Member State". Accordingly, one may find that the blame is too easily directed towards the EU. It is entirely up to national governments to find better ways of involving the legislative branch.

This is not to say that no progress would be made were the Lisbon Treaty to enter into force. Indeed, the Member States have agreed on a set of slightly more affirmative rules. The new Protocol on the role of national parliaments in the EU illustrates a modest but incremental improvement on the Amsterdam rules. The Commission, rather than the national governments, would be directly responsible for forwarding all consultative texts upon publication to national parliaments. National parliaments would also receive the Commission's annual legislative programme, as well as any other instrument of legislative planning or policy strategy. Also, legislative proposals would be sent to national parliaments at the same time as to the European institutions. No change, however, is brought to the eight-week period that must elapse between a legislative proposal being made available to national parliaments and the date when it is placed on an agenda of the Council of Ministers. Yet, for the first time, the new Protocol provides that no agreement may be reached on a draft European legislative act during those eight weeks, another example of a modest but positive upgrading of the current rules.

As for the issue of transparency of the Council's work, the Lisbon Treaty essentially consolidates previous and already quite sufficient reforms. The key principle is that "the Union institutions, bodies and agencies shall conduct their work as openly as possible".[25] The novelty lies in the motivation preceding this declaration: transparency is justified to promote "good governance and ensure the participation of the civil society". Unsurprisingly, the same article reaffirms that the European Parliament as well as the Council, shall meet in public "when considering and voting on a draft legislative act". This is in line with the current obligations for the Council of Ministers to meet in public when it acts under the codecision procedure and to guarantee public access to its documents.[26]

To conclude on the role of national parliaments, the current protocol offers a satisfying set of rules. It clearly affirms the importance of closely informing national parliaments of European policies, while allowing for scrutiny of national governments' actions at Council meetings. In the name of constitutional autonomy, the protocol starts with the affirmation that "scrutiny by individual national parliaments of their own government in relation to the activities of the Union is a matter for the particular constitutional organisation and practice of each Member State". As a result, the protocol merely offers a code of good

---

[25] See new Art 255 TEC (formerly Art I-50(1) EU CT).

[26] Article 255(1) TEC currently states that "any citizen of the Union, and any natural or legal person residing or having its registered office in a Member State, shall have a right of access to European Parliament, Council and Commission documents".

practice. The EU, therefore, cannot be blamed if its Member States fail to make good use of its provisions. As previously stated, it is up to each Member State to modify its own internal organisation to guarantee an effective scrutiny of executive actions at the Council of Ministers level. With the few exceptions of Denmark, Sweden, Finland or Austria, it could easily be argued that should there be an information or accountability deficit, it is a self-inflicted one. Yet, irrespective of the enhancement of the role of the European Parliament as well as the national parliaments since the Amsterdam Treaty, the discourse on the "double democratic deficit" remains. It would be tempting to argue that such rhetoric is simply immune to factual contradiction. In reality, and more fundamentally, it reveals a sentimental attachment to the traditional model of parliamentary democracy, and the inability to think of the EU as something other than a federal state in the making. In such a context, the ultimate goal appears to be the duplication, at the European level, of the political model applied, however imperfectly, in the Member States: the parliamentary model.

(c) The Democratic Model Underlying the Diagnosis

The convergence in the political and judicial discourses on European democracy "shows how deeply anchored a model representative democracy is in the Western European political culture."[27] The main political actors, as well as national and European courts, appear to share a similar view: a democratic deficit currently affects the EU for which the remedy lies essentially in more parliamentary input, the precise dosage of which obviously varies according to the political preferences of each actor. However, what is common in all of these alarming findings, is that democracy is hardly ever defined. Without a definition of the apparent missing object, curing the democratic deficit may bear a resemblance to Sisyphus's work. For that reason, it is imperative to briefly explore the democratic essence of the parliamentary model, before assessing its relevance when applied to the EU.

Having the concept of *Rechtsstaat*, or rule of law, in mind, the Belgian historian Raoul van Caenegem wrote: "the problems ... start with the very word".[28] The same could easily be said of the concept of democracy. The word could be referred to as frequently as the word "freedom" in a George W. Bush sermon and yet, its meaning could still remain obscure for the orator and the public alike. Undeniably, the relative and elusive nature of the concept of democracy renders any definitional exercise a very delicate one. In the well-known Gettysburg address, Abraham Lincoln spoke of a government of the people, by the people, for the people. Article 2 of the French Constitution reproduces literally Lincoln's statement whereas the Constitution of Ireland, in its Art 6 para 1, states that "all

---

[27] R. Dehousse, "European governance in search of legitimacy: the need for a process-based approach", in O. de Schutter, N. Lebessis and J. Paterson (eds), *Governance in the European Union* (Office for Official Publications of the European Communities, Luxembourg, 2001), p 171.

[28] R. van Caenegem, "The 'Rechtsstaat' in Historical Perspective", in R. van Caenegem, *Legal History: A European Perspective* (Hambledon Press, London, 1991), p 185.

powers of government, legislative, executive and judicial derive, under God, from the people, whose right it is to designate the rulers of the State and, in final appeal, to decide all questions of national policy, according to the requirements of the common good". What could be easily deduced from these statements is the centrality of the "People" in a *Demos-Kratos*. This does not come as a surprise since these two Greek words say it all: a democracy is a political regime where the "power" belongs to the people. However, before the concept of a government of, by and for the people could become the cardinal value of the Western world, a key change had to be brought upon the notion of sovereignty, being the legal translation of the word power. In turn, this evolution enabled parliamentary bodies to claim a central role in our modern polities and to act as the exclusive delegates of the sovereign people.

The prominent political change brought about by the French Revolution must be emphasised. Starting a gradual process of transfer of sovereignty from the monarch to a new abstract entity, the 1789 Revolution slowly but irresistibly encompassed the people with the supreme quality of being the "Sovereign". According to Art III of the Declaration of the Rights of Man and of the Citizen of 1789: "The principle of all sovereignty resides essentially in the Nation. No body and no individual may exercise authority which does not derive expressly therefrom." The word "Nation" was used to convey that the sovereignty which used to belong exclusively to the King had now passed to the citizens. Sieyès provided the political rationale for the adoption of such a principle in the first French constitution, the Constitution of 1791. He argued that the people are in fact the Nation and that, in consequence, the people, acting through its representatives, can adopt a constitution and rule the country on behalf of the Nation. If the people are sovereign the people may not, however, exercise directly its sovereign powers, if only for practical reasons. The people must thus delegate the power to govern to its representatives. Such practical necessity led to a situation of parliamentary sovereignty. One major explanation lies in the transposition made by the revolutionaries of the providential qualities which Rousseau, in *Du contrat social* (1762), attributed to laws voted by the people to laws which were passed by representatives. Indeed, in Rousseau's view, as an expression of the general will, law is enacted by the entire populace for the entire populace and is thus "infallible". It follows, then, that the law must be applied as written by judges and by administrative and government officials; it may not be displaced by anyone but the sovereign body politic itself. In other words, it may not be displaced by anyone but the "representatives" of the Sovereign, the members of Parliament.

The sovereignty of Parliament obviously characterised the United Kingdom's political regime before finding its way in France.[29] Undeniably, a different historical development and a distinctive legal tradition produced a distinct interpretation of the concept of

---

[29] On the British doctrine of parliamentary sovereignty, see the enlightening work of J. Goldsworthy, *The Sovereignty of Parliament. History and Philosophy* (Oxford University Press, Oxford, 2001).

sovereignty. Without a revolution in the United Kingdom, the principle of sovereignty could only be vested in the Crown and not in the Nation or People. Despite this, the British Parliament progressively established itself as the institution that exercised absolute public power—in a process that preceded by far the French political evolution—and legitimised it in the name of the people. From Rousseau's perspective, this situation was theoretically difficult to come to terms with, as there could only be one sovereign. Dicey explained it, however, by distinguishing legal from political sovereignty, the latter being vested in the people. From a consequential point of view, the United Kingdom, as well as France, was characterised for a long period of time by the absence of any judicial power to review the legality of Acts of Parliament. Indeed, in the model of parliamentary democracy, the idea of constitutional supremacy could not easily materialise.

Regarding the question of constitutional arrangements, separation of powers was traditionally required as a protection against abuse and tyranny. Looking to the English system as a model, Montesquieu, in *De l'Esprit des Lois* (1748), advocated a constitution based on the principle of separation of powers: "To assure liberty, legislative, executive, and judicial powers must be kept separate." A direct consequence of Montesquieu's influence is to be found in Article XVI of the Declaration of the Rights of Man and of the Citizen of 1789: "Any society in which the guaranty of rights is not assured or the separation of powers established, has no Constitution."

Broadly speaking, in the model of parliamentary democracy, the legitimacy of political authority and of legal norms is exclusively derived from the association of the Parliament with the people, whether or not the People or the Crown is recognised as the ultimate authority. To assess the relevance of the parliamentary model with regard to the EU, it may be useful, beforehand, to identify its underlying assumptions. As Renaud Dehousse perfectly sums it up:

> "First, in its most basic understanding, the system is based on what one could call an input-oriented form of democratic legitimation: people elect their representatives, the latter take decisions affecting the fate of the polity, and they must be accountable for their choices before voters. ... Secondly, laws passed by representative bodies are *par excellence* the instruments whereby such political choices are made. In this vision inherited from Jean-Jacques Rousseau, legislative bills are the expression of an axiomatic 'general will'. Thirdly, there is often an implicit equation between the 'general will' and the common good: what legislators decide is supposed to serve the interests of the whole polity."[30]

In light of these underlying assumptions, the democratic deficit charge is likely to remain. Despite a clear "parliamentarisation" of its decision-making process over the last decade,

---

[30] Dehousse, "European governance in search of legitimacy", pp 170–71.

the Union's institutional architecture is such that it still leaves little margin for the application of the principles of the separation of powers and the responsibility of an elected and single executive body before a "genuine" parliament. Applying the model of parliamentary democracy to the EU is somewhat problematic because it embodies a non-state and a non-nation polity. Before assessing, however, the Union's original system of government from a normative point of view, the relevance of the democratic deficit diagnosis may already be seriously questioned on pragmatic grounds.

(II) EVALUATING THE EVIDENCE

Reviewing the conventional understanding of the democratic deficit thesis leads to the conclusion that the charge is essentially founded upon a "parliamentary tropism": the absence of mechanisms associated with a parliamentary regime justifies the negative diagnosis. The analogy with a majoritarian model of parliamentary democracy is not only widely popular in the media, more worryingly, it also still transpires from numerous scholarly analyses. The following brief excerpt could serve as a perfect illustration of the reproaches addressed to the EU:

> "EC policy-making processes are largely dominated by bureaucracies and governments that provide little scope for parliamentary institutions (whether national parliaments or the EP) to intervene and to exercise roles traditionally believed to be the hallmarks of legislatures in liberal democratic politics."[31]

Certainly, starting with the Maastricht Treaty, the European Parliament's powers were incrementally reinforced in the legislative procedure, while its power to control the European Commission was reaffirmed, most notably with the right to overthrow it by voting a motion of censure, as attempted against the Santer Commission in 1999. In line with the reforms agreed in 2004, the Lisbon Treaty clearly pursues the trend: the European Parliament sees its role of co-legislator formalised and its influence strengthened as the codecision procedure is extended to new areas. The Parliament will also stand as the budgetary authority alongside the Council of Ministers. Nevertheless, the Lisbon Treaty, while enhancing European Parliament's powers as well as the role of national parliaments, does not fundamentally alter the Union's institutional architecture. Consequently, it could be suggested that the Union's democratic deficit has yet to be dealt with.

This diagnosis reflects, to some extent, a romantic understanding of the notion of democracy as well as a profound misapprehension of the EU. Before any "democratic" assessment of the EU is undertaken, the actual functioning of European democracies must

---

[31] J. Lodge (ed), *The European Community and the Challenge of the Future* (Frances Pinter, 1989), quoted in G. Majone, "Europe's 'Democratic Deficit': The Question of Standards", (1998) 4 *European Law Journal* 5, p 8.

first be considered in order to avoid criticism based on an idealised vision of democracy. It is also imperative to recall that the EU is not a nation-state. Although it is certainly difficult to assert its current political and legal nature with complete authority, the EU remains a supranational system of government whose complexity and apparent "isolation" from direct involvement of the European citizenry may be defended, paradoxically, on democratic grounds.

This is not to say that criticising the EU for being insufficiently democratic is an illegitimate exercise. To be fruitful, however, the debate must be based, first of all, on a clear enunciation of what one understands by democracy and how democracies are functioning in reality. Any attempt at defining democracy reveals how difficult the exercise is. To give an edifying example, when the General Lucius D. Clay, the governor of the US-occupied zone in post-war Germany, had to work on the new constitutional framework, he, John Foster Dulles and a group of State Department officials "spent a whole day disagreeing on a definition of democracy" and "this was entirely within the American delegation". In the end, they realised that they "could not agree on any common definition for democracy".[32] The debate on the EU's democratic deficit reveals, nevertheless, that in most cases, democracy is equated with parliamentary democracy. Before considering the relevance of such an association, it may be profitable to overview the development and functioning of national democracies.

Bearing Rousseau's assertion in mind: "Were there a people of gods, their government would be democratic. So perfect a government is not for men", it is not surprising to observe a severe gap between the normative theory of democracy and many contemporary practices of governance.[33] If unaware of such a gap, a citizen could easily feel frustrated or disillusioned with the EU. Indeed, the EU can hardly be defended if it is effectively believed that "at national level, there is a simple chain of command whereby all decisions can be linked to the supreme will of the people, public authority is exerted in an orderly fashion, according to crystal-clear principles enshrined in a constitutional text, which is known to every citizen".[34] Such an idealised version of democracy obviously fails to give an account of the real functioning of modern democracies. One may regret, in particular, the tendency amongst scholars "to analyse the EU in ideal and isolated terms", with comparisons being "drawn between the EU and an ancient, Westminster-style, or frankly utopian form of deliberative democracy".[35] As a result, any scrutiny of the EU is likely to

---

[32] Ferguson, *Colossus*, p 76.

[33] For an instructive introduction to the transformation of the conditions of governance and regulation in contemporary democracies, see the report of T. Burns, *The Future of Parliamentary Democracy: Transition and Challenge in European Governance*, Green Paper prepared for the Conference of the Speakers of EU Parliaments (Rome, 22–24 September 2000). See also T. Burns, "The Evolution of European Parliaments and Societies in Europe: Challenges and Prospects", (1999) 2 *Journal of Social Theory* 167.

[34] R. Dehousse, "Rediscovering Functionalism", in C. Joerges, Y. Mény & J. Weiler (eds), *What kind of Constitution for what kind of Polity?* (The Robert Schuman Centre for Advanced Studies, Florence, 2000), p 199.

[35] Moravcsik, "In Defence of the 'Democratic Deficit'", p 605.

lead to the ensuing inexorable conclusion: Europe is suffering from a democratic deficit. The available evidence, however, does not support this claim. It would be more accurate to argue either that national democracies also suffer from a similar plague or, to put it in a more neutral manner, that the government of modern societies is mutating. Our romantic vision of democracy remains at odds with such mutation and it may be time, therefore, to undertake a "cultural revolution" to reinvent its meaning.[36] In turn, such understanding of the evolving and more plural nature of democracy is more likely to lead to a proper assessment of the EU and its democratic defects, if any.

(a) The Vanishing European Voter

From almost 65 percent in 1979, when the first direct elections for members of the European Parliament were held, the turnout progressively decreased and reached a new record low in June 2004, with just 45.3 percent of EU voters casting ballots. If the steady decrease cannot be denied, the last figure must be interpreted in the context of a dismal turnout of about 27 percent in the 10 new member countries.[37] Voter apathy used to be explained by the European Parliament's lack of powers or overall political insignificance over the decision-making process. As the historian Tony Judt puts it: "Why waste time selecting the monkey when you should be paying attention to the choice of organ grinder instead?"[38] This explanation is now clearly unsatisfactory as the Parliament has been gaining a great deal of powers and influence since the Maastricht Treaty. As a result, the link between power and turnout ought to be revised and the explanation must rely on other factors. And so the lack of pan-European politics is now blamed. In short, the main reason lies in the fact that European political life cannot easily be explained by reference to the classic distinction between a parliamentary majority supporting a government, and a minority opposing it. Worse, voting majorities are flexible within the European Parliament and there is no genuine cleavage between a right-wing and a left-wing. Therefore, a polarised debate is not available with the damaging consequence that the media take little interest in political affairs discussed at the European level.

If the original nature of European politics cannot be denied, the argument of the poor turnout in European elections as evidence of the remoteness of European institutions should also be rejected. Some structural problems certainly exist at the European level. For instance, the proposal that a certain number of MEPs could be elected on the basis of a European constituency, via transnational lists, would certainly increase public interest and help in shaping the discussion on European issues. One may also consider urging the adoption of a uniform electoral procedure in all the Member States and the obligation to hold elections, if not on the same day, at least on the same week. The Treaty of Rome

---

[36] Robert Dahl has argued that "democracy can be independently invented and reinvented whenever appropriate conditions exist", *On Democracy* (Yale University Press, New Haven, 1998), p 9.

[37] See e.g. "Populists, ahoy", *The Economist*, 17 June 2004. With a turnout of about 17 percent, Slovakia set a new abstention record.

[38] T. Judt, *Postwar. A History of Europe since 1945* (William Heinemann, London, 2005), p 731.

actually offers the legal basis for the drawing up "of a proposal for elections by direct universal suffrage in accordance with a uniform procedure in all Member States or in accordance with principles common to all Member States".[39] The Member States, however, have favoured the second option, the less constraining one. Indeed, national governments remain opposed to relaxing their grip on electoral procedure for a mix of grandiose reasons (protecting national sovereignty) and less admirable ones (preserving their freedom to use European elections to get rid of or to reward political opponents or long-term personal "friends"). The Lisbon Treaty still reflects this reluctance and no change in the procedure for European elections is envisaged. The MEPs will continue to be elected for a term of five years by direct universal suffrage in a free and secret ballot while any European citizen (resident in any Member State) has the right to elect (and to stand as candidates) his/her representative. As a result, no progress towards any real pan-European politics is foreseeable in the near future.

Despite the peculiarities of European politics, the poor turnout must also be put into a broader perspective.[40] Decline in voter turnout and rise in electoral support for eccentric or extremist political parties are far from exclusive to European elections. Regarding poor turnout, the European Parliament does not apparently suffer from the comparison with the US Congress: voting rates in congressional elections average 45 percent.[41] One may also mention that it is not unusual for an American President, since the end of the 1960s, and with the exception of the polarised elections of 2004, to be elected with a turnout barely above 50 percent without its legitimacy being contested (as long as his election is not the culmination of curious events recalling a banana republic). Furthermore, the US electoral system may sanction the "election" of a presidential candidate with less popular votes, for instance, George W. Bush in the 2000 elections. Another argument which ought to be taken with a pinch of salt, is that "the European Union badly needs more popular legitimacy, as the big anti-incumbent votes and quite sizeable anti-EU votes"[42] seemingly showed in the 2004 European Parliament elections. "Extremist" votes are not a unique

---

[39] Article 190(4) of the TEC.

[40] See e.g. the interesting proceedings of a seminar organised by Notre Europe and the European University Institute, *Europe and the Crisis of Democracy. Elections in Europe: 1999–2002*, Cahiers Européens de Sciences-Po, no. 6, 2002 (available at: http://www.porteeurope.org).

[41] For a comparison of voter turnout, see e.g. S. Hix, "Elections, Parties and Institutional Design: A Comparative Perspective on European Union Democracy", (1998) 21(3) *West European Politics* 19, p 33. It appears, however, that voter turnout is more likely to be calculated in the United States by reference to the number of Americans of voting-age rather than the number of registered voters, therefore leading to low figures of voter turnout. As a result, a direct comparison between the United States and Europe remains a difficult exercise as long as voter turnout is not precisely defined. For an analysis, according to which, decline in voter participation is an artefact of the way in which it is measured, see the website animated by Dr M. McDonald of George Mason University: http://elections.gmu.edu/voter_turnout.htm. It also offers a direct link to a study he published with S. Popkin, "The Myth of the Vanishing Voter", (2001) 95 *American Political Science Review* 963.

[42] "The right verdict on the constitution", *The Economist*, 24 June 2004.

feature of European elections. The rise of extremist parties is well-documented at the national level and eccentric politicians are not only found at the European level. In the end, the apparent decline in favourable attitudes towards European institutions is very well shared with national institutions.[43] As a final word, assuming that democratic apathy and anti-establishment votes actually reflect a genuine crisis of legitimacy, such a "crisis" is present at all levels of government since the 1970s.

(b) The European Parliament's lack of powers

The European Parliament's alleged lack of powers and, more particularly, the power to legislate and dismiss the executive power, is also brought into play to demonstrate the reality of the EU's democratic deficit. Briefly said, the advocates of this thesis do little justice to the "parliamentarisation"—however incomplete—of the Union's decision-making structure and process. Indeed, since the Amsterdam Treaty came into force, the codecision procedure has progressively governed more and more areas, to the point that it is now considered a standard legislative procedure. The most important aspect of this procedure is that it puts the European Parliament, in principle, on equal footing with the Council of Ministers. If the Parliament does not agree to the adoption of a text, it cannot enter into force. On average, about 10 percent of the texts submitted to the European Parliament are rejected. The adoption of the Lisbon Treaty would extend the codecision procedure, renamed the "ordinary legislative procedure", to almost all cases. As for the power to dismiss the "executive", the current Treaty of Rome provides for a motion of censure against the Commission.[44] It requires a two-thirds majority of the votes cast, representing a majority of Parliament's component members, in which case the Commission must resign.

Notwithstanding its ongoing "parliamentarisation", the EU does not conform entirely to the classic canons of a parliamentary democracy. For instance, the European Parliament has the power to dismiss the Commission. Yet, it cannot dismiss the Council of Ministers which is the most influential executive organ. Additionally, the EU can hardly conform to the mythology of parliamentary democracy where elected representatives control the legislative process and implement the will of the people expressed periodically through elections. In such a scheme, members of the executive are the subverted servants of the people's representatives and could be dismissed for not acting in conformity with the will of the directly-elected assembly. This representation is, unfortunately, profoundly at odds with the real practice of government in modern democracies.

In Western Europe, extensive literature deals with the so-called decline of parliaments, at least since the 1960s. Undeniably, the executive branch has openly triumphed over the legislative branch. Ideological division, structured on a right-left spectrum associated with

---

[43] See e.g. Y. Mény and Y. Surel (eds), *Democracies and the populist challenge* (Palgrave, Basingstoke, 2002).
[44] Article 201 TEC.

the rationalisation of parliamentary life, has produced important consequences for the concrete working of parliamentary democracies. In other words, governments determine the agendas of their parliaments and completely dominate the decision-making process. Bills are now mostly the product of ministerial departments (and other indeterminate actors) and cannot be adopted without the explicit or implicit agreement of the government. For instance, in France, about 95 percent of the Bills ultimately adopted directly originate from ministerial departments. A complete set of rules in the French Constitution goes as far as to allow the government the right to exclude any vote on any Bill emanating from an MP, if it wishes to do so. Examples could easily be multiplied to demonstrate the dramatic marginalisation of parliaments, even as an instrument of mere debate, by the sole willingness of the executive. With relevance to the alleged neutral tradition of Ireland, Proinsias De Rossa recently wondered: "what improvements to our democratic decision-making procedures can we put in place to effectively challenge odious government decisions like the one to allow the US use Shannon Airport for the prosecution of its illegal war in Iraq?"[45] Should the EU be blamed for such blatant sidestepping of the Oireachtas?

Another classic claim is the affirmation that, at the national level, the Executive is accountable to parliament. The existence of a strong bipartite system associated with strong party discipline in the United Kingdom led progressively to a more stable political life, where the cabinet government emerged as the sole real player. Since the end of World War II, only one British government, the Government of M. Callaghan in 1979, has been brought down by a motion of censure. Furthermore, the motion of censure was only successful because an old Labour MP could not cast his vote as he was too weak to leave hospital. The rationalisation of parliamentary rules governing the dismissal of government also produced a dramatic evolution in countries such as France, where governmental instability marked political life since the birth of parliamentary politics. With the entry into force of the Constitution of the Fifth Republic in 1958, only one government has ever been dismissed. It happened in 1962, in exceptional historical circumstances involving a withdrawal from Algeria. Furthermore, the French President, Charles de Gaulle, actually responded to the parliamentary vote by declaring the National Assembly dissolved. After winning the general elections, he nominated the same Prime Minister. The situation in Germany is no different, as the requirement of a "constructive vote of no-confidence" means that once elected by a majority of the Bundestag (the lower house), the chancellor may be forced out only if the Bundestag simultaneously, and by an absolute majority, deposes him and elects a successor.

In the end, the everlasting argument, according to which democracy is suffering since power has been effectively taken out of the hands of national Parliaments and given to Ministers who are not collectively responsible to any representative body, should be read

---

[45] "Ireland's role and responsibilities in the world at large", *The Irish Times*, 11 February 2005.

in the context of a widespread trend. On the one hand, national parliaments were marginalised within their own national political systems and national governments given a complete free hand well before the creation of the EU. On the other hand, each national ministerial representative within the Council of Ministers is today accountable before his or her own parliament whereas the Commission is responsible before the European Parliament. Unless one wants to transform the EU into some federal state, no valid argument can justify a double responsibility for the Council of Ministers. This European body is democratically legitimate since it represents all the national governments, which are "themselves democratically accountable either to their national Parliaments, or to their citizens".[46]

Europe does not need to reproduce a phantasmagorical model of parliamentary democracy nor must it blindly duplicate abstract principles that are not enforced at the national level. To conclude, the balance of power has clearly shifted to the executive branch. This historical development should be kept in mind when the EU is being criticized for the pre-eminence of the Council of Ministers in the decision-making process and its alleged lack of accountability.

(c) The Eurocracy

Another facet of the decline of parliaments in modern democracies is the growth of the "technostructure", to use a term coined by John Kenneth Galbraith in 1967 in a different context. As a result, it would have been surprising not to find a similar pattern at the European level. To put it differently, the subtle influence of the bureaucracy, of technical expertise and of private interests on policy-making cannot be said to exclusively characterise European governance. This is not to say that it is a bed of roses as far as the EU is concerned. The influence of experts and the myriad of committees in the European decision-making process, for instance, could appear unprecedented from the perspective of the layman.[47]

Before elaborating a legislative proposal, the Commission usually consult committees of experts or ad hoc consultation bodies in a wide range of policies. Yet the precise number of these bodies and their influence remain quite unclear. In fairness, the Commission itself recognised that "there is currently a lack of clarity about how consultations are run and to whom the Institutions listen" and stated the need to "rationalise this unwieldy system not to stifle discussion, but to make it more effective and accountable both for those consulted and those receiving the advice".[48] However, with regard to the input of experts in policy-

---

[46] New Art 8A TEU (formerly Art I-46 EU CT).

[47] For a first overview, see e.g. T. Christiansen and E. Kirchner (eds), *Europe in Charge. Committee Governance in the European Union* (Manchester University Press, Manchester, 2000).

[48] White Paper on European Governance, COM(2001) 428 final, 25 July 2001, p 17. According to the Commission itself, it runs nearly 700 ad hoc consultation bodies in a wide range of policies.

making, the lack of clarity should not be interpreted as being peculiar to Brussels. Consultation bodies proliferate at the national level without citizens knowing and worrying about it. Furthermore, in the case of the EU, the phenomenon is, in reality, the result of Member States' choices. Committees and consultation bodies offer Member States the opportunity to control the work of the Commission through national experts sent to these bodies. In addition, one cannot complain about the high number of committees and consultation bodies. It is the direct result of an understaffed European Commission. Once again, the inconsistency of critics who complain about the Union's democratic deficit is genuinely apparent, as they refuse to see the Commission granted with the means to govern without the direct and cumbersome assistance of national experts. In other words, the Commission is a convenient scapegoat when it comes to denouncing the influence of the "expertocracy". Not only is this phenomenon at work in all the Member States, but it is the Member States who have institutionalised a government of committees at the EU level.

Less likely to be the subject of malicious headlines, the Committee of Permanent Representatives is a powerful body whose task is to prepare the work of the Council of Ministers. The Permanent Representatives operate, in practice, as the Ambassadors of the Member States to the EU. They are based in Brussels and provide a continuity of presence which political representatives cannot. The Permanent Representatives, in other words, the Member States, have also asked to be assisted by "working groups" whose number is said to vary between 150 and 250. These groups, composed of national experts, examine legislative proposals from the Commission. Their exact number was said to be "one of the EU's great unsolved mysteries".[49]

To make things worse, a mysterious term, "comitology", is used to describe the procedure under which the Commission consults committees made up of national officials and experts when it has to implement EU laws and policies. In a few words, EU legislation frequently gives the Commission the power to work out technical details. The Member States, once again unwilling to give the Commission *carte blanche* to legislate, oblige the Commission to work within the framework of committees made up of Member States representatives, thus the name comitology. In its details, the procedure is certainly complex and the functioning of these committees is somewhat opaque. The only person who truly understands it may very well be "the doorman at 35 Avenue Brochart in Brussels (the venue for most meetings) who can survey the hundreds of national and EU bureaucrats and experts walking in and out of comitology meetings on a daily basis".[50] Comitology could, all the same, be defended on the grounds that it enables the Commission to establish an efficient and, some authors would argue, a democratic dialogue with national

---

[49] F. Hayes-Renshaw and H. Wallace, *The Council of Ministers* (Palgrave MacMillan, Basingstoke, 1997), p 97.
[50] A. Stubb, H. Walace and J. Peterson, "The Policy-Making Process", in E. Bomberg and A. Stubb (eds), *The European Union: How Does it Work?* (Oxford University Press, Oxford, 2003), p 142.

administrations and diverse interest groups, before adopting implementing measures.[51] Furthermore, a Council decision in 1999 has dramatically increased the oversight of the European Parliament and the transparency of the committee system: committee documents should now be more readily accessible to the citizen.[52] One may hope, as a result, that the hidden "netherworld", the suggestive term suggested by Joseph Weiler to typify comitology, has been brought under more formal control.[53] In the end, it would be unfair to blame the European Commission for a scheme imposed upon it. To get rid of comitology would certainly make the European decision-making process faster and simpler, but, as always, the Member States support this complex scheme of government in the name of national sovereignty. Finally, it would be naive to assume that democratically elected representatives control not only the drafting but also the implementation of legal norms at the national level. Regardless of the specificity and intricacy of the European bureaucracy, it cannot be denied that it remains one element of a general trend where the bureaucracy dominates policy-making. As a result, it could rightly be concluded that "the legitimation of secondary norms is an endemic problem for all domestic political systems".[54]

The same conclusion could easily be drawn from the accusation that the EU increases the influence of private parties in the decision-making process. Distressing examples, where particular interests, especially capitalistic interests, have triumphed over public interest, could easily be exposed.[55] Yet, without much effort, similar examples could be found in most Member States. In reality, the only substantial distinction may be that the EU does not shy away from formalising the participation of private parties and lobbying in general. This may be regretted, as it is possible to argue that the most powerful actors, and not the preferences of most individual citizens, are likely to influence policy-making. Moreover, for this author, public interest ought not to be equated with what could be obtained from

---

[51] On the deliberative (and therefore democratic) nature of comitology, see in particular C. Joerges and J. Neyer, "From Intergovernmental Bargaining to Deliberative Political Process: the Constitutionalisation of Comitology", (1997) 3 *European Law Journal* 273.

[52] Council Decision of 28 June 1999 laying down the procedures for the exercise of implementing powers conferred on the Commission, [1999] OJ L 184/23.

[53] Joseph Weiler has said that instead of supranationalism, "it is time to worry about infranationalism – a complex network of middle level national administrators, Community administrators and an array of private bodies with unequal and unfair access to a process with huge social and economic consequences to everyday life – in matters of public safety, health, and all other dimensions of socio-economic regulation". See J. Weiler, "To be a European Citizen - Eros and Civilisation", *Working Paper Series in European Studies*, Spring 1998, pp 38–39 (available at: http://uw-madison-ces.org/papers/weiler.pdf).

[54] P. Craig, "The Nature of the Community: Integration Theory and Democratic Theory", in P. Craig and G. de Búrca (eds), *The Evolution of EU Law* (Oxford University Press, Oxford, 1999), p 25.

[55] A good example for discussion would certainly be the Directive 2000/36/EC of the European Parliament and of the Council of 23 June 2000, relating to cocoa and chocolate products intended for human consumption. The directive, by allowing products containing vegetable fats other than cocoa butter to be called "chocolate", had extremely damaging consequences for cocoa producers in the Third World and appeared to have been inspired for the sole benefits of multinationals active in that market.

a "free" competition between private parties' conflicting interests. Yet, regardless of one's views on the benefits of associating interest groups, it is difficult to claim that such practice constitutes further evidence of a democratic deficit peculiar to the EU. It simply organises a process that is taking place *sub initio* at each level of government.

Generally speaking, one may regret the tendency towards double-standards whenever the EU is subject to "democratic" scrutiny. In most cases, critics tend to assess the EU in light of an idealised model of majoritarian democracy. This is especially so when the focus is on the "undemocratic" or anti-majoritarian nature of the European Court of Justice or the European Central Bank.

(d) The presence of anti-majoritarian institutions

The undemocratic pedigree of the EU is sometimes argued on the grounds that it organises a peculiar form of government where anti-majoritarian mechanisms are used to "tame" the popular will. One emblematic illustration is the European Court of Justice whose judicial activism is denounced as being undemocratic. One must realise, however, that all European democracies have sought to balance the rule of the majority with the rule of the law since the end of World War II.[56] To do so, most constitutional courts have been conferred with the power to annul legislative acts and, more generally, have been entrusted with the task of defending fundamental rights in order to prevent authoritarian rule. The new strength of the judicial branch has not always been well received, hence the customary and recurring accusation of a government by judges which allegedly threatens the sovereignty of the people. This is especially true in countries such as France where, since the Revolution, the judicial function has been regarded as subservient to the legislative power. How, then, could the "counter-majoritarian" paradox be explained?[57] Democratic societies have come to consider it necessary to associate the democratic ideal of law with a liberal theory of fundamental rights, functioning as an inherent limit to the exercise of public power.[58] Judicial review may well contravene the will of the majority or, more accurately, the will of the parliament,but it could be argued that this departure from the "Rousseauian" tradition actually allows a genuine respect for the constituent will of the sovereign People as embodied in the constitutional text. To quote the French *Conseil Constitutionnel*, it must be affirmed that "the law expresses the general will only when it respects the Constitution."[59] Ultimately, as the sovereign People can always amend its own creation, especially in the situation where constitutional judges would be tempted to act as a committee of philosopher "kings", it can generally be concluded that judicial review is compatible with democracy.[60]

---

[56] See e.g. L. Favoreu, "American and European Models of Constitutional Justice", in *Comparative and Private International Law. Essays in Honor of J.H. Merryman* (Duncker and Humblot, Berlin, 1990).

[57] A. Bickel, *The Least Dangerous Branch* (2nd ed, Yale University Press, New Haven, 1986), p 16.

[58] On such concern, see the classic work of J. Ely, *Democracy and Distrust. A theory of Judicial Review*, (Harvard University Press, Cambridge, 1980).

[59] Decision no. 85-197 DC, 23 August 1985.

[60] See e.g. A. Stone Sweet, *Governing with Judges. Constitutional Politics in Europe* (Oxford University Press, Oxford, 2000).

As for the existence of a Court of Justice at the European level, it merely illustrates that the EC is also based on the rule of law:

> "It must be first emphasised in this regard that the European Economic Community is a Community based on the rule of law, inasmuch as neither its member states nor its institutions can avoid a review of the question whether the measures adopted by them are in conformity with the basic constitutional charter, the treaty."[61]

The institution of a Court of Justice, therefore, guarantees that European institutions are kept in check and that Member States play by the rules they agreed to. If the rule of law is deservedly a cherished and emblematic value of any democracy, one cannot deny that the European Court of Justice has sometimes adopted a dynamic or "flexible" interpretation of the European's "basic constitutional charter", meaning the EC Treaty. On the other hand, the case law of all constitutional courts in Europe similarly reflects a dynamic interpretation of national constitutions. However, it is true that, in some circumstances, the European Court of Justice comes close to exercising law-making power. The most prominent example may be the doctrine of supremacy of EC law. This doctrine could reasonably be described as a judge-made law doctrine. The Member States had several opportunities to amend the Treaty of Rome, to limit the scope of the Court's jurisprudence or to abolish the doctrine of supremacy since it was first formulated by the Court in 1964. They have always refused to do so. On the contrary, the drafting of the Constitutional Treaty led to the conferral of an explicit constitutional basis on the doctrine of supremacy.[62] In this light, the alleged judicial activism of the European Court of Justice can hardly be described as illegitimate.

The autonomy of the European Central Bank and the rise of independent or autonomous regulatory agencies have also been denounced as symbols of the Union's democratic deficit. Nevertheless, European institutions, such as the European Central Bank, the European Court of Justice or the European Food Safety Authority, enjoy the greatest autonomy in precisely those areas "in which many advanced industrial democracies, including most Member States of the EU, insulate themselves from direct political contestation. The apparently 'undemocratic' nature of the EU as a whole is largely a function of this selection effect."[63] Therefore, the existence of what have been called "non-majoritarian" institutions, as they are insulated from direct electoral mechanisms, do not exclusively characterise the EU. On the contrary, there is a general trend at national level towards the delegation of policy-making powers to independent regulatory agencies. This widespread phenomenon demonstrates that the idea of legitimacy is evolving, and

---

[61] Case 294/83 *Les Verts v Parliament* [1986] ECR 1339, para 23.
[62] See Art I-6 EU CT.
[63] Moravcsik, "In Defence of the 'Democratic Deficit'", p 613.

does not have to exclusively derive from election or from parliamentary supervision.[64] Indeed, the main rationale behind the development of these non-majoritarian institutions is to increase efficiency in fields where special expertise is needed or where independence from daily politics is a means to guarantee credibility through long-term commitments. When the "goods are delivered", the political system as a whole should benefit from output legitimacy.[65] Such a trend should not invariably be equated with increasing unaccountability or a democratic deficit.[66] There are always some forms of parliamentary scrutiny. Furthermore, administrative law, media scrutiny and peer pressure, with judicial review as an ultimate check, guarantee that autonomy will not lead to arbitrary regulation.

CHAPTER THREE – CONCLUSION

Whenever the EU is subjected to a democratic assessment, it appears essential that such an exercise should be undertaken in light of the actual development of national democracies. Deep and widespread structural changes have been taking place and have led to a marginalisation of parliaments. To mention but a few of these changes: contemporary societies are increasingly characterised by the growing importance of expertise, the growing influence of the civil society and the overall "privatisation" of policy-making.[67] The impact of globalisation adds to the challenges faced by national parliaments and their powers to shape public policies. As brilliantly condensed by Professor Burns: major legislative and policy-making activities are now "being substantially displaced from parliamentary bodies and central governments to global, regional, and local agents as well as agents operating in the many specialized sectors of a differentiated, modern society. In other words, governance is increasingly diffused — upward, downward and outward — beyond Parliament and its government."[68] Such changes make it "difficult to argue that all decisions affecting the fate of the polity are taken by people's representatives".[69] The striking

---

[64] See generally G. Majone (ed), *Regulating Europe* (Routledge, London, 1996).

[65] The underlying assumption is that when "regulation is made by a majoritarian institution, such as a parliament, bargaining is between rival legislative coalitions, and the outcome is inherently redistributive/zero-sum: in the interest of the majority, against the interests of the minority. However, by delegating regulatory policy to an independent institution, which is required to act in the "public interest", outcomes will be positive-sum", S. Hix, "The Study of the EU II: the 'New Governance' Agenda and its Rival", (1998) 5 *Journal of European Public Policy* 38 at 51.

[66] On the ECB, for instance, two studies could be usefully compared: L. Gormley and J. de Haan, "The Democratic Deficit of the European Central Bank", (1996) 21 *European Law Journal* 95 and P. Magnette, "Towards 'Accountable Independence'? Parliamentary Controls of the European Central Bank and the Rise of a New Democratic Model", (2000) 6 *European Law Journal* 326.

[67] See e.g. L. Pech, "Le droit à l'épreuve de la gouvernance. Légitimation de la privatisation du droit?", in R. Canet and J. Duchastel, *La régulation néolibérale. Crise ou ajustement?* (Athéna editions, Montréal, 2004), p 51.

[68] *The Future of Parliamentary Democracy: Transition and Challenge in European Governance*, Green Paper prepared for the Conference of the Speakers of EU Parliaments (Rome, 22–24 September 2000).

[69] Dehousse, "European governance in search of legitimacy", p 171.

gap between the pre-eminence of the parliamentary model of democracy in our cultural mindset and the reality of policy- and law-making, could only lead to uneasiness within the citizenry. As for parliaments, the sense of malaise described by Peter Riddell, in relation to the United Kingdom, can easily be extrapolated: "the real malaise at Westminster is a sense of exclusion, a belief that the real political debate and decision-making are elsewhere - in European institutions, in the courts, the media, the Bank of England and financial markets, and in the decisions of regulators and those who run quangos."[70]

Equating democracy with an abstract model can only lead to a drastic misunderstanding of how democracy is being practised. It may also justify unrealistic demands. For instance, if some room for criticism is justified with regard to the European Parliament's insufficient powers or the marginalisation of national parliaments, it has to be seriously undertaken. Due regard must be paid to the development of parliamentary democracy at the national level in the context of globalisation.[71] To argue that European integration "perverts" national democracy may be going too far.[72] This is not to deny that the complexity of the decision-making structure and process has allowed national executives to somewhat escape national parliamentary control. But to put it bluntly, national parliaments were being marginalised before the concept of EU was ever thought of. It is even tempting to contend that European integration has acted as a catharsis, progressively allowing national parliaments to regain some influence.[73] In line with the Constitutional Treaty, the Lisbon Treaty, for instance, offers new improved tools for the European and national parliaments to be more effective policy actors. Were the national MPs to adopt an empirical view of European integration, they might come to realise that European integration is a legitimating factor for increased scrutiny of their respective governments, a prerogative which has long been abandoned in most democracies. In light of the widespread decline of national parliaments and of their traditional subservience to the executive power, it is quite astonishing to read that a "deeply retrograde" Constitutional Treaty "would reverse five centuries of struggle to give representative national parliaments control over public finance and governance generally".[74] Such an assertion only illustrates a great deal of ignorance or deeply held prejudices, or both.

More fundamentally, the key question is whether the displacement of legislative and policy-making activities described above is the product of European integration, or whether the EU represents a rational answer from Member States whose regulatory functions are

---

[70] P. Riddell, *Parliament under Blair* (Politicos, London, 2000), p xiv.

[71] For a general introduction to the theme, see A. McGrew (ed), *The Transformation of Democracy?* (Polity Press, London, 1997).

[72] See D. Wincott, "Does the European Union Pervert Democracy? Questions of Democracy in New Constitutionalist Thought on the Future of Europe", (1998) 4 *European Law Journal* 411.

[73] For a study concluding that the EU has helped national parliaments in their functions as regulators of society, see F. Duina and M. Oliver, "National Parliaments in the European Union: Are There Any Benefits to Integration?", (2005) 11 *European Law Journal* 173.

[74] G. Will, "Europe at the Precipice", *The Washington Post*, 29 May 2005.

being challenged by the corrosive effects of globalisation. In the latter case, it would be paradoxical to reject the idea of European integration on democratic grounds as it offers the most democratic experiment at the supranational level, with the additional political and positive perspective of preserving the 'European way of life'. As Jürgen Habermas puts it:

> "The question therefore is: can any of our small or medium, *entangled and accommodating* nation-states preserve a separate capacity to escape enforced assimilation to the social model now imposed by the predominant global economic regime? ... To the extent that European nations seek a certain re-regulation of the global economy, to counterbalance its undesired economic, social and cultural consequences, they have a reason for building a stronger Union with greater international influence."[75]

This is not to say that everything is for the best, in the best of all possible worlds. Our intention, at this point, was to put into perspective the alleged EU's democratic deficit by emphasising the defects associated with the natural tendency to rely on a somewhat mythical model of parliamentary democracy. Since it is now clear that parliamentary democracy does not operate according to Locke's or Rousseau's standards, it may be more constructive to redefine democracy with the view of adapting it to the peculiar nature of the EU.

---

[75] J. Habermas, "Why Europe needs a Constitution", (2001) 11 *New Left Review* 5, pp 11–12.

CHAPTER FOUR

Refining Democracy for a Non-State and a Non-Nation Polity

In its "standard version", the democratic deficit thesis relies on a rather rudimentary understanding of democracy. The model of democracy that transpires from most critical analyses is an idealised model of parliamentary democracy, more precisely, the "Westminster" model with its majoritarian features. It is, therefore, unsurprising that the EU should be described as some sort of undemocratic *Leviathan*. However, from a conceptual point of view, the appropriateness of the model of parliamentary democracy can be contested. To begin with, the current and unique nature of the EU does not allow for a transposition of national analytical grids. And while a "parliamentarisation" of the Union's decision-making process ought to be welcomed to a certain extent, the adoption of majoritarian mechanisms associated with the model of parliamentary democracy may actually undermine the legitimacy of the EU. Some intellectual gymnastics are therefore required. Firstly, the EU must be understood and, dare we say it, accepted in its originality. In turn, the consensual and relative complexity of the Union's institutional architecture is more likely to be positively assessed. Furthermore, although the results are yet uncertain, the suggested reform of "European governance" as well as the introduction of a model of participatory democracy may well offer some room for further optimism. Undeniably, European institutions are trying to take up the legitimacy challenge and in so doing, they may offer a potentially fruitful redefinition of our classic understanding of democracy.

(I) THE EUROPEAN UNION'S ORIGINAL SYSTEM OF GOVERNMENT

A number of factors, including the strong level of integration of the normative system and the considerable advances of a supranational logic in its institutional architecture, point towards an emerging statehood for the EU. Even though this comparison to a state in the making is defective, it explains why the EU is so often analysed with particular regard to the principles of separation of powers and governmental responsibility before the legislative branch. Inexorably, a damaging diagnosis for the EU ensues, as its original institutional architecture leaves little margin for the straightforward application of these two principles. In turn, this diagnosis usually implies that the only way of addressing the Union's democratic deficit "is to insert 'conventional democratic institutions' into the way the EU makes binding decisions, e.g. assert parliamentary sovereignty, institute direct elections for the President of the Commission and, above all, draft and ratify a 'federal' constitution".[1]

---

[1] Schmitter, "What is there to legitimise in the European Union", p 3.

We should refrain from our natural tendency towards isomorphism and, in particular, our habit of evaluating the EU in light of (idealised) national democratic practices.[2] More fundamentally, one may suggest that the model of parliamentary democracy is not the proper yardstick to evaluate the Union's democratic credentials. For instance, it could be argued that the EU must not be analysed as a primitive political model that must evolve towards some kind of federal "United States of Europe", but as a regulatory structure, a special purpose association, whose main object is to offer more efficiency.[3] If the EU is to be conceptualised as a regulatory structure, input-legitimacy matters less than output-legitimacy. In other words, norms are legitimate because they are produced by actors with a democratic mandate derived from elections and this is more important than "delivering the goods".

As we shall see, the ambition of the new governance agenda is to conciliate legitimacy and efficiency in the context of a redefinition of the notion of democracy. At this point, however, further discussion on the implementation of the principles of separation of powers and governmental responsibility before the legislative branch is required. As a matter of fact, the EU has recently been marked by a phase of increased "parliamentarisation", which should be welcomed. However, as previously stated, such development should not lead to an evaluation of the Union's democratic credentials exclusively in light of the Westminster model of parliamentary democracy. The incomplete parliamentarisation of the Union's institutional architecture could actually be defended on democratic grounds. One may even add that, despite its relative complexity, European decision-making—within the first pillar, i.e. the Community pillar—possibly offers more transparency and accountability than national democracies.

(a) The "Institutional Triangle"

To put it concisely, the EU is built on a relatively complex institutional architecture that is the result of a difficult and permanent bargaining process between the defenders of a supranational scheme of integration for Europe, and the defenders of an "intergovernmental" logic which preserves national sovereignty. It is euphemistic to say that the principle of separation of powers is not conventionally applied.[4] In reality, EC decisions are produced within the so-called "institutional triangle" whose functioning does not entirely comply with the classic canons of a parliamentary democracy.

---

[2] For a stimulating introduction to the inadequacy of critical diagnosis based on analogy with the model of parliamentary democracy, see G. Majone, "Europe's 'Democratic Deficit': The Question of Standards", (1998) 4 *European Law Journal* 5.

[3] See e.g. R. Dehousse, "European Institutional Architecture after Amsterdam: Parliamentary System or Regulatory Structure?", (1998) 35 *Common Market Law Review* 595.

[4] See e.g. K. Lenaerts, "Some Reflections on the Separation of Powers in the European Community", (1991) 28 *Common Market Law Review* 11.

In this "institutional triangle", the Commission embodies the supranational logic at work in the EC. In other words, its mission is to "promote the general interest of the Union and take appropriate initiatives to that end".[5] Among its numerous powers, it is well known that it has the right of legislative initiative, meaning that legislative acts may be adopted solely on the basis of a Commission proposal, except when provisions of the EC Treaty provide otherwise. Both the Council of Ministers and the European Parliament have the formal power to ask the Commission to put forward a proposal. And, in practice, the Commission's monopoly over legislative proposals is relative.[6] In most cases, the Commission puts forward proposals to adapt the current legislation (32.5 percent) or to implement international obligations (30 percent). Furthermore, quite a number of proposals are a direct result of Council or of Parliamentary requests (22.5 percent). A minority of legislative proposals (15 per cent) could then be said to originate from the sole initiative of the Commission.

In any case, the Commission's power over the initiation of legislation should be understood in light of the predominant role played by the Council of Ministers in the decision-making process. On its website, the Council of Ministers actually presents itself as "the main decision-making body of the European Union". Formally known as the Council of the European Union, it embodies the intergovernmental logic at work in the EC. Consisting of a representative of each Member State at ministerial level, it has seen its role constantly expanded over the years. It is the Council's responsibility to enact European "legislation", i.e. Regulations, Directives, Decisions, etc. Depending on the area being regulated, the Council adopts legislative proposals by a simple majority, a qualified majority or by unanimous vote. The Council of Ministers is the Union's true legislature, even though, under the codecision procedure, the European Parliament is said to be on equal footing with it. This is precisely the point raised by numerous critics. Although called a "parliament", the European Parliament does not have, strictly speaking, the power to initiate and the exclusive power to enact laws. It is true that since the first direct elections in 1979, the European Parliament has seen its influence and power greatly strengthened. One could easily get a sense of such reinforcement over the years by simply reading the following new provision inserted into the TEU by the Lisbon Treaty and which consolidates the most important rules concerning the Parliament:

> "The European Parliament shall, jointly with the Council, exercise legislative and budgetary functions. It shall exercise functions of political control and consultation as laid down in the Treaties. It shall elect the President of the Commission."[7]

Nonetheless, in practice, the Parliament can only block the decision-making process when in disagreement with the Council. And if it has the power to dismiss the Commission by

---

[5] New Art 9D TEU.
[6] See Magnette, *Le régime politique de l'Union européenne*, p 106.
[7] New Art 9A(1) TEU.

a motion of censure, the Commission is not, in reality, the main decision-making institution within the EU.

This overview of the institutions composing the "institutional triangle", however brief, helps one understand the sensation of unease often felt by citizens when faced, for the first time, with an institutional system which organises an unusual dissociation between organs and functions. Romano Prodi himself, the president of the European Commission from 1999 to 2004, has admitted his initial difficulty in fully understanding the role of the Commission in this complex decision-making process:

> "Nobody understands this job before being inside here. I knew all the aspects that you can know from outside—all the powers, the duties. But to know how this body [the Commission] works, you have to be inside. For me, it was a great surprise how complicated, how delicate this toy is. But this is why it's so fascinating, because it's not a government. It's not only an executive body because it also proposes legislation. It's not a legislative body because it cannot legislate alone."[8]

Undeniably, within the Community, no institution could be said to exercise a function on an exclusive basis; by the same token, no function is assumed by a single institution. Collaboration between institutions is required if action is to be taken. To summarise, interpenetration of powers and multiple actors characterise the functioning of the European political system. As a result, it is not surprising to see specialists referring to mysterious concepts such as "multilevel governance" to explain the overall institutional framework, and other unique principles such as "institutional balance" to make sense of the interplay between European institutions. The main point here is to understand that by organising an institutional system where the decision-making process is extremely consensual as well as interdependent, the Union's architecture excludes, to a great extent, a parliamentary logic. For instance, the executive power is fragmented between the Commission and the Council. As a result, a key aspect of a parliamentary regime cannot be implemented: the power of the legislative branch to dismiss a well-identified executive power. The legislative power is similarly fragmented between the Council and the European Parliament, hence the notion of "co-legislator". One should add, to the probable horror of Montesquieu, the presence of a European Council, politically and judicially unaccountable, that acts as the supreme political organ of the EU.[9]

There are signs, however, of a trend towards an increased "parliamentarisation" of the EU, hence the "semi-parliamentary" label occasionally used to describe it.[10] Such

---

[8] Quoted in D. Staunton, "Irish EU presidency 'paramount' for Prodi", *The Irish Times*, 23 October 2004.
[9] See Art 4 TEU: "The European Council shall provide the Union with the necessary impetus for its development and shall define the general political guidelines thereof. The European Council shall bring together the Heads of State or Government of the Member States and the President of the Commission".
[10] See P. Magnette, "L'Union européenne: Un régime semi-parlementaire", in P. Delwit and J.-M. de Waele and P. Magnette (eds), *A quoi sert le Parlement européen?* (Éditions Complexe, Bruxelles, 1999), p 25.

parliamentarisation cannot, theoretically, be complete under the current institutional architecture and, in turn, it could be suggested that this goal should not be entertained. The current institutional architecture is based on the rightful idea of "dual legitimacy". In other words, the legitimacy of the Community's institutional architecture flows from two sources: the Council of Ministers, which represents the Member States, and the European Parliament, which is directly elected and represents European citizens.[11] The idea of dual legitimacy explains why a complete parliamentarisation of the institutional architecture cannot be achieved. This is not to say that the Union's limited parliamentarisation ought not to be praised. The paradox is that, while the EU does not claim to be a parliamentary regime, it now appears to function in a more transparent and accountable manner than our formal parliamentary regimes. One may refer, for instance, to the Commission's appointment and dismissal.

(b) The appointment of the Commission

Starting with the Maastricht Treaty, the European Parliament has seen its influence gradually enhanced in the process of nominating the President and members of the European Commission. The nomination of the President must be approved by the Parliament, and the Commission, as a body, must be subject to a vote of approval.[12] An additional interesting feature subjects prospective commissioners to individual questioning by the appropriate committee prior to parliamentary approval.

The Buttiglione affair offered interesting insight on Parliament's strength with regard to these different aspects. Mr Buttiglione, the candidate proposed by former Italian Prime Minister Silvio Berlusconi in 2005, did not, contrary to what is claimed, endure any persecution on account of his religious faith. Professor William Reville, writing in *The Irish Times*, argued that intolerant left-wing European MEPs forced the Italian candidate out.[13] This is, however, a revisionist version of what actually happened. Buttiglione conceded that he would oppose any Commission proposal which ran foul of his moral principles. He also expressed his negative views on homosexuality, which he likened to sin, and on single mothers. The crucial element in *l'affaire Buttiglione* was the portfolio sought by the former Italian minister, that of Justice and Home Affairs. Among the core duties of the post is the obligation to guarantee the enforcement of European anti-discrimination law. It would have been simply astonishing to appoint a candidate who openly argued that his deeply-felt beliefs were completely opposed to the law he would have to serve and implement. In short, the Italian nominee was manifestly unsuitable for

---

[11] Article I-1 of the Constitutional Treaty reaffirmed the Union's dual legitimacy by clearly asserting that it is a union of States and of citizens: "Reflecting the will of the citizens and States of Europe to build a common future, this Constitution establishes the European Union."

[12] Article 214 TEC.

[13] See W. Reville, "How middle-class political correctness holds the sway of power", *The Irish Times*, 25 August 2005.

the post of Justice and Home Affairs Commissioner. Moreover, rather than deride the alleged European secular dictatorship, critics should bear in mind that a majority of MEPs were in favour of moving him to a less controversial post, not to get rid of him.

More fundamentally, the possibility of a negative vote against Mr Barroso's Commission, following his refusal to drop the Italian nominee, was described as an institutional crisis. Is that not merely democracy at work? There is no point in having a Parliament if it cannot have any say and not hold accountable the Commission. The customary rule of individual questioning allows for an intensive scrutiny procedure unseen in Europe at the national level. Once the public hearing is held, a letter is sent by each committee to the President of Parliament and a public vote is held. As a result, this procedure considerably improves accountability and furthermore, offers citizens a prior insight on the prospective Commissioners' ideological views and professional competences. It has been far too long since executives were held accountable by their own parliaments. Sadly media commentators seem not to appreciate the relative vitality of Europe's parliamentary life.

With an identical term of five years and a parliamentary vote of approval following extensive individual scrutiny, one may argue that the current rules already confer a high political profile on the Commission. In comparison, the democratic life in each Member State could certainly be improved if candidates for ministerial posts were submitted to individual questioning, even though it may run against the parliamentary tradition throughout Europe. Individual questioning would make it easy to realise the number of occasions where unsuitable persons for a particular portfolio were somehow nominated, and without the national parliament having the option to say a word. Regardless of the recent politicisation of European's political life, the European Council remains, and we would argue rightly so, the master of the appointment process. Should the pre-eminence of the European Council be interpreted as another sign of the legendary European democratic deficit? If convinced by such rhetoric, an alternative should be offered. Could it be a President of the Commission elected by direct election all across Europe? A good example of democratic absolutism can be found in the following passage:

> "The fact that none of the three officials [Mr Barroso, Mr Juncker and Mr Borrell] had been elected by Europeans as a whole, but rather were appointed to their current posts, only strengthened the sense of detachment between voters and EU institutions."[14]

The commentators further complained that direct democracy remains elusive at the European level.

---

[14] J. Dempsey and K. Bennhold, "EU leaders and voters see paths diverge", *The International Herald Tribune*, 18–19 June 2005.

As we shall see below in more detail, Mr Barroso, the former Portuguese Prime Minister and now the President of the European Commission, was "nominated" by the 25 democratically elected governments of the Member States before his nomination was "approved'"by a majority of democratically elected MEPs. As for Mr Juncker, the democratically elected Prime Minister of Luxembourg, he held the presidency of the Council for six months without the need to be appointed. Indeed, in the name of democracy and perfect equality between countries, the current rules allow for the presidency to be held by each Member State in turn for six months. Finally, regarding Mr Borrell, a former Spanish elected official and now the President of the European Parliament, he was elected to this position by his peers after having been elected to Parliament by direct universal suffrage.

More fundamentally, the idea of direct election for the president of the European Commission is another illustration of a cultural mindset unable to escape from state-centric thinking. More worryingly, it also reveals some constitutional ignorance, classically associated with double-standard assessment. In too many instances, extravagant democratic reforms are demanded from the EU under the illusion that national democracies have put into practice similar mechanisms. Whatever about so-called "presidential" parliamentary elections, there is no actual direct election for selecting the Prime Minister in parliamentary regimes. The Prime Minister would certainly be locally elected as an MP. Yet, he or she will become Prime Minister, strictly speaking, on the sole ground of being the victorious leader of a political party, that party having selected his or her leader beforehand, without asking citizens' opinion. In other words, it is wrong to assume that electors directly decide on the identity of the Prime Minister; rather they select the leader of the country from a pool of names put forward by political parties. Similarly, it is also wrong to assume that national ministers are always elected officials. It is relatively pleasant to loudly assert one's preference for more "accountability" and "democracy" as far as the Commission is concerned. As always, the devil lies in the detail. In most cases, unfortunately, democracy-lovers fall short on specifics—apart from relying on their own national model or on an idealised version of the American model of democracy—when details should be put on the table.

Jens-Peter Bonde, a Danish MEP, argues that it is time to allow the people of each state to "elect their own commissioner and make him or her accountable to one's national parliament".[15] Coming from one of the leading eurosceptics in the European Parliament, it appears difficult to reconcile such a proposal with a deep-seated opposition to the emergence of a European "superstate". The direct election of each commissioner would likely lead to the materialisation of a European government that would compete with the representatives of national executives for political leadership at Union level. This position also presupposes some form of direct election by the people as a whole. In most European

---

[15] J.-P. Bonde, "Seven steps to a more democratic, more transparent European Union", *The Irish Times*, 11 August 2005.

democracies, however, the prime minister is, strictly speaking, only locally elected. In other words, the implementation of such a reform would transfigure the EU and grant the Commission unprecedented political capital. Finally, and more pragmatically, it must be said that the most vociferous critics are often from Member States where governments have regularly ruled out any idea of pan-European election for any European official on grounds of sovereignty. One should also stress that the United States, with its famous electoral college, does not offer a better example of "direct democracy". Strictly speaking, not even the President is directly elected by Americans "as a whole", to quote the Union's harsh critics previously mentioned. The European's institutional architecture and decision-making process merely reflect the twofold legitimacy of the EU as a union of States and of citizens. In this context, the consensual and cumbersome process overshadowing the selection of the President of the Commission could be better understood.

In line with the Constitutional Treaty, the Lisbon Treaty embodies the latest evolution towards a stronger politicisation of the institutional triangle's functioning. The European Council, acting by qualified majority, will now have to take into account elections to the European Parliament, as reflected in the proportionate division of ideological allegiances, when proposing a candidate for President of the Commission. In turn, this candidate shall be elected by a majority of the component members of the European Parliament. The term "elected" does not appear in the current EC Treaty, as the President of the Commission should merely be "approved". The obligation for the European Council to consider the results of the European Parliament's elections is also new. Even though these changes are mostly semantic, they show the willingness to remedy the current asymmetry between the Member States and the European Parliament when it comes to selecting the President of the Commission. As for the fact that the Member States do not always nominate the most qualified candidate, it would be unfair to blame "Europe".

As the Taoiseach realised during his search for a candidate in June 2004, the involvement of multiple actors may not absolutely exclude the recruitment of the most competent candidate, but it certainly does not pay to be too smart or too independent-minded. Occasionally, the successful candidate can be both. For instance, Jacques Delors, the venerated Commission president from 1985 to 1994, whose vision and effective leadership remains indisputable, was selected quite awkwardly. His appointment was apparently due to the dislike of the German Chancellor Helmut Kohl for who then appeared to be the "natural" candidate for the post, the German foreign minister, Hans-Dietrich Genscher. François Mitterrand had another man in mind but agreed to Kohl's proposal to nominate Jacques Delors, then the French Finance Minister. In an enlarged and more polarised EU, the task of Bertie Ahern was more challenging: he had to find a candidate who would be neither federalist nor too liberal, with a few additional requirements, such as speaking French and coming from a "small" Member State. In light of these political constraints, it is unsurprising that the selection of José Manuel Durão Barroso in June 2004, the then Portuguese Prime Minister, appeared to reflect the lowest-common denominator.

Critics have also complained about the lack of transparency in the selection process. As already argued, no democracy offers the example of political leaders chosen by the citizens. For instance, in the United Kingdom, Gordon Brown's "coronation" mid-term was not sanctified by a general election. Similarly, although the comparison is imperfect, due to the French Constitution's original parliamentary regime, the French Prime Minister is appointed according to the sovereign choice of the President. Remarkably, one can be appointed without having ever been elected to the national Parliament or to a local assembly. The latest example is Dominique de Villepin. Even worse, in a multi-party system, as opposed to a two-party system, the citizens may find themselves with a government that does not represent the most successful political party, but which is the fruit of arrangements between political parties after the elections are held. With these examples in mind, the selection of a candidate by the European Council cannot be said to be less "democratic" nor less "transparent". On the contrary, the merits of potential candidates were debated for weeks.

The idea of European-wide elections for the President of the Commission, or for the entire team of Commissioners, betrays a profound misunderstanding of the EU. Such a scheme would only be justified if the goal of setting up a federal parliamentary state is regarded as a fruitful one for Europe. Unfortunately, it remains quite common to hear from detractors of a European federal state, even educated ones, unsubstantiated criticism on the grounds that "too much of its laws emanates from an unelected and unaccountable commission for it to enjoy legitimacy".[16] Not only is the Commission accountable, the preservation of the current dual legitimacy of the EU requires that it not be elected. To call for the direct election of the President of the Commission by the European citizens as a whole or by national parliaments, would certainly be an enormous step towards the creation of a federal entity. In other words, critics and, in particular, eurosceptics, should be careful about what they wish for!

The preservation of the current dual legitimacy of the EU implies that the essential goal is to balance the influence of the Member States with a stronger authority for the European Parliament. This goal was satisfactorily achieved by the drafters of the Constitutional Treaty. As previously mentioned, the European Council will be under the obligation to take elections to the European Parliament into account, thus allowing a connection between the choices made by citizens all across Europe with the political colour of the selected candidate to the presidency of the Commission. Certainly, the legitimacy of the EU would not suffer if political parties were to agree, prior to European elections, on a name for the presidency of the Commission. There is no legal obstacle for doing so. As for the composition of the Commission, another reform can be proposed. It would also be positive to see each Member State submitting a list of three persons, in which both genders will be

---

[16] Ferguson, *Colossus*, p 256.

represented.[17] The elected President of the Commission would then have the freedom to choose from among the three names. Such a mechanism would avoid the nomination of controversial national candidates and would offer the President of the Commission the option to shape his team to a greater extent. As always, if the blame game must be played, one should not forget that it is the Member States who are reluctant to increase transparency and efficiency, as the price to be paid would certainly be an attenuation of national control in the appointment process. In other words, more "democracy" would certainly be detrimental to the eurosceptics' most cherished value, national sovereignty.

(c) The dismissal of the Commission

The power of the legislative branch to dismiss the executive—which implies the right of the government to dissolve the Parliament—is often described as the quintessence of a parliamentary democracy. Due to the specific nature of European institutional arrangements, the principle of separation of powers cannot be applied *in extenso*. All the same, since its inception, the EC Treaty permits the European Parliament to pass a motion of censure against the Commission. As with the situation in all Member States, a few conditions surround this possibility: a two-thirds majority of the votes cast is required, representing a majority of Parliament's members, in which case the Commission must resign as a body. One interesting fact is that there have been only seven motions of censure since 1957 and a successful one has yet to be passed. The last unsuccessful motion, involving the Santer Commission, obtained 232 votes to 293 in January 1999. Would the Community suffer from a comparison with the Member States? Certainly not, as the power to dismiss the government has simply been lost at national level for a range of reasons, among them, one may mention the so-called rationalisation of parliamentary rules and a more disciplined partisan system. But to focus exclusively on the European Parliament's political control over the Commission, it could be argued that the Commission is subject to more practical accountability than national governments.

The Santer episode is indicative of the potential for significant scrutiny which hangs over the Commission. The European Parliament, in exercising its supervisory role, set up a Committee of Independent Experts, with a mandate to investigate fraud and mismanagement within the Commission. While no commissioner was found to be directly or personally involved in fraud or in personal enrichment, the publication of the Committee of Independent Experts' first report led to the resignation of the Commission *en bloc*. The 144-page report made clear that it was becoming difficult to find anyone in the Commission with the slightest sense of responsibility. The Santer Commission assumed the criticism and resigned. It would be wrong to presuppose from this episode that only

---

[17] The draft Constitutional Treaty, as submitted in July 2003 to the European Council, provided that each Member State "shall establish a list of three persons, in which both genders shall be represented, whom it considers qualified to be a European Commissioner". Following the opposition of some national governments, this provision was later withdrawn.

European institutions and in particular, the European Commission, are prone to fraud, mismanagement or nepotism.[18] In Ireland, for instance, in the so-called "illegal nursing home charges" case, no minister resigned in a situation where the bill could reach €2 billion (almost two percent of the EC annual budget!). Remarkably, after reading a report of the Oireachtas Health and Children Committee, where it was said that there was "an urgent need" to clarify "the responsibilities of Ministers and the extent to which they can reasonably be held accountable for the actions of the department and agencies under their charge", Mr Kevin Murphy rightly expressed his amazement. The former Ombudsman said he was "appalled" that such a statement could be made after "80 years of parliamentary democracy", adding: "I think that the great parliamentarians that we have had the privilege to serve will be turning, if not squirming, in their grave".[19] To end this brief yet depressing review, it could well be argued that political scrutiny and sense of accountability are more developed at the Commission level. It would be clearly noticeable if incompetence, mismanagement or cases of nepotism were followed by governmental or individual resignation in a majority of Member States. To put it more bluntly, it appears that some media, especially those from the Rupert Murdoch's stable, have developed a high moral sense only with regard to EU institutions.

If the trend towards parliamentarisation is to be praised for raising standards of accountability, it would be unwise to call for total parliamentarisation. What appears to be more important is to politicise the Community's decision making-process, meaning to introduce debate and offer policy alternatives rather than replicate a national model of government. The secret hope of the Community's founding fathers was certainly to see the Commission emerging progressively as some sort of federal government responsible before the European Parliament. It did not happen and is unlikely to happen. It can further be argued that the current system of government must be preserved. It reflects an original balance between two sources of legitimacy: the States in the name of their peoples and the citizens directly represented in the European Parliament. With a European Parliament now standing as a "co-legislator", alongside the Council of Ministers, the Union's institutional architecture does not demonstrate, in any case, less attachment to democratic principles. Both institutions can claim perfect democratic legitimacy: The European Parliament directly represents European citizens at Union level; the Council of Ministers represent national governments which are democratically accountable to their national parliaments and to their citizens. In reality, it would be unwise, and one may even say undemocratic, to push for a complete "democratisation" of the Union's institutional architecture. Contrary to popular wisdom, the strict implementation of a majority rule and

---

[18] For a study concluding that the Commission remains a clean, high-performance bureaucracy when compared with other administrations in Europe, see e.g. J. Peterson, "The Santer Era: The European Commission in Historical, Theoretical and Normative Perspective", (1999) 6 *Journal of European Public Policy* 46.

[19] M. Hennessy, "Murphy wants Ministers to take blame", *The Irish Times*, 6 June 2005.

the transplantation of the mechanisms associated with the national model of parliamentary democracy would, in all likelihood, undermine the Union's legitimacy.

(II) THE PERILS OF A PURELY MAJORITARIAN DEMOCRATIC SYSTEM

In the 2003 version of the Constitutional Treaty presented by the former French President Valéry Giscard d'Estaing, the preamble was headed with an exquisite quotation from Thucydides:

> "Our Constitution … is called a democracy because power is in the hands not of a minority but of the greatest number."

Quoting philosophical ancestors is a common mannerism within the French political élite. To the probable disappointment of the former French President, however, the Taoiseach Bertie Ahern, under the Irish Presidency of the Council, decided not to retain the quotation despite some ultimate desperate attempts from Greece and Cyprus. Some delicate minds had previously argued about the inaccurate translation or the apocryphal character of the quotation from the author of *The History of the Peloponnesian War*. It certainly did not help that Thucydides expressed his admiration for Pericles, whose concept of democracy does not exactly fit modern standards with its exclusion of women, foreigners and slaves from citizenship.

The heart of the discussion was, nonetheless, about the merits of a quotation solely emphasising a demographic criterion, a population principle. Some Member States were keen on insisting that the EU is, first and foremost, a union of States. Needless to say, the quotation finally succumbed to such demand. Indeed, to refer to the reservation formulated by Kalypso Nicolaïdis, one could wonder "how and on which scale should this greatest number be counted in a Union which is closer to the federation of city-states of Thucydides' times than to ancient Athens?"[20] A strong case could be made against encompassing the European Parliament with the sole power of passing legislation to the detriment of the Council of Ministers, no matter how difficult it is to reconcile the intergovernmental body with the separation of powers doctrine of Montesquieu. Interestingly, this view could be defended on legitimacy grounds as opposed to democratic requirements and efficiency imperatives. This is an important point. The usual suspects—democracy and legitimacy—are typically seen as being closely associated. Yet, being too "democratic" may actually undermine the legitimacy of the EU.

(a) Majority-Voting in a Heterogeneous Polity

Could EU law be more "legitimate" solely by being the product of a majoritarian decision-making process? Such democratisation could actually produce more tension than

---

[20] K. Nicolaïdis, "Our European Demoi-cracy. Is this Constitution a Third Way for Europe?", in K. Nicolaïdis and S. Weatherill (eds), *Whose Europe? National Models and the Constitution of the European Union* (Oxford University Press, Oxford, 2003), p 151.

legitimacy for the EU. The key element here is the degree of homogeneity of the European polity. In short, national democracies can only satisfactorily function if there is a sense of common identity and social solidarity, meaning that citizens are willing to obey the rule of the majority and to sacrifice, if necessary, their private interests, in the name of the "general interest" or "national interest". As explained by Fritz Scharpf,

> "[U]nitary legitimation of majority decisions is not an available option under any and all conditions. It presupposes the existence of a 'community' with a collective identity, which implies that in regard to particular issues citizens are in principle prepared to treat their fellow citizens' interests as their own. It is only where this is the case that the minority need not fear exploitation, oppression or annihilation by the ruling majority; and it is only where this is the case that measures amounting to redistribution at the expense of individual interests will be considered acceptable."[21]

The question, therefore, is whether the European polity is "homogeneous" enough, if the sense of solidarity is sufficiently developed for each national polity to obey the rule of a hypothetical European majority. It can safely be affirmed that the European polity is more heterogeneous than homogeneous. Richard Bellamy rightly underscores it:

> "Eurobarometer polls have consistently shown, a very small percentage of European citizens identify themselves as Europeans. Most view themselves as nationals first and foremost, with their allegiance to the EU being linked to (and to some degree conditional upon) its perceived positive benefits for them as citizens of a Member State."[22]

The situation is unlikely to change if only for the simple reason that Member States and their own citizenry remain predominantly proud of their national identities. As the EU is, ultimately, the product of the Member States' will, it is not surprising to find this attachment to national identity solemnly enunciated in the Preamble of the Constitutional Treaty: "CONVINCED that, while remaining proud of their own national identities and history, the peoples of Europe are determined to transcend their former divisions and, united ever more closely, to forge a common destiny." The reference to a common destiny does not imply that the EU pursues the goal of erasing national identities and replacing them with a unique sense of identity, thus reproducing the model of the nation-state. We shall return to this debate. The essential point, here, is that

> "[T]he heterogeneity of the European polity is such that the adoption of a purely majoritarian system, in which decisions can be taken by a majority of representatives

---

[21] F. Scharpf, "Democratic Policy in Europe", (1996) 2 *European Law Journal* 136, p 137.
[22] R. Bellamy, "Which Constitution for What Kind of Europe? Three Models of European Constitutionalism", Paper for the CIDEL Workshop on Constitution-making and Democratic Legitimacy in the EU, London, 12–13 November 2004, p 9 (study available at: http://www.arena.uio.no/cidel).

of the people, is difficult to conceive. The lack of any strong collective identity makes it difficult to believe that minorities would easily accept that their fate be decided against their will."[23]

In short, the adoption of a national model of representative democracy at Union level—direct democracy would not fare better—would likely lead to the demise of European integration.

Viewed in this light, the originality of the Union's institutional architecture, with its complex mix of supranational and intergovernmental elements, could be positively assessed. In other words, to preserve the legitimacy of the EU, it may well be argued that the essential role played by the Member States must be preserved. This is not to say that Member States should overwhelmingly dominate the decision-making process. Such consideration merely underlines the complexity of democratisation at the European level. Critics keen on emphasising the Union's democratic deficit should acknowledge that the legitimacy of European action may sometimes be at odds with the imperatives of efficiency and democracy, especially when the latter concept is equated to traditional parliamentarian mechanisms applied at national level.

For instance, one may refer to the cumbersome rules which govern voting within the Council of Ministers. The Treaties define cases where a simple majority, qualified majority or unanimity votes are required. As a rule, the Council of Ministers must act by a majority of its Members. Yet, in practice, the exception became the rule. A strong search for consensus pervades the entire decision-making process within the Council.[24] Furthermore, in extreme circumstances, Member States could always invoke "the Luxembourg Comprise" to veto a legislative proposal, even though unanimity is not required.[25] Undeniably, a permanent search for consensus may be detrimental to efficient action. As argued by Joseph Weiler, the legitimacy of European action may, all the same, require a thirst for consensual decision-making. The eminent author went as far as to argue, in 1991, that the shift to majority voting might actually be the root cause of the Union's legitimacy problem:

"The legitimacy of the output of the Community decisional process was, thus, at least partially due to the public knowledge that it was controllable through the veto power.

---

[23] Dehousse, "European governance in search of legitimacy", p 171.

[24] See e.g. M. Mattila and J.-E. Lane, "Why Unanimity in the Council? A Roll Call Analysis of Council Voting", (2001) 2 *European Union Politics* 31. The authors argue that unanimous decision-making is much more frequent than commonly assumed and that the probability of voting against the Council majority varies greatly between the Council members.

[25] The Luxembourg compromise brought to an end the so-called "empty chair" crisis initiated by France in 1965 over some financial considerations and majority-voting. The compromise, agreed in January 1966, allows a Member State, in the name of preserving "very important interests", to call for its partners to reach unanimous agreement even though the relevant decision can be taken by majority vote. The legality of the Luxembourg compromise has never been tested.

The current shift to majority voting might therefore exacerbate legitimacy problems. Even an enhanced European Parliament, which would operate on a co-decision principle, will not necessarily solve the legitimacy problem. The legitimacy crisis does not derive principally from the accountability issue at the European level, but from the very redefinition of the European polity."[26]

Majority-voting within the Council, however, is far from a duplication of the classic democratic principle according to which one person equals one vote. It also departs from the principle in international law according to which one State equals one vote, a principle which appears to be favoured by Weiler. In fact, the system of majority-voting is organised on a subtle weighting of votes reflecting population differentials, yet in an adjusted manner, gives appropriate weight to "small" Member States.

Following the entry into force of the Nice Treaty, the "big four" —Germany, France, Italy and the UK—are granted with 29 votes, "medium" states such Belgium, Greece or Portugal are allocated a number of 12 votes. In the "small" camp, one may note the seven votes attributed to Ireland or the four votes attributed to Luxembourg. A qualified majority is reached whenever the following two conditions are met: a majority of Member States approve (some provisions demand a two-thirds majority); or a minimum of 255 votes is cast in favour of the proposal, i.e. 73.9 percent of the total of the number of votes allocated to the 27 Member States. A simple comparison between the number of votes allocated and the size of the population of each "large" Member States makes it easy to realise that the system gives overrepresentation to Member States with small population. For instance, Ireland, with seven votes for four million people, is almost five times better "represented" than Germany with 29 votes for 80 million people. Similarly, the composition of the European Parliament demonstrates strong distortions in representativeness. The rule is that "representation of citizens shall be degressively proportional".[27] In practice, this means that a Luxembourg MEP currently represents approximately 70,000 citizens, while a Swede MEP represents 400,000 citizens, an Italian MEP 660,000 and a German MEP 820,000. "Small" Member States consequently benefit from an *overwhelming* overrepresentation. For that reason, their representatives would be well-advised not to complain too loudly about an alleged democratic deficit. However, the biggest Member States would certainly be entitled to protest about a lack of democracy, on the grounds of imperfect demographic representativeness.

Caution must then be required from the Union's critics, too keen on promoting a model of representative democracy without thinking through the consequences of their mantra. The originality of the decision-making process within the Council must be

---

[26] J. Weiler, "The Transformation of Europe", (1991) 100 *Yale Law Journal* 2403, p 2473.
[27] According to new Art 9A TEU, "representation of citizens shall be degressively proportional, with a minimum threshold of six members per Member State". Article 190 TEC currently speaks of ensuring an "appropriate representation of the peoples of the States brought together in the Community".

understood for what it is: the search for a system constantly guaranteeing that decisions are taken with the largest possible support while avoiding a situation where a coalition of large or small countries could impose its will on the other. The criterion of demographic representativeness has always been secondary to these purposes. To the layman, the majority-voting scheme may certainly appear cumbersome. One must understand, however, that the Council will always search for consensus even where the Treaties provide for a qualified majority vote. Indeed, efficiency is far from being the prime concern of the Member States.[28] This was again evident in 2004 when the Member States refused to adopt the new simplified definition of qualified majority suggested by the European Convention in 2003 and according to which qualified majority would have consisted of the majority of Member States, representing at least three-fifths of the Union's population. The idea of a "double-majority system" was, however, saved after the Member States finally agreed to raise the thresholds required for a decision to be adopted by qualified majority. Reproducing the provisions of the Constitutional Treaty, the Lisbon Treaty requires a decision to be taken by 55 percent of the members of the Council (threshold increased from 50 percent initially), comprising at least 15 of them (new condition) and representing at least 65 percent of the Union's population (from 60 percent initially).[29] Furthermore, to limit the potential blocking power of the most populous countries, it was also agreed that a blocking minority must include at least four Member States. This rule was specifically designed to prevent three out of the four biggest Member States (France, Germany, Italy and the United Kingdom) to block a decision.

Polish opposition to the new voting system on the absurd grounds that it would reduce its influence while increasing Germany's while Nazi Germany was responsible for population losses Poland incurred in 1939–1945, led to an awkward compromise in June 2007: the double majority voting system will only take effect in November 2014, until which date the present qualified majority system will continue to apply.[30] Regardless of the merits of this compromise and without going into the mathematics, it can be argued that the Lisbon Treaty merely offers the promise of a slightly more straightforward and effective voting procedure than the current EC Treaty. The explanation lies in the fact that Member States' first concern is to preserve their room for manoeuvre and, ultimately, their potential power to block decisions. One should also remember that numerous domains — taxation, harmonisation in the field of social security, EU finances, EU membership, etc. — are still formally governed by unanimity voting within the Council of Ministers.

---

[28] On the "politics of size" and the work of the European Convention, see P. Magnette and K. Nicolaïdis, "Large and Small Member States in the European Union: Reinventing the Balance", *Notre Europe*, Research and European Issues, No. 25, 2003.

[29] See new Art 9C TEU. Increased thresholds apply when the Council of Minister does *not* act on the proposal of the Commission or the EU "minister for foreign affairs".

[30] To make things worse, an extra concession was obtained by the twin brothers governing Poland: during a transitional period until March 2017, when a decision is to be adopted by qualified majority, a member of the Council may request that the decision be taken in accordance with the qualified majority as defined in Art 205(2) of the present TEC.

Regarding the democratic credentials of the voting system within the Council of Ministers, it is important to single out two of its most significant features: a strong search for consensus and a positively disproportionate representation of "small" Member States. Accordingly, the voting system could be "democratically" justified if one believes that individuals' primary allegiances remain with their state. It is also possible to defend the current voting system on the grounds that a plurality of majorities actually reinforces Europe as a political entity. If Europe ought to truly respect its proposed constitutional motto "United in Diversity", it is entirely correct to argue, as Philippe Schmitter so convincingly does, that "it is neither feasible nor desirable to try to democratize the European Union *tutto e sùbito*—completely and immediately. Not only would the politicians not know how to do it, but there is also no compelling evidence that Europeans want it."[31] Too often, critics analyse the EU through a national democratic prism without paying due attention to its original "dual legitimacy". It is important, however, to point out that the EU reflects "the will of the citizens and States of Europe to build a common future".[32] The eurosceptics, promoters of the democratic deficit charge, simply do not push their logic to its final consequence. They incessantly complain about a lack of democracy, primarily with reference to an idealised national model of parliamentary democracy, a model they would not actually wish to see emerging. It could lead, indeed, to the quality of statehood being granted to the EU. In essence, what is usually labelled anti-democratic is therefore an institutional architecture which is justified by the original nature of Europe. The argument could be pushed further. What is labelled anti-democratic may well be described as a highly democratic system of government if one understands democracy as a system of government where the rights of minorities are effectively guaranteed. As Kalypso Nicolaïdis argues:

> "[T]he numerous forms of democratic safeguards embedded in its decision making procedures and institutional structures (super-majorities and vetoes, involvement of four different institutions, role of the national capitals in drafting laws) guarantee that no interest will be trampled on. It may be imperfect, but the EU level of democracy compares favorably with the level of democracy in its member states."[33]

As European integration is an experiment in building a common future while preserving Europe's pluralism, it is positive to see a decision-making process effectively guaranteeing that national views are taken into consideration even though the price to pay is a cumbersome decision-making process. With a Europe made of a number of *demoi*, there is no choice but to work with an original and relatively complex institutional architecture which excludes the direct transplantation of constitutional mechanisms associated with national democracies. Perplexingly, however, the very fact that Europe is not made of a

---

[31] Schmitter, "What is there to legitimise in the European Union", p 3.
[32] Article I-1 EU CT.
[33] Nicolaïdis, "Our European Demoi-cracy", p 139.

single *demos* is sometimes considered to be a general obstacle for the EU to ever claim to be democratic.

(b) Democracy Without a *Demos*

According to the argument previously exposed, the adoption of a pure majoritarian democratic system would be fraught with problems and might undermine the overall legitimacy of the EU. That is not to say that the EU cannot be democratic until there is a European *demos*. Nonetheless, this is the claim made by some distinguished authors and, significantly, by the German Federal Constitutional Court. It is difficult to do full justice to the "no-demos" thesis in a few sentences. To put it concisely, this thesis actually pushes the democratic deficit charge further, by arguing that the EU, as a matter of principle, cannot be "democratic" as it is characterised by a weak collective identity.[34] As summarised by Joseph Weiler, in a challenging article dissecting the previously mentioned German Maastricht decision:

"Soft version or hard, the consequences of the No Demos thesis for the European construct are interesting. The rigorous implication of this view would be that absent a demos, there cannot, by definition, be a democracy or democratization at the European level. This is not a semantic proposition. On this reading, European democracy (meaning a minimum binding majoritarian decision-making at the European level) without a demos is no different from the previously mentioned German-Danish anschluss except on a larger scale. Giving the Danes a vote in the Bundestag is, as argued, ice cold comfort. Giving them a vote in the European Parliament or Council is, conceptually, no different."[35]

Concerning the key question on how to guarantee the democratic legitimacy of the EU, the German Constitutional Court argued that it is conceptually impossible for the minority to obey the will of a European majority, as individuals do not belong to the same *demos*. Consequently, democratisation is unlikely until a European *demos* emerges. It is further argued that no European *demos* is likely to emerge as long as certain "subjective" (sense of community and loyalty) and "objective" (common language, common culture, etc.) elements are not met.

Without questioning the desirability of a European people, the German Court's exclusive definition of a "people" is open to criticism. Educated by the reading of Ernest

---

[34] "What obstructs democracy is accordingly not the lack of cohesion of Union citizens as a people, but their weakly developed collective identity and low capacity for transnational discourse. This certainly means that the European democracy deficit is structurally determined", D. Grimm, "Does Europe Need a Constitution?", (1995) 1 *European Law Journal* 282 at 297.

[35] J. Weiler, "Does Europe Need a Constitution? Demos, Telos and the German Maastricht Decision", (1995) 1 *European Law Journal* 219 at 230.

Renan more so than of Johann Fichte,[36] with a positive predisposition towards *ius soli* rather than *ius sanguinis* and the idea of a "civic nation" rather than of an "ethnic nation", we instinctively experience some unease with a vision that predominantly defines collective identity by reference to "objective" elements, such as a common language, a common history, common cultural habits, etc. The ethnic connotations, the emphasis on the necessary homogeneity of a European *demos* are clear. Indeed, a *demos*, i.e. a people deriving from a collective identity, is presumed impossible, without the objective elements mentioned above. Yet, the history of an old nation-state such as France[37] or a more recent one such as Italy,[38] demonstrates that these two countries have formally existed well before developing a strong national identity. Without extensively debating how appropriate the assumed necessary link between ethno-cultural criteria and a sense of collective self-identity and of shared destiny is,[39] it could be suggested that the German vision is considerably at odds with the progressive evolution of modern societies towards increased multiculturalism, notwithstanding the existence of the EU. It may be further argued that citizens may feel a (subjective) sense of community, for instance in plurinational democracies, without sharing predominant ethno-cultural traits with their fellow citizens. A sense of community could also be constructed on what Jürgen Habermas has called "constitutional patriotism" (*Verfassungspatriotismus*). Then, social cohesion is mostly derived from an attachment to the fundamental values of a polity, as embodied in a constitutional text, and from the right to participate in the governing of the polity. In turn, such attachment and participation guarantee loyalty to the polity. The rule of the "majority" is thus obeyed by the "minority" without the need for each individual to be part of an homogeneous *demos*. This is not to deny, however, that the bond of social unity may be more fragile than with a community whose identity is founded on some ethno-cultural criteria.

In any event, one may argue that the possibility or the desirability of a European *demos* or the relevance of the *ethnos-demos-politeia* sequence should not even be contemplated. The crucial, unexpressed syllogism in the no-demos approach is to compare the EU with

---

[36] Even though Ernest Renan argued in his famous speech delivered at the Sorbonne in 1882, *Qu'est-ce qu'une nation*, that a nation presupposes a past (a "glorious heritage") and a readiness to sacrifice oneself, importantly, the French philosopher set aside the notion of race, language or religion as the prerequisite elements of any nation. In his words, a nation's existence is a daily plebiscite. This "romantic" vision can be contrasted with the views of Johann Fichte. Although a supporter of the French Revolution, he finally encouraged the development of German nationalism when Napoleonic armies occupied Berlin. In his *Speeches to the German Nation* (1808), he identified the existence of a German nation on "ethnic" terms.

[37] In 1789, less than 50 percent of the people spoke French. For further references, see J. Rifkin, *The European Dream* (Polity, London, 2004), p 168.

[38] After Italian formal unification in 1861, Massimo d'Azeglio was said to have remarked: "We have made Italy, now we have to make Italians", quoted in J. Rifkin, *ibid.*, p 167.

[39] On the thesis that the nation-state is more an artificial construct created by political and economic élites, than an organic creation rooted in objective elements of collective identity, see B. Anderson, *Imagined Communities: Reflections on the Origin and Spread of Nationalism* (Verso, London, 1991).

a mythical and exclusive vision of the nation-state: "At the root of the No Demos thesis is ultimately a world view which is enslaved to the concepts of *Volk*, *Staat* and *Staatsangehöriger* and cannot perceive the Community or Union in anything other than those terms."[40] This is not the appropriate way of thinking about the EU as a political object. To fruitfully assess the EU, one must go beyond the traditional concepts of constitutional law and realise that conventional dichotomies may not offer the appropriate tools for understanding the European experience. Citizenship, as with other cardinal legal concepts of Western thought, such as the concepts of state and of sovereignty, are historical products, the fruits of contingent circumstances. An exercise of redefinition and of polycentric thinking must, therefore, be undertaken to make sense of Europe. The main argument, here, is that democracy could be put into practice by an association of *demoi*, united around shared values and objectives, without the need to envisage the creation of a European *demos* on the basis of common ethno-cultural traits.

A European sense of community does not have to derive from ethno-cultural similarities. It may be built around shared civic values, embodied in a fundamental text, a social contract that each national *demos* would have approved and from which it is free to withdraw. As Kalypso Nicolaïdis puts it: "The sense of belonging and commitment to the European Union ought to be based on the *doing* more that the *being*, on shared projects and ambitions, both internal and external."[41] Some may argue that there is no European identity, no European political culture. Despite obvious philosophical, religious and cultural bonds, the argument stands if the idea of collective identity is understood in the exclusive context of the nation-state. While a comprehensive case has still to be made, a European layer of identity is emerging, one built on abstract shared values and objectives, adding to our sense of national and local identity originally built on ethno-cultural similarities. For instance, despite the divisions it created among European governments, the illegal war in Iraq appeared to have explicitly demonstrated that a European identity may be emerging, at least by opposition to the values pushed by the Bush administration. Jeremy Rifkin's work may help in the realisation that, regardless of our perpetual and heated debates on the European Union's *finalité*, there is a clear European set of values:

> "The European Dream emphasizes community relationship over individual autonomy, cultural diversity over assimilation, quality of life over the accumulation of wealth, sustainable development over unlimited material growth, deep play over unrelenting toil, universal human rights and the rights of nature over property rights, and global cooperation over the unilateral exercise of power."[42]

The prolific American writer based his work on the progressive crystallisation of a European dream, in light of the values and objectives enshrined in the Constitutional

---

[40] Weiler, "Does Europe Need a Constitution", p 244.
[41] Nicolaïdis, "Our European Demoi-cracy", p 146.
[42] Rifkin, *The European Dream*, p 3.

Treaty. The text, which the Lisbon Treaty mostly reproduces, offers a compelling digest of shared European civic values, around which each of us could develop a sense of constitutional patriotism:

> "The Union is founded on the values of respect for human dignity, freedom, democracy, equality, the rule of law and respect for human rights, including the rights of persons belonging to minorities. These values are common to the Member States in a society in which pluralism, non-discrimination, tolerance, justice, solidarity and equality between women and men prevail."[43]

By attachment to these values, the EU should pursue a certain number of objectives.[44] Internally, the Union's aim is to promote the "well-being" of citizens, to offer them an area of freedom, security and justice, a single market, "to work for the sustainable development of Europe based on balanced economic growth and price stability, a highly competitive social market economy, aiming at full employment and social progress, and a high level of protection and improvement of the quality of the environment". The EU shall also promote scientific and technological innovation, social justice and protection, equality between women and men, solidarity between generations and protection of the rights of the child, economic, social and territorial cohesion and solidarity among Member States. In the international arena, the EU "shall contribute to peace, security, the sustainable development of the Earth, solidarity and mutual respect among peoples, free and fair trade, eradication of poverty and the protection of human rights, in particular the rights of the child, as well as to the strict observance and the development of international law, including respect for the principles of the United Nations Charter".

The clear—and inescapably long—enunciation of these objectives should be praised as it finally offers, in a systematic manner, what the EU stands for. On a sole reading of Art 2 TEU, as amended by the Lisbon Treaty, any citizen could understand the meaning of the Union's unofficial[45] motto: "United in diversity". The word diversity should be understood as the fundamental recognition of our rich national identities and democratic traditions. And while European integration is about building a common future, Europeans do so on the basis of shared abstract values and objectives. It does not and shall not imply giving up one's national sense of identity through the establishment of a "superstate", in which a European *demos* would absorb the European *demoi*. United in diversity is not to be confused, for instance, with the American motto: *E pluribus unum*, "out of many, one". Diversity, in the European context, should be positively praised and preserved.

---

[43] See new Art 1a TEU (formerly Art I-2 EU CT).

[44] See new Art 2 TEU (formerly Art I-3 EU CT).

[45] The Member States agreed in June 2007 that the Lisbon Treaty will not reproduce Art I-8 of the Constitutional Treaty on the "symbols of the Union".

The association of national citizenships with European citizenship offers a fruitful path for the future of the EU by overcoming traditional dichotomies, by going beyond state-centric thinking and by legitimising plurality. Introduced in 1992 by the Maastricht Treaty, the notion of "citizenship of the Union" is additional to national citizenship, in other words, it *complements* and does not replace national citizenship.[46] The Lisbon Treaty does not alter the present, original, yet limited, regime. The rights of European citizens include the traditional rights to move and reside freely within the territory of the Member States;[47] the right to vote and stand as candidates in municipal and European Parliament elections in their Member State of residence under the same conditions as nationals of that state; the right to diplomatic and consular protection by other Member States; and the right to petition the institutions of the EU. In the end, the most fundamental point is that the notion of European citizenship allows for a relative, yet positive, detachment of citizenship from nationality and statehood[48] and further legitimises the possibility for each national of a Member State to claim a plural sense of belonging. After all, to paraphrase Montesquieu, we are all citizens of humanity first and by necessity, and citizens of a specific country second and only by accident.

European citizenship is innovative as it does full justice to the realities and challenges of a globalised world by going beyond the nation-state. Winston Churchill dreamt, in his famous speech, given at Zurich University on 19 September 1946, of "a European group which could give a sense of enlarged patriotism and common citizenship to the distracted peoples of this turbulent and mighty continent". The eminent statesman did not expect common citizenship to mean the end of national citizenship or that it would necessarily conflict with national loyalties. By comparison, Margaret Thatcher's suspicion of the idea of European citizenship assumed somewhat paranoid proportions. During the House of Lords debate on ratification of the Maastricht Treaty, Baroness Thatcher went as far as to argue that:

> "If there is a citizenship, you would all owe a duty of allegiance to the new Union. What else is citizenship about? There will be a duty to uphold its laws. What will happen if the allegiance to the Union comes into conflict with the allegiance to our own country? How would the European Court find them? The Maastricht Treaty gives this new European Union all the attributes of a sovereign state."[49]

Fortunately, the current Treaties as well as the proposed Lisbon Treaty, answer Churchill's call. Offering a promising "third way", a European citizenship *complements* national

---

[46] See Art 17(1) TEC.

[47] These rights are subject to the limitations and conditions laid down in the TEC and to the legislation to give them effect.

[48] The decoupling is relative, as an individual first needs to be a national of a Member State before any claim to European citizenship. Furthermore, Member States remain free to define the conditions presiding over the granting of nationality.

[49] Quoted in R. Koslowski, "A constructivist approach to understanding the European Union as a federal polity", (1999) 6 *Journal of European Policy* 561, p 572.

citizenship, even though it was classically assumed that citizenship ought to be tied with nationality of a state and to exclude, as a matter of principle, plural loyalties. In an evolving world where interdependence is the key feature, European democracy does not need a European *demos*, an exclusive European collective identity based on ethno-cultural traits. As an original political experiment, Europe requires more innovative thinking. Rather than duplicating the model of the nation-state and requiring a homogeneous "community of European citizens", the EU should embrace its current singularity, its "complementary" character, and construct its cohesion on the association of the peoples of Europe around shared values and objectives.[50]

As a final point, while it is not difficult to agree that, "given the historical, linguistic, cultural, ethnic, and institutional diversity of its member states",[51] the European sense of belonging is likely to remain less developed than the "thick" sense of collective identity in national democracies, democratisation does not have to be a vain quest for Europe. The "no-demos" thesis is valuable to the extent that it suggests it may be unwise to set up a European democracy—democracy being understood as a majoritarian decision-making process—due to the original and supplemental character of the European collective self-identity. It can further be argued that, for European integration to flourish, the goal of a European *demos* with its ethno-cultural overtones is not a proper one for the EU. The drafters of the Constitutional Treaty rightly rejected such an ambition. Its Preamble, for instance, recalls that it is the peoples of Europe—the plural is noteworthy—who are determined to transcend their former divisions and to forge a common destiny. The Preamble of the EU Treaty currently speaks of a desire to deepen the solidarity between the peoples of the Member States "while respecting their history, their culture and their traditions" while another provision requires that "the Union shall respect the national identities of its Member States".[52] Remarkably, the Lisbon Treaty goes even a bit further by providing that "the Union shall respect the equality of Member States before the Treaties as well as their national identities, inherent in their fundamental structures, political and constitutional, inclusive of regional and local self-government".[53]

Europe requires a more subtle understanding of democracy than the one professed by most of the Union's critics, according to which democracy means *grosso modo* the rule of the majority in a representative regime organised on the principle of the separation of powers. Surprisingly, this diagnosis is often expressed by eurosceptics opposed to the so-called European superstate. Were the EU to function like a national parliamentary democracy, it would certainly pave the way to its transformation towards a federal State.

---

[50] The author is indebted to Joseph Weiler and in particular, his suggestion to analyse the EU in non-statal, national terms, for the evolution, over the years, of his personal views on the subject of the Union's democratic legitimacy.

[51] F. Scharpf, *Governing in Europe. Effective and Democratic* (Oxford University Press, Oxford, 1999), p 9.

[52] Article 6(3) TEU.

[53] See new Art 3a(2) TEU (formerly Art I-5(1) EU CT).

Regardless of this lack of coherence in the debate about the future of the EU, applying traditional mechanisms, associated with the national model of representative democracy would certainly lead the EU to suffer a crisis of legitimacy, due to the "thin" character of Europe's sense of collective identity. The paradox is that the incomplete implementation of mechanisms associated with the Westminster model of democracy and the ensuing complex and cumbersome characteristics of the European decision-making process, can be defended on democratic grounds:

> "Depoliticisation of European policy-making is the price we have to pay in order to preserve national sovereignty largely intact. As long as the majority of the citizens of the Member States oppose the idea of a European super-state, while supporting far-reaching economic integration, we cannot expect democratic politics to flourish at the European level. These being the preferences of the national electorates, we are forced to conclude that, paradoxically, Europe's 'democratic deficit,' as the expression is usually understood, is democratically justified."[54]

Our diverse history, culture and traditions require an institutional architecture which guarantees a permanent search for consensus, extensive dialogue between diverse interests and above all, the ultimate say for the representatives of the national *demoi*. The resulting original system of government could be a hard sell to the man on the street, as it may differ from his instinctive (and, in most cases, idealised) understanding of what a democracy is. It may, all the same, be defended in the name of democracy, one where the value of consensus (the so-called "consociational" or "consensus" model) trumps the majoritarian features classically associated with the Westminster model of parliamentary or representative democracy. Indeed, some countries such as Belgium, the Netherlands and Switzerland, have already put into practice a corrective version of the Westminster model. Coined by Arend Lijphart,[55] a consociational democracy is generally characterised by the joint management of affairs common to the national group as a whole through broad political coalition; the proportional representation of the main communities; and broad autonomy for each community at the local level. Additionally, a consociational system of government normally grants each community with a constitutional and legislative right to veto when they deem their "vital interests" to be affected.

With regard to the emphasis put on consensual decision-making and the preservation of national interests, the EU appears to typify the consociational or consensus model. This is not to say, obviously, that all is for the best in the best of all possible worlds. In light of Lijphart's work, however, it could be argued that the EU does not appear to suffer from major democratic defects. As with all systems of government, genuine concerns may

---

[54] Majone, "Europe's 'Democratic Deficit'", p 7.
[55] See A. Lijphart, *Patterns of Democracies. Government Forms and Performance in Thirty-Six Countries* (Yale University Press, New Haven, 1999).

certainly be articulated vis-à-vis the European institutional architecture and decision-making process. It would appear imperative, for instance, to further improve the representativeness and accountability of European institutions. In this context, the new emphasis on "participatory democracy" should be considered with interest and not disdain as it may offer a new fruitful path for the EU.

(c) The Proper Balancing Act for the European Union: Associating Representative Democracy with Participatory Democracy

The trouble with democracy is that it means many things to many people. For Ancient Greeks, democracy was a direct form of self-government by citizens. Yet the concept of citizenship was interpreted in a fashion that is, nowadays, considered unacceptable. Thus, it is obvious that the meaning as well as the institutions and values of democracy have changed radically over time. Robert Dahl has spoken of several "revolutions" in its past practice (often without its proponents being aware of it), arguing that "democracy can be independently invented and reinvented whenever appropriate conditions exist".[56] As previously emphasised, the EU is too often analysed in light of an idealised version of the Westminster model of parliamentary democracy and by reference to political or legal concepts which were developed in a specific context: the progressive domination of the nation-state as the paradigmatic model of organisation and exercise of public power. From a descriptive and normative point of view, the relevance of the democratic deficit thesis could seriously be questioned, as it is often implied that the solution resides in the duplication at the European level of the national model of parliamentary democracy, either in its Westminster form or in its "consociational" form. In the debate it is often forgotten that democracy is not a static concept. Its elasticity certainly renders feasible the emergence of alternative views or, at the very least, it authorises the discussion of concurrent or complementary definitions. The relevance of a new democratic model for the EU, the so-called participatory democracy, should accordingly be examined. It appears, indeed, to offer the promise of further democratisation of the Union's decision-making process while respecting the Union's original nature. Despite evident deficiencies and the debatable legitimation scheme being proposed, the participatory model appears, nevertheless, to offer a fruitful path for the EU, and a potentially positive *complement* to the representative model of democracy.

Reproducing the Constitutional Treaty's provisions,[57] the Lisbon Treaty inserts into the EU Treaty a new Title on democratic principles. It first provides that "the functioning of the Union shall be founded on representative democracy".[58] This is a well-established principle. It mostly entails that European citizens are directly represented in the European

---

[56] R. Dahl, *On Democracy* (Yale University Press, New Haven, 1998), p 9.
[57] On the drafting history of the provisions dealing with "The Democratic Life of the Union", see A. Peters, 'European Democracy After the 2003 Convention', (2004) 41 *Common Market Law Review* 37 at 42.
[58] New Art 8A(1) TEU (formerly Art I-46(1) EU CT).

Parliament while "Member States are represented in the European Council by their Heads of State or Government and in the Council [of Ministers] by their governments, themselves democratically accountable either to their national Parliaments, or to their citizens".[59] Such an assertion exposes briefly, yet particularly well, the twofold democratic legitimacy of the EU as traditionally understood. Another provision brings more originality by formalising a model of participatory democracy. It does not, however, affirm that the EU is also founded on participatory democracy but rather impose a certain number of duties on European institutions:

1. The institutions shall, by appropriate means, give citizens and representative associations the opportunity to make known and publicly exchange their views in all areas of Union action.
2. The institutions shall maintain an open, transparent and regular dialogue with representative associations and civil society.
3. The Commission shall carry out broad consultations with parties concerned in order to ensure that the Union's actions are coherent and transparent.[60]

If the proposed model of participatory democracy appears relatively fuzzy at first sight, two key features characterise it: broad participation (see the references to "citizens", "representative associations", "parties concerned", "civil society"); and public deliberation ("publicly exchange", "transparent"). The new provision on participatory democracy reflects the influence of the "governance" exercise, previously undertaken by the European Commission. As a result, it may be helpful to expose the purpose behind the exercise and clarify the meaning of a concept often used interchangeably with the notion of participatory or deliberative democracy.

Among the "strategic objectives" the European Commission decided to pursue in 2000 was the objective to reform "European Governance". The underlying purpose behind this apparently indefinite objective is to go beyond the model of representative democracy and explore alternative ways of increasing the Union's democratic legitimacy. In the words of Romano Prodi, the ultimate ambition is to achieve "a more complete and thoroughgoing democracy" by devising a new relationship between Europe's citizens and its institutions, based on openness and accountability.[61] The influence of the theory of deliberative democracy, under which legitimacy is supposed to flow from access to a deliberative process,[62] is particularly clear when the former President of the European Commission specifies how to better involve citizens:

---

[59] New Art 8A(2) TEU (formerly Art I-46(2) EU CT).

[60] New Art 8B (formerly Art I-47 EU CT).

[61] R. Prodi, "The European Union and its Citizens: a Matter of Democracy", Speech 01/365, European Parliament, Strasbourg, 4 September 2001.

[62] See e.g. E. Eriksen and J. Fossum (eds), *Democracy in the EU: Integration through Deliberation?* (Routledge, London, 2000).

"This does not mean changing the institutional balance or asking unelected bodies to represent the people. ... But it does mean taking on a new challenge ... the citizens' growing call to make their voices heard through other channels; to express themselves more directly via local government and citizens' associations. Our task must not be to oppose this expression of the people's voice and of the complex nature of our societies but rather to channel it, finding new and better ways of entering into a dialogue with local authorities and civil society. ... We must encourage the emergence of a 'network Europe' where all levels of governance are involved in shaping, implementing and monitoring EU policies."[63]

The willingness to increase dialogue, deliberation and the involvement of the citizens at all stages of European decision-making must be praised. Indeed, more than the legislative phase of the Union's decision-making, democratic concerns could be expressed with regard to the drafting and implementation of EU law. In other words, it could be argued that reforms should be aimed primarily at improving the functioning of the current obscure European administrative network, bringing together both national and Community bureaucrats. This problem is compounded by the added weight given to the voices of experts and interest groups in the administrative decision-making process. Such features are certainly not exclusive to the EU but the "supreme" authority of its law makes it important to control. From this perspective, the most productive strategy for improving the Union's legitimacy is not to complete a full "parliamentarisation" of its institutional architecture, but rather to increase the openness and transparency of its decision-making process.

Before exploring the ongoing reforms pursued under the "governance" label in more detail, some conceptual clarification may be useful as too often the word itself is used interchangeably with democracy. For instance, in the words of Romano Prodi, "when we speak of 'governance' we are, in fact, discussing democracy; European democracy, how it works, why it doesn't work better and what its prospects are".[64] However, beneath the term governance one may discover another understanding of democratic legitimacy. Before addressing this issue, the general meaning of governance should first be explained. In most instances, governance is used as shorthand for the idea that the state has to play a new role in complex modern societies. In other words, the state should play a minimal role and policy-making should be opened to all "stakeholders". Viewed in this light, the liberal character of the notion is undeniable.[65] This understanding does not exhaust, however, all

---

[63] Prodi, "The European Union and its citizens".

[64] *ibid.*

[65] See P. Hirst, "Democracy and Governance", in J. Pierre (ed), *Debating Governance: Authority, Steering and Democracy* (Oxford University Press, Oxford, 2000), p 13.

possible meanings of governance as "the term remains a very versatile one".[66] In the context of the EU, the Commission has proposed the following definition in its widely discussed *White Paper on European Governance*, published in 2001:

> "'Governance' means rules, processes and behaviour that affect the way in which powers are exercised at the European level, particularly as regards openness, participation, accountability, effectiveness and coherence."[67]

The most revolutionary aspect of the governance agenda is not the aim being pursued. As always, the ultimate objective is to increase "democratic input" and consolidate the Union's legitimacy. This time, however, the democratic input is not supposed to be derived from the application of mechanisms associated with the model of parliamentary democracy. Indeed, it is assumed that democratic legitimacy could be derived from improved "procedures". To quote Jérôme Vignon, Chief Adviser responsible for the White Paper on European Governance, the Union's democratic legitimacy crisis does not originate from "the absence of a parliamentary institution analogous to that found at the centre of national public life" but "from the procedures of the European Community, which have become formal rather than genuine".[68] Accordingly, "procedural" reforms should be undertaken with the aims of improving public deliberation, consultation and, generally speaking, "active citizenship". In the words of Renaud Dehousse, the main advantages of what he calls the "procedural avenue", another expression for governance, are twofold:

> "An extensive dialogue with the various segments of civil society would obviate some of the shortcomings of representative democracy at the European level, by enabling those who so wish to have a say in the decision-making process. In so doing, one might enhance the legitimacy of decisions taken by European bodies … A greater openness of the decision-making process also improve public awareness of the issues discussed at the European level, thereby contributing to the emergence of a truly pan-European public sphere."[69]

---

[66] "What is governance?" (http://europa.eu.int/comm/governance/governance/index_en.htm, consulted on 1 July 2007). The exact definition of the term is, therefore, likely to vary with each author. According to Roderick Rhodes, whose work is mentioned by the Commission, the concept of governance is currently used in contemporary social sciences with at least six different meanings: the minimal State, corporate governance, new public management, good governance, social-cybernetic systems and self-organised networks. See R. Rhodes, "The New Governance: Governing Without Government", (1996) 44 *Political Studies* 652.

[67] European Commission, *European Governance. A White Paper*, COM(2001) 428 final, 7 July 2001, p 8, n 1. For a first and exhaustive critical appraisal of the White Paper, see C. Joerges, Y. Mény, J. Weiler (eds), *Mountain or Molehill? A Critical Appraisal of the Commission White Paper on Governance*, Jean Monnet Working Paper no. 6/01 (available at: http://www.jeanmonnetprogram.org).

[68] J. Vignon, Preface, in de Schutter, Lebessis and Paterson , *Governance in the European Union*, p 4.

[69] Dehousse, "European governance in search of legitimacy", p 182.

Such potential benefits would make governance a sweet medicine. However, two key questions have yet to be answered. How do the governance promises translate into practice? Is this process-based approach likely to improve the Union's democratic legitimacy?

The Commission's White Paper can be summarised in one essential reform with one basic aim: "to open up policy-making to make it more inclusive and accountable" in order to "connect the EU more closely to its citizens".[70] Such an ambition, unsurprisingly, leads to multiple concrete proposals under four main headings: Better involvement and more openness; Better policies, regulation and delivery; Global governance; Refocused policies and institutions. To focus very briefly on the first two headings, for the Commission, the main challenge is to renovate the so-called "Community method" by following a less top-down approach. Under the (debatable) assumption that "democracy depends on people being able to take part in public debate",[71] the Commission first proposes to guarantee a better involvement of the public through diverse measures: on-line information through all decision-making stages, a more systematic dialogue with regional, local governments and civil society at an early stage in shaping policy and the establishment of "partnership arrangements". Secondly, in the endeavour to improve efficiency, the Commission suggests, among many other things, limiting the number of regulations, promoting co-regulatory mechanisms, encouraging non-binding instruments (e.g. the open method of coordination), simplifying existing EU law and developing the number of regulatory agencies. More interestingly, as it directly answers a concern often expressed about the relative opacity of expert input at the European level, it is proposed to publish guidelines on the use of expert advice at the European level, "so that it is clear what advice is given, where it is coming from, how it is used and the alternative views available".[72]

It would appear difficult to oppose many of the Commission's proposals calling for better involvement of the public, more openness and better regulation. Numerous problems, however, are likely to alter the effectiveness of these proposals. For instance, the willingness to increase public participation is certainly positive. Assuming that citizens are willing to participate more, one essential question is how to guarantee the effective participation of individuals lacking the resources to do so. There are no mechanisms to remedy inequalities between potential participants, and the difficulties in doing so would be immense as it is difficult to see how to measure such "inequality". Accordingly, the decision-making process is likely to "remain the monopoly of already organised groups, while ordinary citizens will not be encouraged to become more active".[73] Nonetheless,

---

[70] European Commission, *European Governance. A White Paper*, COM(2001) 428 final, 7 July 2001, p 8.

[71] *ibid.*, p 11.

[72] *ibid.*, p 5.

[73] P. Magnette, "European Governance and Civic Participation: Can the European Union be politicised?", in Joerges, Mény, Weiler, *Mountain or Molehill?*, p 3. If the author recognises the élitist nature of European citizenship, he argues that from such a fact cannot be derived the conclusion that the system is not democratic. What appears more problematic, to follow his challenging line of reasoning, is that European civic apathy is likely to remain as the governance exercise does not 'politicise' the decision-making process.

such criticism is also valid as far as national consultation mechanisms are concerned. The apparent "privatisation" of policy-making could be another source of concern. Co-regulation, for instance, the process that "combines binding legislative and regulatory action with actions taken by the actors most concerned", may give "wider ownership of the policies in question by involving those most affected by implementing rules in their preparation and enforcement".[74] There is a risk, however, of policy-making being hijacked by private interests without any increase in accountability. Yet again, the inclusion of private actors in the law-making process and the use of soft law instruments are not specific to the EU. The inadequacies and risks one could derive from the governance toolkit also apply at the national level.

If the above concerns are serious enough, the most fundamental issue relates to the democratic pedigree of the governance agenda.[75] Rather than a democratic deficit, several eminent specialists have argued that it would "be more accurate to speak of a more fundamental deficit of mutual awareness between civil society and public authorities and accordingly more appropriate to focus the reform process on options aimed at addressing this problem".[76] In light of this diagnosis, it is clear that the governance agenda embodies a new model of democratic legitimacy where the legitimacy of public action (as well as its efficiency) is made possible by a "proceduralisation" of law. In other words, the legitimacy of European norms ought to be essentially based on the presence of procedural safeguards which guarantee continual discursive and argumentative processes, as well as a pluralist participation of the parties or actors affected by the application of rule. The pursuit of more direct and multiform participation by individuals, or should we say, organised groups, in the European decision-making process is certainly not illegitimate or undesirable. It appears important to balance the influence of non-elected actors (civil servants, experts, lobbyists, etc.) through better involvement at the pre- and post-legislative phases, i.e. when laws are prepared and implemented.

On the other hand, one may wonder whether the philosophy of governance sufficiently embodies the democratic ideal. Strong criticism has been expressed by Erik Eriksen who argues that governance illustrates a "thin" concept of democratic legitimacy, unable to remedy the Union's "legitimacy gap" as it does not spell out the proper standards of democracy: accountability and congruence criteria.[77] Behind such a critical assessment,

---

[74] European Commission, *European Governance. A White Paper*, p 21.

[75] For further references, see e.g. L. Pech, "Le remède au 'déficit démocratique': Une nouvelle gouvernance pour l'Union européenne? ", (2003) 25 *Journal of European Integration* 131.

[76] N. Lebessis and J. Paterson, "Developing new modes of governance", in de Schutter, Lebessis and Paterson, *Governance in the European Union*, pp 279–280.

[77] E. Eriksen, "Democratic or Technocratic Governance?", in Joerges, Mény, Weiler, *Mountain or Molehill?*, pp 11–12. The author defines congruence as the basic democratic principle according to which those affected by decisions should also be responsible for them, and accountability as the possibility for the citizenry to dismiss rulers.

one may recognise the influence of the parliamentary model of democracy. While it remains essential to refrain from the natural tendency to evaluate the EU in light of criteria developed in the context of the nation-state, there is room for legitimate questioning. Indeed, is it still appropriate to speak of democracy when the unitary reign of the *demos*, governed through universal suffrage, is replaced by that of the "participating" individual? The frequent use of "participatory democracy" and "participatory governance" as interchangeable synonyms also raises the possibility of envisioning modern democracy as an art of governing where it does not really matter in whose name our governments exercise their power. While it certainly seems excessive to assert that what the drafters of the White Paper "have in mind amounts to the creation of a benevolent dictatorship",[78] the governance rhetoric certainly has the potential to weaken parliamentary democracy, diluting even further the collective ability of the citizenry to change their rulers.

This does not imply, however, that parliamentary democracy, either in its Westminster or consensus versions,[79] ought to be considered as the exclusive and appropriate analytical model for conceptualising the future of the EU. Its non-state nature and supranational character exclude, to a large extent, any direct transposition. Furthermore, the originality of the Union's institutional architecture is rightfully justified by its twofold legitimacy as a union of States and of citizens. On the other hand, the governance agenda should not be considered a substitute for parliamentary democracy at Union level.[80] The association of representative democracy and participatory democracy is therefore worth exploring. Democratic legitimacy continues to essentially presuppose "that the political will underpinning decisions is arrived at through parliamentary deliberation" and that "legitimacy is ultimately inconceivable without clear attribution of political responsibility and cannot be replaced by 'technical' factors".[81] "Participating" individuals should complement the oversight exercised by their parliamentary representatives at the European level, whose function does not exclude a reinforcement of national parliaments' powers. And even though the challenges of globalisation and, in particular, the subsequent marginalisation of parliamentary bodies must be noted, it does not render illusory or unnecessary the search for a more effective parliamentary involvement and supervision. The imperative to fundamentally rethink democracy in the context of globalisation is surely inescapable.[82] Even if the concept of governance may involve a philosophy of

---

[78] Not without humour, Fritz Scharpf further adds: "Undoubtedly, it is meant to be a well-informed, highly sensitive and very open form of dictatorship", "European Governance: Common Concerns vs. The Challenge of Diversity", in Joerges, Mény, Weiler, *Mountain or Molehill?*, p 9.

[79] To refer to the two models distinguished by Lijphart, *Patterns of Democracies*, p 9 and p 31.

[80] For a recent defence of a parliamentary approach to advance the democratisation and legitimation of the European Union, see C. Lord, "New Governance and Post-Parliamentarism", (2004) POLIS Working Paper No 5 (available at: http://www.leeds.ac.uk/polis/research).

[81] European Parliament, Resolution on the Commission White Paper on European governance, COM(2001) 428–C5-0454/2001 – 2001/2181 (COS), 15 November 2001, point 10.b.

[82] See e.g. D. Held, "The changing contours of political community: rethinking democracy in the context of globalisation", in B. Holden (ed), *Global Democracy – Key Debates* (Routledge, London, 2000), p 17.

government open to criticism, reform is preferable to *status quo*. Were the governance agenda to lead the EU towards increased "openness, participation, accountability, effectiveness and coherence", it would obviously be all for the best. There is no reason, however, to limit the call to open up policy-making to the so-called "stakeholders", i.e. representatives of European institutions and national institutions, representatives of business interests and of the civil society.

In addition to the empowerment of individuals and organisations, the call for a more participatory democracy should also help rediscover the potential for legitimacy by the direct and collective intervention of the European citizenry. In line with the Constitutional Treaty, the Lisbon Treaty provides that one million European citizens coming from "a significant number of Member States may take the initiative of inviting the Commission, within the framework of its powers, to submit any appropriate proposal on matters where citizens consider that a legal act of the Union is required for the purpose of implementing the Treaties".[83] By comparison to national provisions which guarantee the direct intervention of the people through constitutional or legislative referenda, the reform remains, unfortunately, quite timid in its scope. Although the right of citizens to launch a national referendum process is sometimes limited by the non-binding character of the consultation and/or the requirement of a minimum turnout, the European "referendum" still cannot be described as a genuine referendum since it is merely consultative. It will not lead to a vote in which all eligible European citizens of Europe can take part. Furthermore, the fact that the legal outcome of the procedure remains open-ended seriously limits its decisiveness. Indeed, following a popular initiative, the Commission must merely submit a proposal to the Council of Ministers.[84] Such a feature can still be easily explained by the potentially disturbing effect of a genuine European referendum on a sensitive subject. The fear of exacerbating passions and of dividing Europe along geographical lines explains the timid nature of the reform. In any event, the precise evaluation of such a reform remains difficult as the text does not specify the procedures and conditions required for such citizens' initiative, including the minimum number of Member States from which such citizens must come. The implementation of any "citizens' initiative" clause would be a positive step towards the creation of an indispensable European sphere of public debate,

---

[83] New Art 8B TEU (formerly Art I-47(4) EU CT).

[84] The European citizen's initiative resembles the right to petition the Parliament. See Art 194 TEC: "Any citizen of the Union, and any natural or legal person residing or having its registered office in a Member State, shall have the right to address, individually or in association with other citizens or persons, a petition to the European Parliament on a matter which comes within the Community's fields of activity and which affects him, her or it directly." In practice, provided that the subject of the petition falls within the remit of European competences, it will normally be declared admissible and the parliamentary Committee on Petitions will then decide what type of action should be taken. Hence the main difference with the new provision is that the Commission is under the obligation to submit a legislative proposal. By comparison, under Art 192 TEC, the European Parliament may only "request the Commission to submit any appropriate proposal on matters on which it considers that a Community act is required".

and may stimulate within the European population a much-needed sense of political control over the orientation of the Union.

CHAPTER FOUR – CONCLUSION

To argue that the Union's unique institutional architecture is democratically deficient is to assume that the EU shall become "something different" from what it currently is. As Charles Leben put it:

> "The reproach related to the democratic deficit implies that the Community (and beyond it, the Union) is regarded as something different from a mere international organisation. … It supposes that the ultimate basis of the legitimacy of the institution being talked of is the people, the people of the Union, the people who are, in democratic theory, sovereign, taking decisions either by themselves or through their representatives, and controlling the executive."[85]

In other words, the democratic-deficit's diagnosis is often justified by the non-application of familiar political mechanisms. Accordingly, to solve the alleged Union's democratic legitimacy problem, a simple and logical solution appears to be available: duplicate the model of parliamentary democracy in the context of a federal state. In this regard, eurosceptics are particularly inconsistent. They persist in fantasising about a European superstate while criticising the EU for being insufficiently democratic. Were the EU to truly function in the manner of a parliamentary democracy, a decisive step further in the statehood direction would have been made.

Analogies with national democracies should always be used with care. They may help in making sense of the EU but they may also lead to evaluations of the EU in light of an idealised model of democracy, whose development is inextricably linked to the nation-state. Furthermore, critics do not make their understanding of the EU sufficiently clear: it certainly suffers from some democratic deficit if one's assumption is that the Union's *finalité* is to transform itself into some kind of United States of Europe. However, the democratic-deficit charge is likely to become insignificant if the EU is accepted for what it currently is: a set of institutions (and not a state) reflecting the will of the citizens and States of Europe, with conferred and limited competences under the ultimate authority of the Member States, in which the peoples of Europe are said to be united in their diversity in order to build a common future.

In conformity with its dual legitimacy as well as the commands of its founding entities, the Union's institutional architecture organises a unique coexistence of supranational and

---

[85] C. Leben, "A Federation of Nation States or Federal State", in C. Joerges, Y. Mény and J. Weiler (eds), *What kind of Constitution for what kind of Polity?* (The Robert Schuman Centre for Advanced Studies, Florence, 2000), pp 100–101.

intergovernmental mechanisms. It cannot be denied that such a political experiment easily leads to confusion from the citizen's point of view. In our cultural mindset, the state continues to be the paradigmatic model of organisation and exercise of public power. That is why the temptation to analyse the EU as a primitive political entity that must evolve into a genuine federal state is always present. The rapid succession of treaties since the signature of the Single European Act in 1986, and the evolving institutional balance that ensued, did not help dissipate a sense of unease among citizens. An additional complicating factor is the persisting uncertainty about the ultimate purpose of European integration, a debate too often simplified as the opposition between the proponents of a politically integrated Europe and those favouring a mere area of free trade.

It may be time for the EU to embrace its unique nature rather than trying to conform to other models. It should neither become a state, nor should it try to duplicate the functioning of a parliamentary democracy. The stage now reached by the EU—more than an international organisation, less than a state—should not be assessed as an intermediary and temporary stage but as an equilibrium which should be maintained and refined. In this regard, Kalypso Nicolaïdis offers considerable food for thought with her defence of a third way for Europe:

> "Sovereignists need to accept that the EU is indeed a community of peoples and not only of states, peoples who ought to take an unmediated part in European politics. And supranationalists need to accept that democracy in Europe does not require that this community become a single demos, whose will is expressed through traditional state-like institutions. … the EU is and should continue to be a *demoi-cracy* in the making, subject to the rule of its peoples, for its peoples, with its peoples."[86]

In any event, the current "Community method" can be viewed as a satisfying and democratic decision-making process. While the independence and powers of the European Commission allows it to function, not as a government, but as the effective guardian of the European interest, the association of the Council of Ministers and the European Parliament in the adoption of legislative and budgetary acts, under the control of the European Court of Justice, perfectly embodies the dual legitimacy of the Union. How could it not be democratic when the European Parliament directly represents the citizens of Europe whereas the Member States are represented in the Council of Ministers by their governments,[87] themselves democratically accountable either to their national parliaments or to their citizens? There may still be a need to correct the asymmetry between the Council of Ministers and the European Parliament, and to favour a better involvement of national parliaments. Were the Lisbon Treaty to enter into force, these goals would be satisfactorily attained. Briefly said, this latter text fully recognises the European Parliament's role as a co-

---

[86] Nicolaïdis, "Our European Demoi-cracy", p 143.

[87] Not mentioning the decisive role of the European Council in imparting political impetus.

legislator by elevating the existing codecision procedure to the rank of the ordinary legislative procedure. Under the proposed scheme, as a matter of principle, EU law would be adopted by two "chambers": one representing the Member States and one representing European citizens. As for national parliaments, the increased transparency of the Council's work already enables them to better monitor the positions of their governments within the Council. With the foreseen "early warning" mechanism, national parliaments will be offered a substantial tool for directly influencing the legislative process. Therefore, and to put it succinctly, the Constitutional Treaty's successor, appears to offer the maximum "parliamentarisation" one could expect from a polity composed of several *demoi*.

To preserve its legitimacy, the EU must maintain a consociational system of government. To push the majoritarian features of the European decision-making process further in the name of more democracy would certainly be a step too far considering the fact there is no European *demos*. Ultimately, what matters with regard to an entity with conferred and limited competences, is that "constitutional checks and balances, indirect democratic control via national governments, and the increasing powers of the European Parliament are sufficient to ensure that EU policy-making is, in nearly all cases, clean, transparent, effective and potentially responsive to the demands of European citizens".[88] Further steps should certainly be taken to improve the democratic life of the EU. In particular, there may be a need to politicise the decision-making process, to "polarise" political debate at the European level in order to increase civic participation. Modest reforms could be undertaken to satisfy these valid concerns without undermining the consensual features of the Union's decision-making process.[89] The need for additional reforms does not imply, however, that the Union's institutional equilibrium does not currently embody a democratically legitimate entity. The European rulers are all, directly or indirectly, selected by the citizenry and can be held accountable for their actions. To reinforce the democratic pedigree of the EU, the model of parliamentary or representative democracy must, however, be combined with and controlled by elements borrowed from other models. Accordingly, the formal association of the two models of representative democracy and of participatory democracy offers a fruitful framework. It would allow the EU to derive its legitimacy not only from its founding entities—the Member States—and from the peoples of Europe (acting through their representatives) but, also, from the individual and collective participation of the citizens of Europe at each stage of the decision-making process.

---

[88] Moravcsik, "In Defence of the 'Democratic Deficit'", p 605.

[89] For Paul Magnette, "politicising the Union, and creating a clear deliberation of European issues, which could generate public interest, is not so much a question of institutions as a problem of political attitudes". See Magnette, "European Governance and Civic Participation", p 14. One of his interesting suggestions is that the Commission, rather than forging compromise *before* political deliberation takes place, should explain the *different possible options*, and their ideological roots. As a result, the Council and the European Parliament would spend more time deliberating European issues offering more space for public conflicts on the Union's policies.

More than a democratic deficit, it may be more appropriate to speak of a democratic "malaise" or a feeling of disenchantment or alienation. This is, alas, a common feature shared with national democracies in which many citizens seem to have realised that national representatives can hardly pretend to be in control of the country's collective destiny. Beyond the philosophical and institutional intricacies associated with the democracy debate, it may be essential to recognise that European integration is not the real threat to national democracy, but an answer to the current challenges of our times.[90] The shift of power—let's call it globalisation—outside national boundaries and the devolution of responsibilities and decisions to private actors at different levels of government, with its serious consequences for democracy, would have similarly occurred with or without the EU. The irony is that the EU may actually represent the only way for the Member States to effectively respond to the demands of their respective citizenry. As Alan Milward powerfully argued, there is no antithesis between the EU and the nation-state as an organisational framework.[91] On the contrary, the evolution of the EU "has been an integral part of the reassertion of the nation-state as an organizational concept" and in reality, "without the process of integration the west European nation-state might well not have retained the allegiance and support of its citizens in the way it has".[92] Today, the EU offers a democratic system of government where citizens' representatives can confront the destabilising force of global capitalism and other unelected powers. For all its imperfections, the Constitutional Treaty offered the chance of political leadership at a level where the social impact of globalisation could be democratically and effectively managed. The new Lisbon Treaty, a technically awkward compromise which safeguards the substance of the text rejected by French and Dutch voters, is likely to also endure the criticism of the usual left-wing sorcerer-apprentices and right-wing demagogues. One might hope that European citizens will remember, to paraphrase Voltaire, that the best can be the enemy of the good.

---

[90] J.-M. Guéhenno, *The End of the Nation-State* (University of Minnesota Press, Minneapolis, 2000). Literally translated into English, the original title of the book was, in French, "the end of Democracy".
[91] A. Milward, *The European Rescue of the Nation-State* (2nd ed., Routledge, London, 1999).
[92] *ibid.*, pp 2–3.

PART THREE

The European Union: Neither Neo-liberal Nor Socialist

It is clear that the neo-liberal economic agenda is now firmly enshrined within the draft constitution. The thrust of its commercial policy is clearly to optimise profit-making opportunities for business, at the expense of public welfare and the public good.
Patricia McKenna, MEP[1]

In the American Constitution, the Bill of Rights stipulates that individual rights prevail over the collectivist rights and the power of the State. In the European Constitution, the new European statists turn it on its head, and collectivist or group "rights" trump individuals and individual rights. This is the "New Europe". It's the world Orwell, a socialist, warned about 50 years ago.
Richard Pollock[2]

The EU legal framework is neither neo-liberal nor socialist. European Treaties offer a balanced framework embodying the values and objectives of the so-called "European social model".[3] While there is no authoritative definition of such a model, the European Council (hereinafter the "Council") has described it as a model based on good economic performance, competitiveness, a high level of social protection and education and social dialogue.[4] The Council also noted that the European social model allows for a diversity of approaches in order to achieve shared European values and objectives and that this diversity should be treated as an asset and a source of strength.[5]

---

[1] Quoted in P. Cullen, "Warning that treaty could destroy public funding", *The Irish Times*, 12 December 2003.
[2] "The New Europe Looks a Little Like '1984'", Cato Institute, 8 July 2003 (available at http://www.cato.org/dailys/07-08-03.html).
[3] For an argument that similarities in industrial relations, social budgets, social protection systems and the organisation of services of general interest "have sculpted a typically European way of conceptualising and promoting social protection", see M. Jouen and C. Papant, "Social Europe in the throes of enlargement", *Notre Europe*, Policy Papers No 15, July 2005, p 4 (available at: http://www.notre-europe.asso.fr).
[4] European Council of Barcelona, Presidency Conclusions, 15–16 March 2002, p 9 (available at: http://europa.eu.int/european_council/conclusions/index_en.htm).
[5] See European Social Agenda, Annex I, European Council of Nice, Presidency Conclusions, 7–9 December 2002 (available at: http://europa.eu.int/european_council/conclusions/index_en.htm).

The defunct Constitutional Treaty did not depart from this model. Social values and objectives continued to complement economic requirements. Furthermore, the Constitutional Treaty merely restated that the EU had the power to complement the action of the Member States in a certain number of enumerated fields. As with the present Treaties, it did not pre-empt the political direction of future EU intervention. This diagnosis is also valid with regard to the new Lisbon Treaty, which replaces the Constitutional Treaty. To denounce, therefore, the "European project" as a neo-liberal plot is nonsensical. The EU legal framework leaves to European institutions, and in particular the Member States within the Council of Ministers, the task of balancing competing objectives and defining sound public policies. The neo-liberal charge is particularly ludicrous when considered in light of the future insertion into the European Treaties of a provision which will give legal binding value to the EU Charter of Fundamental Rights, a Charter that has been presented (especially in the United Kingdom) as a socialist enterprise with its guarantee of socio-economic rights. Before responding to critics of the EU Charter, the accusation that the EU embodies a neo-liberal bias will first be addressed.

CHAPTER FIVE

The Alleged Neo-Liberal Bias

A brief and preliminary digression into a discussion on liberalism may be useful. The word itself has become quite pejorative in some quarters. This is certainly a troubling trend. Politically speaking, all constitutional democracies embody liberalism. A constitution, for instance, is the emblematic set of rules of any authentic liberal regime. Historically, as a political doctrine, liberalism is characterised by its emphasis on individual freedom, the free selection of governors and economic freedom. As an economic doctrine, the philosophy of liberalism can be summed up by the expression *laissez-faire*, meaning that the advocates of such a philosophy oppose, as a matter of principle, governmental regulation of commerce beyond the minimum necessary for a free-enterprise system to operate according to the laws of supply and demand. Following the crisis of the "welfare state" since the mid-seventies, advocates of liberalism have argued that the state should have a minimal role. In this context, the neologism "neo-liberalism" itself has become extremely popular, in particular since the strengthening of "anti-globalisation" movements in the last decade. But the exact meaning of neo-liberalism remains ambiguous. At a minimum, it can loosely be described as a policy orientation favouring liberalisation, privatisation and deregulation. Irrespective of its precise meaning, it has been used as a powerful rhetorical tool to undermine public support for European integration in general and for the Constitutional Treaty in particular.

(I) THE ENTRENCHMENT OF *LAISSEZ-FAIRE*[1]

One remarkable feature of the French referendum campaign on the Constitutional Treaty in 2005 was the focus of critics on the Third Part of the text, dealing with the policies and the functioning of the EU. Many left-leaning critics were allegedly alarmed to discover detailed provisions guaranteeing not only the free movement of goods and capital but also free and undistorted competition throughout Europe. Those provisions, the argument runs, clearly confirm the neo-liberal bias of the EU. To give a typical example of the prevalent Manichaeism in the debate on the Constitutional Treaty, Susan George, Vice-President of ATTAC France (Association for the Taxation of Financial Transactions for the Aid of Citizens), found the choice to be clear-cut:

---

[1] The following analysis is based on L. Pech, "The European Project: Neither Neo-liberal, Nor Socialist – A Reply to Andy Storey", *The Irish Review*, no 36–37, Winter 2007, p 95.

"I believe people in France have understood a momentous truth. We were being asked to choose between a Europe which would, in the fullness of time, ensure that we were all subjected to an American-style, neo-liberal model based on competition and the survival of the fittest, accompanied by huge inequality; or that we had one final chance to defend a genuine European model of solidarity and social justice."[2]

Such reactions are certainly surprising insofar as the very idea of a common market in Europe demands free movement and free competition. And indeed, since 1957, the aim of the EC Treaty has been to eliminate all obstacles to intra-community trade in order to merge national markets into a single market with the hope of maximising consumer welfare and ensuring the most efficient use of our resources. As we shall see, left-leaning critics have clearly demonstrated their prejudice towards the EU. They have based their "analysis" on a very limited set of legal rules found in the current Treaties and in the Constitutional Treaty, to the exception of the rules likely to demonstrate the fallacious character of their thesis.

This is not to say that the EU cannot be criticised or the range and content of its public policies ought not to be constantly scrutinised and debated. To denounce the inherent neo-liberal nature of European integration does not, however, do justice to the values and objectives upon which the EU is founded and the numerous public policies that illustrate its social dimension. In the end, it must always be remembered that "Brussels" may act only if it has the power to do so. In other words, it is for the Member States to decide whether or not they want to grant the EU more powers in the social field. This could represent a positive evolution but unsurprisingly, most, if not all the Member States, are very reluctant to transfer any of their welfare-state functions. Accordingly, the EU may have a more dominant "economic" dimension mostly because the Member States—and a clear majority of their citizens—want the EU to be an economic entity. One should not confuse these economic responsibilities with a neo-liberal agenda. This charge completely betrays the past and current efforts at balancing the economic and social dimension of European integration. It further illustrates a miscomprehension of the limited mandate of the EU.

(a) The Social Market Economy
The reference to a "social market economy" at Art I-3(3) of the Constitutional Treaty[3] has revealed a misunderstanding by critics as to the existing legal provisions in this area. This reference to a market economy has been presented as a distressing novelty. However, several

---

[2] S. George, "France's 'non' marks just the beginning of our campaign", *Europe's World*, Autumn 2005, p 50.
[3] The Lisbon Treaty reproduces this provisions: see new Art 2(3) TEU.

provisions of the current Treaties already refer to the concept of an open market economy.[4] Particularly misguided was the argument raised by some non-Weberian "experts" equating the Constitutional Treaty to the capitalist equivalent of the USSR Constitution. For those critics, these two texts are the only examples of constitutions which embody the economic principle upon which society is organised. This argument is flawed on many levels. First, and perhaps pragmatically, one may ask if there is an effective alternative to a market economy: a North Korean or a Cuban type of socialism possibly? An astonishing aspect of the French political debate was the violence of the attacks on the constitutional reference to a social market economy. It appears that many advocates of the "Non"-camp chose not to consider that the French economy is also a market economy and quite a productive one. Yet, no major political leader was forthcoming in an explanation that a market economy means no more than an economic system where factors of production are privately owned and where supply and demand determine, to a certain extent, the allocation of resources.

Secondly, the comparison with the USSR Constitution is unsustainable. It is actually in light of the German constitutional experience that the EU Constitutional Treaty was drafted. To the author's knowledge, no reference was ever made in mainstream French media to the German constitutional "principle of social statehood" as embodied in Art 20(1) of the German Basic Law which provides that "The Federal Republic of Germany is a democratic and social federal state".[5] As the EU could not be compared to a state, the drafters of the Constitutional Treaty apparently contented themselves with a reference to a "social market economy". But again, the latter expression is "a concept with a long German history" and "is understood to be an approach to fulfil the task of the German state to perform as a 'social state'".[6] According to a German Professor of Economics, Alfred Müller-Armack, who invented the above term in 1946, a social market economy promotes interventionist state measures and redistributive policies.[7] The subtlety is that social goals cannot be attained through instruments which undermine the functionality of market mechanisms. In any case, it is astonishing to condemn the term "social market economy"

---

[4] Article 4(1) TEC reads as follows: "For the purposes set out in Article 2, the activities of the Member States and the Community shall include … the adoption of an economic policy which is based on the close coordination of Member States' economic policies … and conducted in accordance with the principle of an open market economy with free competition." Article 98 TEC provides that the Member States and the EC, when conducting their economic policies, "shall act in accordance with the principle of an open market economy with free competition, favouring an efficient allocation of resources, and in compliance with the principles set out in Article 4". Finally, according to Art 105(1) TEC, the European system of central banks "shall act in accordance with the principle of an open market economy with free competition, favouring an efficient allocation of resources, and in compliance with the principles set out in Article 4".

[5] See C. Joerges and F. Rödl, "'Social Market Economy' as Europe's Social Model?", EUI Working Paper Law No 2004/8, p 10 (available at: http://www.iue.it).

[6] *ibid.*, p 11. The authors also signal that the expression "social market economy" was legalised in the Treaty on the Unification of Germany (1990) as the basis of the economic unification.

[7] *ibid.*, p 16.

for its alleged neo-liberal overtone. The term in itself does not favour public policies promoting privatisation and deregulation. It merely describes the current economic framework of European countries: they are all market economies with a high level of social protection. To claim, therefore, that "it is not difficult to understand that the 'Constitution' actually aims at making neoliberalism 'irreversible' in the enlarged EU",[8] makes one wonder whether critics have been working on a truncated version of the Constitutional Treaty.

The devious nature of the neo-liberal charge becomes particularly apparent once Art I-3(3) of the Constitutional Treaty on the Union's objectives—the Lisbon Treaty replicates this provision *in extenso*[9]—is read in its entirety:

"The Union shall work for the sustainable development of Europe based on balanced economic growth and price stability, a highly competitive social market economy, aiming at full employment and social progress, and a high level of protection and improvement of the quality of the environment. It shall promote scientific and technological advance.

It shall combat social exclusion and discrimination, and shall promote social justice and protection, equality between women and men, solidarity between generations and protection of the rights of the child.

It shall promote economic, social and territorial cohesion, and solidarity among Member States.

It shall respect its rich cultural and linguistic diversity, and shall ensure that Europe's cultural heritage is safeguarded and enhanced."

The Lisbon Treaty, therefore, speaks of a competitive European market economy because it is actually a means of fulfilling social goals, which happen to be innovative ones. The criticism that a market economy cannot be referred to as a constitutional objective is, as a result, surprising and misguided. The controversial provision merely provides that the EU is *based on* a market economy as this is the best framework to attain a series of social objectives. To answer criticism coming from the self-proclaimed "progressives", who highlight the fact that there is no constitutional precedent with regard to the inclusion of the notion of "market economy", one may ask, *a contrario*, with no historical precedent in national constitutions, should the reference to "social exclusion" or "solidarity between

---

[8] J. Milios, "European Integration as a Vehicle of Neoliberal Hegemony" in A. Saad-Filho and D. Johnston (eds), *Neoliberalism. A Critical Reader* (Pluto Press, London, 2005), p 211.
[9] It adds, however, a new sentence at the beginning of the article: "The Union shall establish an internal market".

generations" also be found illegitimate? Comparisons with current national constitutions should not be one-sided if one's goal is, genuinely, to inform the citizenry.

Leading left-leaning politicians and commentators were curiously selective in their reading of the Constitutional Treaty.[10] If they undertook, in good faith, a genuine reading of this document they might well have discovered among the "provisions of general application",[11] an *unprecedented* affirmation that the EU's policies must contribute to the achievement of a set of social objectives:

> "In defining and implementing the policies and actions referred to in this Part [*Part III on the policies and functioning of the EU*], the Union shall take into account requirements linked to the promotion of a high level of employment, the guarantee of adequate social protection, the fight against social exclusion, and a high level of education, training and protection of human health."[12]

Is it worth mentioning that other "provisions of general application" were contained in the Constitutional Treaty and that they are all reproduced in the Lisbon Treaty. These new provisions allow for the pursuit of the following objectives: to eliminate inequalities, to combat discrimination, to promote sustainable development and take into account consumer protection as well as animal welfare. The added-value of the Lisbon Treaty, like the Constitutional Treaty before it, therefore, is to treat these objectives as *horizontal* ones governing the definition and implementation of all EU policies such as, for instance, monetary policy.

To the likely horror of some ideological defenders of a "free market" the Constitutional Treaty further provided that, in order to achieve these objectives, the EU shall support and complement the activities of the Member States in the following fields: (a) improvement in particular of the working environment to protect workers' health and safety; (b) working conditions; (c) social security and social protection of workers; (d) protection of workers where their employment contract is terminated; (e) the information and consultation of workers; (f) representation and collective defence of the interests of workers and employers, including codetermination, subject to para 6;[13] (g) conditions of employment for third-country nationals legally residing in Union territory; (h) the integration of persons excluded from the labour market, without prejudice to Art III-283; (i) equality between women and men with regard to labour market opportunities and

---

[10] See e.g. L. Fabius, *Une certaine idée de l'Europe* (Plon, Paris, 2004); J. Généreux, *Manuel critique du parfait européen: Les bonnes raisons de dire "Non" à la Constitution* (Seuil, Paris, 2005).
[11] See Arts III-115 to III-122 EU CT.
[12] New Art 5(a) TEC (formerly Article III-117 EU CT).
[13] This article shall not apply to pay, the right of association, the right to strike or the right to impose lockouts.

treatment at work; (j) the combating of social exclusion; (k) the modernisation of social protection systems without prejudice to point (c).[14]

It is important to stress that, in doing this, the Constitutional Treaty only reproduced a provision currently contained in the EC Treaty.[15] It did not alter the present allocation of competence between the EU and the Member States in the area of social policy.[16] The third part of the Constitutional Treaty merely preserved the existing *acquis communautaire*,[17] while better stressing the social dimension of its policies. To give two examples of the preservation of the *acquis*: the constitutional text required each Member State to "ensure that the principle of equal pay for female and male workers for equal work or work of equal value" was applied;[18] the Member States were also encouraged "to maintain the existing equivalence between paid holiday schemes".[19]

As for a better emphasis on the Union's social dimension, the explicit recognition of the role of the social partners[20] serves as a good example. Social partners have always been involved in the European decision-making process and several provisions of the EC Treaty make reference to them. One may refer, for instance, to the creation of the European Economic and Social Committee in 1957, modelled on a similar French body which was created under the French Constitution of 1946 and maintained by the constitutional text now in force in France.[21] In any event, the EC Treaty already guarantees the involvement of social partners. The Commission must consult the representatives of "management and labour" before submitting proposals in the social policy field and Member States may entrust them with the implementation of certain directives.[22] More ambitiously, employee and employer federations can negotiate collective agreements which can be given legal effect by a Council directive.[23] Yet, a general provision recognising their role and the

---

[14] Article III-210 EU CT.

[15] Article 137 TEC.

[16] European social policy has never been intended to replace national social policy. It is not entirely clear if this is the objective actually entertained by those condemning the neo-liberal character of the "European project". If their criticism is based, however, on the fact that the constitutional text does not encompass the creation of a European welfare state, one has to demonstrate, first, that there is a compelling majority of Member States willing to contemplate such a revolutionary objective.

[17] The body of common rights and obligations which bind all the Member States together within the European Union.

[18] Article III-214 EU CT reproduced Art 141 TEC.

[19] Article III-215 EU CT reproduced Art 142 TEC.

[20] Principally the representatives of employers and employees.

[21] The European Economic and Social Committee consists of representatives of the various economic and social components of organised civil society. It appears to function more effectively than its French counterpart which is too often staffed with politicians' cronies.

[22] See Arts 137–139 TEC.

[23] Six agreements, including two sectoral agreements, have been subject to this procedure: agreement on parental leave; agreement on part-time work; agreement on fixed-term contracts; agreement on the organisation of working time of mobile workers in civil aviation; agreement on the organisation of working time of workers at sea; agreement on teleworking.

importance of social dialogue was missing. The Constitutional Treaty remedied this shortcoming by providing that the EU "shall recognise and promote the role of the social partners at its level, taking into account the diversity of national systems" and that it should also facilitate social dialogue.[24] The 2007 Lisbon Treaty reproduces this provision as well as the clause stressing the role played by the "Tripartite Social Summit for Growth and Employment", a product of the so-called "Lisbon strategy".[25] In practice, it means that European institutions should promote the consultation of management and labour and involve them in the decision-making process whenever the topic may be related to employment law and labour market regulation.

With these provisions in mind, it would seem difficult to argue that "Europe" embodies and will continue to embody a neo-liberal model based on the survival of the fittest. One may regret that the Constitutional Treaty did not improve the current status quo on social policy as it merely reproduced provisions of the EC Treaty. Unfortunately, a great deal of voters appeared to have been convinced that, irrespective of the provisions mentioned above, the section on social policy was no more than a fig-leaf on unrestrained neo-liberalism. In particular, two arguments have been advanced repeatedly. First, the EU supposedly leaves social harmonisation to the mercy of the market. Secondly, the EU's social objectives are, in reality, undermined by several references to economic principles.

Regarding the first argument, the focus of most criticism was the assertion that the fulfilment of the EU's social objectives "will ensue not only from the functioning of the internal market, which will favour the harmonisation of social systems, but also from the procedures provided for in the Constitution and from the approximation of provisions laid down by law, regulation or administrative action of the Member States".[26] The reference to the functioning of the internal market as a way to favour harmonisation was denounced by some born-again Marxists of the French socialist party as allowing a diminution of workers' rights and of social protection. This provision duplicated Art 136 TEC. The critique did not do full justice to its exact wording, as the EU allows, and will continue to allow, public authorities to intervene to the extent that market mechanisms have failed to achieve the desired outcome. No change was sought to the current situation: the EU may establish minimum requirements in such areas as workers' health and safety, working conditions, etc. with the sole (and sound) condition that such intervention shall avoid imposing administrative, financial and legal constraints in a way which would hold back the creation and development of small and medium-sized undertakings. Again, "Europe" offers the example of a balanced legal framework: social progress goes hand in hand with the recognition that the existence and nurturing of productive firms is a

---

[24] New Art 136a TEC (formerly Art I-48 EU CT).

[25] In March 2000, the EU Heads of States and Governments agreed in Lisbon to make the EU "the most competitive and dynamic knowledge-driven economy by 2010". Among numerous initiatives, it was agreed that successive European Councils would offer management and labour the opportunity to give their point of view on the issues discussed by the Council.

[26] Article III-209 EU CT.

condition *sine qua non.* The following may be obvious to most people but the French debate makes it worth repeating: lack of wealth creation can only lead to a situation where a welfare state is left without resources or "wealth" to redistribute.

This argument has been criticised on the ground it does not take into account a key-element: the requirement of unanimity voting within the Council of Ministers for many social protection measures.[27] It is argued that European intervention on social matters will continue to be a pure mirage and, therefore, social standards will continue to be left to the mercy of the market. This is certainly one way of looking at the unanimity requirement. However, it could also be interpreted as a guarantee for countries such as France or Sweden, in order to avoid a "neo-liberal" harmonisation of social systems, i.e. harmonisation at a lower level. What if the United Kingdom was to convince a majority of the Member States to harmonise social systems according to its liberal ideological preferences? The French would certainly then call for a unanimous vote. Besides, it is not reasonable for a Member State to denounce unanimity only in those areas where it is willing to go further than others. France, for instance, appears to be the sole Member State keen on defending the notion of "public service". And, as we shall see, its partners have always succumbed to French demands. Indeed, the present Treaties now preserve the freedom for each Member State to reject the liberalisation of major sectors of the national economy. Finally, the unanimity requirement is not in reality prevalent across the board contrary to what is usually stated. Unanimity is and will continue to be reserved to the "sensitive" areas, most notably in the areas of social security; protection of workers where their employment contract is terminated; representation and collective defence of the interests of workers; and conditions of employment for third-country nationals residing within the EU.

More fundamentally, regardless of the unanimity versus majority voting debate, the argument of the French Socialist Party and others lacks sophistication and does not do full justice to the immense complexity of the area. As Fritz Scharpf convincingly explained, the normative and structural diversity of national welfare states makes uniform European legislation in the social-policy arena an impossible goal to reach.[28] If the level of relatively low minimal standards now being defined at the European level is judged not to be

---

[27] As required by Art III-210(3) EU CT. As under the current EC Treaty, *unanimity* in the Council of Ministers remains the norm in the following areas: social security and social protection of workers; protection of workers where their employment contract is terminated; representation and collective defence of the interests of workers and employers, including co-determination subject to para 6; conditions of employment for third-country nationals legally residing in Community territory; financial contributions for promotion of employment and job creation. It is nonetheless possible for the Council of Ministers, since the Nice Treaty, to relinquish unanimity voting in favour of majority voting in the areas of employment-contract termination, of representation and collective defence of the interests of workers and employers and of conditions of employment for third-country nationals.

[28] F. Scharpf, "The European Social Model: Coping with the Challenges of Diversity", (2002) 40 *Journal of Common Market Studies* 645.

acceptable, one has to offer feasible solutions on how to accommodate the existing diversity of national welfare regimes with a potential "Europeanisation" of social policies.[29] Notwithstanding this diversity, it may actually be argued that the transfer by the Member States of their welfare-state obligations to the European level is no solution in any case since it is likely to undermine the legitimacy of the EU. This is no paradox. The explanation, as Giandomenico Majone observed, lies in the fact that "nonhomogeneous polities find it particularly difficult to pursue redistributive and other policies with clearly identified winners and losers".[30] Accordingly, in a transnational federation such as the EU, "all such policies would have to be excluded from the public agenda as being too divisive. This is, in fact, the main reason why redistributive social policy plays such a small role even in the present EU".[31]

As for the undermining of the social objectives enunciated in the Constitutional Treaty, critics have principally focused on references to "the need to maintain the competitiveness of the Union economy" or the commitment to free competition.[32] The merits of this claim, and the changes brought by the Lisbon Treaty, will be addressed below.

(b) A Market where Competition is Free and Undistorted

Often faced with unambiguous provisions that run counter to their thesis, the proponents of the neo-liberal bias generally attempt to demonstrate its validity by referring to the number of times the word "market" or the word "competition" appear in the current Treaties or in the Constitutional Treaty:

> "The Constitution went into enormous detail concerning economic policies, stressing free market [78 references], competition [over 100] and stressed again and again the needs of capital over those of people."[33]

From these numbers, it is hastily concluded that the Constitutional Treaty embodies the quintessence of neo-liberalism. If there is a need to show the futility of this line of reasoning, one could refer to the number of times the words "employment" or "social" are mentioned. "Employment" is mentioned approximately 18 times with "social" (thus

---

[29] The so-called Open Method of Co-ordination is now being presented as *the* panacea to this conundrum. In brief, the Open Method of Coordination is aimed at encouraging Member States to co-ordinate their actions in a number of policy areas on a voluntary basis without resorting to European legislation. For a general overview in the social field, see D. Trubek and L. Trubek, "Hard and Soft Law in the Construction of Social Europe: the Role of the Open Method of Co-ordination", (2005) 11 *European Law Journal* 343.

[30] G. Majone, *Dilemmas of European integration. The Ambiguities and Pitfalls of Integration by Stealth* (Oxford University Press, Oxford, 2005), p 189.

[31] *ibid.*, p 190.

[32] See respectively Art III-209 EU CT and Art III-177 EU CT.

[33] George, "France's 'non' marks just the beginning of our campaign", p 50.

winning the Palm d'Or!) appearing more than 100 times. In truth, it must be said that this huge number of references is explained by the number of times the Economic and Social Committee is alluded to. Yet, the same can be said about the term "market". In most instances, the reference is to the common market, not to the market economy. More depressingly, the dispute about how many times the words "market" and "competition" appear in the Treaties or in the Constitutional Treaty has revealed the depth of popular misunderstanding regarding the current competences conferred on the EU and a common and distressing ignorance about the purpose of competition rules.

(b.1) A Common Market
At the outset, to clarify the term common market, it must firstly be pointed out that the EU was created with the goal of constantly improving, according to the Preamble of the Treaty of Rome, "the living and working conditions of their peoples". To do so, the Member States have recognised the need to remove trade barriers and, accordingly, granted European institutions the necessary powers to supervise their removal. It certainly cannot be denied that, for a long time, the core of European activities were of economic nature hence the formal name, European Economic Community (EEC), used until 1992. The primary objective of the EU was and still is to complete market integration. In other words, since its origin, the goal of creating a "common market" lies at the heart of European integration.[34]

What does the notion more precisely encompass? When the Member States established the EEC in 1957, they agreed to create a market where all impediments to free movement of goods, persons, services and capital among themselves are removed and where a common external policy would govern trade with non-Member States. The underlying assumption is that there are huge economic benefits associated with operating in a wider and open market.[35] Most economic textbooks contend that the free movement of goods, workers, services and capital—the so-called "four freedoms" in the EU context—maximise wealth-creation. In simple terms, the setting up of a common market increases potential sales for each company within that market. Furthermore, an increase in competition leads to more investment to maintain competitiveness, and the bigger dimension of the market leads to economies of scale. In theory, the result is more economic growth and, therefore, more jobs. In their quest for such positive results, European institutions have always been

---

[34] Article 3 TEC elaborates on this goal by detailing further the required activities of the Community: "1. For the purposes set out in Article 2, the activities of the Community shall include, as provided in this Treaty and in accordance with the timetable set out therein: (a) the prohibition, as between Member States, of customs duties and quantitative restrictions on the import and export of goods, and of all other measures having equivalent effect; (b) a common commercial policy; (c) an internal market characterised by the abolition, as between Member States, of obstacles to the free movement of goods, persons, services and capital; ... (g) a system ensuring that competition in the internal market is not distorted; ... "
[35] See P. Cecchini, *The European Challenge 1992: The Benefits of a Single Market* (Wildwood House, Aldershot, 1988).

mostly preoccupied with ensuring that all barriers to European trade are removed. As the European Court of Justice put it, a common market is aimed at—and the negative feature of the enterprise should be noted—eliminating "all obstacles to intra-community trade in order to merge the national markets into a single market bringing about conditions as close as possible to those of a genuine internal market".[36] The signing of the Maastricht Treaty in 1992 illustrated the willingness of a majority of Member States to refine the common market goal by establishing an economic and monetary union. As a result, a single currency now governs the trade of 15 Member States and all the Member States must conduct their economic policies with a view to contributing to the achievement of the objectives of the Community.

To recapitulate, the idea of a common market is inherently liberal and inevitably of an economic nature. This may come as a shock to some. Yet, all democracies are "liberal" regimes functioning with an open market economy. As for the EU's concern with economic matters, it is the result of Member States' continuing choice and of their persistent refusal to transform the EU into some sort of state with a general competence over redistributive policies. Be that as it may, it would be incorrect to assume that European integration has no social dimension or that the goal of establishing a common market trumps everything else. In fact, in 1957, the EC Treaty included a Chapter on social provisions. The European Social Fund was set up in 1958 with the aim of supporting measures which aim to prevent and combat unemployment, develop human resources and foster social integration in the labour market, in particular with regard to the disadvantaged sections of the population. To further contribute to the social and economic cohesion of the EU and to create "a level playing field" following the liberalisation of intra-EU trade, a European Regional Development Fund later provided support mainly for public and private investments in infrastructure.[37]

Ireland is a witness to European generosity and the importance of such policies in helping a national economy making the transition from a status of a relatively low level of economic development to a high and sustainable level. To mention a few figures, during the period 1989–2001, Ireland received €12.4 billion in structural funds from Brussels. This is equivalent to 1.9 percent of annual gross national product.[38] Even though European structural funds did not guarantee economic success, EU membership as well as EU financial grants certainly contributed to the emergence of the Celtic Tiger. This demonstrates that European integration is and ought to be based on solidarity between poor and rich Member States.

---

[36] Case 15/81 *Gaston Schul* [1982] ECR 1409, para 33.

[37] Article 160 TEC: "The European Regional Development Fund is intended to help to redress the main regional imbalances in the Community through participation in the development and structural adjustment of regions whose development is lagging behind and in the conversion of declining industrial regions."

[38] J. Murray Brown, "Ireland proves to be a shining example of membership", *The Financial Times*, 22 April 2004.

Workers' rights have also figured prominently in the Community's work since its origin. On the basis of the EC Treaty, extensive European legislation has been issued to guarantee that any national of a Member State is entitled to take up and engage in gainful employment on the territory of another Member State. Discrimination on the grounds of nationality is strictly prohibited. Furthermore, Community workers are entitled to the same social and tax benefits as national workers. One may also mention that the EC Treaty itself, as early as 1957, provided for the principle of equality between men and women, which means in particular that they should receive equal pay for equal work. One final element worth noting, thanks to an amendment introduced by the Amsterdam Treaty in 1999, the EC Treaty now requires the objectives of the Community's social policy to be consonant with the fundamental social rights set out in the European Social Charter 1961 and the Community Charter of the Fundamental Social Rights of Workers 1989.[39]

Irrespective of these Treaty provisions and European policies, it is nevertheless legitimate to consider that the social dimension of the EU has long remained the focus of less interest than the economic dimension of European integration. The Amsterdam Treaty reflects, however, a clear shift of emphasis. Particularly symbolic was the introduction of a new provision which refers to the adoption of provisions on non-discrimination, and authorises the Council, acting unanimously, "to take appropriate action to combat any discrimination based on sex, race, ethnic origin, religion or belief, disability, age or sexual orientation".[40] The principle of equality between men and women was also added to the list of Community objectives. It is now explicitly provided that in all its activities the Community must aim to eliminate inequalities, and to promote equality between men and women.[41] Among the other innovations introduced by the Amsterdam Treaty, and to specifically answer French concerns, a new Title on Employment was inserted into the Treaty of Rome. Accordingly, employment policies of the Member States ought to be coordinated with a view to better combining economic and social policies in order to achieve full employment. The objective was to reach a "high level of employment". In order to attain this objective, the Community was given a new area of responsibility to complement the activities of the Member States involving the development of a "coordinated strategy" for employment. Again, to answer French concerns, a new article was also introduced to protect "public services".[42] As the issue will be addressed in more detail below, it is enough to mention here that "services of general economic interest"— the EU name for public services—have progressively seen their role recognised in promoting social and territorial cohesion.

In the end, it would appear difficult to deny that the EU has always had a strong social component but another contention needs to be answered. Critics often allege that the

---

[39] See Art 136 TEC.
[40] Article 13 TEC.
[41] See Art 3(2) TEC.
[42] Article 16 TEC.

EU's neo-liberal bias is clearly demonstrated by the fact that EU rules allow the common market goal to trump any other competing (social) objective. This is forgetting that several provisions of the Treaty of Rome authorise the Member States to take national measures restraining the free movement of goods, persons, services or capital.[43] In practice, if national measures severely restraining free trade (e.g. a ban on imports) serve the public interest, they will not be prohibited. In other words, EC law is no obstacle if these measures can be justified in the name of public morality, public security, protection of health, etc. and if they are proportionate and do not constitute a means of disguised discrimination. The European Court of Justice has also developed a list of further justifications in situations where a Member State limits intra-EU trade in goods by imposing non-discriminatory rules which have an adverse impact on goods coming from other Member States. In other words, consumer protection, the protection of the environment, the pluralism of the press, etc. may justify national restrictions on European trade.

The *Schmidberger*[44] ruling shows that the protection of fundamental rights should normally override free movement concerns. In this 2003 case, the Austrian authorities had closed the Brenner motorway for four days in order to allow an environmental group to organise a demonstration. Because the Brenner motorway is the major transit route for trade between Northern Europe and Italy, its closure led to a serious restriction on the free flow of goods between Member States with severe economic consequences for transport companies. The Austrian authorities had, therefore, to demonstrate that their action was justified under EC law. For the European Court of Justice, the protection of fundamental rights is a legitimate public interest which, in principle, justifies a restriction of the obligations imposed by EC law. In light of the facts of the case, the European Court of Justice ruled that a fair balance had been struck between the competing interests, i.e. the free movement of goods and freedom of assembly.

It may still surprise some that fundamental rights, constitutionally protected at the national level, ought to be balanced against the free movement of goods. Certainly, it is a constitutional imperative for Member States to protect fundamental rights. Yet, as always, the European Court of Justice must also make sure in light of the facts of each particular case, that restrictions on free movement rights guaranteed by EC law are not disproportionate to the legitimate objective pursued by the relevant Member State. If not, it would always be tempting for national authorities or private parties to hide protectionist intent behind the legitimate objective of protecting fundamental rights. There should, therefore, be no indignation towards the idea of balancing fundamental rights with competing interests such as the free movement of goods or the free movement of people. What matters is that the European Court of Justice plainly and obviously accepts that the

---

[43] Articles 39(3), 46 and 55 TEC allow Member States to derogate respectively from the principle of free movement of workers, from the freedom of establishment and the freedom to provide and receive services. Article 58 of the TEC does the same regarding the principle of free movement of capital and payments.
[44] Case C-112/00 [2003] ECR 5659.

necessity to respect fundamental rights may justify restrictions on the application of EU rules.

More problematic than the content of the Treaties or the overall direction of the case law is the vocabulary used at European level as it may create unnecessary scepticism about the ideological orientation of the EU. The so-called "four freedoms"—the free movement of goods, persons, services or capital—are also commonly described as the "fundamental freedoms" of the EC Treaty.[45] This can create some unease as it easily leads people to believe that these four freedoms should therefore override any competing public interest. This vocabulary undeniably favours the advocates of the neo-liberal bias thesis as it requires time and effort to make sense of EC law. Accordingly, critics have an easy time arguing that the principle of free movement is merely a ruse to trump the real "fundamental freedoms", meaning human rights. A bit of explanation about the terminology may, therefore, be useful. It is quite common for lawyers, in Germany or in France, to characterise human rights protected by the national constitution as "fundamental rights", a term that includes rights (e.g. right to privacy) as well as freedoms (e.g. freedom of expression) without any distinction between the two. To call the free movement of goods, persons, services or capital, "fundamental freedoms", is unfortunate as it instinctively implies, for the citizens of some Member States at least, that the Community's four freedoms can claim equal status with the human rights that are constitutionally protected. This is difficult to accept as respect for human rights is considered, politically speaking, the supreme value of any modern democratic system.[46] For that reason, it would be beneficial to eventually find a substitute for the use of the term "fundamental freedom" to describe the Community's "four freedoms".

As previously mentioned, in light of its progressive development over the years, the Member States rightly decided in 1992 that it was time to rename the European Economic Community the European Community, to do justice to its transformation into an entity no longer predominantly concerned with the establishment of a common market. Indeed, among the policy areas where the EC may intervene, one may note agriculture asylum and immigration, transport, employment, trade, social welfare, consumer protection, research and technology, the environment and development aid. Furthermore, the EU was also created to incorporate the EC and the policies and forms of intergovernmental co-operation established outside it, i.e. the Common Foreign and Security Policy and Justice and Home Affairs pillars. The current Treaties cannot, therefore, be presented as embodying a framework with an exclusive economic dimension. And when it is stated

---

[45] See e.g. Article I-4(1) EU CT on "fundamental freedoms": "The free movement of persons, services, goods and capital, and freedom of establishment shall be guaranteed within and by the Union, in accordance with the Constitution."

[46] For instance, the German Constitution stipulates that human rights form the basis of every human community and the Preamble of the French Constitution proclaims the French people's attachment to the Rights of Man as defined by the Declaration of 1789.

that the EU's task is to create an area without internal frontiers, it is immediately followed by a provision emphasising the EU's duty to promote a high level of employment and of social protection, equality between men and women, a high level of protection and improvement of the quality of the environment, the raising of the standard of living and quality of life, and economic and social cohesion and solidarity among Member States. To denounce the current Treaties, or the Constitutional Treaty for that matter, as a "liberal corset", to repeat the daring analogy used by a French politician,[47] is misleading. In the same way, the brawl about the reference to free and undistorted competition has revealed a worrying lack of knowledge.

(b.2) Free and Undistorted Competition

Surprisingly, many have labelled the Constitutional Treaty a neo-liberal document on the ground that it included a provision which provided that the Union shall offer its citizens "a single market where competition is free and undistorted".[48] While citizens can be forgiven for not knowing that this commitment in favour of free competition has been in place since 1957, it is a depressing spectacle to see major politicians make loud protests about it even though, in some cases, they previously signed European treaties where the principle of free competition was obviously included. In any case, the principle of free and undistorted competition is a condition *sine qua non* for a European common market. There is no point removing barriers to trade if companies can subsequently allocate markets to each other on a national basis and compartmentalise markets according to national boundaries. Similarly, national public authorities have to be submitted to the scrutiny of an impartial and supranational referee to make sure they will not subsidise inefficient national companies with the result of eliminating more efficient ones from other Member States. And it is precisely because each Member State is fully aware of the imperative of having an impartial actor to check that all the parties are playing by the rules that the European Commission was instituted. Viewed in this light, it may be easier to understand why the EC Treaty has always provided that Europe shall have "a system ensuring that competition in the internal market is not distorted"[49] and why the enforcement of European competition law has long been solely entrusted to the Commission.[50] As for the "constitutional" entrenchment of free competition, most French politicians have shown a singular lack of knowledge about their own law. Indeed, the

---

[47] See J.-P. Chevènement quoted in J.-L. Andreani and T. Ferenczi, "Les six thèmes-clés de la campagne", *Le Monde*, 28 May 2005.

[48] Article I-3(2) EU CT.

[49] Article 3(g) TEC.

[50] The power to enforce EC competition law on anti-competitive restrictions between undertakings and on abuses of a dominant position is shared with the Member State competition authorities and national courts by virtue of Regulation 1/2003. In other areas of competition law, it lies exclusively with the Commission (merger control when the merger has a Community dimension and monitoring of State aid). For an introduction to EC competition law, see e.g. A.-L. Hinds, *Competition Law* (Thomson Round Hall, Dublin, 2006).

French Constitutional Court also protects economic freedoms (freedom of movement and free competition) and, in particular, it has given constitutional value to freedom of enterprise. Accordingly, it is not uncommon for French constitutional judges to balance freedom of enterprise with competing constitutional principles or rights, especially socio-economic rights.

In light of this long-time and widespread commitment to free competition, one may be legitimately surprised by the French demand, in June 2007, that the clause providing that competition is "free and undistorted" in Europe's single market, be dropped from the Lisbon Treaty. This concession to the freshly elected French president, Nicolas Sarkozy, was justified on the grounds that he needed a "victory" over the United Kingdom in order to confront French critics who have been arguing that the EU has become "a free market Anglo-Saxon creature".[51] This "French coup" has led some authoritative voices to fear that "the European court of justice will not be able to assert the principles of competition in judging on individual cases and that will be a gift to all resurgent forms of economic nationalism and protectionism".[52] Such removal, however, is largely symbolic. The current Art 3 TEC, which provides that the activities of the EC shall include "a system ensuring that competition in the internal market in not distorted", will remain. Furthermore, the Member States have agreed that the Lisbon Treaty will include a new protocol on the internal market and competition, a protocol in which they reaffirm their commitment to the principle of undistorted competition. In other words, competition will continue as an EC policy but will not become one of the Union's objectives. This is fine as competition law should always have been considered as a means to achieve goals rather than a goal in itself. It is also important to stress the conversion of competition into an objective by the Constitutional Treaty in 2004, whereas the EC Treaty has always considered it an activity. This conversion was in fact advocated by Germany rather than the United Kingdom.

Regardless of the legal entrenchment of the principle of free competition in most Member States, it may still be argued that such a principle should not be entertained at the European level. Indeed, according to many left-leaning critics in France, Ireland and elsewhere, the EU legal framework opens the door to "untamed competition" (*concurrence sauvage*). The following excerpt is typical of this view:

"European politicians and commentators often speak (admiringly or accusingly) of Europe's supposed 'social model'. But the reality … is that right-wing (or neo-liberal) economic policies are now dominant at EU level. This is evident in, among other things, an EU competition policy that can act against state provision of certain goods

---

[51] P. Wintour, "Brown in London overrules Blair in Brussels on French coup", *The Guardian*, 23 June 2007.
[52] Mario Monti quoted in P. Wintour, *ibid.*

and services. As part of competition policy, the EU limits state aid to businesses (though there are certain egregious exceptions, such as the Common Agricultural Policy)."[53]

It is therefore necessary to ask whether the pursuit of free competition may contradict a genuine respect of the social goals listed in other provisions of the current (and forthcoming) rules governing the EU. To answer the question, the main rationale behind competition policy must be understood—i.e. the promotion of economic efficiency or, as the economists would say, the optimum allocation of resources. The underlying assumption of competition law is that there are economic benefits associated with a market economy organised on a competitive basis: competition favours innovation, reduces production costs and assures the consumer desired goods at the lowest price and the best quality possible, with the sacrifice of the fewest resources. It would be foolish to deny that the law protecting free competition has a direct role in the prosperity of our democratic societies. Similarly, it is difficult to understand why some see competition rules as a neo-liberal plot. In fact, it is because the practical functioning of the market economy is to some extent deficient that competition rules are required. Apparently, this is a point that left-wing critics have a difficulty understanding. If the market could function in a situation of perfect competition,[54] no external referee would be needed. However, because the market does not function perfectly in real life—the number of buyers or sellers is often reduced, information about products and services is never complete, barriers to entry into a specific market often exist, etc. —national public authorities must intervene to make sure that firms as well as local authorities play by the rules of the game. In other words, competition rules are there to regulate the functioning of the market, not to promote "untamed competition".

To "attack", therefore, European Treaties on the ground that they include provisions aimed at ensuring competition serves to illustrate a flawed knowledge of the functioning of a modern economy.[55] If critics were consistent, they should then formulate an alternative to an economy governed by competition under a regulatory framework defined by public authorities. Too often, criticism aimed at "neo-liberal Europe" often masks affection for discredited economic philosophies and systems. It further demonstrates a singular misunderstanding of the objectives of competition law. Briefly explained, European competition law forbids agreements between firms which restrict competition (e.g. price-fixing agreements between competitors) and abuses of a dominant position (e.g. when a

---

[53] A. Storey, "Another EU: possible and necessary", *The Irish Times*, 7 May 2004.

[54] "Perfect competition" is usually broadly defined as a market structure in which they are large numbers of both buyers and sellers, homogeneous products, perfect information about the price of each firm's product and no barriers to market entry.

[55] See generally the website of the Association for the Taxation of Financial Transactions for the Aid of Citizens (ATTAC: http://www.attac.org) for an immense panoply of arguments mainly emphasising the fact that the EU should not be based on the principle of free trade and free competition but rather on a rather vague principle of "cooperation" between the Member States. Although the extent and modes of implementation of free trade and free competition may legitimately be debated, the apparent desire to re-apply the economic doctrine of the defunct USSR may leave one worried.

dominant firm tries to eliminate competition through illegal behaviour). The European Commission also has the power to control mergers between firms to avoid any excessive domination of a particular market. State aid is also monitored in order to make sure no Member State uses public funds to favour national firms or artificially keep a loss-making national firm in business even though there may be no real prospect of recovery. Finally, regardless of the legal debate, it is important to identify those who are the beneficiaries of free and undistorted competition. Rather than big "evil" firms, citizens and small and medium-sized firms are the direct beneficiaries of competition rules. In the words of Mario Monti, the former European Commissioner in charge of competition policy:

> "The competition policy pursued by the European Commission has a direct impact on the daily life of the citizens of the EU. The reduction of telephone charges, wider access to air transport and the possibility of buying a car in the EU country in which prices are lowest are tangible results. … Whether they be consumers, savers, users of public services, employees or taxpayers, the Union's citizens enjoy the fruits of the competition policy in the various aspects of their everyday life."[56]

The example of the European Commission 2004 decision against Microsoft may suffice to prove Mr Monti right.[57] After a long investigation, and despite a huge team of well-paid lawyers employed by Microsoft, the Commission fined Microsoft €497 million, the biggest fine ever levied by the Commission, for abusing its market power. Microsoft abused its dominant position by deliberately restricting the possibility of using its products with the products of other competitors and by tying its Windows Media Player with its ubiquitous Windows operating system. In short, thanks to its virtual monopoly in PC operating systems, as stated by the Commission, Microsoft had been illegally trying to shut competitors out of the market and to artificially deflect consumer choice in favour of Microsoft's products. It should be clear, therefore, that the direct beneficiaries of a strict enforcement of competition rules are certainly consumers and small and medium firms. An additional comment must be made. It could very well be argued that no individual Member State would have had the courage to stand up against Microsoft for fear of economic retaliation, or could have resisted intense lobbying and financial contributions to governing political parties. Thanks to its political clout, Microsoft actually escaped condemnation in the United States.[58] By contrast, the independence of the European Commission has allowed a thorough investigation into well-known suspicious business practices.

European rules on state aid must also be briefly explored as national politicians often deliberately misinterpret them. This time around, though, criticism mainly originates from

---

[56] European Commission, *Competition Policy in Europe and the Citizen* (Office for Official Publications of the European Communities, Luxembourg, 2000), p 4.
[57] Commission Decision of 24 March 2004 relating to a proceeding under Art 82 of the EC Treaty (Case COMP/C-3/37.792 Microsoft).

the right-wing of the political spectrum. What is usually denounced is the interference of "Brussels" in what should be a "sovereign" definition of national industrial policy. More modestly, EC law forbids state aid that distorts intra-Community competition by favouring certain companies or the production of certain goods. The rationale behind such prohibition is straightforward. By giving certain national companies or goods favoured treatment, a Member State unfairly discriminates against companies that operate unaided. Such a policy could lead to unemployment in other Member States where unaided companies may have to close down as they cannot compete with subsidised ones, irrespective of the fact that they may be more efficient. This, in turn, reduces the general competitiveness of Europe as a whole.[59] Efficiency is not, however, the cardinal and unique value of the EU.

Too often, the national media fail to mention that state aid can be considered acceptable when it has useful social purposes, when it contributes to the development of regions with low levels of development, when it encourages certain activities and practices that are of common interest or when it seeks to remedy a serious disturbance in the economy of a Member State.[60] European rules on state aid, therefore, cannot be presented as being of an absolutist nature. In practice, the great majority of aid schemes are approved by the Commission. The hysteria surrounding the proposal to grant state aid to Intel's operation in Ireland was unfathomable.[61] Notwithstanding the subsequent withdrawal of the aid provided by the Irish Government before any formal inquiry by the European Commission, one should stress that giving taxpayer's money (apparently between €50 and €100 million) to a highly *profitable* and *dominant* American giant firm was from the start a questionable choice. Worse, the purpose was not to create new jobs or support innovation but rather to respond to Intel's threat to move its production out of the country, a despicable yet classic business move nowadays. Moreover, one could imagine the nationalist uproar if state subsidies granted by another country would lead to the closure of an Irish plant. To attract foreign investment, the "Celtic Tiger" already benefits from a low tax rate on business profits, a trait already denounced as unfair competition by some Member States.[62] It is hard to see a pressing need to subsidise profitable businesses, other

---

[58] It recently appeared that the top antitrust official at the Justice Department who recently defended Microsoft against accusations of anticompetitive conduct had worked until 2004 at the law firm that has represented Microsoft in several antitrust disputes. Furthermore, the United States delegation to the European Union, which has lobbied on behalf of Microsoft before the European Commission, is also led by a lawyer who had worked for Microsoft. S. Labaton, "Microsoft finds legal defender in Justice Depart.", *The New York Times*, 10 June 2007.

[59] The stud fee tax exemption is a good example. The tax exemption has helped to make the Irish bloodstock industry the biggest in Europe. Not only do Irish taxpayers foot the bill for a cost of approximately of €3 million annually, it has helped decimate the bloodstock industry in other Member States where the sector had less political clout. See M. Brennock, "EU Commission could demand an end to tax free stud fees", *The Irish Times*, 4 February 2005.

[60] See Arts 87(2) and (3) TEC.

[61] Editorial, "New Realities of Investment Aid", *The Irish Times*, 3 March 2005.

than to use public money to enrich private shareholders. More pragmatically, if it were not for the European Commission, Ireland would not be able to compete against bigger economies where the temptation to attract foreign investments may also easily lead to granting huge sums of public subsidies. Finally, while European (or national) competition rules may not be perfect, they are still indispensable tools to retain fair competition and prohibit distorting practices, detrimental to the public as a whole, from public authorities to private actors.

To sum up, contrary to the fear vehemently expressed by many French citizens during the referendum campaign of 2005, competition rules are, in reality, protective of consumers and of taxpayers. It is the lack of competition rules or the lack of robust enforcement of such rules which actually leads to "untamed competition". There is, however, an argument which has yet to be explored. It is often argued that European competition rules are of an "absolutist" nature, meaning that they override any competing public interest. As we shall see below, the European Commission and the European Court of Justice have always sought to balance efficiency concerns and competing goals, such as social objectives. Certainly, competition is only one policy among others, and the maintenance of competition ought to be read in light of the entire EC Treaty. Furthermore, the notion of competition is understood pragmatically. According to the European Court of Justice, the EC Treaty is aimed at achieving a "workable competition".[63] To put it differently, the objective is to attain sufficient competition in a real world where perfect competition is not achievable while taking into account other public interests. Accordingly, European competition rules may be set aside in order for a Member State to fulfil social objectives.

Critics often fail to mention that the European Court of Justice has recognised the social dimension of the common market, and the necessity to give this equal weight to the economic dimension of market integration. A few cases are worth mentioning to demonstrate the one-dimensional character of the neo-liberal thesis. In a case decided in 1999, *Albany International*,[64] the European Court of Justice explicitly recognised the need to balance the social and economic objectives of the EC:

> "[I]t is important to bear in mind that ... the activities of the Community are to include not only a 'system ensuring that competition in the internal market is not distorted' but also 'a policy in the social sphere'. Article 2 of the EC Treaty provides that a particular task of the Community is 'to promote throughout the Community a harmonious and balanced development of economic activities' and 'a high level of employment and of social protection'".[65]

---

[62] For more details on taxation, see below.

[63] Case 26/76 *Metro* [1977] ECR 1875, para 20.

[64] Case C-67/96 *Albany International* [1999] ECR I-5751.

[65] *ibid.*, para 54.

As a result, the Court held that agreements concluded in the context of collective negotiations between management and labour in pursuit of social policy objectives must, by virtue of their nature and purpose, not be subject to competition rules. In this particular case, it was therefore decided that a private employer cannot invoke competition rules to opt-out of a compulsory sectoral pension scheme drawn up by the social partners. As the agreement made a direct contribution to the improvement of work and employment conditions in the EU, this type of agreement cannot be evaluated in light of European competition law.

Another case, *Sievers*,[66] decided in 2000, can also help demonstrate that fundamental rights have primacy over the principle of free competition. Faced with a situation where part-time workers were excluded from a retirement pension scheme, the European Court of Justice recalled a 1976 ruling according to which the principle of equal pay for male and female workers (guaranteed at Art 141 TEC) pursues a twofold purpose both economic and social. First, in view of the different stages of development of social legislation in the various Member States, the aim of the Treaty provision "is to avoid a situation in which undertakings established in States which have actually implemented the principle of equal pay suffer a competitive disadvantage in intra-Community competition as compared with undertakings established in States which have not yet eliminated discrimination against women workers as regards pay".[67] Secondly, the Court has stressed that the principle of equal pay for male and female workers "forms part of the social objectives of the Community, *which is not merely an economic union* [emphasis added] but is at the same time intended, by common action, to ensure social progress and seek constant improvement of the living and working conditions of the peoples of Europe, as is emphasised in the Preamble to the Treaty".[68] In light of these observations, the European Court of Justice concluded that the economic aim pursued by Art 141 is *secondary* to the social aim pursued by the same provision, namely the right not to be discriminated against on the ground of sex, which is a fundamental human right.[69] In other words, regarding the alleged absolutist application of competition rules, the case law of the European Court of Justice demonstrates the bias of those denouncing the allegedly neo-liberal predisposition of European law. The need to balance the goal of a single market where competition is free with a wide range of social objectives has been formally recognised by EU institutions.

(c) The Situation with "Public Services"

Due to a romanticised attachment to "public services" in countries such as France, a critique often heard is that the EU is eager to apply competition rules without paying due

---

[66] Case C-270/97 *Sievers* [2000] ECR I-929.

[67] *ibid.*, para 54, referring to Case 43/75 *Defrenne II* [1976] ECR 455, para 9.

[68] *ibid.*, para 55, referring to *Defrenne II*, para 10.

[69] *ibid.*, para 57. Accordingly, for the European Court of Justice, part-time workers are entitled to retroactive membership of an occupational pension scheme and to receive a pension under that scheme, notwithstanding the risk of distortions of competition between economic operators of the various Member States to the detriment of employers established in the first Member State.

attention to the specifics of those services. For instance, the Constitutional Treaty has been described as the last act before complete privatisation of what remains under public control at the national level. In the author's view, and this is rarely advocated even by neo-liberal economists, it is clear that competition rules ought not to be applied to all sectors of a market economy. It seems obvious that a free market cannot provide all public goods or services a society may be in need of (e.g. defence, public infrastructure, etc.). A free market may also be unable to satisfy needs with limited or no solvency. In any case, the fact that the European Commission has been trying to liberalise some sectors of activities has been constantly presented by left-leaning critics as a threat to the idea of *service public*. Even though the French like to claim paternity over the concept, all societies obviously operate a hierarchy between social activities and exclude some of these from a market where competition is free and undistorted. Such policy choices are contingent on and would vary according to the axiological preferences of each society.

Nonetheless, there may be a public service *à la française* in the sense that this idea is also treated as a legal concept in France. It has been used by some scholars to identify the scope of French administrative law. The unfortunate aspect of the success of the term *service public* is that it tends to be confused with the idea of public monopoly and the exclusive use of public law. Also striking is the fact that most citizens associate public services with the exclusion of market mechanisms and the suppression of choice. To a great extent, this vision amounts to a myth entertained by the Left. Legally speaking, numerous French public services had always been governed by private law by as early as the end of the nineteenth century. Similarly, it was common in the past, and it obviously is common today, to delegate the management of public services to private individuals and firms while imposing a certain number of specific obligations on them.

Viewed in this light, the "threatening" neo-liberal aspect of EU law seems less compelling. Not only are European competition rules *excluded* where the relevant activities are not of an *economic* nature,[70] what EU law essentially requires is the reconciliation of market mechanisms with *commercial* public services, i.e. energy, telecommunication, transport, postal services, etc. Hence, EU law plainly accepts that national public authorities and European institutions may have to restrain the work of market forces. However, they ought to justify the extent to which they do so regarding *commercial* activities "which the public authorities class as being of general interest and subject to specific public services obligations".[71] Ultimately, what is essential is that activities of an

---

[70] For instance, when the activities of a public (or private for that matter) entity, by their nature, their aim and the rules to which they are subject, are connected with the exercise of powers which are typically those of a public authority, European competition rules cannot be applied. See e.g. Case C-364/92 *Eurocontrol* [1994] ECR I-43. The situation is identical for organisations involved in the management of the public social security system, which fulfil an exclusively social function and perform an activity based on the principle of national solidarity which is entirely non-profit-making. See e.g. Case C-159/91 *Poucet* [1993] ECR I-637.

[71] Commission Green Paper of 21 May 2003 on services of general interest, COM (2003) 270 final, para 16.

economic nature, which may be said to be "of general interest", are obliged by public authorities to comply with specific public-service obligations such as universality and equality of access, continuity, affordability, etc. Public ownership and/or the grant of a monopoly should not be seen as being inherent to the idea of public service. In commercial sectors, rather than directly acting as service providers, public authorities should pursue the more effective option to impose on the competing private entities common public-service obligations to guarantee access for all, whatever the economic, social or geographical situation, of a service of a specified quality at an affordable price. Accordingly, rather than excluding the implementation of competition rules to sectors of an economic nature, the objective is always to strike the right balance between public service missions and the operation of market mechanisms, with a view to promoting Europe's general interest.

This conclusion can easily be reached based on Treaty articles and the case law of the European Court of Justice. Article 16 TEC, introduced by the Amsterdam Treaty, deals precisely with services of general economic interest, the EU name for public services, and provides that "the Community and the Member States, each within their respective powers and within the scope of application of this Treaty, shall take care that such services operate on the basis of principles and conditions which enable them to fulfil their missions". This somewhat tortuous formulation might be considered insufficiently protective. Yet, Art 86(2) TEC further protects the position of those firms entrusted with the operation of services of general economic interest. The application of competition rules should *not* "obstruct the performance, in law or in fact, of the particular tasks assigned to them". The same article sets a condition: "the development of trade must not be affected to such an extent as would be contrary to the interests of the Community". This should not lead to excessive worry as this condition has a marginal importance since the Commission has never successfully relied on it before the European Court of Justice. More fundamentally, the European Court of Justice interprets Art 86(2) in a manner that authorises public authorities to temper market forces in all commercial sectors to the extent that it is necessary to fulfil "universal service" obligations, obligations that are not in themselves profitable.[72] Generally speaking, for the European Court of Justice, competition rules can be set aside if their implementation will obstruct the performance of the special obligations incumbent upon the undertaking entrusted with the management of services of general economic interest under economically acceptable conditions.[73] Finally, the European Court of Justice defines the notion of universal service in line with the French tradition. In other words, a common set of obligations governs any undertaking entrusted with the

---

[72] The concept of universal service refers to a set of general interest requirements ensuring that certain services are made available at a specified quality to all consumers and users throughout the territory of a Member State, independently of geographical location, and, in the light of specific national conditions, at an affordable price. It has been developed specifically for some of the network industries (e.g. telecommunications, electricity, and postal services). See Art 3(1) of Directive 2002/22/EC of 7 March 2002 on universal service and users' rights relating to electronic communications networks and services (Universal Service Directive), [2002] OJ L108/51.
[73] See e.g. Case C-159/94 *Commission v France* [1997] ECR I-5815.

management of a public service. In particular, the public service should be made available at a specified quality to all consumers and users throughout the territory of a Member State, independently of geographical location, and, in the light of specific national conditions, at an affordable price.[74]

Contrary to what the defenders of public services *à la française* have been arguing over and over, the Constitutional Treaty strengthened the importance of services of general interest as one of the pillars of the European model of society and the need to ensure the provision of high-quality and affordable services of general interest to all citizens and enterprises in the EU. For instance, access to services of general economic interest, "as provided for in national laws and practices" and in accordance with current EU rules, became a *new* fundamental right.[75] The aim was to promote the social and territorial cohesion of the EU. Furthermore, the Member States agreed to underscore the national competence for the provision of public services.[76] The ratification of the Constitutional Treaty's successor, the Lisbon Treaty, will not alter in any manner the substance of those improvements agreed in 2004. The only change is technical in nature: rather than having several provisions dealing with public services, a new protocol on services of general interest will be annexed to the European Treaties. One may note, in particular, that the protocol reaffirms that the Treaties "do not affect in any way the competence of Member States to provide, commission and organise non-economic services of general interest".[77]

To conclude on the neo-liberal thesis, neither the current Treaties nor the forthcoming Lisbon Treaty, insofar as it reproduces provisions of the Constitutional Treaty, can be seriously identified as instruments of "ultra-liberalism". In most cases, critics actually denounce principles existing since the foundation of the EU in 1957. But one should not condemn, for instance, the principle of a free and undistorted competition, without first understanding its rationale and without linking it to the fact that one essential purpose of the EU was to complete and to guarantee the proper functioning of a common market. The economic dimension of European integration is merely the direct expression of the limited mission conferred on the EU by the Member States, and certainly not the fruit of some mysterious neo-liberal conspiracy. Ironically, in a popular book,[78] it has been argued to the contrary that "behind the formal rules which govern the decision-making process of the European Union, the French have imposed their will to an extraordinary extent". Accordingly, for some, the EU resembles a socialist Leviathan in the image of the French State while, for other critics, it embodies a neo-liberal experiment. Irrespective of the extreme and contradictory nature of both accusations, it has to be said that the Lisbon Treaty offers some progress or, to put it more neutrally, some change, in terms of the

---

[74] See e.g. Case C-393/92 *Almelo* [1994] ECR I-1477.
[75] Article II-96 EU CT.
[76] Article III-122 EU CT.
[77] Article 2 of the Protocol on services of general interest, [2007] OJ C306/158.
[78] L. Siedentop, *Democracy in Europe* (Penguin, London, 2000), p 30.

Union's values and objectives. If ratified, the EU will then be expressly founded on the values of equality and solidarity. Among many other social provisions, the Lisbon Treaty expressly stipulates that the EU shall combat social exclusion and shall promote social justice.[79] Clearly, this amounts to a restatement, yet in a clearer and concise manner, of the current values and objectives of the EU. These values and objectives could hardly belong to a purportedly neo-liberal entity. The fact that the "European project" has suffered the criticism of free-marketers as well as neo-Marxists may amount to the ultimate evidence that it offers a balanced framework. As stated by the working group of the European Convention on Social Europe:

> "European policy in the economic and social sphere is aimed at creating conditions for the fullest development of the individual in society in such a manner that ultimately the free development of each one becomes a condition for the free development of all."[80]

To accuse the EU of being a neo-liberal entity completely betrays the past and current efforts of balancing the economic and social dimension of European integration and further illustrates a profound misapprehension of the limited mandate of the EU. Rather than agreeing to the creation of a European welfare state, the democratically elected representatives of the Member States have agreed to push for the completion of an internal market. The former goal may be legitimately entertained, yet political fiction is not the concern of the present study. Even though current and contemplated European Treaties cannot be seriously described as neo-liberal instruments, such claims have found a special resonance in the hearts and minds of many French voters. Unfortunately but predictably, the EU is now being accused of promoting social or fiscal dumping. This time, it is not the content of the legal provisions governing the EU that is condemned but rather the substance of public policies defined at Union level. The reality of a European-organised "race to the bottom" must be examined. In this instance, the arguments raised against European integration appear prima facie much more substantiated.

(II) THE RACE TO THE BOTTOM

While it has been common to denounce "Brussels" for its neo-liberal policies, widespread fears of social dumping and outsourcing were unanticipated by the proponents of the Constitutional Treaty. Allegations of social dumping and outsourcing have found, however, deep resonance in France. This was unsurprising as the social dumping charge had been asserted for years by an influential association of "alter-globalists" in its fight against the

---

[79] In doing so, the Lisbon Treaty merely reproduces a provision first found in the Constitutional Treaty.
[80] European Convention, Final Report of Working Group XI on Social Europe, CONV 516/1/03, Brussels, 4 February 2003, p 29.

World Trade Organisation.[81] It may well be described as the most effective allegation raised against the "European project". It would be excessive, however, to condemn the EU on the basis that it organises social dumping or to use another popular expression, a race to the bottom leading to the dismantling of the welfare state and the watering down of social standards. The picture is more complex. While it can be affirmed that European integration has placed general constraints on national policy choices, European welfare states are primarily threatened by structural and national problems (e.g. unfavourable demographic trends, massive unemployment, etc.). Moreover, the pressure to reform the welfare state generally originates from national groups unwilling to continue to pay high taxes for preserving existing levels of welfare protection. As for watering down social standards, it is difficult to find a binding piece of European legislation harmonising social standards at the lowest common denominator. This is not to categorically refute the argument that EU rules on free movement of goods, persons, services and capital might favour "regulatory competition" between the Member States and indirectly add downward pressure on workers' salaries. To conclusively prove that this regulatory competition actually leads to a race to the bottom in Europe remains, however, an arduous challenge. I shall try to demonstrate this point in light of the heated debate surrounding European-wide harmonisation of taxation and the so-called "Bolkestein" Directive on services in the internal market, finally adopted in December 2006 and which is aimed at liberalising services throughout Europe.[82]

(a) The European Dimension of the "Delaware Effect"

Before examining the EU's responsibility, if any, in creating a "race to the bottom", the expression must be put into context. This problem is hardly new. In the United States, it is common to debate the so-called "Delaware effect".[83] In short, critics of Delaware's corporate laws have argued that most large American firms establish themselves in this US State simply because its rules are the least demanding. Referring to this problem of companies establishing in states where the cost was lowest and the laws least restrictive, Justice Brandeis spoke in 1933 of a "race" between US states which "was one not of diligence but of laxity".[84]

To explain the origin of the current situation it is necessary to return to the "stagflation" crisis of the seventies. Following the huge increases in oil prices in the seventies and the

---

[81] See http://www.attac.org. The term "alter-globalist" has been recently coined to offer a more positive alternative to the term "anti-globalist" predominantly used by the media. Members of the "alter-globalisation" movement have been denouncing, *inter alia*, the World Trade Organisation and the International Monetary Fund for legislating neo-liberalism. See e.g. I. Wallerstein, "The 'alter-globalists' hit their stride", *The International Herald Tribune*, 2 February 2007.

[82] Directive 2006/123/EC of 12 December 2006 on services in the internal market, [2006] OJ L376/36.

[83] For a good overview of US academic literature, see M. Roe, "Delaware's Competition", (2003) 117 *Harvard Law Review* 588.

[84] *Liggett Co. v Lee*, 288 US 517 (1933), p 559.

implosion of the Bretton Woods regime of fixed exchange rates, all major industrialised nations suffered inflation and unemployment. To deal with the economic crisis the liberalisation of trade and free movement of capital was promoted. Generally speaking, the influence of economic liberalism has greatly benefited from the demise of communism and the apparent failure of classic Keynesian remedies, i.e. the stimulation of the economy through expansionary fiscal policy or monetary policy. Parallel to this trend, the establishment of a common market in Europe has obliged the Member States of the EU to abolish obstacles to the free movement of goods, persons, services and capital.

These developments, it is often alleged, threaten the viability of the welfare state as well as high social standards. The argument goes that in an environment where free trade, free competition and free movement of the factors of production are all promoted and—in the case of the EU—legally guaranteed over national laws, national authorities have no choice but to offer national firms, capital owners or highly skilled workers the best regulatory environment to retain them and eventually attract foreign firms, capital and workers. This process is known as regulatory competition.[85] Although the process can be positively defended from a theoretical point of view,[86] it has been forcefully argued by Fritz Scharpf, in his classic book *Governing in Europe*, that regulatory competition is not without damaging consequences from a social point of view:

> "As all countries are now competing to attract or retain investment capital and producing firms, all are trying to reduce the regulatory and tax burdens on capital and firms, and all are tempted to reduce the claims of those groups—the young, the sick, the unemployed, and the old—that most depend on public services and welfare transfers."[87]

If you add the temptation for national governments, in the name of retaining competitiveness, to make the labour market more "flexible" by lowering, for instance, workers' legal protection against dismissal, this is exactly the race to the bottom that most European citizens instinctively fear. Indeed, it is widely believed today, at least by the citizenry of some Member States in the "old Europe", that regulatory competition is

---

[85] J.-M. Sun and J. Pelkmans define it as follows: "Regulatory competition is the alteration of national regulation in response to the actual or expected impact of internationally mobile goods, services, or factors on national economic activity", "Regulatory Competition in the Single Market", (1995) 33 *Journal of Common Market Studies* 67 at 68–69.

[86] Three justifications are normally given for regulatory competition: "firstly, it allows the content of rules to be matched more effectively to the preferences or *wants* of the consumers of laws (citizens and others affected); secondly, it promotes diversity and experimentation in the search for effective legal solutions; and thirdly, by providing mechanisms for preferences to be expressed and alternative solutions compared, it promotes the flow of information on effective law making", C. Barnard and S. Deakin, "Market Access and Regulatory Competition", in C. Barnard and J. Scott (eds), *The Law of the Single European Market* (Hart, Oxford, 2002), p 199.

[87] F. Scharpf, *Governing in Europe: Effective and Democratic?* (Oxford University Press, Oxford, 1999), p 176.

progressively leading to a situation where Member States compete on the basis of low standards. The recent enlargement contributed decisively to the popularising of this view.

Critics contend that the EU *inherently* favours a race to the bottom by adding to the constraints on policy choices imposed upon nation states by the liberalisation of trade under the auspices of the World Trade Organisation. To understand the nature of Europe's constraints the common distinction between negative integration and positive integration must be understood. In short, negative integration is about removing barriers to trade by imposing prohibitions on the Member States in terms of the free movement of the factors of production. As previously mentioned, the European Court of Justice has always considered that the purpose of the EC Treaty provisions dealing with the "four freedoms" is to eliminate "all obstacles to intra-community trade in order to merge the national markets into a single market bringing about conditions as close as possible to those of a genuine internal market".[88] By contrast, positive integration "refers to the reconstruction of a system of economic regulation at the level of the larger economic unit".[89] According to the dominant view, "the main beneficiary of supranational European law has been negative integration".[90] Undeniably, the European Commission, in association with the European Court of Justice, has greatly favoured market integration by making sure that Member States do not infringe Treaty provisions, prohibiting them from protecting domestic producers or from restricting the freedom of national firms and workers to move to another Member State. In doing so it is correct to contend that the European Commission pushed for an extensive interpretation of the relevant Treaty provisions and that, in most cases, the European Court of Justice concurred.

An examination of the celebrated *Cassis de Dijon* case[91] reveals the force of negative integration as a constraint on a Member State"s regulatory autonomy. Faced with a German law that prohibited selling fruit liqueur unless it contained a certain minimum amount of alcohol content, the European Court of Justice was easily convinced by the Commission that the German law served a protectionist intent rather than the defence of public interests, such as the effectiveness of fiscal supervision, the protection of public health, the fairness of commercial transactions or the defence of the consumer:

> "It is clear ... that the requirements relating to the minimum alcohol content of alcoholic beverages do not serve a purpose which is in the general interest and as such to take precedence over the requirements of the free movement of goods, which constitutes one of the fundamental rules of the Community."[92]

---

[88] Case 15/81 *Gaston Schul* [1982] ECR 1409, para 33.
[89] Scharpf, *Governing in Europe*, p 45.
[90] *ibid.*, p 50.
[91] Case 120/78 [1979] ECR 649.
[92] *ibid.*, para 14. One may note in particular the ludicrous argument raised by the German Government as regards the protection of public health. To defend its legislation, it argued that the purpose of fixing minimum alcohol content is to avoid the proliferation of alcoholic beverages with a low alcohol content since such products, in the view of the German Government, may more easily induce a tolerance towards alcohol than more highly alcoholic beverages.

The case is remarkable less for the protection it afforded *Cassis de Dijon*—a fine French liqueur—against German attempts at restricting its sale than for the European Court of Justice's interpretation of Art 28 TEC, which forbids "quantitative restrictions on imports and all measures having equivalent effect". By setting out the principle that this provision prohibits all national rules which hinder intra-EU trade unless justified, the European Court of Justice granted itself control over the regulatory choices of the Member States. In other words, even where an apparent "neutral" national trading rule, i.e. a non-discriminatory rule, has the effect of restricting intra-EU trade, the Member State must also justify its existence. As we shall see in relation to the "Bolkestein" Directive on Services, the European Court of Justice has adopted a similar approach in the context of free movement of workers and services.

The second remarkable aspect of the *Cassis de Dijon* ruling is that by further announcing the new principle of mutual recognition (i.e. the principle according to which products lawfully manufactured and marketed in one Member State must be admitted in all Member States) the European Court of Justice empowered the consumer and promoted market integration to the detriment of Member States' autonomy to regulate trade in the absence of European harmonisation. To summarise, *Cassis de Dijon* opened the door to European scrutiny of all national regulations that can be viewed as obstacles to the free movement of goods between the Member States. In order to survive European scrutiny, national measures must be "reasonable", meaning they must be justified by the defence of a public interest and must be proportionate in their scope.

Clearly, it is up to the European Court of Justice to ultimately define what should be viewed as an obstacle to free trade and, once an obstacle is identified, to accept or refuse to accept a Member State's defence of it. True to what its critics often assert, the European Court of Justice showed some dogmatism in this exercise. First, it has broadly interpreted the remit of Art 28 TEC. For instance, a ban on advertising alcohol on the radio and television, a law prohibiting magazines containing prize competitions and the temporary closure of a motorway in order to accommodate a demonstration were all found to constitute "measures having equivalent effect to quantitative restrictions" which had to be objectively justified.[93] Secondly, the Court of Justice has frequently adjudicated in favour of market integration rather than in favour of the societal goals raised by the Member States. However, since the beginning of the nineties, its case law illustrates more judicial self-restraint and the readiness of the European Court of Justice to set aside free movement rules in order to preserve national regulatory autonomy. To begin with, all national business regulations dealing with "marketing modalities" or "selling arrangements", e.g. restrictions on advertising, restrictions on sales outlets, etc. are now excluded, as a matter of principle,

---

[93] See respectively Case C-405/98 *Gourmet International* [2001] ECR I-1795; Case C-368/95 *Familiapress* [1997] ECR I-3689; Case Case C-112/00 *Schmidberger* [2003] ECR I-5659.

from European scrutiny.[94] And if a national regulation falls within the scope of Art 28 TEC, a Member State can now refer to an extensive list of public interests to defend it.

In addition to those public interests enunciated in *Cassis*, the European Court of Justice has recognised that a Member State can justify a "neutral" regulation having an adverse impact on trade on the following grounds: the protection of the working environment; the protection of cinema as a form of cultural expression; the protection of national or regional socio-cultural characteristics; the maintenance of the plurality of the press; preventing the risk of seriously undermining the financial balance of the social security system; the protection of fundamental rights.[95] Furthermore, it is important to note that even discriminatory measures can be justified by reference to the exceptions contained in Article 30 of the TEC: public morality; public policy or public security; the protection of health and life of humans, animals or plants; the protection of national treasures and the protection of industrial and commercial policy. Finally, and most importantly, at the balancing stage, when a national measure restricting trade has to be justified, the European Court of Justice now admits more easily that the free movement of goods can be restricted in order to accommodate, for instance, social rights and policies.[96]

To conclude on "negative integration", *Cassis de Dijon* should not be understood as opening the way to a destructive regulatory competition. Undeniably, "if applied without any qualification, there is a danger that mutual recognition would lead to a race to the bottom, and to a deregulation of standards".[97] However, "the danger of a race to the bottom is acknowledged within EC law on free movement"[98] as it allows Member States to preserve discriminatory or indirectly discriminatory regulations when such rules are necessary for the defence of a public interest. The somewhat uncompromising attitude of the European Court of Justice until the beginning of the nineties, in the majority of cases dealing with free movement of goods has to be understood in light of the ever-present temptation for national authorities to unfairly defend national producers by hiding behind the alleged defence of a public interest. A comical example is provided by the "beer purity" case decided in 1987.[99] Germany tried to stop the importation of foreign beers on the ground that they failed to meet its beer purity standards. German authorities defended the

---

[94] See Cases C-267-8/91 *Keck and Mithouard* [1993] ECR I-6097. This is not to say that the case law is always consistent or straightforward.

[95] See respectively Case 155/80 *Oebel* [1981] ECR 3409; Case 60/84 *Cinethèque* [1985] ECR 2605; Case 145/88 *Torfaen Borough Council v B & Q* [1989] ECR 3851; Case C-368/95 *Vereinigte Familiapress* [1997] ECR I-3689; Case C-120/95 *Decker v Caisse de Maladie des Employés Privés* [1998] ECR I-1831; Case C-112/00 *Schmidberger* [2003].

[96] For a stimulating account, see M. P. Maduro, "Striking the Elusive Balance between Economic Freedom and Social Rights in the EU", in P. Alston (ed), *The EU and Human Rights* (Oxford University Press, Oxford, 1999), pp 449–472.

[97] Barnard and Deakin, "Market Access and Regulatory Competition", p 203.

[98] *ibid.*

[99] Case 178/84 *Commission v Germany* [1987] ECR 1227.

legislation by arguing that additives could constitute a public health risk for a person who drinks in excess of 1,000 litres of beer a year![100]

To preserve the benefits of a common market and limit the potentiality of any "free-rider" strategy, the European Court of Justice had to make sure that Member States play by the rules defined in 1957 and which have been further refined by a succession of amending Treaties. It does not mean, for instance, that "pure beers" cannot be produced and consumed in Germany. It merely forbids Germany to prohibit the importation of "impure" beers and leaves to the German consumer the freedom to choose. To be sure, the Member States only express discontent when they are the object of European scrutiny. When their neighbours are censured for hindering the selling of the goods they produce, there is no more talk about the dogmatism of the European Court of Justice. At any event, the Court is now more sensitive to the dangers arising from the direct (legal) effect of negative integration on national problem-solving capacities. In the sectors of social and process regulations discussed in Scharpf's work,[101] the broad picture is one of a careful Court unwilling to condemn national regulations unless the protectionist intent or effect is manifest. Furthermore, as Miguel Poiares Maduro points out, "if one takes the Europe majority policy as the yardstick by which to judge the impact of free movement rules on regulation, then there has been hardly any deregulation as a consequence of the application of free movement provisions".[102]

Even if the EC Treaty provisions aimed at removing trade barriers are now well and effectively balanced with a wide range of competing objectives and interests, it is further argued by social democratic critics of the EU that the ease with which capital and work can move from one state to another continues to lead to regulatory competition, increasing the pressure on the Member States willing to defend existing levels of national regulation and social protection. The allegedly unfortunate aspect of European integration is that national authorities cannot rely on any European "re-regulation" to protect and develop existing regulatory and social policies. Due to the cumbersome character of the European decision-making process and deep ideological differences among Member States, interventionist policies aimed at managing regulatory competition could hardly be defined, much less agreed upon. To quote once again Fritz Scharpf, at the European level, the institutional capacity for negative integration is supposedly "stronger than the capacity for positive integration, interventionist policies, and the interests they could serve, are systematically disadvantaged in the process of European integration".[103]

Before exploring further the reality of a "race to the bottom", a caveat must be introduced. Negative integration should be accompanied by "positive" measures not only

---

[100] See the opinion of the Advocate General Slynn in Case 178/84 ECR 1246, p 1253.
[101] Scharpf, *Governing in Europe.*
[102] Maduro, "Striking the Elusive Balance between Economic Freedom and Social Rights in the EU", p 455.
[103] Scharpf, *Governing in Europe*, p 49.

to make sure the market functions properly but also to eventually correct regulatory competition through harmonisation measures, e.g. in the form of minimum European standards. From such an "interventionist" perspective, European legislation should at the very least provide common standards to guarantee a level playing field and to avoid social or fiscal dumping. Yet, before discussing any eventual European "re-regulation" and the delicate issue of when disparities between the laws of the Member States give a competitive advantage to states with lower standards, the existence of a race to the bottom should first be substantiated.

(b) The Issue of "Fiscal Dumping"

To the probable surprise of many well-intentioned critics, a "race to the top" seems to prevail in Europe in some significant areas such as health and industrial safety, environmental risks, gender equality and consumer protection.[104] Yet, regarding taxation, such a race to the top does not appear to have materialised. On the contrary, Member States give the impression of competing against each other to attract or to retain capital by lowering their corporate tax rate. How can these two different situations be explained? According to Andrew Moravcsik:

> "The major difference between apparently intractable issues of EU discussion such as social and tax harmonization, and similar issues where European regulation is effective, such as worker health and safety, appears not to lie in constitutional structure but in the precise nature of conflicts of interest among national governments. In the case of taxation, some governments remain deeply opposed to the harmonization of taxation and social welfare, whereas there are few die-hard defenders of unilateralism in matters of worker health and safety or pollution abatement."[105]

As a result, the EU cannot be said to *inherently* suffer from a neo-liberal bias, embodied in its constitutional structure. The EU can merely accomplish what a super-majority of Member States want it to accomplish and then a race to the top is feasible. Furthermore, even in the taxation field, it is tempting to argue that the reality of a race to the bottom is not as clear-cut as commonly assumed. It is important to stress that critics here complain about the lack of European harmonisation. When examining the 2004 Commission's proposal on the liberalisation of services, we shall discover that the same critics also complain about European harmonisation when it does not fit their ideological preferences. But let's focus for the moment on the fiscal dumping now allegedly taking place in Europe.

---

[104] On the competitive pressures on national regulatory systems induced by economic integration, see the special issue of the *Journal of European Public Policy* with in particular an introductory presentation by F. Scharpf, "Introduction: The Problem Solving Capacity of Multi-level Governance", (1997) 4 *Journal of European Public Policy* 520.

[105] Moravcsik, "In Defence of the 'Democratic Deficit'", pp 618–619.

Small Member States have been tempted to cut corporate tax rates to attract foreign firms. It is a sensible strategy as long as the reduction is accompanied by an increase in total revenue. Ireland successfully implemented this strategy. Ireland's decision to cut its rate of profits tax from 40 percent to 12.5 percent coincided with a sustained period of impressive economic growth. Several new Member States are now busy trying to emulate the example of the Celtic Tiger.[106] Estonia went as far as abolishing taxation on reinvested profits while other Member States are adopting or contemplating an increasingly popular solution: a flat tax system where income tax, corporation tax, and VAT are subject to the same rate of taxation. To retain their firms, and possibly attract foreign investments, France and Germany have also envisaged bringing down their corporate tax rates (respectively 33.3 and 38.3 percent in 2006). For example, speaking for Angela Merkel, in the 2005 German federal elections campaign, Mr Kirchhof, a university professor, called for a new flat income tax of 25 percent and a corporate tax cut to 22 percent. And in stark contrast to the position adopted by the former German Chancellor Gerhard Schröder, he controversially declared that he "would never support guidelines against so-called tax dumping. Every country has autonomy in the sense of its own legislation and every country should strive to be better than the others".[107] More surprisingly, in January 2007, Jacques Chirac followed suit and called for the French corporate tax rate to be reduced from 33.3 percent to 20 percent. There is also a remarkable consensus on low corporate taxes in the newly self-governing Northern Ireland.

From the point of view of those willing to preserve a sufficiently large tax base to maintain a viable welfare system and convinced that social justice and equity justify substantial taxes on capital, this trend amounts to a vicious circle as all Member States will eventually end up with less revenue from capital owners.[108] Worse still, in the name of job creation or job retention, Member States are always tempted to subsidise firms, as the Intel affair in Ireland demonstrated. The result is that not only do states collect less money from capital owners, they also give away taxpayers' money. Regarding the latter aspect, thanks to the EC Treaty, the European Commission is empowered to control state subsidies with the principle of undistorted competition. However, and this is a legitimate cause for concern, "no such criteria are as yet applied to competitive *general* reductions of the tax

---

[106] For a general overview, see *KPMG's Corporate Tax Rate Survey – An international analysis of corporate tax rates from 1993 to 2006* (published in October 2006 and available at: http://www.kpmg.com).

[107] Quoted in D. Scally, "CDU rejects tax harmonisation", *The Irish Times*, 6 September 2005. The policy choices advocated by Paul Kirchhof proved to be so controversial and politically damaging for Angela Merkel that the shadow Finance Minister had to publicly declare before polling day that he will remain in academia.

[108] For the moment, Ireland still enjoys the benefits of being one of the few countries pursuing a strategy of development based on a low corporation tax rate. In 2002, Ireland raised more corporate taxes as a percentage of GDP (about 3.7 percent) than any of the other 15 countries reviewed in the 2005 Report of the Irish National Competitiveness Council. By contrast, in Germany, corporate taxes do not even reach 1 percent of GDP while, in France, they represent close to 3 percent. See National Competitiveness Council, *The Competitiveness Challenge 2005*, figure 2.1, p 24 (report available at: http://www.forfas.ie/ncc).

rates applying to capital incomes and businesses".[109] It should be noted in passing that this demonstrates, yet again, that competition law should not be seen as the enemy of social protection. On the contrary, what is needed is a stronger enforcement of the current provisions against abuses of private power and unfair public subsidies as well as a broadening of their scope at the European level, to cover "competitive *general* reductions of the tax rates" suggested by Fritz Scharpf. It may then be easier to convince fellow citizens that competition law is all about guaranteeing a level playing field.

However, the vehement opposition from Ireland and the United Kingdom to any harmonisation of corporate taxation at the EU level makes it highly unlikely that Member States will ever agree to such an extension of the scope of European competition law. To remedy what it sees as fiscal or tax dumping, successive French governments have also regularly proposed the harmonisation of the rules under which corporate tax is calculated throughout the EU. This proposal has been taken onboard by the European Commission, which is now working on a legislative proposal that will enable companies to follow the same rules for calculating the tax base for all their EU-wide activities.[110] The continuous opposition of the Irish and British Governments to this idea is based on the fear that this proposal may eventually lead to the emergence of harmonised corporate tax rates through the back door.[111] When questioned in 2004 about a possible harmonisation of corporate tax rules at EU level, Mr McCreevy, then the Irish Finance Minister said: "We are against it. Any methodology that would lead to harmonised tax rates, either through the front door or through the back door, is against the EU constitution."[112] Remarkably, the fear of EU harmonisation is such that it led the Irish Government, when the Constitutional Treaty was being negotiated, to oppose harmonisation in matters relating to tax fraud and tax evasion. The fear of opening the door to more harmonisation overrode any consideration of the common good. On the other hand, it was clear that some governments intended to use this clause as a first step towards tax harmonisation. In any event, the strident Irish opposition has so far paid off: Unanimity voting remains—and will remain under the Lisbon Treaty—the general rule for all tax-related matters. The adoption of the legislative proposal on the "Common Consolidated Corporate Tax Base", now contemplated by the Commission is, therefore, highly unlikely.

Another proposal is worth mentioning. Mr Nicolas Sarkozy, then the French Finance Minister, suggested in 2004 that Member States with unusually low corporate tax rates should not benefit from European structural funds, these funds representing a third of the

---

[109] Scharpf, *Governing in Europe*, p 100.

[110] See European Commission, Communication on Implementing the Community Lisbon Programme: Progress to date and next steps towards a Common Consolidated Corporate Tax Base (CCCTB), COM (2006) 157 final.

[111] M. Coleman, "Bertie gives tax harmonisation 'nul points'", *The Irish Times*, 10 November 2006.

[112] D. Staunton, "Ministers move to harmonise corporate tax rules", *The Irish Times*, 13 September 2004.

EU's budget. This call was widely denounced, and rightly so. First and foremost, policies embodying European solidarity should be preserved and implemented exclusively with regard to socio-economic criteria. Secondly, a country may need to compensate for other disadvantages it suffers in order to attract investment. In the case of Ireland or Estonia, for instance, their geographical isolation ought to be compensated for in some way. Yet, these Member States must realise that they play a dangerous game when they oppose—not on ideological grounds but merely to preserve their competitive advantage—any proposal to introduce a minimum corporate tax throughout the EU, e.g. a 10 percent rate for the poorest countries with a superior threshold for the richest countries. A minimum corporate tax rate would demonstrate that all Member States realise that Europe is now "a community of destiny" and that national well-being cannot be sought at the expense of your neighbours.

Nevertheless, the extent of tax dumping should not be overstated. Investments and the maintenance of jobs do not exclusively depend on taxation rates. France, where you find the most vociferous voices against globalisation, is still among the group of countries receiving the largest share of foreign investments. In 2002, for instance, it ranked number two worldwide for investment inflows just behind China. It also ranked number two in Europe, behind the United Kingdom and in front of Ireland, for job creation from foreign direct investment.[113] In addition, the perceived threat of the exodus of jobs to "low-cost" destinations appears unfounded. A study published in 2005, analysing a period running from 1995 to 2001, claims that only 2.4 percent of the 3.9 million people employed in France in the manufacturing sector have been "outsourced" during this period.[114] To put it differently, merely 0.35 percent of industrial jobs were transferred and created abroad, and that means, in absolute numbers, approximately one job out of 300. Another unexpected conclusion is that only half of these jobs created abroad are actually located in "low-cost" countries. The other jobs migrated to Spain, Italy, Germany and the United States. Although authoritative figures have yet to be offered, it is extremely unlikely that the 2004 enlargement has resulted in a massive exodus of jobs from the "old" to the "new" Europe.

Irrespective of the complex and surprising realities of outsourcing, it cannot be denied that taxes on business and capital incomes, a trend initiated at the beginning of the eighties, have progressively and continuously diminished as a source of government revenue in the "old" Member States with extensive welfare obligations, to the detriment of immobile factors of production, meaning the workers.[115] To guarantee existing levels of public

---

[113] See http://www.investinfrance.org.

[114] See P. Aubert et P. Sillard, *Délocalisations et réductions d'effectifs dans l'industrie française (1995–2001)*, INSEE, No G 2005/03, April 2005 (available at: http://www.insee.fr). Another informative report largely confirms these findings and exposes the numerous myths associated with "outsourcing": Assemblée des Chambres Francaises de Commerce et d'Industrie, "Délocalisations: La peur n'est pas la solution", November 2005 (available at: http://www.acfci.cci.fr).

[115] By contrast, despite the reduction in corporate income tax rates, the revenue from corporate taxation appears to be increasing in Ireland and in the new Member States.

services while maintaining a decent level of public debt, taxes on labour and taxes on consumption have increased to compensate for the amount lost with regard to companies and capital owners. Assuming that regulatory competition between EU countries ought to be blamed for this trend, what are the potential solutions as far as Europe is concerned? A first solution may lie in the setting up of a minimum corporate tax rate at Union level or different thresholds that would be linked to the level of development.[116] Alternatively, if no agreement is possible for ideological or purely selfish reasons, the Member States should seek to develop a law of "unfair regulatory competition". It has been suggested that the Commission and the European Court of Justice should be empowered to intervene "against competitive tax concessions, competitive forms of deregulation, and similar practices. The criterion in every case would be Kantian: given the preferences of the adopting country, would measures of this kind become self-defeating if they were simultaneously adopted by all other countries?"[117]

Ideologically compatible with economic liberalism, it would be much more difficult for Ireland and the United Kingdom to oppose, normatively and politically speaking, the development of a set of rules aimed at guaranteeing fair competition than to reject proposals to directly harmonise taxation at the European level. The EU would then be in the position to limit eventual tax dumping, with the political advantage that citizens may come to better realise that the EU is a genuine community and an effective framework to manage the most disturbing changes brought about by the globalisation of the economy. In the areas of social-policy regulation (e.g. working hours, employment security), ironically, it is not the lack of European rules that many have come to regret. On the contrary, the European Commission has been accused of actively favouring "social dumping" by pushing forward a Directive aimed at liberalising services throughout Europe.

(c) The "Frankenstein" Directive on Services

In addition to propagating fears about imminent job losses to the benefit of the new "low-cost" Member States, some prominent French socialists took advantage of the debate on the Constitutional Treaty to spread, to the visible delight of Jean-Marie Le Pen, fears about the likely invasion of "Polish plumbers". In Ireland, the Labour Party Leader, Pat Rabbitte, decided to emulate his humanist colleagues from the French Left. He suggested, without any hard evidence, that migrant workers from Eastern Europe were causing a displacement of Irish workers and the erosion of pay and working conditions in Ireland; hence the so-called "race to the bottom".[118] However, according to the Central Statistics Office, if

---

[116] See e.g. R. de Mooij, "Does the Enlarged European Union Need a Minimum Corporate Tax Rate?", (2004) 39 *Intereconomics* 180. The author argues that by putting a floor on the tax rate, Europe may avoid a potentially harmful tax race to the bottom. As long as the minimum rate is not too "high", the disciplining impact of tax competition will not be lost.

[117] Scharpf, *Governing in Europe*, p 198.

[118] See e.g. Editorial, "Attitude towards migrant workers", *The Irish Times*, 23 January 2006.

migrant workers make up more than 10 percent of the Irish labour force at the end of 2006, there is no evidence that migrants are displacing Irish workers from their jobs.[119] This is obviously not the first time critics misrepresented the EU in relation to the enlargement in May 2004 when 10 Eastern European countries joined the Union. Before the social dumping discourse, some leaders made it their personal business to emphasise the fact that hordes of "welfare tourists" were about to abuse our cherished national welfare systems. It obviously did not happen and, similarly, the adoption of the so-called "Bolkestein Directive" on services in the internal market—also labelled the "Frankenstein Directive" by some—would not have led to a race to the bottom.

It is important here to note that the following discussion will primarily focus on the draft Directive on services in the internal market as originally proposed by the European Commission in March 2004,[120] rather than the largely revised version adopted at the end of the year 2006.[121] The purpose of Directive 2006/123, on services in the internal market, is still to facilitate the provision of cross-border services but it does so without referring to the controversial country-of-origin principle which was dropped following the opposition of the European Parliament and some Member States. Under this principle, a service provider must be subject only to the law of the country in which he is permanently established and not to the law of the Member State where it wants to provide services on a temporary basis. The infamous principle has now been replaced with a new clause entitled "freedom to provide services" whose added-value remains unclear. The country-of-origin principle is therefore likely to stir up passions for a little while and should be, in any event, further explained since it has been so widely misinterpreted.

Before discussing the country-of-origin principle, it is worth remembering that the free movement of services is one the four fundamental principles underpinning the EU common market since 1957. Yet, 50 years later, cross-border trade in services still lags behind the trade in goods. Indeed, although services account for more than 70 percent of the GDP in most Member States, cross-border trade in services only amounts to about 20 percent of trade within the EU, thanks to a good deal of protectionism and bureaucratic red tape. Convinced that greater economic growth and more jobs would follow greater trade and competition—the number of 600,000 jobs has been put forward—the Commission issued a draft Directive in January 2004. The aim is to encourage greater cross-border trade in services by providing a legal framework that will eliminate obstacles to the *freedom of establishment* (the right for service providers to establish their business in any Member State for an indefinite period), and to the *freedom to provide services* (the right to provide services on a temporary basis in a Member State in which the provider of services is not established).

---

[119] C. Madden, "Migrant not displacing Irish Workers – CSO", *The Irish Times*, 23 February 2007.
[120] Proposal for a Directive of the European Parliament and of the Council on Services in the Internal Market SEC(2004)21.
[121] Directive 2006/123/EC of 12 December 2006 on services in the internal market, [2006] OJ L 376/36.

In its initial version, the "Bolkestein Directive" raised strident protests as regards the second objective. According to the dominant allegation at the time, the proposed liberalisation of the freedom to provide services, under the auspices of the country-of-origin principle, was likely to initiate a race to the bottom. A characteristic example of the (inaccurate) claims one may effortlessly find in the press is given by David Begg, General Secretary of the Irish Congress of Trade Unions (hereinafter "ICTU"):

> "What does not make sense is to allow service industries to base themselves in the low-cost accession countries and from there outsource jobs to provide services in the EU 15, on pay rates and conditions of employment which apply in the base country. This is a crazy proposition which would cause great resentment and potentially undermine support for the European project. … Unless our social model is robust enough to protect these most vulnerable people, it is only a matter of time before everyone joins the 'race to the bottom'".[122]

Rather than promoting "social dumping", the country-of-origin principle is aimed at helping small and medium-sized enterprises to test the market before eventually setting up business on a permanent basis. In other words, to ease the burdens involved with doing business in another Member State, the Commission initially advocated the following principle: any company which provides services in one country should be automatically qualified to provide services in any other Member State on the basis—here is the Gordian knot—of home-country regulation. Under this principle, a business which provides services in the Member State in which it is established is qualified to provide services on a *temporary* basis in any other Member State according to the regulations of its home Member State. Although the draft Directive included provision for a number of important exceptions to the application of the principle (consumer contracts, for instance) as well as complete derogations (23 in total) for sectors such as health and other "public services", opponents expressed fears about "social dumping". In short, it was argued "that if the new EU Member States can compete in the market for services on an equal basis without applying the often higher social rights as well as health and safety and environmental standards of some of the EU 15, the lowest level of standards in the European Union will become the norm".[123]

The key issue is how to clearly interpret the country-of-origin principle and whether or not it is a new principle. It is well established that EC law guarantees the right of establishment and the freedom to provide services. As previously mentioned, the right of establishment ensures that nationals and companies of one Member State can freely move to another Member State in order to carry out activities as self-employed persons and to

---

[122] D. Begg, "Barroso intent on shifting EU to right of centre", *The Irish Times*, 7 February 2005.

[123] House of Lords, EU Committee, *Completing the Internal Market in Services*, 6th Report of Session 2005–06 (HL Paper 23), para 7. This Report should be singled out not only for the brilliant synthesis it operates but also for the diversity of evidence it offers.

set up and manage companies.[124] Also protected by EC law since 1957, the freedom to provide services implies that any self-employed person has the right to undertake, *on a temporary basis*—an important feature often neglected by critics—any economic activity normally performed for remuneration within the EU.[125] In both cases, it is clear that EU law prohibits, unless justified by a public interest requirement, discriminatory and indirectly discriminatory national measures. Non-discriminatory national measures are also prohibited when they constitute an impediment to freedom of movement.

The country-of-origin principle is only concerned with the freedom to provide services and *not* the right of establishment. This is an important point, too often misunderstood. Indeed, in the latter case, any company willing to do business on a *permanent* basis in any Member State must do so through a fixed establishment and comply with all the rules of the host Member State. As for the fact that Directive 2006/123 protects the right of companies to provide services on a *temporary* basis, i.e. without the need to establish themselves in the Member States where they trade, there is nothing new here. It is argued, however, that Directive 2006/123, in its draft version, went further to the extent that the right to provide services was deemed to protect a brand new country-of-origin principle. This is not entirely accurate. Not only does the principle already appear in several pieces of legislation,[126] the European Court of Justice has applied a similar principle in the field of goods since 1978. As we have seen, in *Cassis de Dijon*,[127] the European Court of Justice ruled that, in the absence of European rules, goods should freely circulate between Member States, provided that they have been lawfully produced and marketed in one of the Member States. This idea is known as the principle of mutual recognition. The application of national rules hindering trade can only be justified by reference to a mandatory public interest. A similar logic governs the case law dealing with the freedom to provide services. For the European Court of Justice, in the absence of European-wide harmonisation, national rules hindering the freedom to provide services violate EU law unless they can be justified by the regulating state with overriding reasons relating to the public interest. More specifically, the Court has held that the application of national legislation to foreign persons providing services ought to be strictly justified whenever the requirements embodied in legislation "are already satisfied by the rules imposed on those persons in the Member State in which they are established".[128]

Even though the country-of-origin principle is not a complete novelty, it is still reasonable to consider that Directive 2006/123, in its initial version, denoted an important policy shift as far as the regulation of the internal market was concerned. Faced with the political and legal intricacies of any attempt to harmonise the provision of services across

---

[124] See Arts 43 to 48 TEC.
[125] See Arts 49 to 55 TEC.
[126] See the TV without frontiers Directive (89/552/CEE) and the E-Commerce Directive (2000/31/CE).
[127] Case 120/78 [1979] ECR 649.
[128] Case C-288/89 *Gouda* [1991] ECR I-4007, para 13.

Europe through a set of sectoral Directives, the Commission appears to have considered the country-of-origin principle to be an acceptable means of revitalising EU's economy in one go. By eliminating a great deal of prior administrative authorisations, any EU-based company would have been automatically qualified (unless the sector fell within one of the many derogations provided for by the Directive) to provide services in any other Member State on the basis of home-country regulation. As a result, the "Bolkestein Directive" has been presented as a neo-liberal plot. More worrisome, some French left-wing humanists have propagated the view that it paves the way for an invasion of "Polish plumbers". In less xenophobic terms, the argument runs that the application of the country-of-origin principle is going to lead to a race to the bottom, most notably in the fields of workers' rights and health and safety standards.

The potential impact of the "Bolkestein Directive" has been deliberately exaggerated. Critics tend to forget that there is a great deal of European legislation setting minimum health and safety standards. The same is true regarding environmental protection. Accordingly, "full" liberalisation of services cannot lead to a situation where a Member State lowers its health and safety standards or environmental standards to gain competitive advantage by being below the current European minimum standards. As for workers' rights, most critics failed to realise that the Posted Workers Directive issued in 1996 regulates this area and precisely *excludes* the country-of-origin principle.[129] In the terms of this Directive, the EU must promote the transnational provision of services in a "climate of fair competition and measures guaranteeing respect for the rights of workers".[130] Accordingly, posted workers must enjoy the application of certain minimum protective provisions in force in the Member State to which they are posted, regardless of the law applicable to the employment relationship. The 1996 Directive further provides that employees who are posted temporarily to a Member State other than their own, will be subject to the labour law of the country in which they are employed. Rules dealing with working time, minimum paid annual holidays, minimum rates of pay, the conditions of hiring-out of workers and health, safety and hygiene at work should therefore be governed by the Member State in which they are employed.[131] On the basis of this Directive, the European Court of Justice has constantly emphasised that "Community law does not preclude a Member State from requiring an undertaking established in another Member State which provides services in the territory of the first Member State to pay its workers

---

[129] Directive 96/71/EC. A posted worker is defined as one who, for a limited period, carries out his work in the territory of a Member State other than the State in which he normally works.

[130] Recital 5.

[131] Article 3(1) of the Directive lays down the mandatory rules to be observed by employers during the period of posting in regard to the following issues: maximum work periods and minimum rest periods; minimum paid annual holidays; minimum rates of pay; the conditions of hiring-out of workers, in particular the supply of workers by temporary employment undertakings; health, safety and hygiene at work; protective measures with regard to the terms and conditions of employment of pregnant women or women who have recently given birth, of children and of young people.

the minimum remuneration laid down by the national rules of that State".[132] When a Portuguese firm was caught employing Portuguese workers on a permanent basis in France in almost Dickensian-type conditions on behalf of a major French firm, France Telecom, it was an obvious and shocking violation of French *as well as* European law.[133] The trouble in France—and this is certainly true in most Member States—is that the manpower of the labour inspectorate, the department whose mission is to inspect companies for potential violation of labour regulations, has shrunk considerably over the years. Accordingly, numerous labour abuses that are unlawful under national as well as European law go undetected. Furthermore, in a situation of high unemployment, it is far from unusual to see politicians exerting great pressure on civil servants in order to convince them to show some "flexibility" when dealing with violating firms. They are often told that they should not behave so as to "discourage" investment.

Detractors of the "Bolkestein Directive" seem unaware that the Directive has always been intended to be *only* applicable to services provided temporarily and by those who are not employed by others, i.e. self-employed persons rather than employees.[134] Accordingly, no firm would have been able to send a contingent of low-paid workers to do a job (requiring a stay of more than seven days) in another Member State without being bound by the laws of the host country. As for the situation of self-employed persons, the "Bolkestein Directive" initially excluded the country-of-origin principle where self-employed persons work directly for consumers. In other words, self-employed persons would have still been obliged to provide services under Irish law in Ireland, under French law in France, etc. So much, therefore, for the "Polish plumber".[135] In the end, *only* those who take on self-employed businesses providing a "commercial" service on a temporary basis for a business customer in a different Member State were supposed to come under the auspices of the country-of-origin principle. The scope of liberalisation was, therefore, limited.

Finally, the argument according to which the "Bolkestein Directive" was going to favour "outsourcing", (i.e. the evasion of national law by national companies or self-employed persons as they move abroad to more "welcoming" Member States), again reveals a misunderstanding of the true scope of the Directive 2006/123. Companies already have

---

[132] See recently Case C-341/02 *Commission v Germany* [2005], para 24. The European Court of Justice requires, however, that the application of such rules must be appropriate for securing the attainment of the objective which they pursue, that is to say, the protection of posted workers, and must not go beyond what is necessary in order to attain that objective. A case-by-case assessment is therefore required.

[133] See "Manifestations contre le travail au rabais", *Le Monde*, 24 May 2005.

[134] As previously discussed, the 1996 Posting of Workers Directive regulates the situation of employees.

[135] The Polish Embassy in Paris should be congratulated for its sense of humour. After all the unpleasant comments heard during the 2005 French referendum campaign, it launched a tourist campaign advertising an attractive blonde man carrying a monkey-wrench, presumably a Polish plumber, who beckoned French people to visit his country with the following slogan: "I am staying in Poland. Come on over."

the freedom to establish themselves wherever they want with great ease.[136] A Member State is nonetheless entitled to take measures to prevent its citizens from attempting to use the EC Treaty to improperly circumvent national legislation or to prevent individuals from improperly or fraudulently taking advantage of provisions of EC law.[137] This is known as the "abuse evasion theory".[138] As a result, an Irish company registering its permanent office in Latvia, while it is clear that it intends to carry out most of its business in Ireland, cannot rely on Latvian law in Ireland. This is not a legal option today and it would not have been allowed under the Services Directive in its draft version. As soon as a company (and its employees) carries out business in a Member State on a permanent basis, it is bound by national rules, no matter where it is formally established. In the field of services the fears were also overblown. It was indeed difficult to imagine Irish plumbers establishing themselves in Slovakia and willing to fly from time to time to work in Ireland for a business customer. Certainly, they would have been covered by Slovakian law under the country-of-origin principle but the benefit of so doing would appear highly elusive.

The discourse on "social dumping" has been singularly misguided. The draft Directive on Services neither compelled the Member States to liberalise public services nor did it regulate the situation of posted workers. It is understandable therefore that Charlie McCreevy, the European Commissioner for Internal Market and Services, has shown some irritation and said, in a statement to the European Parliament: "I don't want to hear any more talk about so-called social dumping. This not what this proposal is about and we should put an end to this confusion."[139] The Commissioner is right. Directive 2006/123 on services in the internal market does not bring any change regarding the conditions and standards for workers. The European Commission never intended to allow companies to bring in "cheap" workers from other Member States and create a type of unfair competition with national companies who play by the rules. In addition, Directive 2006/123 does not prevent Member States from supervising companies and workers operating in their territory. For instance, national authorities are free to enforce national labour laws by means of on-the-spot checks or by demanding all relevant information from the company that posts workers in the country.

---

[136] See e.g. Case C-56/96 *VT4* [1997] ECR I-1459, para 22: "The Treaty does not prohibit an undertaking from exercising the freedom to provide services if it does not offer services in the Member State in which it is established."

[137] See e.g. C-23/93 *TV 10* [1994] ECR I-4795.

[138] However, the European Court of Justice has held, somewhat unconvincingly, that the mere fact that a company does not conduct any business in the Member State in which it has its registered office but instead pursues its activities only in the Member State where its branch is established, is not sufficient to prove the existence of abuse or fraudulent conduct. This does not mean that the Member State where business is being exclusively conducted cannot deny that company the benefit of the provisions of Community law relating to the right of establishment. The Court requires instead that national authorities must prove, on a case-by-case basis, abuse or fraudulent conduct on the part of the persons concerned. See Case C-212/97 *Centros* [1999] ECR I-1459

[139] Statement to the European Parliament on Services Directive, speech/05/149, Strasbourg, 8 March 2005.

Rather than obsessively focusing on the liberalisation of services in Europe, it is the insufficient enforcement *by each individual Member State* of the 1996 Posting of Workers Directive which must be addressed. In this regard, it is essential to repeat that it is the responsibility of the host Member State to conduct inspections and to enforce its employment and working rules as well as the relevant EU standards. It cannot be denied that the posting of workers is an important economic phenomenon. Before enlargement in 2004, about 120,000 workers had been posted in France.[140] Such a phenomenon, however, does not have any link with lasting high unemployment', even though it may be tempting for failed national élites to use this as a way of detracting attention from their incompetence. The main problem, today, is the political unwillingness of most national governments to enforce these rules even in situations where violations of national rules are committed by or on behalf of national companies. Rather than deploring the fact that companies do not abide by the law, national governments would be better advised to hire more workplace inspectors.[141] The EU should not be blamed for the political preferences of national governments or their incompetence.

The controversy surrounding Irish Ferries was a distressing demonstration that the EU can be blamed, even in situations where there is not the slightest reason to assign blame in that direction. In September 2005, the General Secretary of ICTU, David Begg, was bold enough to inaccurately state that if the EU Services Directive becomes reality, "the grotesque Irish Ferries scenario will become the norm" and added:

> "If anybody was in any doubt as to the impact of this crazy proposition—the Services Directive—they need look no further than Irish Ferries. The chief executive of Irish Ferries earned €687,000 last year. But he wants to dump 543 workers and replace them with people on around €3 per hour ... there's something deeply obscene about that."[142]

It is important to stress that the EU, a body with limited powers, does not possess the power to pass legislation on salaries. Likewise, it would be impossible to link the EU with the fact

---

[140] See the report issued by the French Sénat on the Bolkestein Directive: Rapport d'information No 206, session 2004–2005, 18 February 2005, p 16.

[141] The "Gama affair" illustrates this particularly well. See e.g. C. Dooley, "Gama secured 70% of PAYE relief scheme", *The Irish Times*, 18 May 2005. Thanks to Mr Higgins, Socialist Party TD, Irish citizens were astonished to learn that Turkish construction workers on Irish projects were being paid between €2 and €3 an hour while working for about 80 hours per week. Despite several complaints, the Turkish company has been successful in securing nearly €200 million worth of State contracts since its arrival at the end of 2000. EC law bears no responsibility whatsoever for this disgrace. Nor is it a question of insufficiently protective national legislation. The crux of the matter is that Ireland only employs about 21 inspectors to police approximately two million workers. The Minister for Enterprise, Micheál Martin, has since announced the appointment of 10 new labour inspectors, specifically to combat exploitation. See P. Cullen, "Expansion of labour inspectorate planned", *The Irish Times*, 9 April 2005.

[142] Quoted in P. McGarry, "Ahern sees no cause for gloom over EU's future", *The Irish Times*, 28 September 2005.

that the average CEO in most developed nations now generally makes between 300 and 500 times as much in pay as the average production-worker.[143] As for the Services Directive, one has to show an astonishing lack of understanding to find a connection between what it aims to achieve and the Irish Ferries scenario. It would be more appropriate to emphasise the shameful acceptance by all governments of the practice of "flag-hopping". It is a well-known fact that the world's largest fleets belong to the Bahamas, Panama and Liberia, allowing ship-owners to avoid paying taxes and to avoid labour and safety standards.

Rather than challenging these capitalist deviances, trade unionists spend a great deal of time portraying the EU as some sort of neo-liberal Leviathan. Both terms are false. Trade unionists, and the workers they allegedly represent, have really nothing to gain from putting forward a representation of the EU as "the enemy". In the case of Ireland, it is indisputable that workers have gained more rights thanks to the EU. Regarding the fear of social dumping, one may note that the Celtic Tiger miracle partially derives from the initial "low-cost" of its labour force. In any case, it is regrettable that the media do not rigorously scrutinise the "arguments" put forward by the opponents to the liberalisation of services in Europe. In all the cases of labour abuses which have agitated the media in Ireland and elsewhere, the abuses do not originate from the implementation of EU norms but rather from the failure of the Member States to properly apply them alongside protective national legal standards.

CHAPTER FIVE – CONCLUSION

The EU, as a political project, has suffered immense damage from the accusation of being a neo-liberal entity pursuing neo-liberal policies. Even its long-time devotees in Ireland or elsewhere lament the fact that the EU, "potentially the most civilised political project of our times", has become the vehicle of a race to the bottom.[144] In claiming, however, that EU law allows for Latvian workers to work on less than half the minimum wage and without the protection of Irish labour law, or in arguing that the Services Directive is waved "around like holy scripture in which the almighty commission decrees that you can't protect national standards of employment",[145] commentators seem to trade stylistic considerations for accuracy. The neo-liberal caricature is deeply unfortunate as not only do the legal provisions upon which the EU is founded *not* embody any neo-liberal bias, there is also little evidence to support the assertion that EU policies encourage a race to the bottom. In most instances, fantasies rather than facts govern the discussion as it is politically more convenient to blame an indeterminate "foreign" entity, and eventually foreigners, than to confront national vested interests or address national failures to enforce

---

[143] Compare this to the situation in the seventies, when the average CEO pay represented about 25 times the pay of an average production-worker. See "Executive pay. Too many turkeys", *The Economist*, 26 November 2005.
[144] F. O'Toole, "A lot hangs on outcome of dispute", *The Irish Times*, 29 November 2005.
[145] *ibid.*

the law of the land. Persisting and massive unemployment and the financial troubles of our welfare systems are structural problems that have little to do with economic globalisation or enlargement. Unfortunately, the temptation is always present for national governments to point the finger at the EU for all their countries' ills. The EU should not be seen, however, as a foreign body with its own (neo-liberal) will. It is, above all, a framework that the Member States can rely on to confront collective challenges and threats. It is up to the Member States to ultimately agree on the definition of sound policies in order for Europe to preserve itself from unregulated economic competition.

Instead of denouncing the supposed neo-liberal nature of the European Treaties, critics should realise that ideological conflicts and divergent national interests are the genuine obstacles to European "re-regulation" in the direction of a more "social Europe". As for the cases of labour exploitation, European law should not be blamed. Such cases are due to companies not abiding by the law or abusing it in a context of persisting high unemployment and illegal immigration and can only continue thanks to an extraordinary unwillingness by national authorities to enforce their own labour standards. To point the finger at European integration, the Lisbon Treaty or the new Member States may be too tempting for unprincipled politicians, yet the situation is unfortunately more complex and, in most cases, the first step will be to hold national authorities accountable for their failure to enforce their own law and put an end to legal loopholes. Ultimately, the key question, as far as the EU is concerned, is a relatively simple one: who would benefit from its weakening or worse, its demise? Certainly not the weakest and smallest?

CHAPTER SIX

The EU Charter of Fundamental Rights as a Socialist Trojan Horse[1]

The most intriguing feature of the debate surrounding the EU Charter of Fundamental Rights (hereinafter the "Charter"), first agreed in December 2000 and to be given legally binding effect by the Lisbon Treaty, is the fact that it has been the subject of plainly contradictory views. To a great extent, reporting in the British or Irish press reflects—or maybe rather explains—the reluctance of the British and Irish governments to fully accept the Charter. Accordingly, the discussion has been mainly negative. Rather than highlighting the benefits for European citizens and the EU of having a proper Bill of Rights, the dangers of making it legally binding have been constantly emphasised. Three major arguments can be distinguished.

For eurosceptics, many elements of the Charter are matters for the Member States and have nothing to do with the EU as it has developed up to now, e.g. the death penalty or reproductive cloning. For the defenders of national sovereignty, the fear is that the Charter may lead the way towards a "federal" common standard. Not only will the Charter allow the European Court of Justice to expand its jurisdictional empire, the argument runs, but it will also enable it to define a common standard applicable right across the EU. In other words, it is alleged that the European Court of Justice is about to gain the power to enforce a uniform standard of rights akin to that of the US Supreme Court. Finally, employers' organisations are keen to stress the potential negative impact of the Charter on business. In particular, the socio-economic rights protected by its "solidarity" title have been widely denounced as threatening Britain's liberal labour laws. By contrast, the referendum campaign in France showed the prevalence of strikingly divergent interpretations. There, the same Charter was widely denounced as embodying a "neo-liberal" conception of rights while, at the same time, decried for its toothless character. Before addressing the arguments raised against the Charter, a discussion of the protection of fundamental rights within the EU legal order is required in order to dispel some common misunderstandings. It should also help to understand why it was deemed necessary for the EU to finally have its own catalogue of rights.

---

[1] This title is directly inspired by the stimulating account given by L. Betten, "The EU Charter of Fundamental Rights: a Trojan Horse or a Mouse?", (2001) 17 *International Journal of Comparative Labour Law and Industrial Relations* 151.

(I) THE EU CHARTER'S OFFICIAL PURPOSE: A REMEDY TO THE PERCEIVED RIGHTS DEFICIT OF THE UNION

When the EC was first established in 1957 its primary goal was the attainment of economic integration. Although the EC Treaty guaranteed the protection of some workers' rights, the Treaty did not and still does not contain a written Bill of Rights.[2] This is not to say that the lack of express and exhaustive provisions for the protection of human rights has meant the absence of any protection. As early as 1969, the European Court of Justice held that fundamental rights were enshrined in the general principles of EU law—strictly speaking EC law[3]—that the Court protects.[4] The European Court of Justice's motivation for protecting fundamental rights did not derive from a sudden passion for rights. It is generally accepted that the European Court of Justice did so under German pressure. More precisely, in 1967, the German Federal Constitutional Court threatened not to accept the principle of the supremacy of EU law so long as the Community legal order lacked specific protection for fundamental rights.[5] To answer the German Court's concern, the European Court of Justice ruled in 1969 that fundamental rights formed an integral part of the general principles of EU law. It followed that the European Court of Justice must proscribe measures which were incompatible with the observance of human rights as recognised and guaranteed under EU law.[6] In the end, as two noted scholars of the EU, Phillip Alston and Joseph Weiler put it: "the European Court of Justice deserves immense credit for pioneering the protection of fundamental human rights within the legal order of the Community when the Treaties themselves were silent on this matter."[7] Furthermore, it is also important to note that by the early 1970s the European Court of Justice had confirmed that, in protecting such rights, it was inspired by the constitutional traditions of the Member States[8] and by the guidelines supplied by international human rights treaties

---

[2] It can also be argued that the EC Treaty did not contain any detailed provisions on fundamental rights for the simple reason that another organisation was already in charge of protecting fundamental rights in Europe: the Council of Europe, founded in 1949. Interestingly, no country has ever joined the European Union without first belonging to the Council of Europe. Among the numerous conventions concluded by the Council of Europe, the most famous is the European Convention for the Protection of Human Rights and Fundamental Freedoms (known as the "ECHR" for European Convention on Human Rights). Part of the institutional framework of the Council of Europe, the European Court of Human Rights, located in Strasbourg—the European Court is often called the "Strasbourg Court"—has jurisdiction to guarantee observance by the contracting states of the European Convention on Human Rights, signed in 1950. For an instructive overview, see G. Quinn, "The European Union and the Council of Europe on the Issue of Human Rights: Twins Separated at Birth?", (2001) 46 *McGill Law Journal* 849.

[3] For didactic reasons, the term EU will be preferred to EC.

[4] Case 29/69 *Stauder v City of Ulm* [1969] ECR 419.

[5] See the so-called *Solange I* case [1974] 2 CMLR 540.

[6] The German Constitutional Court considered these developments adequate. It therefore overruled its earlier decision in holding that it will no longer exercise its (theoretical) jurisdiction over EU law in the field of fundamental rights. See the *Solange II* case [1987] 3 CMLR 225.

[7] P. Alston and J. Weiler, "An 'Ever Closer Union' in Need of a Human Rights Policy: The European Union and Human Rights", in P. Alston (ed), *The EU and Human Rights* (Oxford University Press, Oxford, 1999), p 52.

[8] Case 11/70 *Internationale Handelsgesellschaft* [1970] ECR 1125.

on which the Member States had collaborated or to which they were signatories.[9] In particular, the European Convention for the Protection of Human Rights and Fundamental Freedoms of 4 November 1950 (hereinafter the "ECHR") was explicitly referred to in several rulings. In fact, the European Court of Justice has recognised its "special significance" amongst international treaties on the protection of human rights.[10] One should not deduce from this "special significance" that the ECHR is a direct source of EU law. As a matter of fact, the European Court of Justice has no jurisdiction to apply the ECHR when reviewing EU law because the ECHR is not itself part of EU law. In practice, however, the European Court of Justice now refers extensively to provisions of the ECHR,[11] as well as to the case law of the European Court of Human Rights,[12] to decisively guide its interpretation of EU law whenever it is argued that it violates fundamental rights.

If one can praise the European Court of Justice for protecting fundamental rights, notwithstanding the silence of the Treaties, it implies that it is left to the Court to identify the fundamental rights protected under EU law on a case-by-case basis. This situation has left some commentators uneasy. Indeed, despite the self-imposed restraints used by the Court and important amendments brought by the Maastricht Treaty and the Amsterdam Treaty, the Court of Justice remains the ultimate arbiter as regards the identification of fundamental rights that ought to be protected under EU law. These amendments were somewhat significant insofar as they formally obliged the Union to "respect fundamental rights, as guaranteed by the European Convention for the Protection of Human Rights and Fundamental Freedoms signed in Rome on 4 November 1950 and as they result from the constitutional traditions common to the Member States, as general principles of Community law",[13] and gave an express legal basis for the EU "to combat discrimination based on sex, racial or ethnic origin, religion or belief, disability, age or sexual orientation".[14] The Amsterdam Treaty also gave the EU the power to act against a Member State that had seriously and persistently violated fundamental rights. It also confirmed that, with the Turkish prospective candidacy in mind, continued respect for those rights is a condition of membership of the EU.[15] Also of significance was the willingness of all the Member States, including the United Kingdom following the election of Tony Blair, to finally include in the EC Treaty the EU's commitment to fundamental social rights as defined in the European Social Charter, signed in Turin on 18 October 1961, and in the 1989 Community Charter of the Fundamental Social Rights of Workers.[16]

---

[9] Case 4/73 *Nold v Commission* [1974] ECR 491.

[10] Case 44/79 *Hauer v Land Rheinland-Pfalz* [1979] ECR 3727.

[11] See e.g. Case 222/84 *Johnston v Chief Constable of the Royal Ulster Constabulary* [1986] ECR 1651.

[12] See e.g. Case C-274/99 *Connolly v Commission* [2001] ECR I-1611.

[13] Article 6 TEU.

[14] Article 13 TEC.

[15] See respectively Arts 7 and 49 TEU.

[16] In 1997, the United Kingdom decided to sign the 1989 Community Charter and to cancel the British "opt-out", clearing the way for the incorporation into the EC Treaty of the Protocol on Social Policy adopted in 1992 by all the other Member States which was, until then, merely annexed to the EC Treaty and did not apply to the United Kingdom.

Yet for of all these developments, the EU still lacked a Bill of Rights of its own.[17] The sudden urgency in the late nineties to give the EU a Charter of Fundamental Rights has to be understood in light of the fact that the previous overriding idea, proposed by the European Commission as early as 1979, and since supported by influential actors, has been to urge accession by the European Community to the ECHR. However, by ruling in 1996 that unless the EC Treaty is amended the EU does not have the power to accede to the ECHR,[18] the European Court of Justice obliged European institutions to rethink how to affirm the EU's commitment towards fundamental rights and how to clarify the sometimes uneasy relationship between the fundamental rights protected by EU law and the ones protected by the ECHR, as well as the fundamental rights protected by national constitutions. The European Parliament actually did so, well before the Court's judgment in 1996. It has pressed in 1989 and in 1994 for the adoption of a declaration of fundamental rights as part of a "Constitution" for the Communities.[19] The idea of an EU Bill of Rights, however, was only successfully revived on a German initiative. On 12 January 1999, the German Foreign Affairs Minister Joschka Fischer told the European Parliament: "In order to increase the citizen's rights, Germany is proposing the long-term development of a European Charter of Basic Rights. ... For us, it is a question of consolidating the legitimacy and identity of the EU."[20] Hence, to solve the perceived rights deficit of the EU, the European Council decided in 1999 that it was time to consolidate, in other words to codify, the fundamental rights applicable at EU level in a single text. It was hoped that a Bill of Rights would strengthen the Union's legitimacy by making it easier for the layperson to quickly and clearly identify his or her fundamental rights under EU law. According to the decision adopted by the European Council in Cologne in June 1999:

> "Protection of fundamental rights is a founding principle of the Union and an indispensable prerequisite for her legitimacy. ... There appears to be a need, at the present stage of the Union's development, to establish a Charter of fundamental rights in order to make their overriding importance and relevance more visible to the Union's citizens."[21]

In a process similar to that which preceded the Constitutional Treaty, the EU Charter was drafted by what became known as "the Convention", an ad hoc body composed of

---

[17] For further developments and references on the origins of the EU Charter, see among a plethora of comments, G. de Búrca, "The drafting of the European Union Charter of fundamental rights", (2001) 26 *European Law Review* 126.

[18] See Opinion 2/94 *Accession by the Communities to the European Convention for the Protection of Human Rights and Fundamental Freedoms* [1996] ECR I-1759.

[19] See OJ C120/51 of 16 May 1989; OJ C61/155 of 28 February 1994.

[20] European Parliament Minutes, 12 January 1999, quoted in House of Lords, EU Select Committee, *EU Charter of Fundamental Rights*, 8th Report 1999–2000, HL Paper 67, para 29.

[21] European Council of Cologne, Presidency Conclusions, 3–4 June 1999.

62 members representing the Heads of State and Government, the President of the European Commission, the European Parliament and the national parliaments. As for the content of the Charter,[22] the fundamental rights it guarantees are set out in six distinct titles: Dignity; Freedoms; Equality; Solidarity; Citizens' Rights and Justice. The Charter's articles thus encompass a wide range of civil, political, economic and social rights. Its drafters did not limit themselves to a simple compilation of existing rights. Indeed, even though the Charter substantially reproduces the rights contained in the ECHR of 1950, its content is, at times, broader. Whereas the ECHR is mainly limited to civil and political rights, the Charter covers other areas such as the right to good administration, the rights of the disabled, the social rights of workers, the right to a clean environment, the protection of personal data and bioethical rights. Even though those rights already have a variable degree of protection under EU law and in most Member States, their consecration as "fundamental" rights was still missing. Finally, in addition to the six titles previously mentioned, a concluding title contains the so-called "horizontal clauses", i.e. the general provisions describing in particular the field of application of the Charter and how the rights and principles protected ought to be interpreted.

Rather than fighting specific provisions of the EU Charter, the British Government (supported by the Irish Government) originally sought in 2000 to neutralise its legal effects by opposing any incorporation into the current Treaties.[23] Essentially, the crucial preliminary legal question was whether and, if so, how the Charter should be integrated into the Treaties. The initial intransigence of the British Government paid off. No agreement was reached at the European Council in Nice in December 2000 on the final legal status of the Charter. Rather, the Member States decided to solemnly "proclaim" it in association with the European Commission and the European Parliament. The ambiguous character of the notion of "proclamation" has been somewhat confusingly interpreted as meaning that the Charter is not legally binding but has nonetheless legal effects. In a clearer fashion, Advocate General Tizzano observed:

> "[I]n proceedings concerned with the nature and scope of a fundamental right, the relevant statements of the Charter cannot be ignored; in particular, we cannot ignore its clear purpose of serving, where its provisions so allow, as a substantive point of

---

[22] For an exhaustive and authoritative presentation, see K. Lenaerts and E. de Smijter, "A Bill of Rights for the European Union", (2001) 38 *Common Market Law Review* 273.

[23] For an instructive analysis comparing the United Kingdom's approach to the ECHR and the EU Charter, see e.g. E. Wicks, "'Declaratory of Existing Rights'" – The United Kingdom's Role in Drafting a European Bill of Rights, Mark II", (2001) *Public Law* 527.

reference for all those involved—Member States, institutions, natural and legal persons —in the Community context."[24]

In other words, the EU Courts, i.e. the European Court of First Instance and the European Court of Justice, may refer to the Charter to guide their interpretation even though it is not legally binding.[25]

In 2004, the Member States decided to incorporate the EU Charter into the Constitutional Treaty. The unanimous decision to abandon this latter text in June 2007 did not lead, however, to the abandonment of the Charter as well. While the Charter will not be incorporated *in extenso* into the current European Treaties, the Lisbon Treaty will replace the current Art 6 TEU on fundamental rights with a new provision which will itself contain a "cross reference" to the Charter.[26] One may regret the change from a stylistic point of view but from a legal point of view the final result remains identical: the Charter will become a legally binding core element of the Union's legal order once the Lisbon Treaty is unanimously ratified. The fact that the Charter will soon have the same legal value as the European Treaties, however, is not without its numerous critics.

(II) Tackling Myths About the EU Charter[27]

The EU Charter has been denounced, above all in the United Kingdom, as an expansionist tool for the EU, a text threatening the national definition of fundamental rights as well as a potential hindrance for businesses by allegedly making socio-economic rights equally as enforceable as political and civil rights. The three main arguments raised against the Charter will be addressed in turn. Before doing so, it should be pointed out that the proposed binding character of the Charter does not inspire the same criticism on the continent. This is not to say that the Charter has been generally praised. During the French referendum campaign, in the broader context of a prevalent anti-globalisation mood, the

---

[24] Case C-173/99 *BECTU* ECR I-4881, Opinion delivered on 8 February 2001, para 28. See also the opinion of Advocate General Kokott in Case C-540/03 *Parliament v Council* [2006] ECR I-5769, para 108: "While the Charter still does not produce binding legal effects comparable to primary law, it does, as a material legal source, shed light on the fundamental rights which are protected by the Community legal order".

[25] The Court of First Instance has used the Charter as a point of reference in several of its judgments. See e.g. Case T-177/01 *Jégo-Quéré v Commission* [2002] ECR II-2365. The approach of the Court of Justice has been more cautious: It referred for the first time to the Charter in 2006 when the European Parliament sought the annulment of Directive 2003/86 on the right to family reunification and which itself refers to the Charter. See Case C-540/03 *Parliament v Council* [2006] ECR I-5769.

[26] Following the abandonment of the Constitutional Treaty, the version of the Charter, as agreed in the 2004 Intergovernmental Conference, was re-enacted in 2007 and published in the Official Journal: [2007] OJ C303/1. Any reference in the Charter's text to the term "constitution" was dropped.

[27] In February 2005, Jack Straw, then the British Foreign Secretary, launched a series of factsheets "tackling common myths" about the EU Constitutional Treaty (see http://www.fco.gov.uk). This section includes my own effort to take on "the mythology of the eurosceptics which distort so much of the European Union".

Charter was widely depicted as a neo-liberal document threatening to lower national and/or international standards of protection. On the other hand, the same text has been criticised for being incapable of judicial enforcement, often by the same persons arguing that it embodies a menacing neo-liberal conception of rights. This striking contrast between all these different views is certainly intriguing and calls for a careful assessment of the Charter. Even though its provisions may seem at times ambiguous—all Bills of Rights offer ambiguous provisions—most critics appear to be quite selective in their analysis and quite regularly demonstrate their ignorance on how fundamental rights are protected at national and European levels.

(a) Enlarging the European Union's Powers by the Back Door?

To the delight of eurosceptics, Andrew Duff, a British MEP and a convinced federalist, accused Tony Blair of trying to disguise the revolutionary implications of the EU Charter. Mr Duff, a genuine constitutional expert, said in 2003 that the incorporation of the Charter was "profoundly federalising" and would extend the European Court of Justice's reach into ordinary life.[28] It would be unfair, however, to accuse the former British Prime Minister, on this occasion at least, of deliberately misleading his citizens. The fact that the Charter will be given legally binding value should not be equated with an enlargement of the EU's powers through the back door.

Decisively, as amended by the Lisbon Treaty, Art 6 TEU provides that "the provisions of the Charter shall not extend in any way the competences of the Union as defined in the Treaties". Furthermore, the Charter itself, in one provision which was aimed at specifically answering British concerns in 2004, provides that it "does not extend the field of application of Union law beyond the powers of the Union or establish any new power or task for the Union, or modify powers and tasks" as defined by the Treaties.[29] The wording of this provision is extremely restrictive and should be compared to the initial version agreed in 2000: "This Charter does not establish any new power or task for the Community or the Union, or modify powers and tasks defined by the Treaties." It should, therefore, be clear that the Charter will apply primarily to the institutions and bodies of the EU, in compliance with the principle of subsidiarity, and cannot offer, *in itself*, a legal basis for the EU to legislate. The fact that certain Charter rights concern areas in which the EU has little or no competence to act is no contradiction: "although the Union's *competences* are limited, it must *respect* all fundamental rights wherever it acts and therefore avoid indirect interference also with such fundamental rights on which it would not have

---

[28] Quoted by A. Evans-Pritchard, "Dutch warn of federal police", *The Daily Telegraph*, 31 May 2003.

[29] Article 51(2) EU Charter (formerly Art II-111(2) EU CT). Rather pointlessly, the Member States also agreed to a Declaration where they declare yet again that "The Charter does not extend the field of application of Union law beyond the powers of the Union or establish any new power or task for the Union, or modify powers and tasks as defined by the Treaties."

the competence to legislate",[30] e.g. the death penalty, the right to strike or the right to a fair trial.

To focus solely on the right to strike, the EC Treaty expressly prohibits and will continue to prohibit EU legislative intervention in this area. Therefore, the Charter simply cannot be relied on by litigants at the national level. Even in areas where the EU has legislative power, the reach of the Charter should not be exaggerated. Contrary to the affirmations of Mr Duff, the Charter is meant essentially to guard against the misuse and abuse of public power by European institutions in the design of EU law, not to supersede national practices. It shall not affect the allocation of powers between the EU and Member States *per se*: the Charter merely reflects the EU's present commitment to respect fundamental rights.[31] It also pursues the goal of answering the concern expressed by some that there was an apparent rights deficit at the EU level. This contention, however unjustified, motivated the drafting of a clear catalogue of fundamental rights that each European citizen could easily consult.

In addition to the fear that the EU might overstep its powers on the basis of the Charter, the British and Irish Governments fought hard to make it clear that the Charter would not impact upon national legal systems. Other Member States never intended to do otherwise. In any case, the Charter reiterates that, outside the current scope of EU law, the Member States are not bound by its provisions. In other words, its provisions are addressed to the Member States *only* when they are implementing EU law. This is in conformity with the case law of the European Court of Justice.[32] The key question, therefore, is to determine the situations where the Member States "implement" EU law. This question is closely linked to the argument that the EU Charter is going to enable the European Court of Justice to act in a similar fashion to the US Supreme Court, that is, to define a common "federal" standard against which all national rules may be evaluated and eventually struck down.

(b) A (Weak) Federal Standard?

A plethora of detractors have complained that the Charter will empower the European Court of Justice to get hold of "our" fundamental rights as a key step in advancing its secret project of creating an EU superstate through a judicial harmonisation of national legal systems. This is largely a fantasy. An American-style incorporation of "federal" human rights into the "state" or national legal order has yet to happen in Europe.

---

[30] European Convention, Final Report of Working Group II on Incorporation of the Charter/Accession to the ECHR, CONV 354/02, Brussels, 22 October 2002, p 5.
[31] Article 6(2) TEU.
[32] See Case 5/88 *Wachauf* [1989] ECR 2609.

Over the years, the European Court of Justice has gradually extended the scope of its review to include not only acts of EU institutions, but also acts of the Member States when they act under EU law. Yet it is still a condition for the European Court of Justice in exercising its jurisdiction that the national measures fall "within the scope of Community law". It is legitimate to criticise the uncertain limits of this rather vague notion but it is simply wrong to affirm that individuals will be able to rely on any provision of the Charter, in any situation, against any national public authority. As a matter of principle, the European Court of Justice has no fundamental rights jurisdiction with regard to national legislation lying *outside* the scope of EU law. For instance, contrary to popular opinion, the European Court of Justice refused, in 1991, to offer an opinion on whether the Irish legal provisions, then prohibiting the dissemination of information about abortion services abroad violated the right to freedom of expression protected under EU law. As a matter of fact, the Court ruled that the challenged Irish rule fell outside the scope of EU law.[33] On the other hand, it also clear that Member States must now not only comply with EU fundamental rights when they enforce EU policies but also when they interpret EU law or when they invoke EU derogation rules relating to the fundamental economic freedoms such as the free movement of goods. A surprising aspect of the Charter is that it appears to narrow the current reach of EU Human Rights law[34] as it contains a provision which provides that the Member States must respect EU fundamental rights *only* "when they are implementing Union law".[35]

It is already apparent that, unlike the system in the US, the EU system for the protection of fundamental rights does not apply "irrespective of the subject-matter at issue, that is to say irrespective of whether it falls within federal or State competence".[36] Koen Lenaerts, now a judge at the European Court of Justice, has convincingly suggested that such a degree of coherence or harmonisation could only be achieved if the Member States decide "to entrust to the Court of Justice the task performed by the US Supreme Court, that of protecting any individual citizen, on the basis of a 'federal' standard of respect for fundamental rights, against any public authority of any kind and in any area of substantive law".[37] Critics of the European Court of Justice may, however, point to US history to justify their fears. Indeed, in the first half of the 20th century, the US Supreme Court decided, on its own initiative, to "incorporate" the federal Bill of Rights through an expansive interpretation of the fourteenth amendment to the US Constitution.[38] In short,

---

[33] C-159/90 *SPUC v Grogan* [1991] ECR I-4685.
[34] de Búrca, "The drafting of the European Union Charter of fundamental rights", p 137.
[35] Article 51(1) EU Charter.
[36] K. Lenaerts, "Respect for Fundamental Rights as a Constitutional Principle of the European Union", (2000) 6 *Columbia Journal of European Law* 1 at 21.
[37] *ibid.* at 24. See also A. Toth, "The European Union and Human Rights: The Way Forward", (1997) 34 *Common Market Law Review* 493.
[38] Particularly important is the first paragraph of the fourteenth amendment which was passed in 1868 after the conclusion of the Civil War. It reads as follows: "No State shall make or enforce any law which shall abridge the privileges or immunities of citizens of the United States; nor shall any State deprive any person of life, liberty, or property, without due process of law; nor deny to any person within its jurisdiction the equal protection of the laws."

the fourteenth amendment, a constitutional provision addressed to all the US States, served as a legal basis to justify the progressive expansion of the federal Bill of Rights' field of application to all state norms, even when the states act within their own sphere of competence. Thanks to this judicial reinterpretation of the federal Constitution, the US Supreme Court, through its power to review any violation of the federal Bill of Rights by state authorities, has built a unified constitutional order. Irrespective of the merits of such "federal" harmonisation in the field of fundamental rights, the Member States have agreed to explicitly prohibit the European Court of Justice from conferring upon itself the power to review Member States' actions on the basis of a "federal" fundamental rights standard in areas outside the scope of EU law. The Charter hence stipulates that its provisions are addressed to the Member States *only* when they are implementing EU law. An "American" evolution to be achieved by judicial activism is, therefore, plainly excluded.

It may even be argued that eurosceptics should actually rejoice at the idea of ratifying the EU Charter of Fundamental Rights. Not only is the wording of the Charter somewhat more restrictive than what the current case law of the European Court of Justice would suggest, once the scope of its fundamental rights jurisdiction is formalised, the European Court of Justice will be prohibited from extending its review of national measures on the grounds that they may violate fundamental rights protected under EU law. By contrast, the US Supreme Court was only successful in its "expansionist" strategy thanks to an open-ended constitutional text. From a political point of view, the legitimacy of the Supreme Court's "legal coup" also benefited from specific historical circumstances—the persistent segregationist practices in Southern States—which required, in turn, a revolutionary expansion of the scope of the US Bill of Rights. In the absence of similar and exceptional historical circumstances, it was predictable that some Member States, and in particular the United Kingdom, would try to take advantage of the constitutional drafting process to further constrain the interpretative power of the European Court of Justice. They did so in 2004, by including a new provision in the EU Charter stressing the importance of the constitutional traditions of the Member States: "Insofar as this Charter recognises fundamental rights as they result from the constitutional traditions common to the Member States, those rights shall be interpreted in harmony with those traditions."[39] Accordingly, once the Lisbon Treaty enters into force, the European Court of Justice will be formally obliged—for the first time—to interpret EU fundamental rights derived from national constitutional traditions in light of the interpretation given by national constitutional courts, with the view of guaranteeing a "harmonious" interpretation. One should not assume, however, that this provision was entirely necessary. Indeed, the European Court of Justice clearly ruled in 1970 that it should always find "inspiration" in the constitutional traditions common to Member States when it comes to protect fundamental rights at the European level in the absence of an EU Bill of Rights.[40] For

---

[39] Article 52(4) EU Charter (formerly Art II-112(4) of the EU CT).
[40] Case 11/70 *Internationale Handelsgesellschaft* [1970] ECR 1125, para 4.

instance, while the European Court of Justice was not compelled to define the so-called general principles of EU law, it did so with due regard to the general principles and fundamental values embodied in the national constitutional traditions of the Member States.

The crucial point is that fundamental rights guaranteed by national constitutions are merely complemented, not superseded by the Charter. The Charter will certainly apply to EU institutions but to the Member States *only* when they implement EU law. Rather than illustrating a desire to impose a uniform interpretation of human rights standards across Europe, the Charter offers a long-awaited codification of fundamental rights protected under EU law and makes it clear that the EU takes fundamental rights seriously. While one may legitimately express some concerns with regard to the possibility of future activism on the part of the European Court of Justice, it must be stressed that the Court, like any constitutional court in Europe or the US Supreme Court, has demonstrated sensitivity to political concerns and social consensus, not to mention its own credibility in the eyes of national supreme courts and academics or lawyers. Unquestionably, the European Court of Justice will show self-restraint in the interpretation of the Charter's horizontal clauses and will not let the fundamental rights "genie" get out of the bottle.

As for the argument, often heard in France, that the entry into force of the Charter will weaken fundamental rights' protection because it sanctifies weaker standards than the European Convention of Human Rights or national constitutions, this makes little sense. As amended by the Lisbon Treaty, the new Art 6 TEU specifically provides that "fundamental rights, as guaranteed by the European Convention for the Protection of Human Rights and Fundamental Freedoms and as they result from the constitutional traditions common to the Member States, shall constitute general principles of the Union's law". In addition, the Charter clearly affirms that insofar as it "contains rights which correspond to rights guaranteed by the Convention for the Protection of Human Rights and Fundamental Freedoms, the meaning and scope of those rights shall be the same as those laid down by the said Convention".[41] It is further specified that this provision does not prevent EU law providing more extensive protection. As a matter of fact, the Charter already provides an important number of provisions providing a slightly higher level of protection than the corresponding rights in the ECHR of 1950. It is worth mentioning a few of these articles where the meaning is the same as the corresponding articles of the ECHR, but where the scope of protection is wider.[42] The right to marry and found a family, for instance, covers the same field as the corresponding article of the ECHR, but its scope may be extended to other forms of marriage if these are established by national legislation. The Charter also allows EU institutions to eventually extend the scope of

---

[41] Article 52(3) EU Charter.

[42] See the explanations relating to the complete text of the Charter, European Convention, CHARTE 4473/00, CONVENT 49, Brussels, 11 October 2000.

freedom of assembly and of association at Union level. Regarding the right to education, its scope is extended to cover access to vocational and continuing training. It is further stipulated that "this right includes the possibility to receive free compulsory education". As for the right to an effective remedy and to a fair trial, also based on the ECHR, it offers a more extensive protection since it guarantees the right to an effective remedy before a court. Similarly, in EU law, the right to a fair hearing is not confined to disputes relating to civil law rights and obligations. Therefore, the Charter can be said to offer a more extensive protection than that provided for in the ECHR.

In any event, it is particularly ironic for French politicians to spread fears about the level of protection guaranteed by the EU Charter as these are the same people who refuse to extend the jurisdiction of the French *Conseil constitutionnel*. In France, constitutional review of legislation exclusively operates on *ex ante* mode on the basis of requests submitted by the main political actors (and not by individuals). This means, in practice, that once a statute comes into force, it can no longer be subject to constitutional challenge, even though, as is sometimes clear, serious constitutional questions may arise in its application. French critics also ignore the fact that France only ratified the ECHR thanks to an "abuse of power" committed by Alain Poher on 3 May 1974. Mr Poher was then the interim French President following the death of Georges Pompidou on the 2 April. He left the presidency on the 24 May after the election of Valéry Giscard d'Estaing. His decision to ratify a far-reaching international agreement, during his two months presidential term, may certainly be questioned on legitimacy grounds.

When confronted with the manifestly groundless nature of their claim, left-wing critics usually invoke the provision dealing with the limitation of fundamental rights. Surprisingly, the "*liberticide*" character of the following provision has been denounced:

> "Any limitation on the exercise of the rights and freedoms recognised by this Charter
> must be provided for by law and respect the essence of those rights and freedoms.
> Subject to the principle of proportionality, limitations may be made only if they are
> necessary and genuinely meet objectives of general interest recognised by the Union or
> the need to protect the rights and freedoms of others."[43]

For some this is a "bizarre clause" as it states that "all rights can be suspended 'where necessary in the general interests of the union', which creates a '*raison d'état*' prerogative that does not exist in English common law".[44] In other words, the main argument here is to say that this allegedly vague provision will authorise undue, abusive limitations on the exercise of fundamental rights. This view only reveals a profound lack of knowledge and

---

[43] Article 52(1) EU Charter.
[44] G. Jones and A. Evans-Pritchard, "Irish commissioner says basic rights charter is badly drafted", *The Daily Telegraph*, 6 September 2003.

this can easily be demonstrated by quoting directly from the ECHR itself. Most fundamental rights that it protects, e.g. right to respect for private and family life, freedom of expression, etc. are subject to limitations, meaning that public interferences with the exercise of those fundamental rights will not violate the ECHR as long as they are provided by law, meet objectives of general interest and are necessary in a democratic society.[45] The EU Charter merely reproduces the usual conditions governing the limitations on the exercise of rights and freedoms. The only original aspect of the Charter is that instead of repeating these conditions, for stylistic reasons, its drafters decided to adopt a general "derogation" scheme. This is no basis for arguing that the European Court of Justice will show any less inclination to strictly interpret any limitation on fundamental rights while, at the same time, preserving, as with the ECHR, some margin of appreciation for national authorities. To further demonstrate the unfounded basis for this criticism, it may be useful to bear in mind that the Universal Declaration of Human Rights adopted in 1948 contains a similar provision to the EU Charter and provides that "in the exercise of his rights and freedoms, everyone shall be subject only to such limitations as are determined by law solely for the purpose of securing due recognition and respect for the rights and freedoms of others and of meeting the just requirements of morality, public order and the general welfare in a democratic society".[46] In any case, the following provision should be enough of a guarantee that the EU Charter will not be interpreted as restricting or adversely affecting human rights and fundamental freedoms in comparison to the ECHR and/or Member States' constitutions:

> "Nothing in this Charter shall be interpreted as restricting or adversely affecting human rights and fundamental freedoms as recognised, in their respective fields of application, by Union law and international law and by international agreements to which the Union or all the Member States are party, including the European Convention for the Protection of Human Rights and Fundamental Freedoms, and by the Member States' constitutions."[47]

Finally, in line with what the Constitutional Treaty guaranteed, the Lisbon Treaty also paves the way for a possible accession of the EU to the ECHR. The EU will be entitled to accede

---

[45] For instance, Art 10 para 2 of the ECHR reads as follows: "The exercise of these freedoms [freedom to hold opinions and to receive and impart information and ideas], since it carries with it duties and responsibilities, may be subject to such formalities, conditions, restrictions or penalties as are prescribed by law and are necessary in a democratic society, in the interests of national security, territorial integrity or public safety, for the prevention of disorder or crime, for the protection of health or morals, for the protection of the reputation or rights of others, for preventing the disclosure of information received in confidence, or for maintaining the authority and impartiality of the judiciary."

[46] Art 29 para 2. More recently, the 1982 Canadian Charter of Rights and Freedoms also contains a general derogation clause which stipulates that "the rights and freedoms set out in it subject only to such reasonable limits prescribed by law as can be demonstrably justified in a free and democratic society" (Art 1).

[47] Article 53 EU Charter.

to the ECHR on the basis of a unanimous decision of the Council of Ministers and the assent of the European Parliament.[48] This legal obligation reflects the clear consensus which emerged during the drafting of the Constitutional Treaty. The transformation of the Charter into a legally binding instrument and the EU's future accession to the ECHR were thought to be complementary steps rather than to be regarded as alternatives.[49] Once a party to the Council of Europe, the actions of the EU, including the rulings of the European Court of Justice, will then be subject to the additional external human rights check of the Strasbourg system and in particular the control of the European Court of Human Rights. It is therefore unfortunate or, arguably, incoherent, to disapprove of the Charter on the ground that it endangers human rights standards as protected by the ECHR.

(c) A Bad Impact on Business?

According to Arthur Forbes, from the Irish Business and Employers Confederation (IBEC), "one of the most significant implications, if not the single most important issue for business resulting from the EU Constitution, is the legal recognition it gives to the Charter of Fundamental Rights".[50] Quite strikingly, while the EU Charter has been denounced in France as a neo-liberal Bill of Rights, the Confederation of British Industry (CBI) has tirelessly repeated its disappointment with the text and claimed that it will have a bad impact on business. To single out a characteristic utterance, John Cridland, Director of Human Resources at the CBI said: "We do not believe that the Charter should make social policy by the back door. ... It's a Trojan horse and we believe the business community is right to be concerned about it."[51] Generally unfamiliar with the concept of socio-economic rights, a category of rights that the Charter protects, British politicians and commentators have multiplied extravagant claims. A few are worth mentioning. It has been said that the Charter will help to restore the right to secondary picketing in Britain, will make it impossible to dismiss workers, will open the door to a host of legal actions as workers from one Member State may be able to claim equal pay with workers from other Member States and, more generally, that the Charter will undermine Ireland and Britain's free-market economies.[52]

To compare the Constitutional Treaty, in light of its incorporation of the EU Charter, to "a giant ball and chain around the ankle of British business",[53] to quote Michael

---

[48] New Article 6(2) TEU.

[49] See European Convention, Final Report of Working Group II on Incorporation of the Charter/Accession to the ECHR, CONV 354/02, Brussels, 22 October 2002, p 12.

[50] A. Forbes, "What Does Business Think of the EU Constitution?", Working Paper 2005/W/06, European Institute of Public Administration, p 8.

[51] Quoted in R. Watson, "Employers fear jobs would be put at risk", *The Times*, 1 June 2000.

[52] See e.g. Editorial, "Put it to the people", *The Sunday Times*, 17 June 2007: "The flexible labour laws that have turned Ireland and Britain into two of the continent's most successful economies and magnets for foreign direct investment, could be open to legal challenges by unions" if the Charter is given legal recognition.

[53] Quoted in D. Borak, "EU Constitution: good or bad for business?", *The Washington Times*, 10 February 2005.

Howard, then leader of the British Conservative Party, only illustrates the politicians' tendency towards hyperbole and misrepresentation when they are desperate to make headlines. The discussion surrounding the EU Charter is actually reminiscent of the debate when the UK Human Rights Act was introduced in 1998 by Tony Blair's Government. The incorporation of the ECHR into English law was commonly presented by xenophobic tabloid newspapers as opening the gate to frivolous litigation from asylum-seekers, gypsies and prisoners likely "to trample everyone else's liberties".[54] As with the UK Human Rights Act, the precise content of the EU Charter deserves a more thoughtful assessment. Most of its provisions essentially reproduce the rights contained in the ECHR but sometimes go beyond these by including certain economic and social rights. The "Solidarity" title,[55] in particular, guarantees the following fundamental rights:

- The Worker's right to information and consultation within the undertaking;
- Right of collective bargaining and action;
- Right of access to placement services;
- Protection in the event of unjustified dismissal;
- Fair and just working conditions;
- Prohibition of child labour and protection of young people at work;
- Family and professional life;
- Social security and social assistance;
- Health care;
- Access to services of general economic interest;
- Environmental protection;
- Consumer protection.

These rights did not fall from the sky in 2000 but are mainly drawn from the 1961 Council of Europe's Social Charter (revised in 1996), the 1989 Community Charter of Fundamental Social Rights of Workers and several EC Directives.[56] For instance, the so-called worker's right to information and consultation within an undertaking already appears in the European Social Charter and in the Community Charter on the rights of workers.[57] And several Directives, Directives 98/59/EC (collective redundancies), 77/187/EEC (transfers of undertakings) and 94/45/EC (European works councils), have specified the legal rights one may derive from this right to information and consultation. To give another example, the article protecting "fair and just working conditions", meaning the right to working conditions which respect his or her health, safety and dignity as well

---

[54] See "The menace that wasn't", *The Economist*, 13 November 2004.
[55] See Title IV of the Charter.
[56] See generally Note from the Praesidium, *Explanations relating to the complete text of the Charter*, Charte 4473/00, CONVENT 49, Brussels, 11 October 2000.
[57] Article 27 EU Charter: "Workers or their representatives must, at the appropriate levels, be guaranteed information and consultation in good time in the cases and under the conditions provided for by Union law and national laws and practices."

as the right to limitation of maximum working hours, to daily and weekly rest periods and to an annual period of paid leave draws again on provisions of the Social Charter and of the Community Charter on the rights of workers. Its legal implications have already been detailed by two Directives: Directive 89/391/EEC on the introduction of measures to encourage improvements in the safety and health of workers at work and Directive 93/104/EC concerning certain aspects of the organisation of working time. Even what may appear to be the least "fundamental" of these fundamental rights—the right of access to placement services—is based on provisions of the European Social Charter and of the Community Charter of the Fundamental Social Rights of Workers.

The number and scope of the fundamental rights protected under the Solidarity title have created a wave of anxiety in the United Kingdom as well as in Ireland. Jack Straw, Britain's Foreign Secretary at the time, made a special point of demanding "legal certainty" so that the EU Charter would not upset Britain's liberal industrial and social laws. Yet, as Lord Goldsmith concisely puts it, the Charter "is not a mine for new human rights".[58] In most cases, criticism of the Charter, an allegedly socialist Trojan horse for most British or American critics, can be traced back to a legal tradition unfamiliar with the notion of socio-economic rights of constitutional status.

According to David Byrne, a former Irish Attorney-General and former European Commissioner, the EU Charter includes issues which could not be described as fundamental rights "by any lawyer who understands the term".[59] Certainly, the "typical" fundamental rights are those implying a (political or civic) freedom to act, as well as the idea of inherent limits on state power. The primary function of these political and civic fundamental rights is to protect the so-called *status negativus* of the citizen. In other words, in the sphere of liberty protected by the constitution, the individual must be protected from undue intervention by public authorities. To argue, however, that socio-economic rights are not "rights" to be included in a Bill of Rights illustrates a rather limited knowledge of comparative law and of international standards. Most constitutional texts in "old Europe" protect an extensive list of socio-economic rights. One should also mention the adoption, in 1966, of the International Covenant on Economic, Social and Cultural Rights. In addition, the so-called "aspirational" nature of several rights contained in the EU Charter is not novel. Economic and social rights can, therefore, be labelled "fundamental rights" and benefit from constitutional consecration, without fear of the imposition of some kind of "socialist central planning" in Brussels, as Mr Duff ironically put it before the House of Lords.[60] On the other

---

[58] Lord Goldsmith, "The Charter of Rights – a Brake not an Accelerator", (2004) 5 *European Human Rights Law Review* 473 at 474. Compare with Roy W. Davis, "A Brake? The Union's New Bill of Rights", (2005) 5 *European Human Rights Law Review* 449.

[59] Quoted in G. Jones and A. Evans-Pritchard, "Irish commissioner says basic rights charter is badly drafted", *The Daily Telegraph*, 6 September 2003.

[60] House of Lords, EU Select Committee, *EU Charter of Fundamental Rights*, 8th Report 1999–2000, HL Paper 67, para 88.

hand, the relatively complex concept of justiciability, i.e. the quality of a legal provision of being actionable before a court, explains most of the misrepresentations made in relation to the Charter.

Only classic fundamental rights (e.g. freedom of expression) are said to be fully justiciable, meaning that they confer on any legal person an individual prerogative that can be judicially enforced on a third party and, in particular, on public authorities without the need for legislative implementation. However, it is important to realise that some socio-economic rights are also capable of "hard" legal enforcement. That is the case, for instance, for rights relating to the worker's status such as the right to strike or the right to join a union. The situation gets more complex as regards *positive* socio-economic rights (e.g. right to education, right to engage in work, right to decent working conditions, right to adequate housing, etc.), rights that imply, as a matter of principle, *positive* action from public authorities to secure access to the benefits or services these rights guarantee. It is far from unusual to see scholars and judges denying their justiciability or regretting the fact that their programmatic nature undermines the concept of subjective rights and the concept of human rights itself.[61] In the author's view, positive socio-economic rights can claim constitutional protection. It is important, however, to clarify their practical scope in order not to disappoint some or worry others. A distinction between justiciability (the notion of direct effect) and invocability (the notion of indirect effect) may be useful. In a few words, without legislative implementation, positive socio-economic rights do not have direct effect. This is a decisive aspect. Accordingly, private parties cannot *directly* rely on them before a court to claim access to or the creation of a particular benefit or service from public authorities. This will be the situation under the EU Charter and this aspect should reassure "liberals". Yet, as Guy Braibant, the French representative to the European Convention in charge of drafting the EU Charter, puts it, positive socio-economic rights have a "normative justiciability". In other words, judges can set aside or nullify legal norms that undermine their implementation.[62] It means that even if these socio-economic rights are not justiciable *per se* courts have to apply them as "principles" to be taken into account in particular when reviewing the legality of EU legislation.

Interestingly, Guy Braibant recalls the conflicts he encountered with the German, Spanish and, in particular, the British representatives, when he suggested including a set of social rights. Among the British representatives, Lord Goldsmith, in particular, had a much more restrictive vision of the notion of justiciability and fought hard not to give the

---

[61] For a surprising study from a well-known American academic arguing, at a time when Eastern European countries were drafting new constitutional texts, that positive socio-economic rights should not be constitutionally guaranteed on the grounds that governments should not be compelled to interfere with free markets and that many positive rights are unenforceable by courts, see C. Sunstein, "Against Positive Rights", (2001) 2/1 *East European Constitutional Review* 35.

[62] G. Braibant, *La Charte des droits fondamentaux de l'Union européenne* (Seuil, Paris, 2001), p 46.

name of "right" to what French lawyers commonly call *droits-créances* or positive socio-economic rights, therefore the use of the term "principle" as a solution of compromise.[63] Not completely satisfied by its success on the semantic front, the British Government pushed later on for additional amendments to dilute the potential scope of the Charter once it became legally binding, to the public consternation of Guy Braibant. The French press therefore widely presented the addition of a set of amendments to the EU Charter in 2004 as a British "victory". In particular, the insertion of the following paragraph has been severely criticised:

> "The provisions of this Charter which contain principles may be implemented by legislative and executive acts taken by institutions, bodies, offices and agencies of the Union, and by acts of Member States when they are implementing Union law, in the exercise of their respective powers. They shall be judicially cognisable only in the interpretation of such acts and in the ruling on their legality."[64]

In light of this paragraph and the strident criticism of the French Left, it would appear difficult to argue convincingly that the Charter is a socialist instrument. On the contrary, the Charter clearly operates a (typical) distinction between directly enforceable "rights" and programmatic "principles". For instance, the Irish Constitution distinguishes between "fundamental rights" (such as the right to free speech and the right to private property) and "directive principles of social policy" (such as the right to an adequate means of livelihood and the principle that the State should safeguard the economic interests of the weaker sections of the Community).[65] While fundamental rights are fully justiciable, the Irish Constitution states that application of the principles of social policy "shall be the care of the Oireachtas exclusively, and shall not be cognisable by any Court".[66] Similarly, the "principles" protected under the EU Charter, as with the positive socio-economic rights protected in most continental countries (including France), are different from subjective rights. They call, in fact, for "concretisation" through legislative or executive acts. As previously shown, it does not mean that they completely lack legal effect. They will become significant for courts when implementing legislative acts are interpreted or reviewed.

Not completely satisfied with the express limitation on the interpretation of the notion of "principles", Tony Blair's government also successfully lobbied for the inclusion of several additional clauses clarifying that the transformation of the Charter into a legally binding instrument cannot enlarge EU competence over national legislation. Most provisions in the Solidarity title expressly stipulate that rights must be guaranteed "… in the cases and

---

[63] *ibid.*, p 46.
[64] Article 52(5) EU Charter.
[65] For an instructive study, see J. O'Dowd, "Boston or Berlin? EU Charter of Fundamental Rights: Some Irish Perspectives", (2002) 14 *European Review of Public Law 427*.
[66] See Art 45 of the Irish Constitution.

under the conditions provided for by Community law *and national laws and practices* [emphasis added]". This is a direct consequence of British insistence although it does not make much sense because the Charter, by definition, can only apply to situations governed by EU law. And if Member States agree that EU law should govern a particular situation, national law must then comply with it regardless of specific and eventually contrary national provisions and practices. The reference to national laws and practices may oblige, however, EU institutions to formally take them into account before agreeing on a new European legislative norm.

In any case, the British Government's mistrust of socio-economic rights did not stop there. It led in 2004 to the incorporation of another new paragraph with the same goal in mind and which states that "full account shall be taken of national laws and practices as specified in this Charter".[67] All these successful attempts aimed at specifically restricting the potential scope of the Charter convinced the Confederation of the British Industry to drop most of its objections to the text: "Nobody should pretend that this draft is perfect, but the [British] Government has fought hard for business and come up with a result we can live with."[68] Yet, the opportunity to further reduce the Charter's scope, and preclude its application in Britain, proved too tempting in June 2007 when Member States had to convene to agree on a successor to the Constitutional Treaty. As a farewell present to Tony Blair, the Member States reluctantly agreed to annex a new Protocol to the Treaties in order to satisfy "the wish of the United Kingdom to clarify certain aspects of the application of the Charter".[69]

Article 1(1) of this Protocol provides that the Charter does not extend the ability of the Court of Justice, or any court or tribunal of the United Kingdom to find that UK legal norms or administrative practices "are inconsistent with the fundamental rights, freedoms and principles that it reaffirms". The added value of such a clause, from a legal point of view, is not obvious. On the one hand, it merely restates what the Charter already provides. Several of its provisions unambiguously indicate that the Charter does not establish any new power or task for the Union. It does so, however, in an incredibly awkward manner by referring to the puzzling notion of "ability" rather than the traditional notion of jurisdiction. On the other hand, Art 1(1) of the Protocol will not preclude the European Court of Justice from ruling that UK legal norms or administrative practices are contrary to EU fundamental rights which are guaranteed or further developed by other provisions of EU law. Finally, one may be tempted to argue that there is a subtle difference between extending the "ability" of the Court of Justice and denying the "ability" of the Court to act. If one agrees that the Court of Justice already has the "ability" to scrutinise

---

[67] Article 52(6) EU Charter.

[68] Quoted in M. Fletcher, "Britain approves charter of right", *The Times*, 3 October 2000.

[69] See Presidency Conclusions of the Brussels European Council, 21–22 June 2007, Doc No 11177/07, Concl. 2, 23 June 2007, p 25 and Protocol on the application of the Charter of Fundamental Rights of the European Union to Poland and to the United Kingdom, [2007] OJ C306/156.

UK laws or practices in light of EU fundamental rights the new reservation obtained by the United Kingdom is rather pointless.

Paragraph 2 of the same article states that "for the avoidance of doubt, nothing in [the Solidarity's title] of the Charter creates justiciable rights" applicable to the United Kingdom except in so far as the United Kingdom "has provided for such rights in its national law". This provision seems both superfluous and misleading. First of all, the Charter's Title IV on Solidarity does not create justiciable rights but lists a series of principles. These principles must guide the legislative action of EU institutions and may guide the European Court of Justice when it has to review the legality of EU legislation. Secondly, the provision will be clearly ineffective with regard to the "solidarity" rights which are *already* guaranteed on the basis of current provisions of the EC Treaty and have been further developed by several European Regulations and Directives. Those socio-economic rights will continue to be exercised under the conditions and within the limits defined by EU law regardless of the entry into force of the Charter. And, as is well known, any provision of EU law which is clear, precise and unconditional must be given direct effect, i.e. must be justiciable. In other words, Art 1(2) of the Protocol should not be understood as giving the United Kingdom a licence not to comply with its other obligations under the European Treaties and EU law generally. In the situation where the Charter guarantees a solidarity right, which no other legally binding provision of EU law already guarantees or develops (e.g. the right to strike, a right of access to preventive healthcare), one may assume it is because the EU has not been granted the competence to legislate in this particular area. The clarification obtained by the United Kingdom then serves no legal purpose since, by definition, the EU does not have the legal power to transform a "solidarity" right into a justiciable right by issuing more detailed legislation in order to give it a concrete meaning.

Finally, according to Art 2 of the Protocol, any provision of the Charter referring to national laws and practices shall only apply in the United Kingdom to the extent that the rights or principles that it contains are recognised in the law or practices of the United Kingdom. On British insistence, when the Charter was finalised in 2000, it was agreed that those rights for which the EU has little or no competence will be guaranteed "in accordance with in the cases and under the conditions provided for by Community law and national laws and practices". This wording was justified on the ground that it was critical to preserve the current allocation of powers between the EU and the Member States and the principle of subsidiarity. In practice, it means, for instance, that the right to protection against unjustified dismissal, unless further developed by EU legislation, must be interpreted and implemented in light of national law. The additional clarification obtained in 2007, therefore, only restates the obvious.

In the end, the Protocol on the Charter appears to be useful only as a public relations exercise. It may help deflect unprincipled criticism from British tabloids. It is important to stress, however, that contrary to what one could read in the press, the United Kingdom has not obtained the right to "opt-out" of the Charter. The Member States only agreed to clarify "the application of the Charter in relation to the laws and administrative action of the United Kingdom and of its justiciability within the United Kingdom", not to render the Charter wholly inapplicable in the United Kingdom. Ireland, which initially reserved alongside Poland, its right to join in this Protocol,[70] finally resisted the populist temptation to present the EU as a threat to its economic success on the ludicrous ground that it includes a list of socio-economic rights. This attitude is hardly reconcilable with the proclaimed goals of bringing Europe closer to its citizens and ending the perceived rights deficit of the EU. As is clear from the reaction of Irish trade unions to this suggestion, it is not reconcilable with their understanding of social partnership. One can therefore be pleased that the Taoiseach finally agreed to unambiguously state that the Irish government has "no difficulty with the scope and application of the charter".[71]

(d) A neo-liberal Charter?

Thanks to the explicit watering down of the Charter's scope of application (on British insistence), it has often been presented, in France, as something of a compromise when compared with the protection offered by French constitutional law and the Council of Europe's legal instruments. If one may regret the eagerness of some national governments to deprive socio-economic rights of any justiciable effect, double standards should not be used when assessing the Charter. French critics often fail to realise that positive socio-economic rights are hardly justiciable under French constitutional law. This diagnosis is also valid with regard to the Council of Europe's European Social Charter. It is not enforced by individual rights of complaint but by an obligation on the governments of countries having ratified it to submit reports on their implementation of the Social Charter over time and by an evolving collective complaints procedure.[72]

The substance of the fundamental rights protected by the EU Charter has also been criticised. Some misguided "experts" went so far as to say that the Charter threatens the right to abortion on the ground that one of its provisions stipulates that "everyone has the right to life".[73] They simply forgot to say that this provision reproduces the first sentence of Art 2(1) of the ECHR and has the same scope and meaning. It is essentially aimed at prohibiting the death penalty and the unnecessary use of lethal force. Furthermore, the European Court of Human Rights has consistently refused to consider that the expression "everyone" covers the unborn child. It has also been claimed that the constitutional notion of *laïcité*, i.e. the principle of separation of church and state as interpreted in France, is threatened by the provision protecting the right to "manifest religion" in public or in private places.[74] Once

---

[70] J. Smyth, "State gets opt-out clause in EU rights charter", *The Irish Times*, 26 June 2007.
[71] Editorial, "The EU charter", *The Irish Times*, 29 June 2007.
[72] See generally G. de Búrca and B. de Witte, *Social Rights in Europe* (Oxford University Press, Oxford, 2005).
[73] Article 2 EU Charter.

again, the right guaranteed by the Charter corresponds to the right guaranteed in Art 9 of the ECHR and has the same meaning and scope.[75] During the referendum campaign, French secularists simply forgot to mention that the European Court of Human Rights unambiguously ruled in 2004 that a Turkish ban on wearing the Islamic headscarf in teaching institutions does not violate Art 9 of the ECHR. The Court held that the protection of secularism and pluralism in a university may be seen as meeting a "pressing social need" and is not a disproportionate measure in light of the legitimate aims pursued.[76]

Unsurprisingly, the neo-liberal charge has also been widely used. This is particularly ironic since, as we know, the Charter has been usually derided in the United Kingdom and the United States for opposite reasons. Gerard Baker, then an Associate Editor of the *Financial Times*, exemplified perfectly this dominant viewpoint in the English-speaking press when he described the EU Charter as a "Bill of Rights in socialist garb".[77] In France, left-leaning critics read the Charter quite differently and denounced the clause guaranteeing the freedom to conduct a business.[78] In doing so, these critics revealed—yet again—their gaps in constitutional knowledge. Despite many affirmations to the contrary, "freedom of enterprise" is constitutionally protected by the French *Conseil constitutionnel*. In 2002, to give a single but well-known example, the socialist Government put forward a new legislative definition of the notion of redundancy for economic motive. In the view of the French constitutional judges, the legislative proposal excessively affected freedom of enterprise and was therefore struck down.[79] Bizarrely, British detractors of the Charter never mention the existence of this right to conduct a business, so abhorrent to the new-born Marxists who are so plentiful within the French Socialist Party.

Another claim, particularly unreasonable yet constantly repeated without much repudiation, is that instead of protecting "a right to employment" (*droit d'obtenir un emploi* in French), the Charter purportedly guarantees a neo-liberal "right to engage in work" or *droit de travailler*.[80] To put this debate into context, one should note that a provision of the preamble to the 1946 Constitution, a text legally binding in France, stipulates that "each person has the duty to work and the right to employment". Although it is obvious, the Charter's critics fail to to remind the public that the French constitutional right to employment has never led to the creation of a single job. It is not a subjective right that is judicially enforceable but a constitutional objective that the legislature should seek to attain. To argue that the Charter's right to engage in work illustrates neo-liberalism in action requires, therefore, a great deal of bad faith. A right to work or a right to

---

[74] Article 10 EU Charter.
[75] See Art 52(3) EU Charter.
[76] ECHR, *Sahin v Turkey*, 29 June 2004.
[77] G. Baker, "Against United Europe", *The Weekly Standard*, 22 September 2003.
[78] Article 16 EU Charter.
[79] CC, 12 January 2002, No 2001-455 DC, para 50.
[80] Article 15 EU Charter.

employment were never intended to guarantee a job. Both "rights" merely inform about a society's values. Rather than a difference of substance, one may simply detect in the different formulation the result of a compromise between "realists" who did not initially want to include political objectives in a Charter of "rights" and those who have no objection to guaranteeing rights without worrying about judicial remedies. If French left-wing critics were serious about the right to employment, they would also have to consider legally binding the "duty" for each person to work, technically also of constitutional value under the French Constitution.

CHAPTER SIX – CONCLUSION

The EU Charter of Fundamental Rights, by bringing political, civil, economic, social and cultural rights together into a single and concise document, is relatively innovative and should certainly be welcomed by those who support the rule of law. Its structure and content is the fruit of compromises between different philosophies and national traditions. It was, therefore, predictable that critics would lament its "eurobabble" style[81] and operate a selective and partial reading of its provisions to force "facts" into the bed that has been prepared for them beforehand. In light of national constitutions and the numerous texts governing fundamental rights at the European and international levels, the EU Charter can be said to represent a gifted crystallisation of existing rights. Were it to become legally binding, its impact is unlikely to be revolutionary. Its main purpose, indeed, is to consolidate the legitimacy and identity of the EU through the adoption of a Bill of Rights making the importance and relevance of fundamental rights more directly visible to the Union's citizens. One should note in passing that, since 2001, the Commission scrutinises its own legislative proposals for compatibility with the EU Charter. The Commission also decided in 2005 that legislative proposals and draft instruments having a specific link to fundamental rights would incorporate a recital as a formal statement of compatibility.[82] Finally, one should note that the EU decided to set up a Fundamental Rights Agency in 2007. The agency's principal tasks are to collect information and data, provide advice to the EU and its Member States and promote dialogue with civil society to raise public awareness of fundamental rights.[83] The promotion of a fundamental rights culture at Union level can hardly be criticised by those always keen to warn European's citizenry against the emergence of an authoritarian European superstate.

---

[81] For *The Economist*, the Charter "is written in exactly the sort of eurobabble that nobody except lawyers, interest groups and other *connoisseurs* of the genre will ever read", "Draft-dodging", 17 August 2000.

[82] To make the results of the Commission's monitoring more visible to other institutions and to the general public, the Commission has recently proposed to formally set out a methodology for ensuring that the Charter is properly implemented in Commission proposals. See Commission Communication on compliance with the Charter of Fundamental Rights in Commission legislative proposals – Methodology for systematic and rigorous monitoring, COM(2005) 172 final.

[83] See P. Alston and O. de Schutter (eds), *Monitoring Fundamental Rights in the EU. The Contribution of the Fundamental Rights Agency* (Hart, Oxford, 2005).

Were eurosceptics not blinded by their uncompromising rejection of the EU, they would realise that the Charter is qualified by a series of "horizontal provisions" which severely and precisely limit its field of application and the way it ought to be interpreted. To call it a "job-destroying charter that should have been vetoed"[84] is similarly a good example of limitless dogmatic fanaticism and of limited legal knowledge. It may be useful to bear in mind that the European Treaties, which shall soon include this supposedly "socialist" Charter, have been accused by left-leaning critics of furthering neo-liberal policies that could destroy publicly funded education, health and cultural services, of encouraging the abandonment of the "welfare state" model in favour of globalisation.[85] These assertions illustrate all too well the tendency towards overstatement, which often characterises any discussion on the EU. For marginal political forces keen to attract attention, EU-bashing represents an effective strategy as the media favour oversimplification and controversy. The EU Charter of Fundamental Rights deserves better than Manichean analysis. Commentators uneasy with its title protecting a certain number of socio-economic rights, rather than raising the spectres of Orwell's 1984 and that of the defunct USSR, should remember the time when, under the sound leadership of the United States, it was decided that the Universal Declaration of Human Rights, signed in 1948, should include socio-economic rights.[86] Rather than being the fruit of socialist thought, or of neo-liberal philosophy, as even more absurdly claimed in France, the EU Charter of Fundamental Rights is heir to the balanced vision expressed by President Roosevelt in 1944:

> "We have come to a clear realization of the fact that true individual freedom cannot exist without economic security and independence. 'Necessitous men are not free men.' People who are out of a job are the stuff of which dictatorships are made."[87]

---

[84] F. Maude, then Shadow Foreign Secretary, quoted in M. Fletcher, "Britain approves charter of right", *The Times*, 3 October 2000.

[85] Some went as far as saying that it could lead to the Hill of Tara being sold to a US company. See P. Cullen, "Warning that treaty could destroy public funding", *The Irish Times*, 12 December 2003.

[86] It is also particularly hypocritical or inconsistent for the British Government to oppose socio-economic rights for EU citizens while granting them to Iraqi citizens. In fact, to the likely surprise of many, the latest Iraqi Constitution, drafted under the auspices of the American and British occupying powers and approved by referendum in October 2005, contains an exhaustive section on economic, social and cultural liberties. Among the rights and principles constitutionally protected, the right to work (Art 22(1)) so as to guarantee all Iraqis a decent living. There is also a provision according to which the State guarantees the protection of motherhood, childhood and old age and shall care for children and youth and provides them with the appropriate conditions to further their talents and abilities (Art 29). One may also note this very "progressive" provision according to which the State guarantees the social and health security to Iraqis in cases of old age, sickness, employment disability, homelessness, orphanage or unemployment (Art 30). Interestingly, and certainly an anathema for most "neo-liberals", the Iraqi Constitution also states that the law shall regulate the relationship between employees and employers on economic basis and with regard to the foundations of social justice (Art 22(2)).

[87] State of the Union address, reproduced in H. Steiner and P. Alston, *International Human Rights in Context* (Oxford University Press, Oxford, 2000), p 243.

CONCLUSION

Europe at Fifty: An Occasion for Dancing in the Streets?[1]

> For centuries Europe has been an idea, holding out hope of peace and understanding. That hope has been fulfilled. European unification has made peace and prosperity possible. It has brought about a sense of community and overcome differences. Each Member State has helped to unite Europe and to strengthen democracy and the rule of law. Thanks to the yearning for freedom of the peoples of Central and Eastern Europe the unnatural division of Europe is now consigned to the past. European integration shows that we have learnt the painful lessons of a history marked by bloody conflict. Today we live together as was never possible before.
> "Berlin Declaration" on the occasion of the 50th anniversary of the signature of the Treaties of Rome, 25 March 2007

In 1957 "the idea of European union, in one form or another, was not new".[2] The idea of fostering European integration through economic means was more innovative. Far from establishing a fearful European superstate, the Treaty establishing the European Economic Community signed in Rome on 25 March 1957 had a more limited ambition: the establishment of a common market with the aim of preserving peace and enhancing economic growth.

Viewed from a historical perspective, the success of this original venture can hardly be denied. In what is now called the European Union, 27 Member States are committed to deepening economic integration and 15[3] of these countries already share a common currency. They are also obliged to define a common foreign and security policy, as well as to develop the Union as an area of freedom, security and justice. Despite these tremendous achievements, or maybe because of the challenges they present, the current ambience in

---

[1] I am grateful to Dermot Cahill (Senior Lecturer in European Law at UCD Dublin) and Brendan Flynn (Lecturer in European Politics at NUI Galway) for providing valuable comments on this section of the book.

[2] T. Judt, *Postwar. A History of Europe since 1945* (William Heinemann, London, 2005), p 153.

[3] On 1 January 2008, Cyprus and Malta adopted the Euro as their currency. Initially, the Euro area consisted of the following Member States: Austria, Belgium, Germany, Greece, Finland, France, Ireland, Italy, Luxembourg, the Netherlands, Portugal and Spain. Slovenia adopted the Euro on 1 January 2007.

Europe is rather gloomy. To use an analogy which is now gaining ground, the EU is said to be in something of a "mid-life crisis".[4]

Going from one crisis to another seems, however, to be a way of life for the EU. This may explain why a good dose of pessimism has always accompanied the slow and, at times, the "invisible progress" of European integration. In 1982, the President of the European Parliament, Piet Dankert, observed that the "anniversary of the European Community does not seem to be an occasion for much celebration", adding that the "infant which held so much promise 25 years ago has changed into a feeble cardiac patient".[5] However, less than 10 years later, it was agreed to adopt a single currency and to dramatically expand Europe's areas of competence. In 2007, the "feeble cardiac patient" is still alive and kicking notwithstanding the melodrama which followed the rejection of the European "Constitution" in the Netherlands and in France.

What is, in reality, surprising about European integration is that, fundamentally, it continues to work and deepen. The reason must be that the Member States have always realised that the EU represents the most effective institutionalised venue they can use to respond to the demands of their citizens and the internationally trading business community.

Without a doubt, the EC's founding fathers were animated by a high sense of idealism and genuinely believed that advancing the cause of European integration would foster peace among old enemies. Some even believed the EEC (as it was originally constituted), might in time lead to the establishment of a federal state. However, the EEC was very much a product of national bargaining, especially between France and Germany! Germany acquiesced in the idea of financing a Common Agricultural Policy (which still represents 35 percent of the EU budget down from close to 70 percent in the 1970s) and, in return, obtained from France the right to participate as an equal partner in a pan-European supranational organisation. It is also important to stress that the EC Treaty offered at first a rather modest set of provisions which were primarily aimed at setting up a common market between its signatories. It actually took more than 30 years and the launch of the so-called 1992 campaign for an EC without internal borders to complete the creation of a European market in which the free movement of goods, persons, services and capital was ensured.

That membership of the EU has continued to expand ever since suggests that the EU continues to be seen as a club which guarantees economic prosperity and peace. This is probably the greatest consequence of the project commenced in Rome in 1957.

---

[4] See e.g. N. Walker, "Europe at 50 – A Mid-life Crisis", NUIG Faculty of Law Annual Distinguished Lecture, 23 March 2007 (text available at: http://www.nuigalway.ie/law/documents/publications/walker_lecture.pdf).
[5] Quoted in I. Ward, *A Critical Introduction to European Law* (2nd ed., LexisNexis Butterworths, London, 2003), p 28.

Membership of the EU club or the mere promise of joining the club in the future has also proven to be spectacularly successful in consolidating democracy and the rule of law in previously authoritarian countries. Of course, the positive role in this area of the Council of Europe should be acknowledged. Furthermore, in today's interdependent world, national governments are well aware that they must collectively confront the global economic and political challenges of our times. History has taught the most powerful European countries that unrepressed *hubris* ineluctably leads to tragedy.

Remarkably, the "widening" of the EU's membership has not prevented further "deepening" of the EU's competences. Indeed, from a narrow focus on economic matters, the EU has grown beyond recognition. Among the objectives it now pursues, one may mention the promotion of balanced and sustainable development of economic activities; a high level of employment and of social protection; a high level of protection of the environment; the implementation of a common foreign and security policy; the tackling of cross-border crime, etc. In order to effectively pursue these objectives, the EU has gradually gained the power to legislate in the areas of trade, monetary policy, social policy, environment, consumer protection, transport, asylum and immigration, among other things. The EU may also complement Member States' action in the areas of industry, culture, tourism, education, and so on.

These developments did not come about without controversy. More recently, the continuous expansion of the EU, both in terms of geographical and regulatory expansion, seems to have produced a general popular backlash. Public opinion, in several Member States, has clearly turned against the EU. To put it succinctly, some citizens of the "old Europe" have grown sceptical of its added-value, and are frustrated at what they see to be an uncontrolled expansion of the club. The widespread disillusion is particularly worrying as it is taking root in a context where two major risks threatening the future progress of the EU have yet to be effectively tackled: relative economic decline and institutional paralysis. The so-called Lisbon Strategy is supposed to answer the former concern, the Constitutional Treaty was a response to the latter.

Taking the Lisbon Strategy first, the European Council in Lisbon in 2000 agreed to define long-term policies to create a highly competitive and knowledge-based society in Europe. The trouble is that the EU has not been given the power to legislate in the areas of employment, social protection and education but can merely complement national policies. But European citizens are unlikely to take note of this subtle distinction, and will certainly come to blame the EU rather than the Member States for the currently disappointing outcomes of the Lisbon strategy.

As for the defunct Constitutional Treaty, it suffered from being called a "constitution". However imperfect, it would have enhanced the efficiency and democratic legitimacy of the EU much more than its successor, the Lisbon Treaty. Regardless of the respective merits of these two texts, one vital lesson of the ratification mess has been that unanimity in an

EU of 27 countries does not work. It allows any one, or a small number of nations to hold up all the others on such a crucial issue of the EU's basic rules and institutional reform. It plunges the EU into periodic and anguished uncertainty thus feeding public distrust of the EU and is the best recipe for lowest-common denominator compromises between the Member States for which the EU is, alas, ultimately blamed. Unfortunately, the Lisbon Treaty must also be ratified by all the Member States.

But to avoid another ratification mess, European leaders implicitly agreed that no Member State, with the exception of Ireland for constitutional reasons, should hold a referendum. In France, for instance, President Nicolas Sarkozy has already indicated that the Lisbon Treaty will be subject to parliamentary ratification in spring 2008. This is regrettable. One may object that direct democracy is not normatively superior to representative democracy and that referendums may not always be suitable instruments when it comes to voting on incomprehensible EU treaties. These are respectable arguments but they fail to consider that referendums confer on the EU much-needed popular legitimacy and that parliamentary ratification of the Lisbon Treaty may alienate further those who voted "no" the Constitutional Treaty and would have voted "no" if given the chance. This is why it would have been preferable to discover some mechanism to overcome the unanimity problem and put the Lisbon Treaty directly to the peoples of Europe. Possible suggestions here include what the Americans simply did in 1787, by allowing ratification via roughly a two-thirds majority of the Member States in accordance with their respective national constitutional requirements. Another (and better) option would be to hold an EU-wide referendum on the same day in all the Member States. The required majority for ratification could then be defined as at least two-thirds of the Member States, comprising at least two thirds of the EU population. As for the Member States that voted "no", they should be given the choice to go ahead with the new treaty, seek an ad hoc exemption from the application of the new rules or exercise their right to withdraw from the EU. Such a radical reform could lead to a genuine pan-European public debate and increase the chance of having a discussion focusing on the merits of any new European text rather than issues of domestic politics. In the long-run, Member States would also be well-advised to emulate Ireland with its National Forum on Europe.[6] There is a need for a politically-neutral public space offering, in each Member State, a regular, popular and comprehensible debate on the "European project" and European policies. Such a space may help citizens realise that even respectable politicians often hide behind "Brussels" to justify unpopular policies.

Overall, few would deny that the EU is a success story, albeit a qualified one. It represents the most successful interstate venture in modern times. Contrary to what critics allege, the EU is no super-state in the making but an original and unprecedented system

---

[6] See http://www.forumoneurope.ie.

of government by, of, and for the Member States, with *conferred* and *limited* powers, which is perfectly democratic in light of its "consociational" nature. Through economic means, it has obliged old and heterogeneous nation-states to learn how to peacefully coexist while pursuing common goals through ongoing compromises.

REFERENCES

Alston, P. and Weiler, J. "An 'Ever Closer Union' in Need of a Human Rights Policy: The European Union and Human Rights", in P. Alston (ed), *The EU and Human Rights* (Oxford University Press, Oxford, 1999), pp 3–68.

Alston, P. and de Schutter, O. (eds) *Monitoring Fundamental Rights in the EU. The Contribution of the Fundamental Rights Agency* (Hart, Oxford, 2005).

Ahern, B. "Neither neo-liberal nor socialist, but a balanced Constitution for Europe", *The Irish Times*, 29 November 2004.

Anderson, B. *Imagined Communities: Reflections on the Origin and Spread of Nationalism* (Verso, London, 1991).

Andreani, J.-L. and Ferenczi, T. "Les six thèmes-clés de la campagne", *Le Monde*, 28 May 2005.

Armstrong, K. "United Kingdom – Divided on Sovereignty", in N. Walker (ed), *Sovereignty in Transition* (Hart, Oxford, 2003), pp 327–350.

Arnull, A. "A Preemptive Strike from the Palais Royal", (2005) 30 *European Law Review* 1.

Assemblée des Chambres Francaises de Commerce et d'Industrie, "Délocalisations: La peur n'est pas la solution", November 2005. Available at: http://www.acfci.cci.fr.

Aubert, P., Sillard, P. *Délocalisations et réductions d'effectifs dans l'industrie française (1995–2001)*, INSEE, No G 2005/03, April 2005. Available at: http://www.insee.fr.

Bache, I. and Flinders, M. (eds), *Multi-Level Governance* (Oxford University Press, Oxford, 2004).

Backer, L. "The Extra-National State: American Confederate Federalism and the European Union", (2001) 7 *Columbia Journal of European Law* 173.

Baker, G, "Against United Europe", *The Weekly Standard*, 22 September 2003.

Baker, K. "Constitution", in F. Furet and M. Ozouf (eds), *A Critical Dictionary of the French Revolution* (Harvard University Press, Cambridge, 1989), pp 479–493.

Barnard, C. and Deakin, S. "Market Access and Regulatory Competition", in C. Barnard and J. Scott (eds), *The Law of the Single European Market* (Hart, Oxford, 2002), pp 197–224.

Beaud, O. "Fédéralisme et souveraineté : notes pour une théorie constitutionnelle de la Fédération", (1998) *Revue du droit public* 115.

Begg, D. "Barroso intent on shifting EU to right of centre", *The Irish Times*, 7 February 2005.

Bellamy, R. "Which Constitution for What Kind of Europe? Three Models of European Constitutionalism", Paper for the CIDEL Workshop on Constitution-making and

Democratic Legitimacy in the EU, London, 12–13 November 2004. Available at: http://www.arena.uio.no/cidel.

Betten, L. "The EU Charter of Fundamental Rights: a Trojan Horse or a Mouse?", (2001) 17 *International Journal of Comparative Labour Law and Industrial Relations* 151.

Bickel, A. *The Least Dangerous Branch* (2nd ed., Yale University Press, New Haven, 1986).

Biehler, G. *International Law in Practice: An Irish Perspective* (Thomson Round Hall, Dublin, 2005).

Bogdanor, V. "A Constitution for a House without Windows", EU Constitution Project Newsletter, The Federal Trust, July 2004, p 6.

Bonde, J.-P. "Seven steps to a more democratic, more transparent European Union", *The Irish Times*, 11 August 2005.

Borak, D. "EU Constitution: good or bad for business?", *The Washington Times*, 10 February 2005.

Braibant, G. *La Charte des droits fondamentaux de l'Union européenne* (Seuil, Paris, 2001).

Brennock, M. "EU Commission could demand an end to tax free stud fees", *The Irish Times*, 4 February 2005.

Brennock, M. and Staunton, D. "Proposal to curtail referendum rule on EU issues", *The Irish Times*, 6 May 2005.

Burgess, M. *Federalism and the EU: Building of Europe, 1950–2000* (Routledge, London, 2000).

Burns, T. "The Evolution of European Parliaments and Societies in Europe: Challenges and Prospects", (1999) 2 *Journal of Social Theory* 167.

Burns, T. (ed) *The Future of Parliamentary Democracy: Transition and Challenge in European Governance*, Green Paper prepared for the Conference of the Speakers of EU Parliaments (Rome, 22–24 September 2000). Available at: http://www.camera.it/_cppueg/ing/conferenza_odg_Conclusioni_gruppoesperti.asp

Caporaso, J. "The European Union and Forms of State: Westphalian, Regulatory or Post-Modern", (1996) 34 *Journal of Common Market Studies* 29.

Carré de Malberg, R. *Contribution à la théorie générale de l'État* (Sirey, Paris, 1920–1922).

Cassia, P. "L'article I-6 du traité établissant une Constitution pour l'Europe et la hiérarchie des normes", (2004) *Europe*, étude 12.

Cecchini, P. *The European Challenge 1992: The Benefits of a Single Market* (Wildwood House, Aldershot, 1988).

Chalmers, D., Hadjiemmanuil, C., Monti, G., Tomkins, A. *European Union Law* (Cambridge University Press, Cambridge, 2006).

Chopin, T., *L'héritage du fédéralisme? Etats-Unis/Europe* (Notes de la Fondation Robert Schuman, Paris, 2002). Available at: http://www.robert-schuman.org/notes/notes8.pdf.

Christiansen, T. and Kirchner, E. (eds), *Europe in Charge. Committee Governance in the European Union* (Manchester University Press, Manchester, 2000).

Christiansen, T. and Tonra, B. (eds), *Rethinking European Union Foreign Policy* (Manchester University Press, Manchester, 2004).

Cimbalo, J. "Saving NATO from Europe. A Threat from Within", *Foreign Affairs*, 83, November–December 2004, pp 111–120.

Coleman, M. "Bertie gives tax harmonisation 'nul points'", *The Irish Times*, 10 November 2006.

Constantinesco, V. "Europe fédérale ou Fédération d'Etats-nations", in R. Dehousse (ed), *Une Constitution pour l'Europe* (Presses de Sciences Po, Paris, 2002), pp 115–149.

Costello, C. "Ireland's Nice Referenda", (2005) 1 *European Constitutional Law Review* 357.

Coughlan, A. "New EU Constitution would establish a federation", Letters Section, *The Irish Times*, 11 November 2004.

Coughlan, A. "Revised EU agreement has radical implications", *The Irish Times*, 28 June 2007.

Craig, P. "The Nature of the Community: Integration Theory and Democratic Theory", in P. Craig and G. de Búrca (eds), *The Evolution of EU Law* (Oxford University Press, Oxford, 1999), pp 1–54.

Craig, P. "Competence: clarity, conferrral, containment and consideration", (2004) 29 *European Law Review* 323.

Cullen, P. "Warning that treaty could destroy public funding", *The Irish Times*, 12 December 2003.

Cullen, P. "Expansion of labour inspectorate planned", *The Irish Times*, 9 April 2005.

Dahl, R. *On Democracy* (Yale University Press, New Haven, 1998).

Davis, R. W. "A Brake? The Union's New Bill of Rights", (2005) 5 *European Human Rights Law Review* 449.

Dashwood, A. "States in the European Union", (1998) 23 *European Law Review* 201.

de Bréadún, D. "Euro-sceptic wants deferral of Irish vote on EU constitution", *The Irish Times*, 30 August 2004.

de Búrca, G. "The Drafting of the European Union Charter of Fundamental Rights", (2001) 26 *European Law Review* 126.

de Búrca, G. "The Drafting of a Constitution for the European Union: Europe's Madisonian Moment or a Moment of Madness?", (2004) 61 *Washington and Lee Law Review* 555.

de Búrca, G. and de Witte, B. *Social Rights in Europe* (Oxford University Press, Oxford, 2005).

Dehousse, R. "European Institutional Architecture after Amsterdam: Parliamentary System or Regulatory Structure?", (1998) 35 *Common Market Law Review* 595.

Dehousse, R. "Rediscovering Functionalism", in C. Joerges, Y. Mény and J. Weiler (eds), *What kind of Constitution for what kind of Polity?* (The Robert Schuman Centre for Advanced Studies, Florence, 2000), pp 195–201.

Dehousse, R. "European governance in search of legitimacy: the need for a process-based approach", in O. de Schutter, N. Lebessis and J. Paterson (eds), *Governance in the European Union* (Office for Official Publications of the European Communities, Luxembourg, 2001), pp 169–187.

de Mooij, R. "Does the Enlarged European Union Need a Minimum Corporate Tax Rate?", (2004) 39 *Intereconomics* 180.

Dempsey, J. and Bennhold, K. "EU leaders and voters see paths diverge", *The International Herald Tribune*, 18–19 June 2005.

de Witte, B. "The Pillar Structure and the Nature of the European Union: Greek Temple or French Gothik Cathedral ?", in T. Heukels, N. Blokker and M. Brus (eds), *The European Union after Amsterdam – A Legal Analysis* (Kluwer Law International, The Hague, 1998), pp 51–68.

de Witte, B. "Sovereignty and European Integration: The Weight of Legal Tradition", in A.-M. Slaughter *et al.* (eds), *The European Court and National Courts–Doctrine and Jurisprudence* (Hart Publishing, Oxford, 1998), pp 277–304.

Diez-Picazo, L. "Treaty or Constitution? The Status of the Constitution for Europe", in J. Weiler and C. Eisgruber (eds), *Altneuland: The EU Constitution in a Contextual Perspective*, Jean Monnet Working Paper 5/04. Available at: http://www.jeanmonnetprogram.org/papers.

Dooley, C. "Gama secured 70% of PAYE relief scheme", *The Irish Times*, 18 May 2005.

Duff, A. and Voggenhuber, J. *Report on the period of reflection: the structure, subjects and context for an assessment of the debate on the European Union*, European Parliament, A6-0414/2005, 16 December 2005.

Duina, F. and Oliver, M. "National Parliaments in the European Union: Are There Any Benefits to Integration?", (2005) 11 *European Law Journal* 173.

Editorial, "Europe et démocratie", *Le Monde*, 29 October 2004.

Editorial, "New Realities of Investment Aid", *The Irish Times*, 3 March 2005.

Editorial, "Time to clean up on waste", *The Irish Times*, 27 April 2005

Editorial, "Attitude towards migrant workers", *The Irish Times*, 23 January 2006.

Editorial, "Put it to the people", *The Sunday Times*, 17 June 2007.

Editorial, "Constitution no more", *The Irish Times*, 25 June 2007.

Eleftheriadis, P. "Constitution or Treaty?", *The Federal Trust Online Paper* 12/04, July 2004. Available at: http://www.fedtrust.co.uk/eu_constitution.

Ely, J. *Democracy and Distrust. A theory of Judicial Review* (Harvard University Press, Cambridge, 1980).

Enderlein, H. *et al.*, "The EU Budget. How Much Scope for Institutional Reform", European Central Bank, Occasional Paper No 27, April 2005. Available at: http://www.ecb.int/pub/pdf/scpops/ecbocp27.pdf.

Eriksen, E. and Fossum, J. (eds), *Democracy in the EU: Integration through Deliberation?* (Routledge, London, 2000).

Eriksen, E. "Democratic or Technocratic Governance?", in C. Joerges, Y. Mény, J. Weiler (eds), *Mountain or Molehill? A Critical Appraisal of the Commission White Paper on Governance*, Jean Monnet Working Paper No. 6/01. Available at: http://www.jeanmonnetprogram.org.

European Commission, *Competition Policy in Europe and the Citizen* (Office for Official Publications of the European Communities, Luxembourg, 2000). Available at: http://competitionpolicy.ww.am/about_conf/competition_europe.pdf.

European Commission, Green Paper on Criminal Law Protection of the Financial Interests of the Community and the Establishment of a European Prosecutor, COM(2001) 715 final. Available at: http://europa.eu/scadplus/leg/en/lvb/l33159.htm.

European Commission, Recommendation of the European Commission on Turkey's progress towards accession, COM (2004) 656 final. Available at: http://ec.europa.eu/enlargement/turkey/key_documents_en.htm.

European Commission, White Paper on European Governance, COM (2001) 428 final. Available at: http://ec.europa.eu/governance/white_paper/index_en.htm.

European Commission, Green Paper of 21 May 2003 on Services of General Interest, COM(2003) 270 final. Available at: http://europa.eu/scadplus/leg/en/lvb/l23013.htm.

European Commission, Communication on compliance with the Charter of Fundamental Rights in Commission legislative proposals – Methodology for systematic and rigorous monitoring, COM (2005) 172 final. Available at: http://eur-lex.europa.eu (Celex no 52005DC0172).

European Commission, Communication on Implementing the Community Lisbon Programme: Progress to date and next steps towards a Common Consolidated Corporate Tax Base (CCCTB), COM (2006) 157 final. Available at: http://ec.europa.eu/taxation_customs/resources/documents/taxation/company_tax/common_tax_base/COM_2006_157_en.pdf.

European Commission Communication, Enlargement Strategy and Main Challenges 2006–2007, Annex 1 – Special Report on the EU's capacity to integrate new members, COM (2006) 649 final. Available at: http://ec.europa.eu/enlargement/key_documents/reports_nov_2006_en.htm.

European Convention, Note from the Praesidium, Explanations relating to the complete text of the Charter, Charte 4473/00, CONVENT 49, Brussels, 11 October 2000. Available at: http://www.europarl.europa.eu/charter/pdf/04473_en.pdf.

European Convention, Final report of Working Group III on Legal Personality, CONV 305/02, Brussels, 1 October 2002. Available at: http://register.consilium.eu.int/pdf/en/02/cv00/00305en2.pdf.

European Convention, Final Report of Working Group II on Incorporation of the Charter/Accession to the ECHR, CONV 354/02, Brussels, 22 October 2002. Available at: http://register.consilium.eu.int/pdf/en/02/cv00/00354en2.pdf.

European Convention, Final report of working group IV on the role of national parliaments, CONV 353/02, Brussels, 22 October 2002. Available at: http://register.consilium.eu.int/pdf/en/02/cv00/00353en2.pdf.

European Convention, Preliminary draft Constitutional Treaty, CONV. 369/02, Brussels, 28 October 2002. Available at: http://register.consilium.eu.int/pdf/en/02/cv00/00369en2.pdf.

European Convention, Final report of Working Group V on Complementary Competencies, CONV 375/1/02, Brussels, 4 November 2002. Available at: http://register.consilium.eu.int/pdf/en/02/cv00/00375-r1en2.pdf.

European Convention, Final report of Working Group X "Freedom, Security and Justice", CONV 426/02, Brussels, 2 December 2002. Available at: http://register.consilium.eu.int/pdf/en/02/cv00/00426en2.pdf.

European Convention, Final Report of Working Group XI on Social Europe, CONV 516/1/03, Brussels, 4 February 2003. Available at: http://register.consilium.eu.int/pdf/en/03/cv00/CV00516-re01en03.pdf.

European Council of Cologne, Presidency Conclusions, 3–4 June 1999. Available at: http://europa.eu.int/european_council/conclusions/index_en.htm.

European Council of Laeken, Presidency Conclusions, 14–15 December 2001.

European Council of Barcelona, Presidency Conclusions, 15–16 March 2002. Available at: http://europa.eu.int/european_council/conclusions/index_en.htm.

European Council of Nice, Presidency Conclusions, 7–9 December 2002. Available at: http://europa.eu.int/european_council/conclusions/index_en.htm.

European Council of Brussels, Presidency Conclusions, 21–22 June 2007. Available at: http://europa.eu.int/european_council/conclusions/index_en.htm.

European Parliament, Resolution on the democratic deficit [1988] OJ C187/229.

European Parliament, Resolution on the Commission White Paper on European governance [2002] OJ C153E/314.

Evans-Pritchard, A. "Dutch warn of federal police", *The Daily Telegraph*, 31 May 2003.

Fabius, L. *Une certaine idée de l'Europe* (Plon, Paris, 2004).

Favoreu, L. "American and European Models of Constitutional Justice", in *Comparative and Private International Law. Essays in Honor of J.H. Merryman* (Duncker and Humblot, Berlin, 1990), pp 105–120.

Ferguson, N. *Colossus. The Rise and Fall of the American Empire* (Penguin Books, New York, 2004).

Ferris, M. "Transfer of power to Brussels is bad for democracy", *The Irish Times*, 28 August 2004.

Fischer, J. "From Confederacy to Federation: Thoughts on the Finality of European Integration", in C. Joerges, Y. Mény and J. Weiler (eds), *What Kind of Constitution for What Kind of Polity? – Responses to Joschka Fischer* (The Robert Schuman Centre for Advanced Studies, Florence, 2000), pp 19–30.

Fletcher, M. "Britain approves charter of right", *The Times*, 3 October 2000.

Flynn, B. *The Blame Game: Rethinking Ireland's Sustainable Development And Environmental Performance* (Irish Academic Press, Dublin, 2006).

Folsom, R. *European Union Law in a Nutshell* (3rd ed., West Group, 1999).

Forbes, A. "What Does Business Think of the EU Constitution?", Working Paper 2005/W/06, European Institute of Public Administration. Available at: http://www.eipa.eu/en/publications/workingpapers/.

Foreign and Commonwealth Office, *A Constitutional Treaty for the EU: The British Approach to the EU Intergovernmental Conference*, White Paper, September 2003.

Généreux, J. *Manuel critique du parfait européen: Les bonnes raisons de dire "Non" à la Constitution* (Seuil, Paris, 2005).

George, S. "France's 'non' marks just the beginning of our campaign", *Europe's World*, Autumn 2005, pp 49–51.

Giscard d'Estaing, V. "Pour ou contre l'adhésion de la Turquie à l'Union Européenne", *Le Monde*, 9 November 2002.

Giscard d'Estaing, V., Oral report presented to the European Council in Thessaloniki, European Convention, 20 June 2003. Available at: http://european-convention.eu.int/docs/speeches/9604.pdf.

Goldsworthy, J. *The Sovereignty of Parliament. History and Philosophy* (Oxford University Press, Oxford, 2001).

Goldsworthy, J. "The Debate About Sovereignty in the United States: A Historical and Comparative Perspective", in N. Walker (ed), *Sovereignty in Transition* (Hart, Oxford, 2003), pp 423–446.

Gormley, L. and de Haan, J. "The Democratic Deficit of the European Central Bank", (1996) 21 *European Law Journal* 95.

Grimm, D. "Does Europe Need a Constitution?", (1995) 1 *European Law Journal* 282.

Grimm, D. "The European Court of Justice and National Courts: The German Constitutional Perspective after the Maastricht Decision", (1997) 3 *Columbia Journal of European Law* 229.

Groom, B. "Forging a united future", *Financial Times*, 27/28 March 2004.

Guéhenno, J.-M. *The End of the Nation-State* (University of Minnesota Press, Minneapolis, 2000).

Habermas, J. "Why Europe needs a Constitution", (2001) 11 *New Left Review* 5.

Hayes-Renshaw, F. and Wallace, H. *The Council of Ministers* (Palgrave MacMillan, Basingstoke, 1997).

Held, D. "The changing contours of political community: rethinking democracy in the context of globalisation", in B. Holden (ed), *Global Democracy – Key Debates* (Routledge, London, 2000), pp 17–31.

Hennessy, M. "Adams says citizenship poll 'is about the rights of children'", *The Irish Times*, 25 May 2004.

Hennessy, M. "Murphy wants Ministers to take blame", *The Irish Times*, 6 June 2005.

Hinds, A.-L. *Competition Law* (Thomson Round Hall, Dublin, 2006).

Hirst, P. "Democracy and Governance", in J. Pierre (ed), *Debating Governance: Authority, Steering and Democracy* (Oxford University Press, Oxford, 2000), pp 13–35.

Hix, S. "Elections, Parties and Institutional Design: A Comparative Perspective on European Union Democracy", (1998) 21(3) *West European Politics* 19.

Hix, S. "The Study of the EU II: the 'New Governance' Agenda and its Rival", (1998) 5 *Journal of European Public Policy* 38.

Hogan, G. and Whyte, G. *J.M. Kelly: The Irish Constitution* (4th ed, LexisNexis Butterworths, Dublin, 2003).

House of Lords, Select Committee on European Communities, *Political Union. Law-Making Powers and Procedures*, 17th Report, Session 1990–1991 (HL Paper 80).

House of Lords, EU Committee, *EU Charter of Fundamental Rights*, 8th Report of Session 1999–2000 (HL Paper 67). Available at: http://www.publications.parliament.uk/pa/ld199900/ldselect/ldeucom/67/6701.htm.

House of Lords, EU Committee, *The Future Role of the European Court of Justice*, 6th Report of Session 2003–2004 (HL Paper 47). Available at: http://www.publications.parliament.uk/pa/ld200304/ldselect/ldeucom/47/47.pdf.

House of Lords, EU Committee, *Strengthening national parliamentary scrutiny of the EU– the Constitution's subsidiarity early warning mechanism*, 14th Report of Session 2004-2005 (HL Paper 101). Available at: http://www.publications.parliament.uk/pa/ld200405/ldselect/ldeucom/101/101.pdf.

House of Lords, EU Committee, *Future Financing of the European Union*, 6th Report of Session 2004–2005 (HL Paper 62). Available at: http://www.publications. parliament.uk/pa/ld200405/ldselect/ldeucom/62/62.pdf.

House of Lords, EU Committee, *Completing the Internal Market in Services*, 6th Report of Session 2005–2006 (HL Paper 23). Available at: http://www.publications.parliament. uk/pa/ld200506/ldselect/ldeucom/23/23.pdf.

House of the Oireachtas, Sub-Committee on European Scrutiny, First Annual Report on the Operation of the European Union Scrutiny Act 2002, October 2004. Available at: http://www.oireachtas.ie/viewdoc.asp?DocID=3231.

Hussein, K. "The Europeanization of Member State Institutions", in S. Bulmer and C. Lequesne (eds), *The Member States of the European Union* (Oxford University Press, Oxford, 2005), pp 285–316.

Joerges, C. and Neyer, J. "From Intergovernmental Bargaining to Deliberative Political Process: the Constitutionalisation of Comitology", (1997) 3 *European Law Journal* 273.

Joerges, C., Mény, Y. and Weiler, J. (eds) *Mountain or Molehill? A Critical Appraisal of the Commission White Paper on Governance*, Jean Monnet Working Paper No. 6/01. Available at: http://www.jeanmonnetprogram.org.

Joerges, C. and Rödl, F. "'Social Market Economy' as Europe's Social Model?", EUI Working Paper Law No 2004/8. Available at: http://www.iue.it.

Jones, G. and Evans-Pritchard, A. "Irish commissioner says basic rights charter is badly drafted", *The Daily Telegraph*, 6 September 2003.

Jouen, M. and Papant, C. "Social Europe in the throes of enlargement", *Notre Europe*, Policy Papers No 15, July 2005. Available at: http://www.notre-europe.asso.fr.

Judt, T. *Postwar. A History of Europe since 1945* (William Heinemann, London, 2005).

Kagan, R. *Of Paradise and Power: American and Europe in the New World Order* (Knopf, New York, 2003).

Kerr, J. "Best on offer", EU Constitution Project Newsletter, The Federal Trust, July 2004, pp 9–10.

Koslowski, R. "A constructivist approach to understanding the European Union as a federal polity", (1999) 6 *Journal of European Policy* 561.

KPMG, *Corporate Tax Rate Survey – An international analysis of corporate tax rates from 1993 to 2006*, October 2006. Available at: http://www.kpmg.com.

Kumm, M. "The Jurisprudence of Constitutional Conflict: Constitutional Supremacy in Europe before and after the Constitutional Treaty", (2005) 11 *European Law Journal* 262.

Labaton, S. "Microsoft finds legal defender in Justice Depart.", *The New York Times*, 10 June 2007.

Laffan, B. and Langan, A. "Securing a "Yes": From Nice I to Nice II", *Notre Europe*, Policy Paper No 13, April 2005. Available at: http://www.notre-europe.eu/uploads/tx_publication/Policypaper13.pdf.

Laprat, G. "Réforme des Traités: Le risque du double déficit démocratique", (1991) 351 *Revue du Marché Commun* 710.

Leben, C. "A Federation of Nation States or Federal State", in C. Joerges, Y. Mény and J. Weiler (eds), *What kind of Constitution for what kind of Polity?* (The Robert Schuman Centre for Advanced Studies, Florence, 2000), pp 99–116.

Lebessis, N. and Paterson, J. "Developing new modes of governance", in O. de Schutter, N. Lebessis and J. Paterson (eds), *Governance in the European Union* (Office for Official Publications of the European Communities, Luxembourg, 2001), pp 259–294.

Le Fur, L. *État fédéral et confédération d'États* (Panthéon-Assas, Paris, 2000).

Lenaerts, K. "Some Reflections on the Separation of Powers in the European Community", (1991) 28 *Common Market Law Review* 11.

Lenaerts, K. "Respect for Fundamental Rights as a Constitutional Principle of the European Union", (2000) 6 *Columbia Journal of European Law* 1.

Lenaerts, K. and de Smijter, E. "A Bill of Rights for the European Union", (2001) 38 *Common Market Law Review* 273.

Leonard, M. *Why Europe will run the 21st century* (Fourth Estate, London, 2005).

Lijphart, A. *Patterns of Democracies. Government Forms and Performance in Thirty-Six Countries* (Yale University Press, New Haven, 1999).

Lord, C. *Democracy in the European Union* (Sheffield Academic Press, Sheffield, 1998).

Lord, C. "New Governance and Post-Parliamentarism", (2004) POLIS Working Paper No 5. Available at: http://www.leeds.ac.uk/polis/research.

Lord Goldsmith, "The Charter of Rights – a Brake not an Accelerator", (2004) 5 *European Human Rights Law Review* 473.

McDonald, M. and Popkin, S. "The Myth of the Vanishing Voter", (2001) 95 *American Political Science Review* 963.

McGarry, P. "Ahern sees no cause for gloom over EU's future", *The Irish Times*, 28 September 2005.

McGrew, A. (ed), *The Transformation of Democracy?* (Polity Press, London, 1997).

Madden, C. "Migrant not displacing Irish Workers – CSO", *The Irish Times*, 23 February 2007.

Maduro, M. P. "Striking the Elusive Balance between Economic Freedom and Social Rights in the EU", in P. Alston (ed), *The EU and Human Rights* (Oxford University Press, Oxford, 1999), pp 449–472.

Maduro, M. P. "Contrapuntal Law: Europe's Constitutional Pluralism in Action", in Neil Walker (ed), *Sovereignty in Transition* (Oxford, Hart, 2003), pp 501–538.

Maduro, M. P. "The Importance of being called a constitution: Constitutional authority and the authority of constitutionalism", (2005) *International Journal of Constitutional Law* 357.

Magnette, P. "L'Union européenne: Un régime semi-parlementaire", in P. Delwit and J.-M. de Waele and P. Magnette (eds), *A quoi sert le Parlement européen?* (Éditions Complexe, Bruxelles, 1999), pp 25–54.

Magnette, P. "Towards 'Accountable Independence'? Parliamentary Controls of the European Central Bank and the Rise of a New Democratic Model", (2000) 6 *European Law Journal* 326.

Magnette, P. "European Governance and Civic Participation: Can the European Union be politicised?", in C. Joerges, Y. Mény, J. Weiler (eds), *Mountain or Molehill? A Critical*

Appraisal of the Commission White Paper on Governance, Jean Monnet Working Paper No 6/01, pp 23–31. Available at: http://www.jeanmonnetprogram.org.

Magnette, P. *Le régime politique de l'Union européenne* (Presses de Sciences Po, Paris, 2003).

Magnette, P. and Nicolaïdis, K. "Large and Small Member States in the European Union: Reinventing the Balance", *Notre Europe*, Research and European Issues, No 25, 2003.

Majone, G. (ed), *Regulating Europe* (Routledge, London, 1996).

Majone, G. "Europe's 'Democratic Deficit': The Question of Standards", (1998) 4 *European Law Journal* 5.

Majone, G. *Dilemmas of European integration. The Ambiguities and Pitfalls of Integration by Stealth* (Oxford University Press, Oxford, 2005).

Marks, G., Scharpf, F., Schmitter, P. and Streek, W. (eds), *Governance in the European Union* (Sage, London, 1996).

Mattila, M. and Lane, J.-E. "Why Unanimity in the Council? A Roll Call Analysis of Council Voting", (2001) 2 *European Union Politics* 31.

Mayer, F. "Powers-Reloaded? The Vertical Division of Powers in the EU and the New European Constitution", (2005) *International Journal of Constitutional Law* 493.

Maurer, A. "National Parliaments in the European Architecture: Elements for Establishing a Best Practice Mechanism", European Convention, Working Group IV, Working document 8, Brussels, 9 July 2002. Available at: http://european-convention.eu.int/docs/wd4/1380.pdf.

Mény, Y. and Surel, Y. (eds), *Democracies and the populist challenge* (Palgrave, Basingstoke, 2002).

Milios, J. "European Integration as a Vehicle of Neoliberal Hegemony" in A. Saad-Filho and D. Johnston (eds), *Neoliberalism. A Critical Reader* (Pluto Press, London, 2005), pp 208–214.

Milward, A. *The European Rescue of the Nation-State* (2nd ed., London, Routledge, 1999).

Monnet, J. "A Ferment of Change", (1962) 1 *Journal of Common Market Studies* 203, reproduced in B. Nelsen and A. Stubb, *The European Union. Readings on the Theory and Practice of European Integration* (2nd ed., Lynne Rienner Publishers, London, 1998), pp 19–26.

Moravcsik, A. "In Defence of the 'Democratic Deficit': Reassessing Legitimacy in the European Union", (2002) 40 *Journal of Common Market Studies* 603.

Moravcsik, A. "Europe without illusions", *Prospect*, July 2005. Available at: http://www.prospect-magazine.co.uk.

Myers, K. An Irishman's Diary, *The Irish Times*, 20 May 2005.

Murray Brown, J. "Ireland proves to be a shining example of membership", *The Financial Times*, 22 April 2004.

National Competitiveness Council, *The Competitiveness Challenge 2005*. Available at: http://www.forfas.ie/ncc.

Nicolaïdis, K. "Our European Demoi-cracy. Is this Constitution a Third Way for Europe?", in K. Nicolaidis and S. Weatherill (eds), *Whose Europe? National Models and the Constitution of the European Union* (Oxford University Press, Oxford, 2003), pp 137–152.

Norman, P. *The Accidental Constitution. The Making of Europe's Constitutional Treaty* (2ⁿᵈ ed., EuroComment, Brussels, 2005)

Notre Europe and the European University Institute, *Europe and the Crisis of Democracy. Elections in Europe: 1999–2002*, Cahiers Européens de Sciences-Po, no. 6, 2002. Available at: http://www.porteeurope.org.

O'Dowd, J. "Boston or Berlin? EU Charter of Fundamental Rights: Some Irish Perspectives", (2002) 14 *European Review of Public Law* 427.

O'Toole, F. "A lot hangs on outcome of dispute", *The Irish Times*, 29 November 2005.

Pech, L. "Le remède au 'déficit démocratique': Une nouvelle gouvernance pour l'Union européenne?", (2003) 25 *Journal of European Integration* 131.

Pech, L. "Rule of Law in France", in R. Peerenboom (ed), *Asian Discourses of Rule of Law* (Routledge, London, 2004), pp 79–112.

Pech, L. "Le droit à l'épreuve de la gouvernance. Légitimation de la privatisation du droit?", in R. Canet and J. Duchastel, *La régulation néolibérale. Crise ou ajustement?* (Athéna editions, Montréal, 2004), pp 51–80.

Pech, L. "The European Project: Neither Neo-liberal, Nor Socialist – A Reply to Andy Storey", (2007) 36–37 *The Irish Review* 95.

Pernice, I. "Multilevel constitutionalism in the European Union", (2002) 27 *European Law Review* 511.

Peters, A. "European Democracy After the 2003 Convention", (2004) 41 *Common Market Law Review* 37.

Peterson, J. "The Santer Era: The European Commission in Historical, Theoretical and Normative Perspective", (1999) 6 *Journal of European Public Policy* 46.

Phelan, D. R. "Right to Life of the Unborn v. Promotion of Trade in Services: The European Court of Justice and the Normative Shaping of the European Union", (1992) 55 *The Modern Law Review* 670.

Piris, J.-C. "L'Union européenne a-t-elle une constitution? Lui en faut-il une?", (1999) *Revue trimestrielle de droit européen*, p 599.

Piris, J.-C. "Does the European Union have a Constitution? Does it need one?", *Harvard Jean Monnet Working Paper* 5/00. Available at: http://www.jeanmonnetprogram.org/papers.

Piris, J.-C. *The Constitution for Europe. A Legal Analysis* (Cambridge University Press, Cambridge, 2006).

Pollock, R. "The New Europe Looks a Little Like '1984'", Cato Institute, 8 July 2003. Available at http://www.cato.org/dailys/07-08-03.html.

Prodi, R. "The European Union and its Citizens: a Matter of Democracy", Speech 01/365, European Parliament, Strasbourg, 4 September 2001.

Quermonne, J.-L. "The Question of a European Government", Notre Europe, Research and European Issues No 20, November 2002. Available at: http://www.notre-europe.eu/uploads/tx_publication/Etud20-en.pdf.

Quinn, G. "The European Union and the Council of Europe on the Issue of Human Rights: Twins Separated at Birth?", (2001) 46 *McGill Law Journal* 849.

Reid, T. *The United States of Europe* (The Penguin Press, New York, 2004).

Renan, E. "Qu'est-ce qu'une nation", reproduced in G. Eley and R. Grigor Suny (ed), *Becoming National: A Reader* (Oxford University Press, New York, 1996), pp 42–55.

Reville, W. "How middle-class political correctness holds the sway of power", *The Irish Times*, 25 August 2005.

Rhodes, R. "The New Governance: Governing Without Government", (1996) 44 *Political Studies* 652.

Riddell, P. *Parliament under Blair* (Politicos, London, 2000).

Rifkin, J. *The European Dream* (Polity, London, 2004).

Roe, M. "Delaware's Competition", (2003) 117 *Harvard Law Review* 590.

Rosanvallon, P. *Le peuple introuvable: Histoire de la représentation démocratique en France* (Gallimard, Paris, 1998).

Sarkozy, N. "EU reform: What we need to do", *Europe's World*, Autumn 2006, p 56. Available at: http://www.europesworld.org.

Scally, D. "CDU rejects tax harmonisation", *The Irish Times*, 6 September 2005.

Scallon, D. "Vote on EU constitution should not be rushed", *The Irish Times*, 1 November 2004.

Scallon, D. "Debate on the EU Constitution", Letters section, *The Irish Times*, 23 November 2004.

Scharpf, F. "Democratic Policy in Europe", (1996) 2 *European Law Journal* 136.

Scharpf, F. "Introduction: The Problem Solving Capacity of Multi-level Governance", (1997) 4 *Journal of European Public Policy* 520.

Scharpf, F. *Governing in Europe. Effective and Democratic* (Oxford University Press, Oxford, 1999).

Scharpf, F. "European Governance: Common Concerns vs. The Challenge of Diversity", in C. Joerges, Y. Mény, J. Weiler (eds), *Mountain or Molehill? A Critical Appraisal of the Commission White Paper on Governance*, Jean Monnet Working Paper No. 6/01. Available at: http://www.jeanmonnetprogram.org.

Scharpf, F. "The European Social Model: Coping with the Challenges of Diversity", (2002) 40 *Journal of Common Market Studies* 645.

Schmitter, P. *How to Democratize the European Union... And Why Bother?* (Rowman & Littlefield, Lanham, 2000).

Schmitter, P. "What is there to legitimise in the European Union... And how might this be accomplished?", in C. Joerges, Y. Mény, J. Weiler (eds), *Mountain or Molehill? A Critical Appraisal of the Commission White Paper on Governance*, Jean Monnet Working Paper No 6/01.. Available at: http://www.jeanmonnetprogram.org.

Sénat, "Que penser de la directive 'Bolkestein Directive'?", Rapport d'information No 206, session 2004–2005, 18 February 2005. Available at: http://www.senat.fr/rap/r04-206/r04-206.html.

Shaw, J. "Postnational Constitutionalism in the European Union", (1999) 6 *Journal of European Public Policy* 579.

Shaw, J. and Wiener, A. "Paradox of the European Polity", in M. Green Cowles and M. Smith (eds), *The State of the European Union: Risks, Reform, Resistance, and Revival* (Oxford University Press, New York, 2000), pp 64–89.

Siedentop, L. *Democracy in Europe* (Penguin, London, 2000).

Slaughter, A.-M. *A New World Order* (Princeton University Press, Princeton, 2004).

Smyth, J. "State gets opt-out clause in EU rights charter", *The Irish Times*, 26 June 2007.

Staunton, D. "Ministers move to harmonise corporate tax rules", *The Irish Times*, 13 September 2004.

Staunton, D. "Irish EU presidency 'paramount' for Prodi", *The Irish Times*, 23 October 2004.

Steiner, H. and Alston, P. *International Human Rights in Context* (Oxford University Press, Oxford, 2000).

Stone Sweet, A. *Governing with Judges. Constitutional Politics in Europe* (Oxford University Press, Oxford, 2000).

Storey, A. "Another EU: possible and necessary", *The Irish Times*, 7 May 2004.

Straw, J. "A constitution for Europe", *The Economist*, 10 October 2002.

Straw, J. Charlemagne, *The Economist*, 8 July 2004.

Stubb, A., Walace, H. and Peterson, J. "The Policy-Making Process", in E. Bomberg and A. Stubb (eds), *The European Union: How Does it Work?* (Oxford University Press, Oxford, 2003), pp 136–155.

Sun, J.-M. and Pelkmans, J. "Regulatory Competition in the Single Market", (1995) 33 *Journal of Common Market Studies* 67.

Sunstein, C. "Against Positive Rights", (2001) 2/1 *East European Constitutional Review* 35.

The Economist, "Draft-dodging", 17 August 2000.

The Economist, Charlemagne, "Snoring while a superstate emerges?", 8 May 2003.

The Economist, Charlemagne, "Government by judges?", 17 January 2004.

The Economist, "Populists, ahoy", 17 June 2004.

The Economist, Leaders, "The right verdict on the constitution", 24 June 2004.

The Economist, "The menace that wasn't", 13 November 2004.

Thym, D. "Reforming Europe's Common Foreign and Security Policy", (2004) 10 *European Law Journal* 5.

Tizzano, A. "La personnalité internationale de l'Union européenne", (1998) 4 *Revue du marché unique européen* 11.

Toth, A. "Is Subsidiarity Justiciable", (1994) 19 *European Law Review* 268.

Toth, A. "The European Union and Human Rights: The Way Forward", (1997) 34 *Common Market Law Review* 493.

Trubek, D. and Trubek, L. "Hard and Soft Law in the Construction of Social Europe: the Role of the Open Method of Co-ordination", (2005) 11 *European Law Journal* 343.

Trybus, M. "Sister in Arms: European Community Law and Sex Equality in the Armed Forces", (2003) 9 *European Law Journal* 631.

van Caenegem, R. "The "Rechtsstaat" in Historical Perspective", in R. van Caenegem, *Legal History: A European Perspective* (Hambledon Press, London, 1991), pp 185–199.

Walker, N. "Postnational constitutionalism and the problem of translation", in J. Weiler and M. Wind (eds), *European Constitutionalism Beyond the State* (Cambridge University Press, Cambridge, 2003), pp 27–54.

Walker, N. "Europe at 50 – A Mid-life Crisis", NUIG Faculty of Law Annual Distinguished Lecture, 23 March 2007. Available at: http://www.nuigalway.ie/law/documents/publications/walker_lecture.pdf.

Wallace, H. "Designing Institutions for an Enlarging European Union", in B. de Witte (ed), *Ten Reflections on the Constitutional Treaty for Europe* (Robert Schuman Centre for Advanced Studies, Florence, 2003), pp 85–105.

Wallace, W. "Where does Europe End? Dilemmas of Inclusion and Exclusion", in J. Zielonka (ed), *Europe Unbound. Enlarging and Reshaping the Boundaries of the European Union* (Routledge, London, 2002), pp 78–92.

Ward, I. *A Critical Introduction to European Law* (2nd ed., LexisNexis Butterworths, London, 2003).

Watson, R. "Employers fear jobs would be put at risk", *The Times*, 1 June 2000.

Weatherill, S. "Competence", in B. de Witte (ed), *Ten Reflections on the Constitutional Treaty for Europe* (Robert Schuman Centre for Advanced Studies, Florence, 2003), pp 45–66.

Weiler, J. "The Transformation of Europe", (1991) 100 *Yale Law Journal* 2403.

Weiler, J. "Does Europe Need a Constitution? Demos, Telos and the German Maastricht Decision", (1995) 1 *European Law Journal* 219.

Weiler, J. "The European Union Belongs to its Citizens: Three Immodest Proposals", (1997) 22 *European Law Review* 150.

Weiler, J. "To be a European Citizen–Eros and Civilisation", *Working Paper Series in European Studies*, Spring 1998. Available at: http://uw-madison-ces.org/papers/weiler.pdf.

Weiler, J., Haltern, U. and Mayer, F. "European Democracy and Its Critique", (1998) 18(3) *West European Politics* 4.

Weiler, J. "Fischer: The Dark Side", in C. Joerges, Y. Mény & J. Weiler (eds), *What kind of Constitution for what kind of Polity?* (The Robert Schuman Centre for Advanced Studies, Florence, 2000), pp 235–247.

Weiler, J. "In defence of the status quo: Europe's Constitutional *Sonderweg*", in J. Weiler and M. Wind (eds), *European Constitutionalism beyond the State* (Cambridge University Press, Cambridge, 2003), pp 7–23.

Wessels, W. "A 'Saut constitutionnel' out of an intergovernmental trap? The provisions of the Constitutional Treaty for the Common Foreign, Security and Defence Policy", in J. Weiler and C. Eisgruber (eds), *Altneuland: The EU Constitution in a Contextual Perspective*, Jean Monnet Working Paper 5/04. Available at: http://www.jeanmonnetprogram.org/papers/04/040501-17.htm.

Wicks, E. "'Declaratory of Existing Rights' – The United Kingdom's Role in Drafting a European Bill of Rights, Mark II", (2001) *Public Law* 527.

Will, G. "Europe at the Precipice", *The Washington Post*, 29 May 2005.

Wincott, D. "Does the European Union Pervert Democracy? Questions of Democracy in New Constitutionalist Thought on the Future of Europe", (1998) 4 *European Law Journal* 411.

Wintour, P. "Brown in London overrules Blair in Brussels on French coup", *The Guardian*, 23 June 2007.

Zielonka, J. "How New Enlarged Borders Will Reshape the European Union", (2001) 39 *Journal of Common Market Studies* 507.

INDEX